PASSION

PAUL POLSON

ISBN 978-1-959182-65-8 (paperback)
ISBN 978-1-959182-66-5 (hardcover)
ISBN 978-1-959182-67-2 (digital)

This is a work of fiction. Names, characters, places, and incidents either are products of the author's imagination or are used fictitiously. Any resemblances to actual events or locales or persons, living or dead, are entirely coincidental.

Passion
paulp@3dair.com

Printed in the United States of America

1

PASSION

Paul drove the company truck to the Pacific Beach *Fine Art Store* to deliver art supplies and framed art pieces. The recipients of his deliveries are galleries, colleges, illustrators, military designers, and anyone who needs art supplies in the San Diego Area.

Xavier is one of the three owners that runs the most extensive art supply chain in Southern California.

Every workday, Paul delivers framing and art supplies to the Pacific Beach store. On this particular day, Xavier called him before he began his deliveries and made it a point that they need to talk.

This request didn't worry Paul because he has always gotten along with Xavier, and he developed friendships with most of the 35 employees. They all had common interests, and together, they have a fantastic social life! They enjoy working together, and are a great team.

Paul loves this job.

Xavier does the hiring for all three stores. His criteria is to hire employees with a degree in art or who are proficient in their abilities. Doing this is smart on his part since all his workers are familiar with art supplies. Xavier knows it's a long shot for them to get a decent job because of their chosen career.

Paul felt secure in his job, but in life, strange things can happen. He never assumes anything.

Paul drove the Fine Art Store truck up to the back door. Opening the van's side door, he moved the framing from the Kearny Mesa store into the storage area near the back entrance. He has several boxes of art supplies: tubes of paint, oil and watercolors, brushes, and different types of paper.

Xavier heard the truck drive up, and he came out back as Paul is carrying the last box through the door.

"Morning, Paul," Xavier said. "Come back to my office."

Paul walked back and sat in the chair across from him. Xavier didn't look Paul in the eye at first. He cleared his desk of annoying paperwork, then rested his forearms on his desk. After a few long seconds, Xavier leaned back in his chair and locked his hands behind his head. He has a slight smile on his face.

"I've decided to lay you off," Xavier said.

"Oh, shit!" Paul thought to himself.

⸺ ❋ ⸺

Paul had recently arrived in San Diego at the age of 23. Born and raised in Wyoming, he received his bachelor's degree in art education from the University of Wyoming in 1970. Paul also joined the Army National Guard and completed his active duty before heading to San Diego. Southern California was not his destination, but he ended up here—flowing with whatever happens next. He has a close friend in San Diego who is delighted that Paul showed up.

Oh yeah. Paul also left a failed marriage. He has always dreamed of pursuing an art career, and his spouse supposedly had the same goal. They agreed that they needed to move to a large city and dive into the art scene. After being married for three years, she changes her mind and insists that Paul's art is now to be his hobby.

To deny Paul's intended future is a big mistake. Paul has always focused on his art. There is nothing that can change his mind. It's called PASSION!

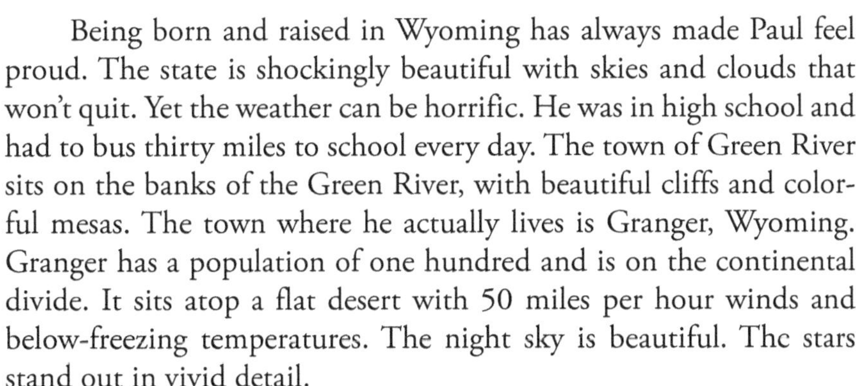

Passion—What is passion?

In his youth, Paul didn't mention or ascribe to that word. He is who he is. A youthful energy drove him to pick up a pencil and draw and draw and draw—mostly in his notebooks and textbooks. Any paper surface worked for him.

As he grew and matured, he saw passion in people. Sports is a good one. Some people had a passion for participating in sports or are fixated on watching sports.

Is loving someone a passion? I guess you can passionately fall in love. Is it temporary or forever? Paul's brother has been passionate about refurbishing muscle cars since the late 60s.

Here is one definition of passion: The state or capacity of being acted on by external agents or forces.

Emotions as distinguished from reason.

Passion can be good or evil—destructive or productive—or just there, taking up your time.

Being born and raised in Wyoming has always made Paul feel proud. The state is shockingly beautiful with skies and clouds that won't quit. Yet the weather can be horrific. He was in high school and had to bus thirty miles to school every day. The town of Green River sits on the banks of the Green River, with beautiful cliffs and colorful mesas. The town where he actually lives is Granger, Wyoming. Granger has a population of one hundred and is on the continental divide. It sits atop a flat desert with 50 miles per hour winds and below-freezing temperatures. The night sky is beautiful. The stars stand out in vivid detail.

Since he left this beautiful state, Paul has experienced much of the world and realized that he commonly uses the term "I didn't know any better" in conversations about his loving upbringing.

The people of Wyoming are hard-working but can't understand the importance of art. They are supportive of it but not as a career. There is work to be done. Paul would get a pat on the head for his artistic accomplishments, but he needs to get a real job.

At age twelve, Paul created his first oil painting and never stopped. They were mostly landscapes, not painted from life but memory. He painted forests and deserts, skies and clouds, winters and summers.

He was obsessed with drawing and painting when he attended the University of Wyoming. Instead of getting a fine art degree, he decided on a teaching degree in art education. What he "really" wants to do is paint.

All he knows are the expectations he feels compelled to follow, resulting in a failed marriage and a commitment to the Army National Guard. It was the late sixties. Paul drew a number 8 in the first lottery and immediately received a letter saying he needed to report for his physical in Denver, Colorado. They will draft him into the army upon graduation from the university.

Paul is married at the time (most people in Wyoming married at too young an age). At first, he is smitten but realized after a year that he was not really in love. Paul also found that he has a partner that contradicted his dreams and goals.

Things all worked for the best in the long run because her father was a WW2 veteran. Now he is a chief warrant officer in the national guard. Regardless of Paul's willingness (even excitement) to do his duty in Viet Nam, his father-in-law grabbed him by the ear and found him a coveted position in the guard. He wasn't going to let him go to war. After all, he married his daughter and had a grandson on the way.

Needless to say, the marriage didn't work out. Paul knew what he had to do, and her motive was to stop it.

"Your art is a hobby. Get a real job. You need to support us."

Realizing that he has this overwhelming "passion" to pursue the arts, Paul knew he needed world experience. He needed to find himself and his potential by surrounding his life with good art and artists. He needed to leave this state.

2

SAN DIEGO

When Paul left Wyoming for the great unknown, he didn't have a destination in mind. It was the first of February, and the weather was cold with icy roads. His van has a bed with all his necessities packed around it (drum set, motorcycle).

Inserting an eight-track tape into the stereo system, he headed straight for San Francisco. The tape is The Best of Rock and Roll with Bob Dylan, Cat Stevens, and Neil Young—to name a few.

The sun is rising as America's "A Horse with No Name" blares in the speakers, followed by Paul Simon's "Mother and Child Reunion." Tears roll down his cheeks. Paul feels an overwhelming sadness.

On a positive note, a great weight has been lifted from his shoulders. Paul looks forward to the upcoming adventure. The trip begins with the beautiful and familiar Wasatch Mountains. He passes through Salt Lake City, followed by the salt flats, heading toward Reno. Even though he had driven a lot around southern Wyoming, Utah, and down to Las Vegas, he has never taken this road. The landscape is new.

Between Reno and Sacramento, the weather drastically changed. It went from below freezing to tee-shirt weather and clear blue skies. The most apparent sensation is the salt smell in the air. Paul had only seen the ocean once in the last twenty years on a quick trip to San Diego.

Nearing San Francisco, he finds himself in the mayhem of rush-hour traffic. It's not the bumper-to-bumper crawl he later became familiar with after moving to San Diego. It is fast, over the speed limit—still bumper-to-bumper—craziness that he had never experienced in Wyoming. Cars and trucks crowded the lanes on both sides. He gripped the steering wheel and stayed in the same lane.

The freeway led him south of San Francisco. He headed straight to the ocean. Pulling off the road at the first opportunity, Paul walked to the ocean's edge and sat down, awestruck by the beautiful sight. The sunset was beyond description. His mind felt the same peace he had experienced while looking up at the stars or standing amid the falling snow. It definitely recharged his batteries.

Climbing back in his van, he found a rest area just a couple of miles further south. The long day had caught up with him. He pulled over and settled into his bed for the night.

Waking to the fresh salty ocean air with the sound of waves breaking and crashing against the rocks was music to Paul's ears. He climbed out of his van and sat on the rocky ledge above the shore. What a beautiful sight! What a wonderful feeling! Paul, born and raised in Wyoming, had never experienced the warmth and sensations that converged on his senses. He could sit here all day, smelling the air and watching the waves' hypnotic motions and details.

It was decision time. Does Paul drive north to experience San Francisco and then on to Seattle? Seattle seems a magical place to Paul. He didn't know why it was so appealing, except that it was pulling him like a magnet.

South is his choice. He plans to go to Seattle eventually. He might as well explore the coast and then end in the Northwest. The coastline is mesmerizing. He saw the film *Play Misty for Me* before leaving Wyoming. Big Sur, Carmel, and Monterey looked like paradise—and they were—like being on an alien planet. Everything was lush and green. The cliffs turned him into a speck on the hillside, and surfers skimmed along the waves, then paddled vigorously through the white water to the swells forming outside. Paul wanted to find a job in that area and settle into this lifestyle, but he was much too antsy. His wanderlust had not been satisfied.

As he drove farther south, the population increased, and he found himself back in the world of jammed freeways. Los Angeles is enormous, an ant colony of scattered direction and purpose. Paul isn't drawn to this area at all. A person could get swallowed up and lost.

Then came San Diego. It was in the early seventies, and the atmosphere was much more relaxed. Each area was like a small town.

Paul's friend Steve Lytle from Evanston, Wyoming, had moved here. He spent a lot of time with him at Sam's Tavern (Pete's Rock & Rye). He talked a lot about the beautiful San Diego area.

He knew his marriage was falling apart when he rejoined the Navy. He also knew his passion for the arts. San Diego is no New York or San Francisco, but it offers the outlets he is looking to find. But, then again, he is not planning to stay here.

Paul found Steve's home in a section of town called Hillcrest and knocked on the door. When the door opened, there is Steve with a huge smile on his face. "I knew you would come to your senses and end up here," he said as he put an arm around Paul's shoulders and led him inside.

That evening, they cruised by a liquor store and bought a bottle of red wine, continued north to La Jolla, and found a small secluded cove. Steve opened the bottle, and they sat back to watch the sunset.

"I had a feeling you would show up sooner or later," Steve said, as he leaned back on a rock wall while sitting on the warm sand. "I'll show you around tomorrow."

"Sounds good." Paul still has his mindset in Seattle. "My money won't last forever. I need to get a job."

"Save your money. You can stay rent-free with me for a few months until you have the time to see what's happening. My guess is that you will be here a while. I'll cover your food too. Buy some art supplies and start painting."

Paul's style at the time is oil painting on wood panels. He would buy a sheet of Masonite, sand it down, and apply two coats of gesso. Using a cross stroke with a flat brush, he applied the primer so it would have a loose textured background. He placed the panel on the floor, leaned it against the wall, and dove into it. Whenever Paul visited his parents, he would do the same thing—buy the materials, push the furniture aside, and paint. His mom and dad loved it!

Being away from the Wyoming environment, Paul found himself with patience and a focus on detail never experienced before. The paintings he did turned out better than he could have imagined. The enjoyment he felt in the act of painting is through the roof!

Steve took Paul to the San Diego Art Institute in Balboa Park. Their gallery has regular monthly juried shows. They also have weekly figure-drawing workshops. Paul is excited about the workshops.

The first month, after becoming a member, he entered a painting in the monthly juried competition. It was accepted and immediately sold. The next month, they had a Southern California juried show. Paul is accepted, received a purchase award, and they called Paul to bring in another painting, which sold immediately.

"Wow, what a great start!" Paul thought, "and all in the first two months in San Diego!"

The phone ringing tempers all of this excitement. It's Barbara, Paul's ex-wife. He calls his children weekly, and they are excited to hear from their dad. He missed them.

When Paul answered the phone, the first thing out of Barb's mouth was, "Now that you realize you're a failure, why don't you come back?"

"Actually, things are going great! Why would you assume it wouldn't be? Why don't you pack the kids in the car and move out here? We could start fresh and leave all the Wyoming baggage behind."

"Nope," was her curt reply.

Nope became a regular reply of hers. Unfortunately, it became the word Barbara used from that point on whenever he called and asked to speak to the kids. "Nope."

— * ❋ * —

Paul loves a small art supply store in Pacific Beach. It is his favorite place to buy needed art materials. It is old and rustic and had an aura about it that felt like all the ghosts of art history were hanging out there. Xavier Romano owns the shop. Since Paul had lived at Steve's for three months, it is time for him to find his own studio and a source of income. He asked Xavier if they were hiring.

Xavier went to his office and returned with an application. Paul filled it out while at the store, then bought his needed supplies and headed home (after a stop at the beach to watch the surfers and the gorgeous babes in bikinis).

Besides the therapeutic value, Paul's association with Steve turned out to be a drinking one. He felt that it was "much-needed" medication at the time. Just before leaving Evanston, he had become acquainted with pot. Steve didn't use it—it's alcohol, all the way, for him.

Now and then, Steve and Paul would visit their favorite spot in La Jolla, but mostly, they went to bars and taverns. Paul enjoyed the differences in the people living in Southern California compared to Wyoming. Their attitudes and their humor are alien to him but exciting. Everyone is tan, and the women are beautiful and flirty.

That could have been because Steve carried this aura, or magic, that drew women to him. Women's response to him was all because of his intelligence and wit. He's a little homely. He wore large glasses and had a larger than average nose. The back of his hair is cut in military fashion, but the front is combed over one eye. All it took is a little wink and a verbal taunt to lure a woman into a conversation, and they had a female drinking partner for the evening.

— ❈ —

Paul received a call from the Fine Art Store as he is sitting on the floor of Steve's apartment with his legs crossed in front of a painting.

It's Xavier. "We would like to hire you, but it will be at the main store in Kearny Mesa."

Paul is delighted.

So he started in retail, which he had never done before. He learned a lot since it was the largest art supply store in Southern California. He didn't know why, but he felt uncomfortable. The owner of that particular store noticed his struggle.

There were several areas of the store. The front retail space is where the art supplies are sold. There is also a design room where customers bring their artwork to be framed. The back is a sizeable fitting area where they cut mats and fit the pieces into the frames. The largest space is stocked with every type of frame molding you can imagine, and two employees cut and joined the frames. The rest of the building is an open warehouse where the art supplies are stored. An order desk is in a central location where Melinda packed orders for delivery to various locations.

The Fine Art Store is the major supplier to all the galleries, schools, navy bases, and other art-related businesses, such as illustrators and designers.

The owner of the Kearny Mesa store (another Steve) asked if he would drive the delivery truck. Paul jumped at the chance. It allowed him to know the San Diego area intimately.

He eventually came to know the owners and employees of all the art supplies and framing customers. It also gave him access to all of the store's work areas. Paul is free to roam around the warehouse when he isn't driving. The other employees are always joking as they greeted each other with smiles. Flirting with the women who worked there was a blast. They flirted back

3

THE STUDIO

The bottom dropped out of Paul's stomach. He just lost his job.

He was so happy! Paul enjoyed this job and loved the people he worked around. He never saw this coming. He always thought he was a responsible worker.

All these feelings rushed through his mind. Xavier sat back in his chair with a smile on his face—"a smile!"

Xavier saw the distress on Paul's face.

He immediately rocked forward and said, "I have an opportunity for you.

I have always admired your devotion to your work—and you are productive. Maybe I should say obsessed."

"I have an artist friend who just passed away. Before he died, he built a fabulous studio. His widow wants another artist to use it. She trusts me. Here, this is the address; it's a couple of blocks from the beach. Introduce yourself to her, and tell her Xavier sent you. Offer her 100 dollars a month."

"By the way, you need to sign up for unemployment. That should get you by for a year. Then I'll hire you back."

—— * ❋ * ——

The studio Paul rented is well-equipped. The whole north side of the building is all windows. There are huge bookshelves packed with hundreds of art books. Drawers are full of brushes, palette knives, and tubes of unopened paint. The only problem with the studio is that it has no shower or bath. It did have a toilet, a kitchen sink, and a refrigerator.

That studio became Paul's home for three years, and he did tons (lots) of work. He bought a bicycle and put high-rise handlebars on it. He cruised the beach on his bike and did his surfing thing every morning. In the afternoon, Paul took a break from painting and rode down the Mission Beach boardwalk. He would peddle down the ocean side and peddle back on the bayside—three miles each way.

Once a week, he biked to La Jolla, following the coast north past Windansea to watch the surfers, then on to the La Jolla Cove.

On the way back, he visits the Museum of Modern Art and makes a stop at his favorite bookstore where he would browse or buy. It is a fabulous bookstore with a great environment.

There is no problem finding a place to shower. His friends seem more than happy to accommodate him. They gave him keys to their houses, so he could bathe when needed even if they aren't there. They also had showers at the beach. After spending the morning surfing, Paul would shower to get the saltwater off before returning to the studio.

—— * ❋ * ——

While working at the Fine Art Store, Paul met Melinda.

Melinda works closely with Paul so that he understands what needs to be delivered and knows its destination. She receives the orders, collects the items and has them stacked in the delivery entrance to be loaded on the truck. She and Bob (another close friend who worked at the store) became involved and moved into a house in Ocean Beach. Through Melinda, Paul met her younger sister Karen. Karen is a gorgeous blond, and she began giving him attention.

When Paul moved into his studio, Karen, jumped in and helped him without being asked. He was fine with the many ferns and plants she hung in his huge north-facing window. A bar with stools appeared out of nowhere. She brought cooking supplies and prepared meals.

Later that evening, they finally got the space looking good and ready to function—everything is in place.

"Alright," said Karen, "this place is looking good. I'm famished!"

"It looks terrific, Karen," Paul said. "Thank you so much for the help."

"No problem," she said, "It's late; let's go to bed." She walked into the small bedroom that we had partitioned off, took off her clothes, and climbed in.

Paul isn't surprised. They had slept together on another occasion after a party. She is the Southern California icon you expect to see when visiting the beaches of California. It's a great way to end the day.

This arrangement continued. Karen took care of him and even modeled now and then. They never argued. Paul didn't interfere with Karen's freedom, and she didn't interfere with his. They worked and lived well together.

Karen has a good job and is not a financial burden at all. Since he knew her, it became easy to ignore her and dive into building stretcher bars, stretching and sizing the canvases, and painting.

Karen is in and out—doing her thing as if they had always been together. She also carried a 35-millimeter camera with her. She's a talented photographer.

Their relationship continued for the fifteen years Paul spent in San Diego, but not always in the same way. She would disappear on occasion, and about eight years later, she married another man. Paul and Karen stayed close even if it wasn't sexual. Karen bought several of his paintings.

Paul also became acquainted with Karen's mother, Trish. Karen and Paul often went there for dinner. Trish allowed him to use her shower since he didn't have one in his studio. He is part of the family.

4

CARL JUNG

Up until that time, Paul painted on gesso-covered Masonite. His work was surrealistic, with a strong influence from weekly figure drawing. He also painted landscapes and continued to draw—doing sketches as he biked around town or while hanging around the beaches.

When Paul moved into the Pacific Beach studio, he was still painting on Masonite. Within a few months, he began buying wood, making stretcher bars, and then stretching canvas over it to be primed and prepared for the initial wash. Paul learned modern techniques but also studied the old masters and how they prepared their canvases. Paul realized the superior methods of the old days. He covered the canvas with rabbit skin glue and then used a lead primer (not the healthiest materials but durable and flexible). In later years, he found that some of the gesso-primed canvases cracked, while the old master techniques were standing the test of time, even when rolled and stored.

Paul also enjoyed doing larger works, averaging four feet by six feet, but he also painted small works.

The hardest part of transferring from wood panels to canvas was to get the same background textures and washes that he had been using. A flexible fabric surface seemed to react differently. His technique was essential to him, and he eventually was able to bring out the same detailed background but not as smooth a surface as he wanted.

⟹ ❋ ⟸

As Xavier promised, the year went by fast, and he rehired Paul at the Fine Art Store. Paul kept the studio for two more years and accomplished a lot. He had stacks of paintings leaning against the walls.

All of Paul's paintings developed into a consistent and philosophical technique. His way of doing his work is not on purpose. Although his works are scattered, from figures to landscapes to non-objective abstracts, his painting method developed into an engaging style. He felt more like a scientist in a laboratory running experiment after experiment.

Paul read Carl Gustav Jung's twenty-one volume set and is awed by the information in these books. They became the basis for all of Paul's artwork.

Jung intensely studied dreams, symbols, religious beliefs, and aspects of the male/female in humanity and the collective and personal unconscious.

Paul's work is like a Rorschach test. He would begin with turpentine splatters and textures. Then he would set it on an easel, sit at a distance, and pick out shapes and objects that he would bring out and define. At the same time, he had his original idea of what he wanted to paint. He began his painting, allowing the wash's textures and shapes to intermix with Paul's intended painting. Paul would allow these two forces to interact. The forces of the universe and the unconscious collided with the artist's structure and intent. It's like a relationship with the opposite sex—like a marriage. If you tried to control the side you didn't understand, it would die.

The result was always unexpected. The finished painting turned out better than intended and became a life unto itself as if birthing a child.

— * ✳ * —

While working at the Fine Art Store, Paul developed a friendship with Martin. You would need to know Martin to understand that he *is* a character—not always good. There are many snags in their relationship. He had a knack for causing trouble, but the good came with the bad.

They bought guitars at the same time and played music together. Paul would hang at his house often and shower there when he needed to. In 1977, Martin quit the art store and got a job at the Reutter Gallery in the Gaslamp Quarter. A year later, he contacted Paul and said that David Reutter, the owner, is looking for more help. Martin told Paul that David, the owner, is interested in meeting him. Martin had already sold him on Paul's abilities, so he had the job if he wanted it.

Paul quit the Fine Art Store and started work at The Reutter Gallery a few days later.

The Gaslamp is in the middle of downtown San Diego. The Gaslamp district is the old part of town with beautiful buildings from the late 1800s. This area of San Diego was never able to pass the new earthquake codes. Great studio spaces are available.

Paul obtained a lead on a fantastic space above San Diego Hardware on Fifth Avenue. He grabbed it. It was a 6,000 square foot ballroom.

5

THE BALLROOM

Winter nights in San Diego can be chilly—more so with a breeze blowing in off the ocean. But for Paul, it is perfect. It's late January 1979, and the sun had set two hours ago.

He had heard about a nice intimate bar just a few blocks from the bright lights and action of Fifth Avenue—The Gaslamp Quarter.

Ten Downing is the name of this so-called English pub. Paul decided to check it out. When he arrives, he walks down a short flight of stairs that ends five feet under the street level.

As Paul opens the door, he is a little taken aback.

His initial thought of what an English pub might look like is something dark with warm colors. Maybe it will have soft lighting and a wood interior. Paul expected to hear friendly chatter with English accents inundating the room with short bursts of laughter and raised voices from friendly disagreements.

It isn't like that at all. It is dimly lit alright but seems classy American with its white walls and scattered tables—each with a candle on a white tablecloth.

A glittery bar occupies the center of the room with sparkling wine glasses and snifters hanging upside down from thin metallic racks. The colors are vibrant from backlighting and look as if each bottle of liquor has its internal light of amber, soft yellows, or darker reddish browns.

The place is empty except for the bartender buffing a wine glass with a white cloth. He is wearing a black vest over a maroon dress shirt and looks to be in his early thirties. There is a distinguished air about him. His mustache is thick and neatly trimmed; he had combed his hair, leaving a tuft of unruliness playing across his forehead.

"Ello, mate," he said as he hung the wine glass in its place. "What can I do fer ya?"

"I'll have brandy in a snifter. Heat the glass, please," Paul said as he settled onto a barstool in front of him. "Just heat the glass, then pour the brandy."

"Alright, a geezer who knows 'ow ter drink 'is brandy."

"Actually, make that a Cognac."

"Right-o."

"I've heard British accents before. Yours is pretty strong. Where are you from?" Paul asked.

"Jus Sowfeast ov London. It's cockney."

He took a snifter from the overhead rack, filled it with hot water from the coffee pot, and set it on the counter.

Reaching for the Cognac, he said, "I've jus been in America fer a week. I'm pracicin speaken wiv an American accent."

He opens the bottle, dumps the hot water, and pours in the Cognac. With his left hand, he plops down a coaster followed by the drink with his right—all in a confident and fluid motion.

The grand finale is a glass of ice water.

"Name's Steve," he said as he held out his hand.

"Paul." They give each other a firm grip.

"So," Paul said as he looked around. "Where's the crowd?"

"This is me first day, but I 'ear i' comes an' goes. Happy 'aaahrs an' lunches are supposed ter be popular. The bookstawer upstairs also owns da pub. Befawer an' after readings an' events, da place fills up. There are also banquets an' dinner par'ese."

"And wha do yew do?" he asked.

"I'm a painter," Paul said. "Like an artist painter. I live in my studio in the Gaslamp."

"Can yew make a livin?"

"I work part time in a gallery and frame shop. Sometimes, I sell paintings or teach figure drawing. What do you do besides bartending?"

"Usually, I travel around an' en'er bartendin' competishuns—plan ter se'le down 'ere fer a while. Jus got me green card."

Paul savors the Cognac as they chat about the attributes of San Diego, life growing up in London, and the questionable decision of pursuing an art career in the United States.

As Paul takes the last sip, Steve asks if I want another.

"I think I'll have a Keoke coffee."

Steve removes a glass coffee cup and expertly combines the brandy and Kahlua with coffee and tops it off with whipped cream and a half shot of Crème de cacao. Oh yeah, and a cherry on top.

"Ya' must be plannin' ter stay up for a while tonight," Steve said with a smile. He places the drink on the bar.

⁕

Paul knows his limits. He strolls the three blocks back to the Gaslamp Quarter as opposed to staggering. There is a slow transition from dark, quiet streets to the lively activity under Fifth Avenue's lights.

It's a Sunday evening, yet the sidewalks flow with people from diverse races. The bums huddle in the nooks and crannies of closed shops. They recognize the locals but don't hit them up for money or favors. They are all family.

Cars cruise the street checking out the action.

Small groups of sailors stagger among the tattoo parlors, X-rated video stores, and rowdy bars.

Hookers roam the street chatting and laughing with each other while their pimps walk on the other side of the avenue keeping their eyes peeled for opportunities or trouble.

Artists thrive in the Gaslamp, fitting in well with the shady elements. The artists and street people greet each other with friendly nods and, in many cases, call each other by name.

The buildings were built in the late eighteen hundreds and had beautiful facades. The majority of these are closed, partly due to the lack of interest by business owners (because of the seedy elements) and partly because the buildings require major rehabilitation if they are to meet the city's codes.

If you are familiar with San Diego in the seventies, you will be used to the fact that most of the activities and the best restaurants are at the beach communities and the valleys.

The owners of the buildings in the Gaslamp area lease out spaces to artists at amazingly low rates. Rather than leave the premises abandoned, they prefer to have them occupied. The water is running, and the electricity works.

The art shows, events, and art walks organized by the art community draw the people of society who are well-educated, well-to-do, and into the arts—the expression of our culture.

Many see the artistic lifestyle as romantic and sacrificial—which it is. The Gaslamp is considered a seedy place and shunned by the people who have heard of or experienced it. People from the suburbs walk into an artist's studio and are immediately struck with envy, experiencing a beautiful studio with ample space and high ceilings. The energy of creating *"art"* develops a craving for such a lifestyle.

The artists' creations have brought the once-depressing space *"who would want to live here?"* to heightened levels of awareness and creativity. The work is unique to each individual's obsession. Images spew from their minds—a reflection of the angels and demons that live inside their heads.

There is a need to go beyond decoration. Each artist has a toolbox of experience and training that stands naked before everyone who views their work, baring their abilities from naïve to spectacular imagery and technique.

The inevitable is sure to happen. People who can afford fabulous studios or apartments are willing to pay to have their dreams become a reality. The businesses will follow, and the artists will no longer be able to afford the artistic environment and energy that such a place had provided.

As Paul nears his studio entrance, he hears a familiar raspy voice.

"Hello, artist," said the bum who had pressed himself inside the doorway of an unused establishment.

Charlie sits among his few necessities—an old ratty sleeping bag and a blanket. He has a dirty red backpack at his side and wears a torn military jacket. Cradled in his arms is a bottle of cheap liquor. He is unshaven and his hair is long with clumps and knots due to a lack of grooming.

"Hello, Charlie," Paul said. "You look cozy."

"My mind's in a good place. I've been watching gorgeous women in black tights entering your studio. What you got that I don't have?" he asked with a grin, revealing his lack of teeth and the brown remnants of those that remained.

"There's a ballet troupe renting the second floor," Paul said. "I'm on the third floor."

"Well," said Charlie. "If you can pick one out and tell her there's a lonely genius willing to share his bottle, send her my way, I'd much appreciate it."

"If the opportunity presents itself, I'll do that," Paul said as he smiled and walked to the next door and entered.

He climbed the stairs and can feel the vibrations and slight movement of the building as the dancers move and jump to their routines.

The door is open to the dance studio, and seven young women are dancing in front of giant mirrors. Megan, the instructor, sees Paul and slightly lifts a hand and smiles at him as the group performs their steps in perfect unison.

The third floor opens up to the vast expanse of an old wartime ballroom with two massive skylights.

Paul walks to the large doors that swing inwards and steps up to the sill. He walks out on the fire escape where a person can see all of Fifth Avenue, both north and south. It is impossible to take in all of the activities of this vibrant street's diverse characters.

A thin, shaky ladder leads to the roof. If you want to be alone and still feel the massiveness of the city, you can take the climb with a bottle of wine, sit by one of the skylights, and feel fine.

Stepping back down to the floor, Paul walks toward his painting area in the far corner where a small stage rises two feet above the floor. The many dance bands that once frequented this place, during the war years, haunt the stage. The whole ballroom has a subliminal aura, or energy, to it. The young people of that time have since passed away or are close to drawing their last breaths in this unforgiving world.

Paul can hear the din of the street as it echoes through the ballroom.

At this point in time, four artists have studios in this space. Carole Frye is working in hers. Large hanging curtains enclose her little creative world. They are not really curtains but large sheets made of tissue paper that are rolled out on a table and painted with pearlescent acrylics that buckle the surface. They provide a diversity of texture and color. To help dry her work, awaiting the next coat, she hangs each piece from the lofty ceiling surrounding her space. The lights inside her studio strike the translucent hangings, and they glow like an enormous Chinese lantern. She paints them in soft blues, pinks, and purples that play off their surface in ever-changing patterns and reflections depending on their movement and the angle they are viewed.

"Hello, Carole," Paul calls out as he passes.

"Hi, Paul. Come check out these new colors I ordered. I'm so excited!"

Entering Carole's space is like walking into a sacred church as the environment changes to her energy and aura. A box lies open on her table with large plastic bottles organized around it.

"These are a new line of colors. Instead of the usual, these have more of a silvery gray tint."

She holds up some sample pieces. "I can't wait to try them out!"

"Wow!" Paul responded. "They're beautiful!"

6

RICHARD

There was one main reason Paul was able to find such a fantastic space.

Gary Ghirardi has the lease on the ballroom. He also has a small room in the ballroom that they once used to project images or films in its hay day. Gary also has another small studio a couple of blocks away.

He subleases space for no profit to himself.

Gary opened another space called Installation Gallery. He shows artists with unusual talents that most galleries wouldn't bother exhibiting. The art is similar to what you would see in *"Artforum"* magazine—avant-garde, environmental, and experimental—not just pictures on the wall. Paul admires the man. He has a selfless attitude and an avid interest in the arts.

Gary is an unusual character—somewhat short with black medium-length hair and a lazy eye that you can't help but notice. It is a bit of a distraction when you talk with him. He is a philosophical person, and Paul enjoys their discussions.

Paul's studio has divisions to enclose his space. Unlike Carole, he hangs large paintings from the ceiling. He also has a hanging wall section made of used palettes. Since he works at a gallery frame shop,

Paul brings the damaged and scratched acrylic sheets from reframed artwork to his studio. He backs it with a white mat board and places it on an old TV stand with wheels. They make great palettes.

Hanging an image on the wall is Paul's forte. He does three-dimensional work as well, but not hanging. He loves sculpting and will always be involved in it. It's just that sculpting combines laborious patience. You work away on it to reach each little objective. Earth clay is pretty spontaneous—the work comes afterward when you cast or prepare for firing in a kiln.

Now painting—that's spontaneous! You paint and get results at the same moment you think of it. It is a fluid eye, to brain, to hand, to canvas activity. Paul loves that! Allowing his psychic self to spontaneously express itself without thinking reveals his soul.

Paul firmly believes that he needs to learn as the old masters did. Figure drawing, painting, and anatomy are essential. Continually drawing and painting landscapes is necessary. *Still lifes* and portraits should be common exercises to train your artistic mind so you can perform confidently. Using many mediums greatly adds to your toolbox of knowledge. Try everything.

Living with his work is essential. Paul puts his bed in the same room that he paints.

His last studio was the same. So what if he doesn't have a shower? Friends give him the keys to their homes to bathe. There are also showers at the beach after surfing or membership in a gym works.

Just running water and a toilet that works is all he needs in his workplace. The ballroom has a toilet and sink room downstairs on the second floor.

The painting Paul's working on is visually coming together. His brush dances between the surface of the canvas and the palette with no hesitation. He knows what he wants to do. It's great to have his mind in this place. It's as if time doesn't exist.

Sitting back in his chair, about fifteen feet away, in deep thought and contemplation, he gazes at his work to decide the next move. There are many directions to go at any point in time, and when the decision is made, Paul pops up and dives in with no hesitation. He knows where he wants to go, or he randomly picks a path to see what adventures will befall him.

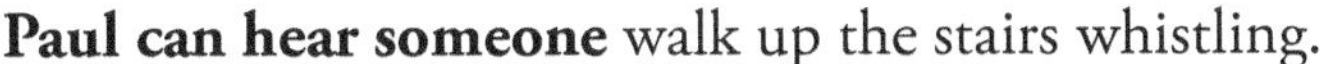

Paul can hear someone walk up the stairs whistling.

It's Richard. He has a dancing gait and a smile on his face, as he usually does. Richard is tall and lanky—not real tall though—about six feet. He wears a tam cocked a bit to the side and says he's from Philadelphia, or maybe it's Pittsburg.

Paul met Richard for the first time after showering at a friend's house in Pacific Beach. He was a friend of Steve Goldblatt—AKA "Gold"—who shares a home with Martin. Martin worked with Paul at the Fine Art Store before he moved to the ballroom.

Richard was in the house when Paul came out of the shower, and the subject came up that he lived in a painting studio that was devoid of the luxuries of life.

Talking about the attributes of an artist's lifestyle is a subject Paul loves to carry on about. People are used to the materialistic rewards in our country. Their goals are more than just financial security. Success is buying a house, having a high-end automobile along with other toys, a sailboat, traveling in luxury, maybe an airplane, a swimming pool—the list can go on forever.

Paul's values are just the opposite. He believes material possessions enslave a person. As an artist, he needs freedom. His lifestyle confuses a lot of people. They can't comprehend a non-materialistic life but not Richard. Paul's diatribe convinced him that he wanted to be an artist. At the time, he thought he was trying to be an interior decorator.

Deep in thought, Richard asked, "So, do you have to go to school and learn to draw and paint?"

"I believe that to learn the basics and the teaching of the old masters is essential," Paul said. "That's the guideline that inspires me."

"But no. A lot of artists these days find a gimmick, like crashing a car into a brick wall and then proudly display the pieces on a gallery wall. Then they say, 'Look what I made or unmade. Who says art is about creation? How about tearing things apart? That is expression, isn't it?'"

"Their artistic pursuit has more to do with verbal diatribes and bullshit than learning to draw and paint, sculpt, discover composition and the potential of color. It's all been done before, and since the discovery of the camera, why paint realistically?"

"Wow!" said Richard. "I want to do that!"

Anyway, Paul didn't think much about it. After his shower and conversation, they all sat back and enjoyed a beer. Gold is a cook on a fishing boat. He made dinner while Paul and Martin played their guitars. After three years of painting like a mad man in the Pacific Beach studio, he heard through Richard that there are unique studios available in the Gas Lamp Quarter in downtown San Diego. Deciding to pursue the arts, Richard found a ballroom above San Diego Hardware. Spaces are available.

Paul didn't need to think about it. He grabbed a space as well.

At the time, Paul is in an environment of peace and tranquility. He is extraordinarily prolific and busy with his work, but he wanted energy around him. He yearned for the craziness of city streets and the power of anti-societal lifestyles. There is something about the continual noise—something about the pimps and hookers, the drug deals, the crime and partying sailors.

For the politicians, the place is like an oozing sore that refused to scab over. The city keeps applying bandages that continually fall off. It is the society we live in and the refusal to deal with the reality of the situation, the powers that be either ignored or punished if it rears its ugly head.

Paul noticed that none of the artists renting studio space at the ballroom lived in their studios. They had their homes in the suburbs. They were all inspired artists but couldn't let go of the American lifestyle.

When Paul met Gary Ghirardi, he immediately said he wanted to move in. He only had a bed, his guitar, and his drum kit. The rest was art supplies and his paintings.

"Of course, you can move in!" exclaimed Gary.

Gary thought like Paul did. He found a studio and moved in with minimal materialistic crutches.

Richard had been living in the burbs, but when he heard that Paul had moved into the ballroom, he decided to move in too.

—— * ✳ * ——

Carole already left her studio to go back home to her husband.

Paul could hear Richard walk into the studio. His whistling changed to a barely audible song as he rummaged around. His head suddenly appeared from behind one of my paintings, and his smile and demeanor expressed a little caution as he addressed Paul.

"Can I come in and talk?" he asked.

Paul had just sat down in his chair after cleaning his brush and laying it on the palette.

"Sure, Richard. Come on in."

Richard entered and sat on the edge of the stage. "I had an excellent evening!" he said with his usual grin. "I ran into a couple of artists at the bar around the corner. They took me to their studio and showed me their work. It was amazing!"

"Their studio or their work?" Paul asked.

"Both. We sat around drinking tequila and talking art for a couple of hours."

Paul laughed. "I'm sure anything would look good after a bottle of tequila."

It is almost midnight, but Paul is still wide awake from his coffee and the energy from his painting.

"I've decided what I want to paint," Richard said.

"And what did you decide?"

"I'm going to paint the street."

"You mean you are going outside with cans of paint and do graffiti all over the street?" Paul asked, a little perplexed.

"No, not a bad idea, though," he said with a laugh. "I'm going to stretch some large canvases and paint the street—like looking down at it from above—left-turn arrows, center lines, maybe even manhole covers."

"Wow, Richard! I think you have something there," Paul said in all seriousness.

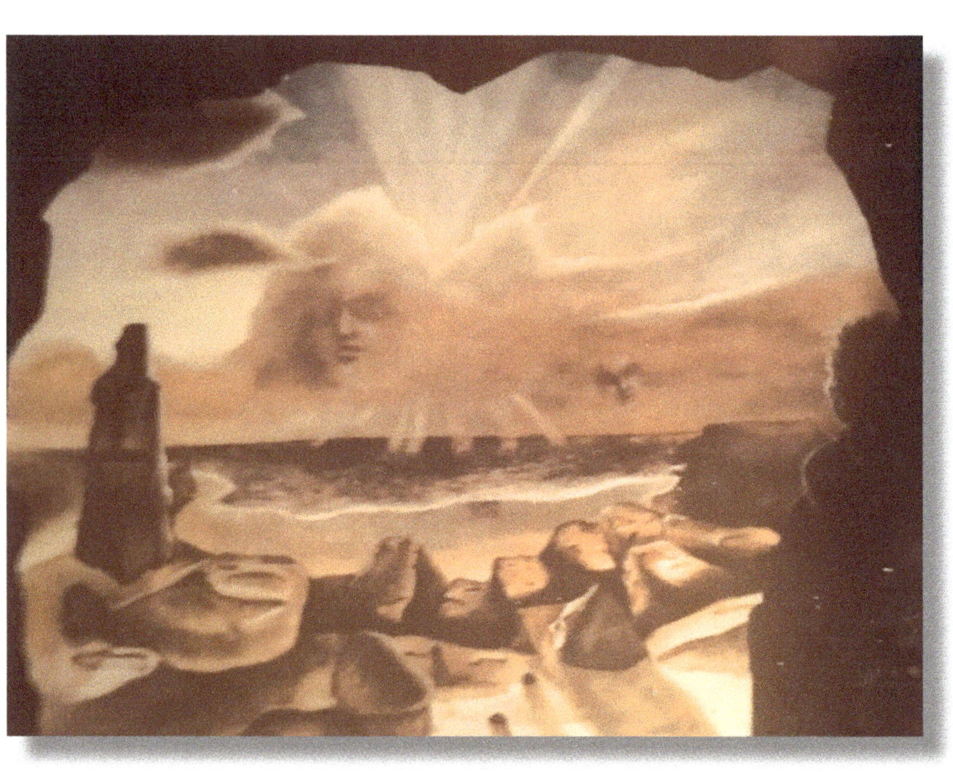

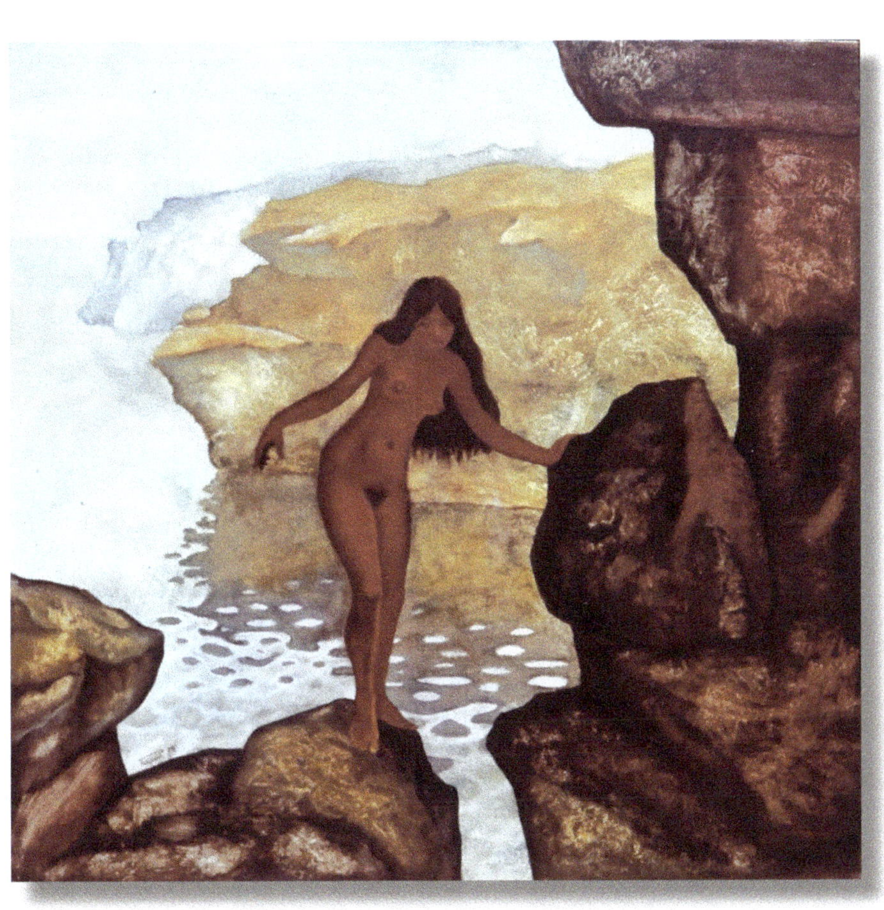

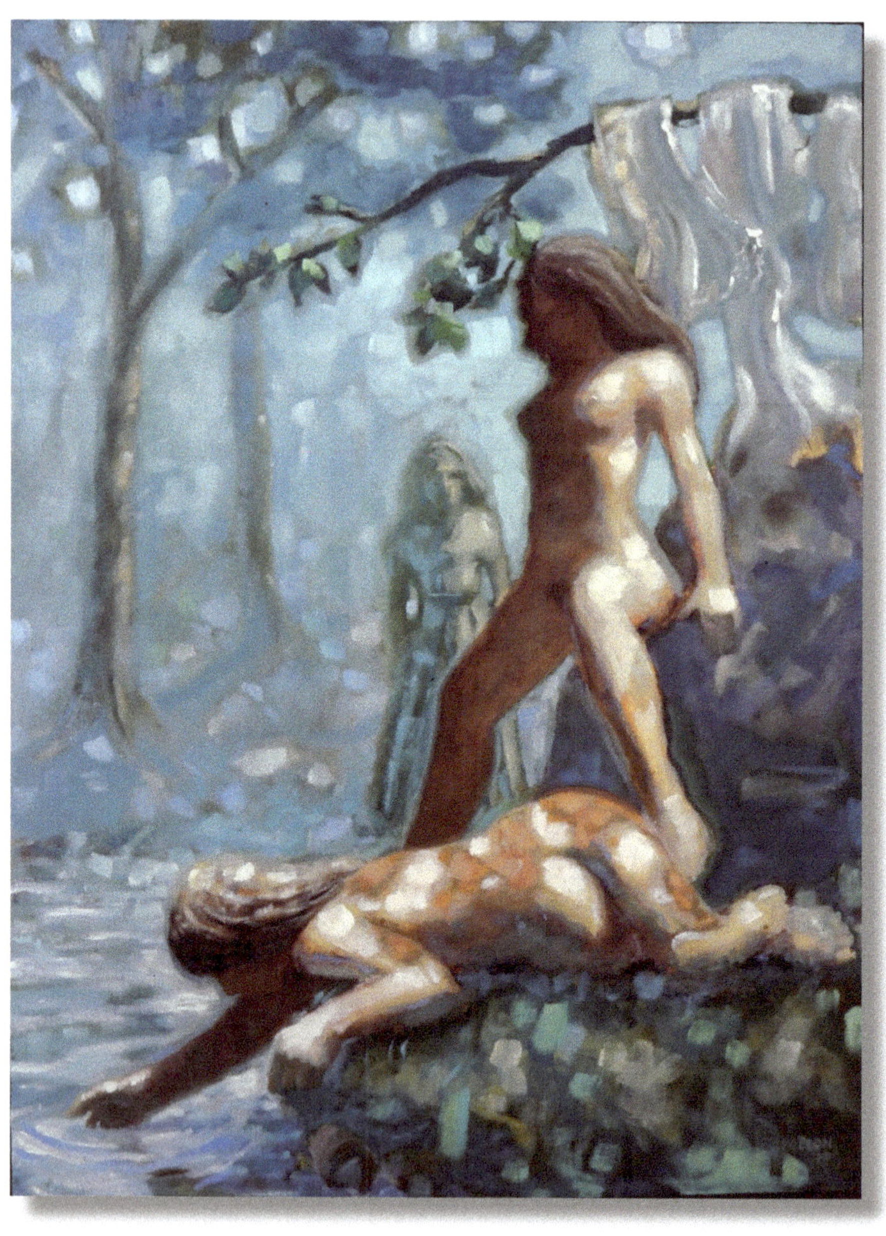

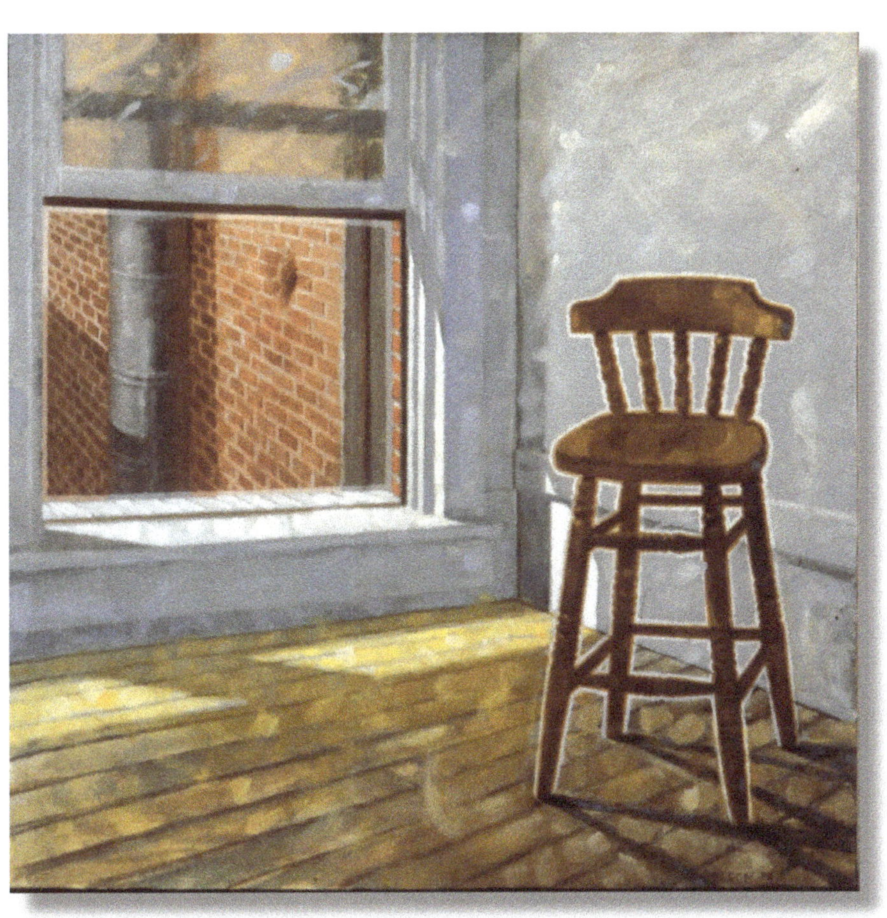

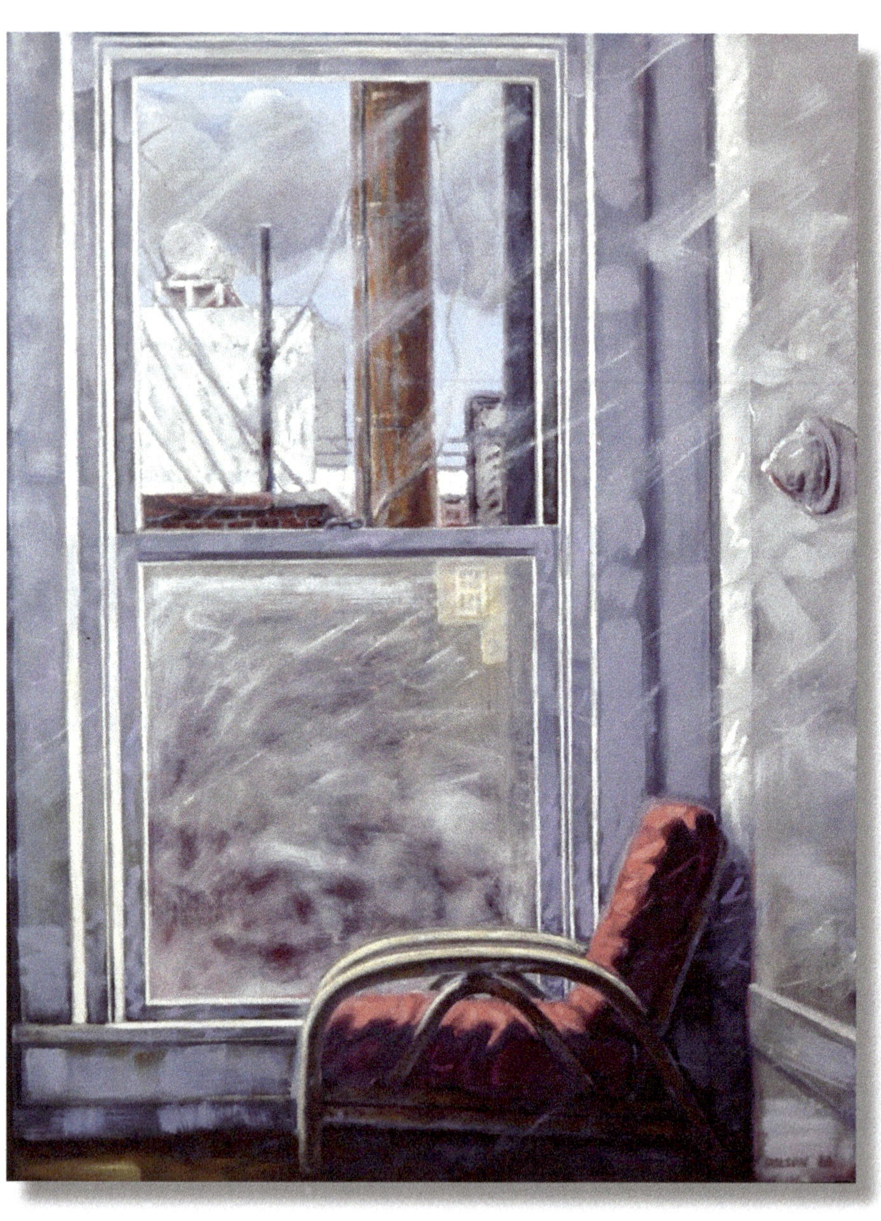

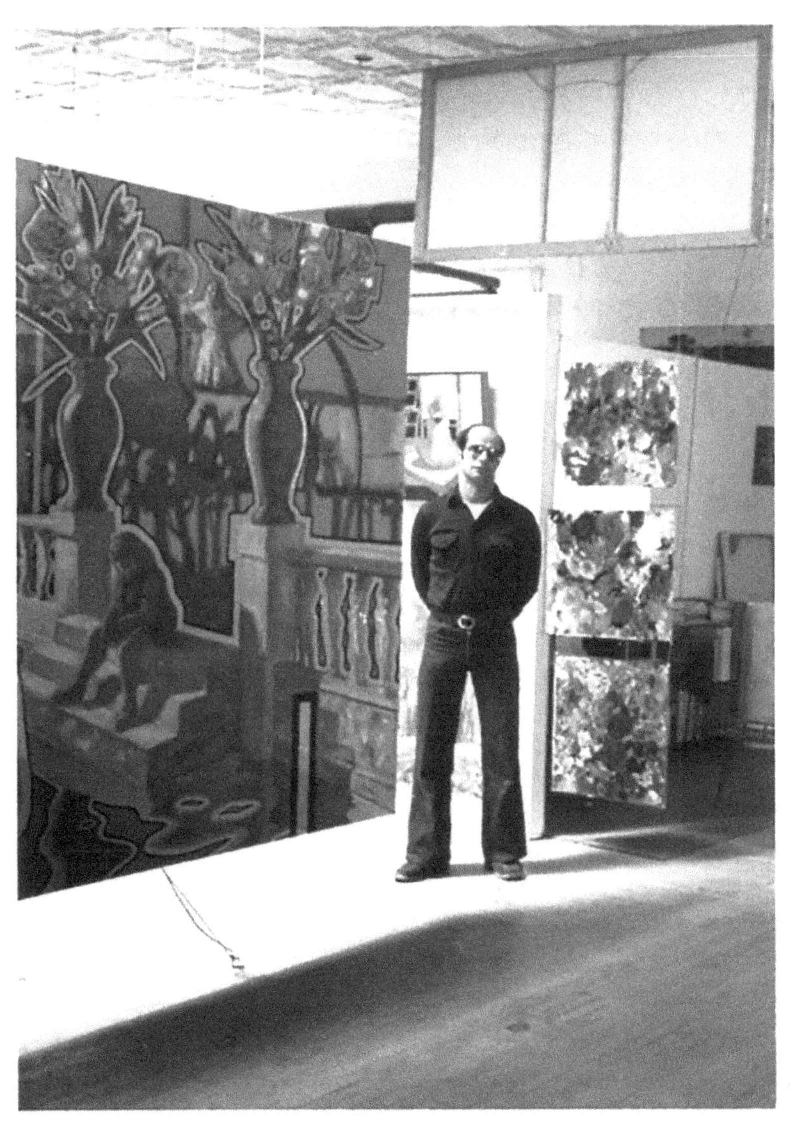

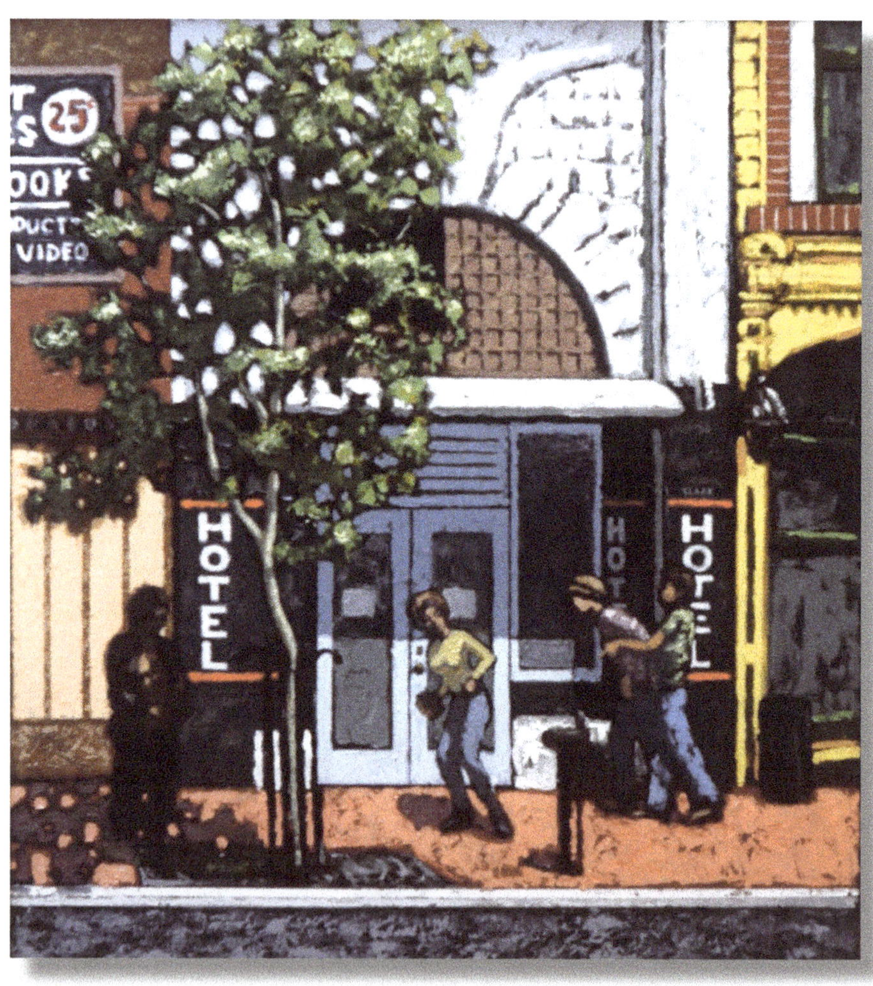
25¢
OOK
DUCT
VIDEO
HOTEL
HOTEL
HOTEL

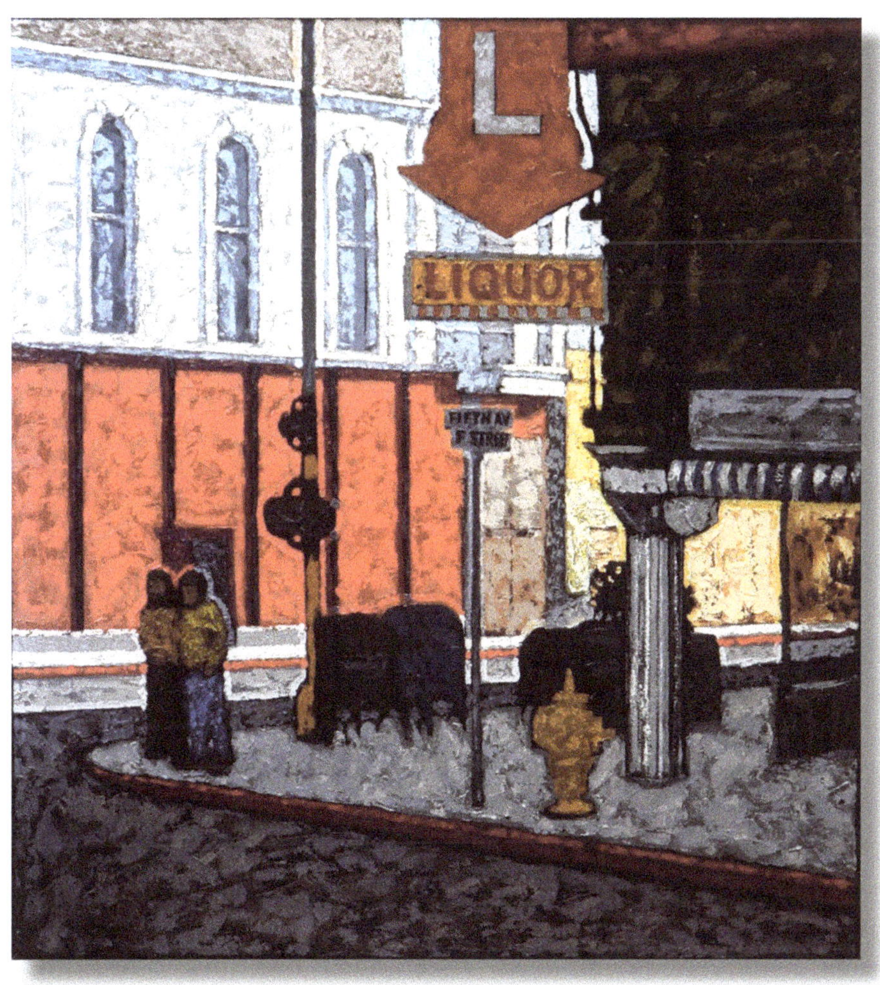
L
LIQUOR
FIFTH AV
E STREE

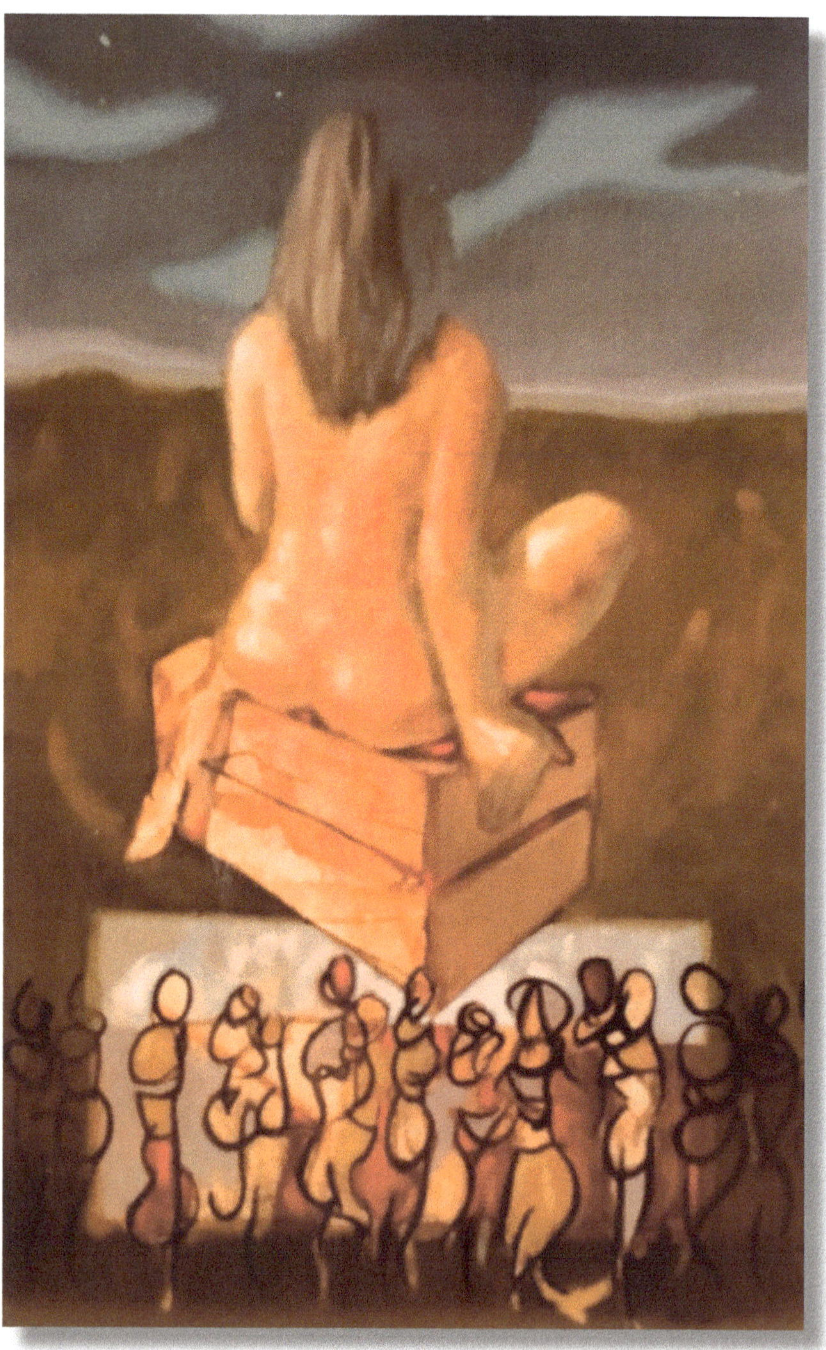

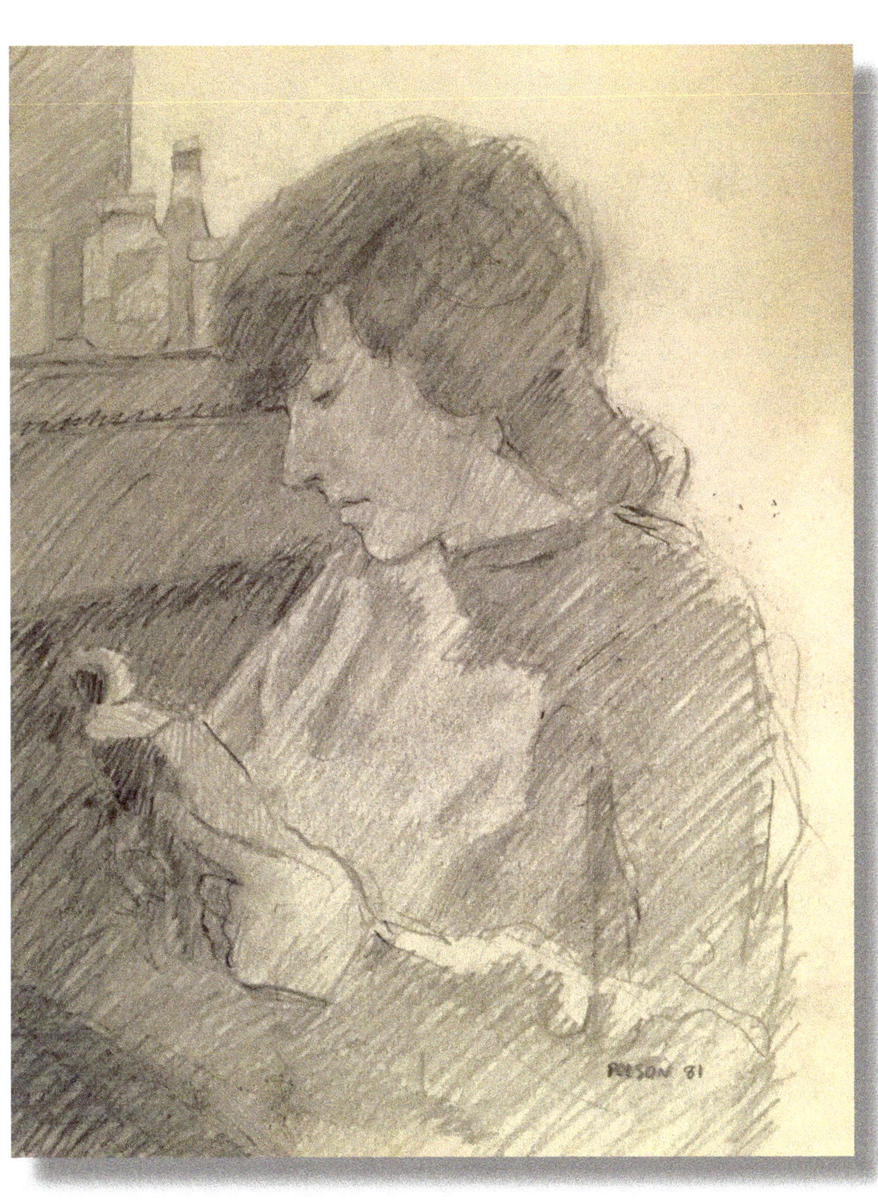

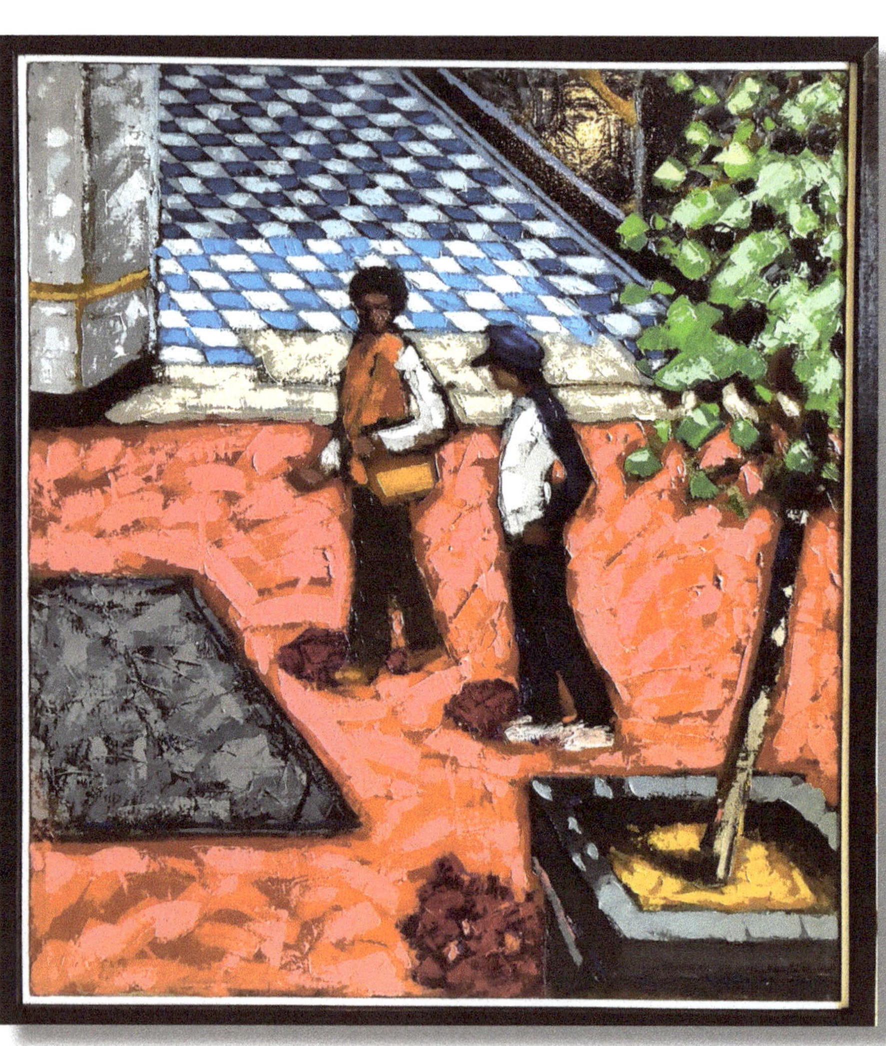

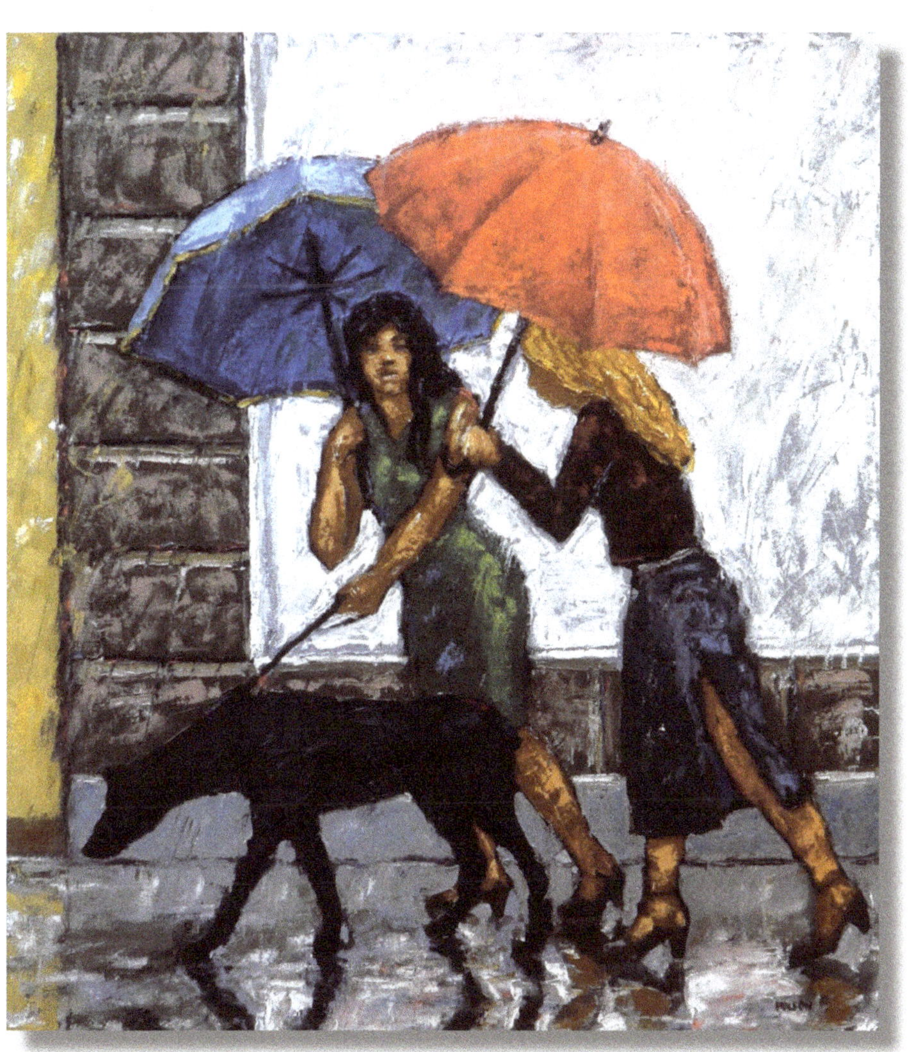

7

REUTTER GALLERY

Whiskers tickled Paul's face as his eyes opened to another beautiful Southern California morning. Gorky, Paul's newly acquired black and white cat, accomplished her goal of making sure he was awake and curled up three inches from his face. The only sound was her soft purr. The ballroom was deafly quiet, as was Fifth Avenue—a sharp contrast from the night before.

The light in the ballroom cast soft shadows from the tall windows and skylights. It was bright enough to render any artificial light useless.

Paul had a productive couple of days painting and he dressed while eyeing his new canvas. It is Tuesday morning, and he has to be at the Reutter Gallery at 9:00 am. The gallery opened at 10:00, giving Paul and Martin a little quiet time to organize framing jobs and plan their day. Or, if they are working on a deadline for a show, they dove into the work at hand.

It is still early. Paul walked to the front end of the ballroom and opened the massive doors to the fire escape. Looking down on a silent street, he could see the remnants and trash littering the street and sidewalks from the night before—the homeless cuddle under blankets in doorways.

Until Paul had to leave for work, he walked back to his stage and sat in his contemplation chair. His easel sits on the stage too—this is his performance, so what if he had no audience? C G Jung would approve of this symbolic platform where his inner expressions played out on a two-dimensional surface. A large window, eight feet tall, is twenty inches away to his right, looking out over an alley. He painted this corner window several times. The old brickwork and angles make for an interesting composition, plus the lighting is beautiful.

In front of him is his yet-to-be-completed painting. Certain areas nagged at him, so he picked up a brush and resolved some of them. He is almost finished.

The gallery is a four-block walk south on 5th Avenue to an old, historic, five-story building that sold and restored antiques, mostly furniture. The gallery is on the third floor. Paul took an old-fashion elevator that opened directly in front of the gallery.

Martin is already there, framing some art that needed to be finished by the end of this week.

A few months after leaving the Fine Art Store for this job, Martin called him and said that David, the owner, needed to hire someone else. The pay is better, and the environment and work are intimate and enjoyable. Paul jumped at the opportunity. It inspired him to frame good artists' work. This change of jobs happened at the same time he acquired his studio space. It's incredible how things work out.

Martin is fitting a group of lithographs from the art deco artist "*Erte.*"

"We still have plenty of time to finish these lithos for the show in Old Town. You can help if you want. There are still mats to be cut and I need to join a couple of more frames."

The pieces are somewhat large, made even larger by the wide mats. David designed the framing with acid-free mats, the same color of white the images are printed on. A quarter-inch spacer lifts the mat above the work, casting a subtle shadow on the litho. The presentation is finished with a simple shiny black two-inch enamel frame.

Erte's work consisted of women in fabulous gowns. The framing sets off these images quite well. The art is so decorative that it would be overkill to do elaborate designer framing. This project is for a one-person show at the "Old Town Gallery" at the base of Mission hills.

"Where's the music?" Paul asked. "Usually, that's your first order of business when you arrive at work."

"I got here just before you did," Martin replied. "I was looking at Erte's lithos. They are so perfect and clean. He's like a fashion designer or something. Do you like it?"

"Not really," Paul said. "It's well done, but I like artwork that is a little looser and painterly. That's just personal. He covers a particular genre. Like Warhol painting soup cans."

"It's called *art deco,*" Martin said as he inserted a cassette of the Doobie Brothers. "*Take it to the Streets.*"

"I know what it's called Marty," Paul said, rolling his eyes.

Martin also knew that Paul was familiar with *Art Deco.* He just has to be an asshole now and then. He wouldn't be Martin if he didn't act this way.

You could hear the elevator gears whining and the door opening.

Seconds later, David pokes his head around the corner with his usual grin.

"It's nice to see you two working so hard. How's the Old Town Gallery show coming?"

"It's going good," Martin said.

"I know it's early, but I think it's break time. Let's go up on the roof." David still has his backpack slung over one shoulder.

The three of them make their way to the elevator.

David is a little shorter than Martin and Paul and pretty stocky. He's the best boss they ever had. They work hard for him, and he appreciates it.

David is an "out of the closet" gay man.

Martin and Paul enjoy his persona and feel no discomfort even though they are outright rabid heterosexuals.

David is also an artist. He took a trip to Amsterdam and had been painting quaint little Amsterdam scenes—quite good, really. They were all in a similar style.

The three of them filed out on the roof to a 360-degree view from the south end of Fifth Avenue. San Diego Harbor is to the West and South with Point Loma in the background. To the North and Northwest, the high-rise buildings formed a wall of steel and glass.

David swings his backpack around and opens a small pocket. He pulls out a large joint, lights it, takes a strong toke, and then hands it to Paul. They finish smoking, then return to their floor and begin the day.

For Paul and Martin, it helps them focus with patience for the job at hand. The fantastic stereo system blasts the Electric Light Orchestra and Bob Seger. Time goes by fast.

David works with clients who love him, and they continue to give him business. Being high is okay with him. If his clients knew it, they didn't care either.

At one in the afternoon, it is time for their lunch break. Lunch means a trip to the roof with the addition of artisan bread slathered with brie cheese—compliments of David.

6:00 pm brings the end of their day as Martin and Paul clean the fitting room so they can return to an organized shop the next morning.

As they are leaving, Martin said, "Hey, want to go to *Sushi* on Friday?"

"What's happening Friday?" Paul asked.

Martin isn't talking about dinner. *Sushi* is a performance space known for its avant-garde and sometimes shocking performances. It is a block east of Fifth Avenue.

"I'm not sure. The performance opens on Friday. I heard it's a good show."

"Sure!" Paul said. "I'm always up for the unusual."

As they are leaving, David is sitting at his desk. Phillip, his male friend, sits in a chair next to him, rocking back on the two back legs.

Phillip is smiling with his hands clasped behind his head. He glances in our direction.

"Here comes trouble," he said

If you are a fan of performance art, Phillip-Dimitri Galas is a playwright and performance artist himself and a damn good one. He is well known in the area, but his sister is more unusual. Diamanda Galas is well known internationally and based in New York City. She started her career early in San Diego and is an avant-garde solo vocalist with multiple skills as a composer, musician, painter, and performer.

"You two are invited to the Old Town Gallery opening with me this weekend," David said. "If you want to meet me at my house, we can go together. Also, being the first of the month, we need to make invitations for the March show Sunday or Monday."

Martin and Paul do this every month. David makes omelets, freshly brewed coffee, and then they dive into the invitations, hand-labeling and stamping each one. They smoke weed and have interesting conversations while listening to David's fantastic music collection.

8

FIGURE DRAWING

artin hops in his car and heads for home as Paul begins his four-block stroll to his studio.

He arrived to the sound of hammering. Richard is building stretcher bars to begin his street series.

Paul goes immediately to his "in progress" painting. He has been thinking about it all day and dives in. Two hours later, he is finished, even satisfied.

He has two canvases ready to work on, and eight other canvases stretched and primed.

The two he has ready to paint are covered with an initial coat. One is 58" tall and 30" wide. The other is 84" tall and 144" wide.

Paul's first act of starting a painting is to attack the surface, like a Jackson Pollock, but not with thick paint. He applies washes with burnt umber, yellow ocher, cerulean blue (or cobalt), and red color—most likely alizarin crimson. He spreads the colors on the canvas with lots of turpentine, showing the brush strokes, then he splatters the canvas with pure turpentine. Paul follows up by blotting the wash with a towel or old tee shirt to add more texture.

So, that's what Paul means by ready to paint. The initial wash was painted yesterday and is now dry enough to begin the actual painting.

Paul puts a painting on his easel and looks at the images.

Not the large canvas. That one is hanging from the ceiling.

He usually has an idea of what he wants to paint, but it is important to see what the base painting has to say first. At this point, it is a world of images and potential.

Paul sees dragons and faces. There are figures, mountains, and animals. He sees a raging river roaring down a canyon and a bird struggling to break free from the splatters and brush strokes.

Richard pokes his head in Paul's studio and asks if he wants to go out for a beer.

"Sure!" Paul said.

After finishing his last painting, he is ready for a break. He is also interested in Richard's new endeavor and wants to be supportive.

There is a bar just around the corner from the studio. A couple of ex-cons owns it. The place is usually packed as it is this evening. Sitting at the bar, they each order a beer.

"I'm excited about my paintings!" Richard gushed over his beer with a big grin on his face.

"Good," I said. "Sounds like you're busy."

"I have two stretcher bars finished and enough wood to do more."

How big are you making them?"

"One is four feet by five," he said. "The other a little larger. I still need to buy a roll of canvas. I plan to do that first thing in the morning. I want to paint now!"

"Be patient," Paul said. "You're off to a good start. You'll be underway by the end of the week. I always start by making sure my stretcher bars are square and made well. Don't forget to sand the inside edge, so it doesn't leave a line on the canvas."

"I won't. One of my paintings will be a 'slow' image—all stretched out—you know, like it is on the street and is readable by drivers. I also want to paint an elongated left turn arrow next to a yellow line!"

"Sounds like fun," I said. "How do you plan to paint the road?"

"I was thinking of dipping rags in paint and dabbing it all over the surface or just splattering paint to look like pavement."

"You should draw from the figure, Richard. It's good for you," I said. "My figure drawing workshop is tomorrow. You should join us. I noticed you were working in your studio during our last session."

"Yeah. I was going to ask you about that. Does it cost?"

"We all chip in for the model. Some are paying for the class through 'ACCESS'—an adult education course. I help them get started. The others chip in about $5 or $10. It depends on how many people show up."

The modeling stand is about nine feet by six feet and two feet high. Paul found a huge theater light with an amazingly bright bulb sitting in the corner of the ballroom. It stands nine feet tall and is perfect for lighting one side of the model—ideal for drawing. The light defines the shapes making it easy to study the shadows as they flow across the human body.

The models Paul uses are from the same source, acquired from the art schools and universities in the area. They all use the same list. These models always show up on time and know the routine. They start with one-minute poses and slowly work up to thirty-minute poses by the end of three hours. On occasion, they have an hour pose at the end.

At a quarter to six in the evening on Wednesday, people begin entering the ballroom with their 24" X 30" drawing boards. Each has a metal clip to fasten a large tablet of newsprint used for quick gestures. Some have another tablet of better-quality paper for the longer poses. Paul always starts with one-minute drawings to capture the motion and feeling of each pose. You can compare these drawings to the warm-up exercises of an athlete before the final event.

The models vary from male to female, old to young (at least eighteen), and fat to skinny—the full spectrum of the human body. On occasion, Paul has a male and female together—usually a couple, married or not. He even has pregnant women models for the workshops.

Figure drawing workshops last three hours, and there are breaks between each hour session. For the most part, it's a routine Paul felt the need to follow.

This particular evening, Paul called a model who has been here several times. Her name is Angela, and she is a beautiful woman with long, full blond hair. Angela didn't have the overly thin body of a swimsuit fashion model depicted in photo shoots on California beaches. She has a slight fullness that you wouldn't call too heavy. She is the type of model that reminded him of renaissance nudes but not as full as a Rubens.

There are five new student participants that Paul acquired through "ACCESS." He took them aside and explained the procedure, starting with one-minute drawings. He preferred to start with 15 seconds, but one minute is fast for someone who hasn't done this before.

Angela walked out to the stand in a robe, took off her robe, and immediately began her poses.

Everyone, including Paul, began drawing. Richard entered the room, sat down, and started as well.

After a few minutes, Paul stood up and walked around, checking on the new people. Four of them dove in as everyone else did, but one young man, tall, blond, and well dressed, sat there staring at the model.

"Do you need help?" Paul asked.

He continued to stare. And, as if Paul startled him awake, he stood up and stared at him in shock.

"I can't do this," he said. He looked wide-eyed and frightened.

"Sure you can," Paul said. "Sit down, and I'll help you."

"No, I can't do this," he repeated. "I need to go."

Then it dawned on him. "You know we work from a nude model, don't you? It's in the information for the class."

"I know, but I didn't realize it was a real nude model. I have to go."

The poor guy turned red, and his look of overwhelming anxiety convinced Paul that he really did need to go.

"Oh, okay." Paul pulled out his wallet and said, "Here, you can have your money back."

"No, that's okay, you keep it. I need to go." He turned and quickly headed to the exit.

Paul was a little taken aback. He had never experienced this before.

Checking the work in the rest of the class, he realized that Richard seemed a bit in disarray.

He looked up at Paul with a sheepish grin and said, "I don't think I'm very good at this."

"You have to start somewhere, Richard. Don't worry about making it look like a finished figure. The idea is to catch the motion in just a few lines." Paul sat next to him and, in five strokes, caught the motion of the model. "You can work on the detail in the longer poses. When we get to that point, I will show you the next step."

Richard tilted his head as he looked at his drawing pad with a weary smile. "Okay."

"Just hang in there. I always think I'm doing a horrible job until I look at my work the next day."

———— * ✳ * ————

After the workshop, people said their goodbyes. The ones who needed to pay made sure the model received her money before they left. There are various comments about the great model, and everyone seemed upbeat.

The environment couldn't be beaten. The atmosphere of an old ballroom added to the magic of the evening. They love coming here as did the models.

Richard walked back to his studio as he looked at his pad, shaking his head.

Paul noticed that Angela hadn't left. She is still in her robe, sitting on the bench that surrounded the giant room.

"I love coming here!" she said as her eyes roamed the room. She was absorbing the skylights and tiled ceiling—the wood floor and the paintings he had scattered around or hanging from the ceiling.

"The place has a lot of history," Paul said. "It's easy to visualize the 40s dance bands and the sailors and marines holding women close as they danced across the floor. I can almost see their hairdos and long skirts, imagining their smiles and giggles."

"And check this out!" Paul added as he brought his fist down hard on the edge of the bench. Four little tiny objects fell to the floor. They were rock hard, and a couple had tooth marks on them. "Petrified chewing gum! They stuck it under the bench when asked to dance."

He has always wondered what these servicemen had experienced. Where are they going to be shipped, and to what war zones? Maybe to the Philippines or the many islands that dotted the West Pacific?

Or maybe they just returned and were beside themselves in thankfulness and the relief of being back in the states with stories to tell, wounds and tattoos to display. Was there sorrow in their eyes from the friends and companions they lost? Did they experience the depth of un-surfaced horrors they had yet to understand or realize?

Angela looked at him and smiled. She reached for his hand as she stood and led him to his bed. Her hand was soft and pale, matching her body. Her natural blond hair went perfect with her porcelain skin.

Looking back on it, he thought she was an angel.

9

---

10 DOWNING

Paul entered *Ten Downing* for the second time, and for the second time, it was empty except for Steve the bartender, buffing and shining the glassware.

After walking Angela to her car, Paul realized he is only a block from Ten Downing. Energy and happiness surge through his body. He didn't need a Keoke coffee to stay up and paint.

Ten Downing sucked him in like a magnet. The environment seemed right for the moment. He isn't ready to go back to the studio.

Paul sat on the same barstool as before. "Hello, Steve."

"Hello, mate. Or maybe I can call yew Paul since we me' befawer."

"Either works for me," said Paul. "Still busy, I see."

"Aah, American sarcasm. I love it. Shall we start wi' a Cognac? Nuff said, yeah?"

"Sure, that would be a good start."

"Lawd above! We do 'ave aaahr busy times, innit," said Steve as he did his heat the glass routine. "But ter be 'onest, deese slow times drive me crazy. Know what I mean? I'm an' all good ov a bartender ter work in a low key place, I'm best when it's crazy busy. So what brings yew in?"

"I host a figure drawing workshop, and we just finished. It lasts three hours. I'm a little too wound up to go to bed."

"Do yew draw from a real model?" Steve asked with a raise of one eyebrow.

"Oh yeah. I've been doing this every week for ten years."

"I'd like ter see yaaahr work sometime."

"I'd love to show it to you."

"So I take i' yew' 'ave no in'erest in doin' da routine like ge'in' a money makin' job, ge'in' married an' 'avin' a brood ov kids?"

"I tried that once," Paul said as he put one elbow on the bar and rested his chin on his palm. "I have son Kevin and a daughter Kim."

"So, what 'appened?"

"I was young and stupid. I married the first girl I had sex with."

"Wyoming values encourage you to get married soon—have kids, get a good job, and settle down."

"Not yer soul mate 'uh?"

"I guess not. We were both in the arts. My ex was into music, voice, and performance, and I majored in the visual arts. I thought it would help us to pursue our paths in our own genre. We even talked about how great it would be to have our kids experience their parents pursuing their dreams. It would give them a unique upbringing, and they would develop the right values, not to make money to support kids who then grew up to make money to support their kids. They need to find a reason and ambition for life."

"So what 'appened mate?"

"When we had kids, she said my art was a hobby, and I needed to get a good-paying job. She said she was too small and didn't have the lungpower for opera anyway. Obviously, she was looking for an excuse."

"Lor' luv a duck. So you divorced her?"

"Pretty much," Paul said. "She didn't realize my passion. To me, that's what life was about. If I had a money-making career, she would have gone along with it. She was afraid of failure."

Paul finished his Cognac, and Steve glanced at the empty glass as he finished the last sip.

"Keoke coffee?"

"Oh, what the hell, sure."

"It must be 'ard ter make a livin as an artist," Steve said as he made the drink.

"It depends on how you approach it. If you're serious, you think of it as a lifelong career of learning and growing, kind of like a philosophy. You don't look at it as your goal to be famous. You look at it like a lifestyle and a personal endeavor."

"So, 'ow do yew make money ter survive?"

"I get art-related jobs," Paul said. "Right now, I'm working at a gallery and frame shop here in the Gaslamp. I still make money selling art and teaching."

"Blimey! Do yew see yaaahr kids often?"

"I tried for three years. At first, I called them once a week, but my ex cut that off. I went to Laramie to visit, and she only let me see them for twenty minutes. She remarried, and I gave up. Maybe when they are old enough, they will visit when they can make their own decisions. The State of Wyoming always gives the children to the mother. If I leave the state, I have no rights at all."

"Wow. Sorry, mate. It can be a cruel world. She's 'urtin 'em ter 'urt you."

"Yup, you hit the nail on the head with that remark. She wants to convince people I'm a deserter. It will ruin her story if she let me actually see and talk to them."

———— ✳ ————

When Paul returned to the studio, Richard was still awake. He poked his head in his studio. His figure drawings are spread out around the room.

"Hey, Richard, I see you survived the workshop."

"Yeah, and you were right. My drawings look a lot better afterward. Can I see yours?"

"Sure!" Paul said. He went to his space and came back with his tablet.

As he leafed through the pad, he shook his head. "Your drawings are nice! I don't know if I'll be able to draw that well."

"Don't compare," Paul said. "Keep it up, and your drawings will progress in your own style."

Paul glanced at the solid wall in Richard's studio. He had a taut rope extending from it and attaching to the other side of his space. There were a couple of pairs of jeans, two shirts, and a pair of old sneakers hanging from the rope.

Paul couldn't help but laugh. "Is this your new art? I thought you were painting the street."

All of the items were splattered and dripping with paint. The jeans had holes in the knees and rips up the side.

"Oh yeah." Richard blushed. "You need to play the part to convince the galleries and critics you are a serious artist. It's called marketing."

Paul shook his head and walked back to his space.

Looking at his drawings, Paul sighed, partly because he could never be as good as he wants to be, and partly because of that beautiful woman, Angela. The drawings weren't that bad, but he didn't think he could ever portray that beauty and the feelings running through his veins from an experience whose reality he will always question.

Paul decided not to paint into the night and went to bed, savoring his thoughts.

He also had to go to work in the morning.

⁕

It was Friday, and the Reutter Gallery crew had a busy day ahead of them. The framed Erte lithographs needed to be wrapped and delivered to The Old Town Gallery who would hang them. The opening was tomorrow evening.

Tonight was the show at *Sushi*. Paul met Martin and his girlfriend, Becky, at the venue.

The show didn't begin until nine, so Paul worked on a painting that he started the evening before. He loves the beginning of a painting and the decisions he makes as he throws things in on a whim and brings images out from the background that make no sense.

Time goes by too fast. He grabbed his jacket and headed downstairs but stops abruptly when he looks out the door window. There is a crowd of people in a horseshoe shape around the door with a police officer in the middle taking notes.

Paul slowly opens the door. There is a young man, maybe a sailor dressed in his civies. He is lying on his side as if sleeping. The man is wearing a white tee-shirt and shorts with white tennis shoes.

The odd thing is that there is a pool cue sticking up his nose. Paul's first thought was that it was a short pool cue. Then it dawned on him that the rest was in the back of his skull.

"Excuse me," Paul said as if everything was normal.

The policeman moved aside. Paul stepped over the body and began his trek to the performance space three blocks away.

When Paul arrived at the performance venue, Martin and Becky were waiting. They climbed a flight of stairs to a room with five rows of fold-out chairs. Over half the seats are occupied. When they sat down, they were looking at a huge projection screen.

Several more people sauntered in and claimed their place, no one Paul recognized. The art community can seem small when you have been here a while. The performance crowd was probably composed of a different group than the visual artists. Paul heard that Whoopi Goldberg was in the Gaslamp District at the time, but he still hadn't seen her. In all fairness, he hadn't been to any theatrical performances in the area either.

After another ten minutes, the lights began to dim. No introduction was necessary. The lights dimmed to the point of complete darkness as the music slowly gained in volume.

Suddenly, there was a flash of light from a slide projector behind the audience. A beautiful mountain scene appeared. It looked a bit odd in that there are parts of the image that seem three-dimensional. The projected image went dark, then flashed again to a cityscape with a large bridge.

Paul finally noticed a human figure in the center of the stage, changing positions for each image. It is beautifully choreographed. The human form complemented each slide so that the body almost disappeared because of the pose the figure took. He then realized that it is not just a human figure. It is a nude woman.

One slide showed a large dog with its sad eyes fitting perfectly over her breasts, and its nose fit in the triangle of her crotch. She turned sideways and thrust her arms ahead of her when another bridge lit the environment. Her arms stretched perfectly along the roadway as cables seemed to hang down and connect to them. Her slight squat matched the shoreline.

On and on it went until the lights came on. The woman stood there erect with her chin held high and her arms out. She bowed at the waist and then scurried off the stage.

That was it—short and sweet. Paul and his friends went out for a beer, talked about the performance, and said their goodbyes. Paul strolled back to the studio. When he approached the door to his space, he stopped and looked down, not even a blood spot. Maybe that was performance art too.

As he reached the top of the stairs, he could hear the sound of a staple gun. Paul walked by Richard's studio and noticed he was kneeling on the floor, stretching one of his two canvases. He didn't see Paul as he quietly entered his own space, sat in his contemplation chair, and stared at his painting. There are so many directions he can go.

10

TECHNIQUE

There is a confident and robust base for Paul's art. His reasons are deeply implanted in his psyche. Paul's motivation is unshakable, and he sees it as the reason for his existence.

After returning from active duty in the Army, Paul landed a job at the Wyoming State Hospital in Evanston, as an assistant to an occupational therapist.

Judy is from New Jersey, Paul's age, and it was one of her goals to move out west, get a horse, and live the western lifestyle. As a registered occupational therapist, she could pretty much choose where she wanted to work. Such was the need for her occupation.

It's an excellent job for Paul's interests as well. He worked in a huge shop and taught arts and crafts—lapidary, ceramics, weaving, and leatherwork, to name a few. He even taught patients how to knit.

After a short vacation to visit her fiancé in New Jersey, Judy returned with a gift for Paul.

It is a book: *"Jackson Pollock: Psychoanalytic drawings"* by CL Wysuph.

Paul is amazed by this book! Being familiar with his splatter paintings, he had enjoyed reading Jung's biography and learning about his work, as well as the other abstract expressionists.

This book is full of Pollock's drawings that he had created for his psychiatrist. It was a bit different from the work Paul was used to seeing. The drawings are filled with images, dream images—animals and deformed figures done in a loose and expressive style—messages from his unconscious.

Jackson's therapist was Dr. Joseph Henderson—a Jungian psychologist.

"Jungian? What the heck is Jungian?"

The book sparked Paul's interest so much that he began researching Jung's way of thought.

Carl Gustav Jung was a contemporary of Sigmund Freud. He found the work of Jung to be more rational and believable than Freud.

Jung's studies were related to dreams. He was comparing the symbolism in dreams from American Indians, African tribes, Europeans, and many other diverse cultures. He found astonishing similarities. Jung studied new and old religions, and again, the similarities of their symbols and beliefs overwhelmed the differences.

He saw humans not as individuals but as a part of a much higher organism. He studied and developed theories (actually, more realities than theories) about the masculine and the feminine. Not in a sexual way, as Freud would, but in the psychological makeup. He also wrote of the feminine inside the man and the masculine inside the woman. He talked of understanding and working with the anima and the animus to become a more aware and complete person. He also expressed the symbolism of the feminine and masculine principles portrayed in dreams and "*art.*"

Yes, "*art.*"

Jung also studied everything from cave drawings to the renaissance to the abstract. And then there is music.

There is an opening quote by Sigmund Freud at the beginning of this book gifted to me by Judy:

"*Before art, psychoanalysis lays down its arms.*"—Sigmund Freud

Paul discovered C G Jung's volume set. It was huge, but he read all the books throughout his twenties. He also found books written by more contemporary Jungian psychologists. To top that,

Paul found novelists whose works are based on Jungian psychology: Herman Hess is one, author of *Siddhartha, Demian, Magister Ludi,* etc.

So, absolutely, C G Yung formed the basis and energy behind Paul's work.

When he does a painting as he describes, Paul begins with splattering paint on the canvas to see what images present themselves—an inkblot test, each one—complicated and full of images that his internal self pulls out, adding to the complexity of his paintings.

They become living participants that Paul battles and works with as he would with another human being. He allows these other forces to "have their way" sometimes, and sometimes, he overpowers them with his will.

Like a relationship, if you control it, it dies.

When Paul finishes one of these works, he finds himself wide awake and full of energy. He even enjoys looking at the painting when it's finished. Paul feels like he birthed a child to have a life and a presence while existing on Earth.

When he forces a painting to become exactly what he wants, he finds himself drained and exhausted.

* ❈ *

There was another event that had occurred several times during his life that he believes was life-changing. This event was instrumental in his decision to pursue the arts with no hesitation or fear. Why? Because Paul knew he could succeed in whatever he chose to do.

He describes this from an excerpt from his Memoir *"The Vision" A painter's Legacy*:

"My body is wracked with fever. I am only nine years old.

A world of darkness enveloped me. Huge dark spheres began to close in. I felt a fear that I had never felt before, and the reality I usually experienced is transformed. There was an overwhelming feeling of no upside down or right side up. The spheres had no size—nor did I.

I could hold a sphere between my thumb and forefinger and roll it in circles as it diminished to nothing, yet the spheres are larger than the universe itself—all at the same instant.

Suddenly, the universe around me is filled with light. Orbs are floating in the void. One sphere has a shape emerging within it. The shape became a human figure, and my fear turned to calmness, peace, and enlightenment.

There it was! Right before me! It was the answer to our existence. It all made sense."

This vision repeated itself every year until Paul was nineteen, with no fever. He could come back to reality when he chose, but if he relaxed, the vision returned. Paul always wanted to write down the answer to what life is. He left a notebook and pencil next to his bed so he could do that. The problem is that Paul knows what it means only while having the vision, and there is no reason to write it down. The moment Paul woke to reality, his vision made no sense, nor could he remember it.

Even though he could not put this answer into words, he felt that the yearly repetition of this vision was meant to impart some wisdom and awareness to his life. One of its effects was to give him strength and confidence. Neither life nor death scared him. He felt the actual reality of our existence, even though he cannot describe it.

The decision to pursue a life in the arts is not a light one. If it is a quest to become famous and sell his work so he can make a vast fortune, there is a good chance Paul will be disappointed, especially if he chooses to become a studio artist.

There are countless employment opportunities in the arts—teaching is one. To commercialize yourself in this capitalist system, you are asking for other more powerful people to stick their fingers in your pie and tell you what to create. Or they may highly suggest the direction you should take if you wish to become financially successful, and you still might not be.

Paul's art is his alone. He makes all the decisions and chooses his path. He makes the sacrifices so he can do this.

So, to the point of his description of being a studio artist, Paul is no different than a scientist in a laboratory, a philosopher, an explorer, or a knight with a quest to find the ultimate Holy Grail.

He does this, not for fame or riches, but to learn about this world. He also wants to discover himself. It's a life quest where he will gain the ultimate fortune. He will take this with him to the most mysterious place life has to offer—the place where he will ultimately go, after his death.

11

ERTE OPENING

The opening at Old Town Gallery has well-dressed viewers who are in awe of the *Erte* Lithos.

The show looks great! Of course, Martin and Paul had seen every piece up close for at least a month, and instead of looking at the art, they are carefully scrutinizing the mats to see if any dust particles snuck in and if the corners are clean with no overcuts.

They also chatted with the crowd. It made for a fun evening. It is tempting to lead the conversations to the excellent framing—only to realize that viewers didn't care much about it. They are there to see the lithos.

That is a testament to the great job Paul and Martin did. If people noticed the framing, they probably did something wrong.

Earlier that day, since the work had already been delivered and hung, Martin and Paul had a busy Saturday, framing the work from individual clients and artists that they had neglected. There is more than enough work to keep them busy for a month. Nothing is overdue yet. Martin and Paul know what they are doing, and they are capable of kicking butt and meeting the deadlines.

After work, Martin and Paul met at David's apartment early to do another monthly ritual before they went to the opening at Old Town Gallery.

David treats them to their favorite Old Town Mexican Restaurant on the first of each month. The tables are placed in a large patio, and heaters are positioned between the tables.

Comparing winters here to Wyoming, San Diego is pretty mild. When Paul first arrived, he never wore a jacket, but after five years, his body acclimated, and he felt a chill in the air. The patio, being somewhat temperate, didn't take much heat to make the area comfortable.

They all ordered their favorite dishes and had their usual fun conversation with bits of humor, mostly instigated by Martin's sarcasm.

This evening, David had an announcement to make.

"So," said David, "I've decided to move my business."

"What?" Paul commented, "I love our place. How could you find a better spot? The antiques and environment are great."

"And the roof," Martin chimed in, "where will we smoke and still have such a great view?"

"The location of this gallery is ideal," Paul said, "How can you find a better place?"

"Whoa! Relax," said David as he threw his arms up in surrender "The place we are moving to has a great gallery. It's above *Pegasus.* They roast coffee beans. It's just a couple of blocks from here, and the aroma is fantastic."

It turned out to be a smart move. The Reutter Gallery has the whole second floor. The frame shop is on the north side—all windows—with great natural lighting to do their work.

It isn't hard to get used to our new location.

When they arrived at work, they poured themselves a cup of fantastic coffee, much better than anything store-bought. David is right about the aroma. The smell, when they walked in, was to die for.

On the first day of work, David arrived late as usual.

"Hey, you two! Check these out," David said as he plopped two CDs on the fitting table.

"Wow!" Martin exclaimed, *"The Police* and *B-52s!"*

The sound system had excellent speakers, and with the two new CDs added to their library, they rocked out all day.

To kick off the first gallery opening, Martin and Paul framed fifteen of David's Amsterdam paintings. They are a big hit, and he sold six of them.

------ * ❈ * ------

After working for two months, Paul dropped a request on David, one he had been thinking about for a while.

"Hey David, is there any chance I could work three days a week? If you get busy, I'll work full time until things slow down."

Paul had been planning this for a while. Martin and Paul talked about introducing Mary to David as a potential framer. She is experienced, and they worked with her at the Fine Art Store. Paul hated doing this to David, but David understood. He wanted to spend more time painting.

Mary Webster is an unusual character. She is a low-key and quiet person but had quite the mouth on her. Your feelings are the last thing she cared about. Martin and Paul had known her long enough that it didn't bother them. They just laughed and threw it back at her. We can always put a smile on her dour expression. She is a bit of a tomboy, and if she had a more erect posture and a big smile, it would put her more in the gorgeous category, but that isn't Mary. Paul prefers her look. You might say she is our buddy since they hung out a lot together, minus any sexual overtures.

Mary is a talented artist, fixated on doing etchings of women's shoes. They were very well done—loose and expressive with lines and cross-hatching that added life to a still life.

------ * ❈ * ------

Back at the studio, Paul focused on his large painting. It is too big to fit on his easel—84 inches tall and 144 inches wide—so he built a wall and painted it white. It is like an alcove with side-walls. These walls helped distribute the light, so the brightness on the painting was more even as opposed to having open space on either side.

The painting itself has lots of faces and figures. On the left side, there are reclining nudes that look like mountain ranges in that the flesh is painted in purples with higher values as they reached the distant horizon. Hands with forearms came down from the top as if groping for the individuals in the crowd below.

Richard's work is coming along also. He is doing a good job making the canvas look like the dark grays and blacks of the road. Not in a photo-realistic way but loose and suggestive. He painted the white and yellow lines along with the letters and images. They played well with each other.

Separate from his street series, Richard did a painting of a hand. Paul, being a serious figure painter, cringed and avoided bringing it up. It is pretty naïve—anatomically incorrect—even though Paul thought he intended to make it realistic.

Looking around his studio, it dawned on Paul that he is amassing a large body of work—many of them are large canvases.

Since arriving in San Diego in 1973, Paul had been heavily involved in *the San Diego Art Institute* in Balboa Park. That worked well for him because they continually showed his work and accepted him in many juried exhibits. They also sponsored a weekly figure-drawing workshop.

Before moving into the ballroom, Paul joined an artist's coop (named *"The Artists Cooperative Gallery"*). They have a small but lovely gallery on the west side of Hillcrest overlooking Highway 5. He still had his fantastic studio two blocks from the shores of Pacific Beach at the time.

His work is being shown, and sales did happen, but not to the point that he could upgrade his standard of living to middle-class requirements. However, that is fine with him. He adjusted his life-style to his measly income. Paul is getting out of life what he wants.

His studios are his castles. Having such a low income and living in the beautiful environments he works and lives in made him realize that income did not need to be a deciding factor.

During openings at his studio, friends and more well-to-do supporters of the art world gaped at Paul's beautiful surroundings that only cost $200 a month.

Paul is in heaven.

Several close friends bought Paul's work and allowed him to use their shower (bathing facilities are absent in his PB studio and the ballroom studio he is now living in). This support is valuable to him. To be loved and encouraged by these people did not go unnoticed. They had the ultimate faith in his obsessive drive in the arts. They validated him—more so than his accomplishments in the San Diego art scene.

12

ABSTRACT EXPRESSIONISM

So it became time to consider using the Gaslamp environment and its potential to show Paul's work. Since moving to the area, he realized that there are fantastic performances and visual arts exhibits that arose and disappeared all around the Gaslamp Quarter.

The owners of these old historical buildings are allowing artists to show art in their buildings.

When Paul opens the doors to the fire escape in the ballroom, the view is taken up by the most beautiful building in the Gaslamp Quarter. He walked downstairs, crossed the street, and read the notice on the door. The phone number of the owner is prominently displayed along with other information on the property.

When he called the number, the owner answered. Paul explained that he is an artist in the Gaslamp, and has a studio directly across the street. He popped the question about using the main floor for an art exhibit. Paul would need to build some walls to partition the space and, along with the existing walls, would exhibit his work. He would also need to install temporary lighting.

To his surprise, the owner immediately agreed. As long as Paul left the space in the same condition, he is welcome to use it.

Later that day, he met the owner at the front door, and Paul is given a tour of the main floor. After showing him around the space, Paul showed him his studio. The owner was delighted and gave him the keys.

"Have at it," he said, "no charge, just make sure it looks the same when you leave, and send me an invite."

Paul couldn't believe it! He had the most amazing space in the Gaslamp area to show his work. The walls were already white, and the ceiling must be fourteen feet high.

The show will take place in a month and a half. That gave Paul time to do more work. He would frame the smaller pieces and paint the edges of the larger paintings black. Partition walls need to be built for the open spaces and painted white, and the final touch will be to add some directed lighting.

＊✳＊

Allan Morrow is the fourth person using the ballroom as his studio.

Allan is a graduate of *San Diego State University*, and like Paul, he is a painter. Unlike Paul, he is heavily into abstract expressionism—you know—like De Kooning and Pollock. Of course, that movement started decades ago, so Allan's work is different, but it did follow the same conceptual parameters.

Paul loves abstract expressionism. Having seen several shows of these masters, in Los Angeles and San Francisco, he is fascinated by their art. In a large rectangular space, they would pit color against color, shape against shape, and line against line—and each against each other—without any emphasis on materialistic or realistic imagery.

However, Paul has seen figurative images in De Kooning's paintings and beasts in Pollock's works. Still, the abstract emphasis of the paintings made the imagery secondary or unimportant compared to the other elements in the work.

The composition is excellent and freer compared to a painting of a landscape, figure, or still life. Paintings of realistic images are restricted by a horizon, or vertical shapes, like trees or buildings. Streams did their part in curves and perspective—all of these controlled by a concept of gravity.

Abstract expressionism did not need to conform, and as a result, the surface of the canvas became a playground that denied these restrictions and refused gravity.

Even though Paul loves this era of painting and genuinely likes Allan, he didn't always agree.

One evening, after we both worked late into the evening, Paul walked into his studio and found him sitting back and contemplating his work.

"Hey, Paul. Want a beer?" Allan said as he opened the lid to his cooler.

"Sure," Paul said, "Am I interrupting anything?"

"No, I'm ready to call it a night."

"Nice work, Allan!"

"Thanks," he said.

Paul never heard Allan verbally justify his work.

He'll have to honor that. Words demean a painting that is beyond words. In this context, words are like chicken scratches compared to a novel. Abstract expressionism has its own language.

However, they did discuss the concept of abstract expressionism as compared to other types of art—like Paul's work.

Paul and Allan did discuss a painting he did of a nude on a 42" X 43" canvas—almost square, it was loosely painted similar to his work genre.

It was a profile of a figure curled up in a sitting position, head bowed, one arm wrapped around her shins while the other touching her forehead.

"You know, a friend of mine who I went to school with was looking at this painting the other day," Allan said as he massaged his chin with his left hand.

"That shadow across her body wouldn't look like that. That's why we don't use images in our work. It is impossible to capture what a camera can do better."

In his defense, Paul held his ground.

"Actually, Allan, this was painted directly from a model. I put that shadow there because that is how it looked. Studying the way shadows play across the body is an important part of drawing from the model. If the light moves only a quarter-inch, or if the model slightly moves, that shadow would change dramatically."

Allan seemed to comprehend this as he nodded his head.

Paul continued, "Let's say I draw the contour of this figure, ignoring how the shadow actually looks, and then logically place the shadow where I think it should be. If I then move the light to try and make the shadow work with what I just drew, the chances are 100% that I could not make the shadow appear like what I imagined."

"That is why I paint the way I do," Allan countered. "Why struggle with copying what a shadow looks like if a camera would show it exactly as it is."

Paul's comeback is, "I think your mind and body needs to act as its own camera. Distortion and the quick expression of a figure or landscape can make an image come alive. It doesn't need to be exact. Look at Picasso and cubism."

"Yes, but all the variations and movements in the arts have already been done. What else is there?" said Allan.

"I don't look at art that way. To me, it's a personal journey. You learn from other artists, art movements, and studio work. Then see where it takes you. A canvas is like a playground, and imagery gives you more to work with, not discounting abstract expressionism. They both have elements that add interest and excitement to a painting. Why not use them together?"

Paul also added a fundamental belief in his goals to become an accomplished painter.

"I believe it is essential to begin a career in art by learning from the old masters. Then determine where painting has gone since then. Fill your head with knowledge and then strike out on your own. Just painting abstracts and neglecting the figure, landscapes, composition, color, and the essentials are like building a house with no foundation."

✳

Richard has been busy doing his street paintings and amassed enough to have a show of his own—about nine pieces. A couple of them are relatively large.

Gary Ghirardi saw his work and offered him a one-person show at Installation Gallery. The small space Gary had conceived is for conceptual work to be exhibited and used as an outlet for artists who did not prescribe to traditional art accepted in most galleries.

Richard is excited. The show is coming up fast, and the opening is the first week of the coming month, during the monthly art walk. Richard's show is a month before Paul has his show across the street.

"I'm getting excited," Richard said when Paul crossed paths with him on the stairs. He is on the way out as Paul is heading upstairs. "An art critic from San Diego Magazine will be interviewing an artist I met the other day. She's meeting him at his studio, and he said I should come meet her!"

Richard is wearing his splattered paint garb. He is really into the marketing aspect of being a painter. "Artists need to meet the right people to make it in the art world. That's what I heard anyway."

Paul didn't prescribe to that philosophy but each to his own. He agreed that knowing the right people would help an artist get exposure and opportunities, but Paul wanted to spend his time painting and learning. His focus is to develop his work, not to play-act for social reasons, especially when you aren't willing to put work into developing your own style.

When Paul has a show, he does the usual press releases showing the details: time, place, and why he is showing his work; what he hopes to achieve; where he is going. Paul doesn't feel like he needs to pursue it further than that. He wants his work to speak for itself.

He doesn't paint to impress critics or other artists for that matter. Paul's whole concept of painting is like being a scientist in a laboratory. He wants to discover visual elements and concepts—search for techniques used by the masters and find his own way by painting and experimenting. Paul wants to dig deep into his psyche to understand and grow as a complete person. It's a search for the Holy Grail. Like an alchemist, he is in a quest to turn base metals into gold, or the symbolic equivalent.

13

RICHARD'S THREAT

Working three days a week is perfect.

Paul has been in situations before when he didn't need to work since he had enough money to sustain his artistic life. That means living as minimally as you can. Occasionally, a painting sold, or he made some money from private lessons or figure drawing workshops.

Initially, he was in heaven. Paul is painting a lot and enjoying his surroundings. He would ride his bike by the harbors and beaches. Once a week, Paul visited Balboa Park and its galleries and would bike up the coast to La Jolla to visit the *Museum of Modern Art* and hang out in his favorite bookstore. He would sit on the rocks of beautiful coastal areas and watch the waves and the surfers. He even surfed now and then, like early mornings or at sunset, regardless of the waves.

Looking at the shapes in water intrigued Paul. The continuing dance and changing patterns were mesmerizing.

Paul carried a sketchpad and drew the world and people around him. He also wrote down his dreams, poetry, ideas, and profound revelations. Sometimes, Paul took his watercolor block and painted these beautiful scenes around him.

Taking a short toke of marijuana on occasion kept him in a state of patience and wonderment with his surroundings. He never liked to indulge as his friends did—smoking joint after joint. Just a little toke is perfect.

Then there is his studio work. Paul stretched large canvases and did what he believed to be his most important work—painting from his mind; forgetting reality and combining images, thoughts, and ideas. Experimenting with colors and associating images that didn't go together is a challenge and adventure, like dreams that continually change and surprise.

Unfortunately, after some time, Paul became less productive when he worked a full-time job—forty hours a week. He felt starved and useless. Working three days a week is perfect.

His work needed to be an art-related job, like working in a gallery hanging shows or picture framing, which forced him to socialize with collectors and other artists instead of confining himself inside his head with no interaction with people or responsibilities.

Working three days a week built up his anxiety to paint. He felt like he is kept from his creative side while being around art-related tasks without producing art itself. After working a three-day job and then having extra days off, Paul found himself to be much more productive. He did twice the work than when he wasn't working a job at all.

Preparing for his show is an ordeal unto itself. Paul knows what he needs to do. He is a very organized person and has always been able to think long-term steps at a time.

To prepare for his opening, Paul had several friends and acquaintances who are excited to help.

Trish had a man friend, Clarence, who spent his life in construction and building houses. When it came time to make partitions in the space where Paul is having his show, Clarence showed up in a truck. He framed and paneled about forty feet of walls in three hours. All Paul has to do is cover the floor and paint the walls white.

For the lighting, he used clamp lights, connected by extension cords placed in strategic places.

Press releases are sent to different publications. His show would take place during the art walk on the first Friday of the month. Paul addressed and sent invitations to people he knows and to people he doesn't know. He also contacted people who followed the arts and events in San Diego.

Richard's show went well. The art walk drew a lot of artists and art lovers as usual.

Paul dropped by *Installation Gallery*; Richard's paintings are well hung. It's an interesting exhibit. He portrayed his agenda well and offered a view of our society that people often take for granted yet experience every day.

Paul couldn't attend the opening since the Reutter Gallery is having an opening of its own. These are David's paintings taken from images of his Amsterdam trip. The work is stylized to be consistent in size and technique. Martin and Paul spent the past week framing his work. There are no figures, just the old iconic Dutch buildings and canals simply painted. The consistency of his style portrayed Amsterdam well in general terms, almost cartoonish but effective. They are fun to look at, and he sold five pieces.

The next day, Richard had a decent write-up from the critic he had met. Richard had a huge smile on his face from the euphoria of his opening. Paul was happy for him.

Things changed as they continued their work as studio mates. He didn't continue with his series. After his experience, he felt relief from his hard work and wanted to relax and bathe in the glory of success.

Paul is working on his paintings and preparing them for his show.

After a few days, Richard walked into Paul's studio with his usual smile. Paul is working intently on a large painting.

"So," he said, "in Philadelphia, each neighborhood is controlled by one person who watches over his territory. Everyone does what this person says or pays the price."

"Sounds interesting but a little weird," Paul said. "What does that have to do with anything?'

"It means that this is my neighborhood, and I'm controlling this studio. You need to do what I say, especially if you want to have a successful show next month. This is my territory."

Paul couldn't help but blurt out a quick short laugh. It looks like this experience went to his head. I guess he's God's gift to the art world now.

"Don't pull this power game on me, Richard. I'm not from Philadelphia, I'm from Wyoming, and I won't put up with that bullshit." Paul said. He didn't bother looking away from his canvas.

Richard turned away and stomped out.

That is the beginning of the end for any relationship they might have had.

They didn't talk after their little chat. Little bits of passive-aggressive behavior began to arise. Like not spending the night at the studio but setting his stereo alarm so that it would go on, full blast, at 2:00 AM, or running around the Gaslamp bad-mouthing him—as reported by friends.

But Richard's behavior doesn't bother Paul, and he stays focused on his work. Paul is, however, confused by his behavior. Maybe his success at Installation Gallery and his successful schmoozing of an art critic went to his head—*ego running rampant.*

Paul tries to give any artist support and credit for original work. He always encourages other artists whether he agrees with them or not. Each has his or her own approach, or what you might call their myth.

Paul's internal unexpressed feelings about Richard is that he is looking for a gimmick. He has no interest in working on art essentials that would take years of study and painting.

Thinking back on the artist's biographies that Paul has read, two different relationships come to mind of painters having irreconcilable differences.

One was Vincent Van Gogh and Paul Gauguin. They were roommates and painted together but had many stormy disagreements to the point of intolerance.

The other was Jackson Pollock and Willem De Kooning. A faint memory arises in his mind where Jackson punched De Kooning, knocking him off a barstool as they were frequenting their favorite drinking establishment. Paul read a lot on Pollock who had issues including violent behavior.

So, maybe there is a common thread here in the collective unconscious that we all need to deal with for our growth and understanding. Human conflict is a reality.

When Paul runs into this kind of situation, he finds himself spending more time on his painting—a constructive diversion so he doesn't need to deal with an issue, especially if it can't be solved with logical discussion or agreeable arrangements.

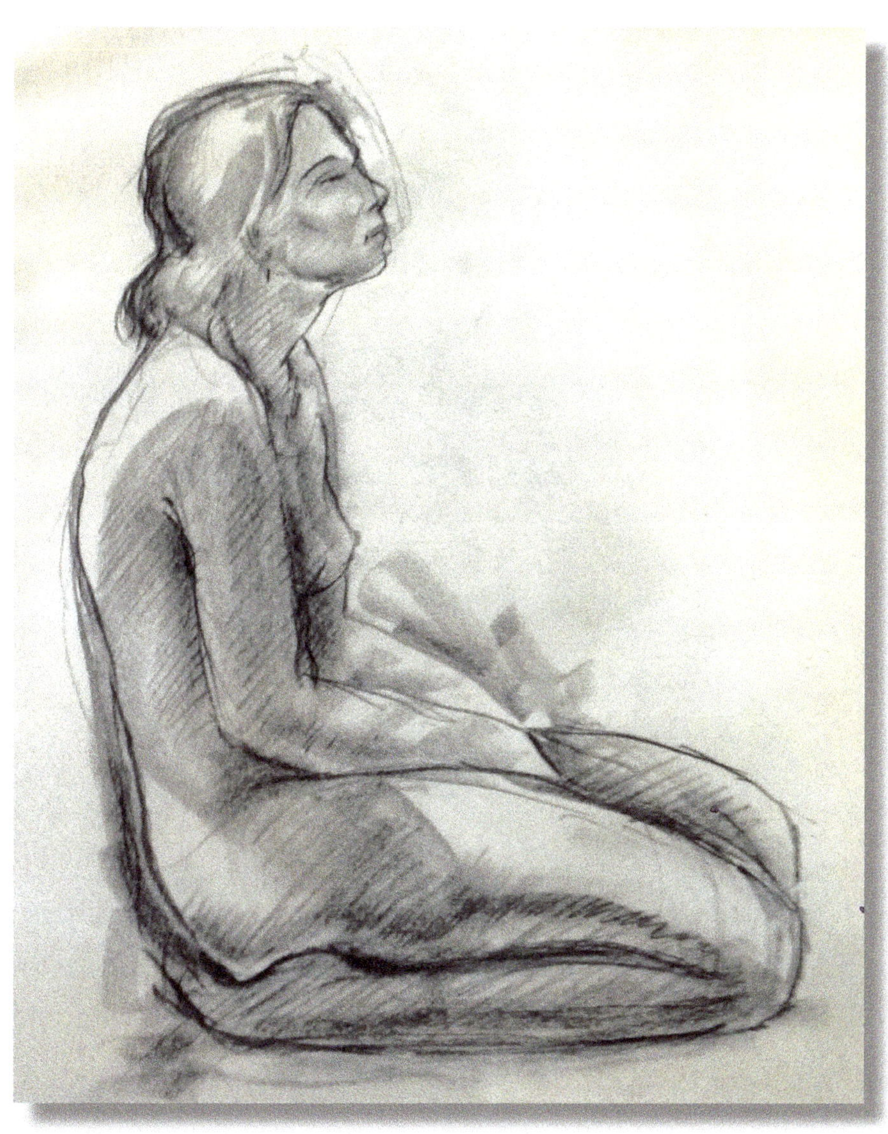

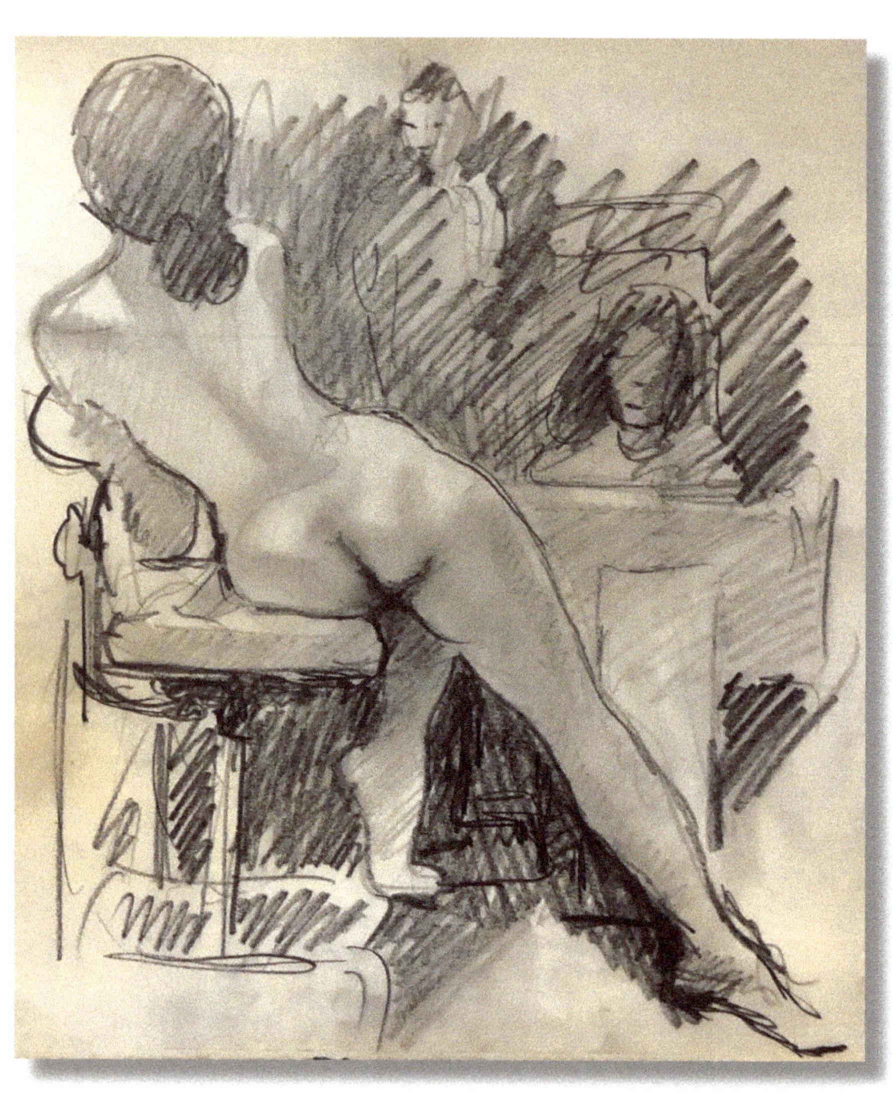

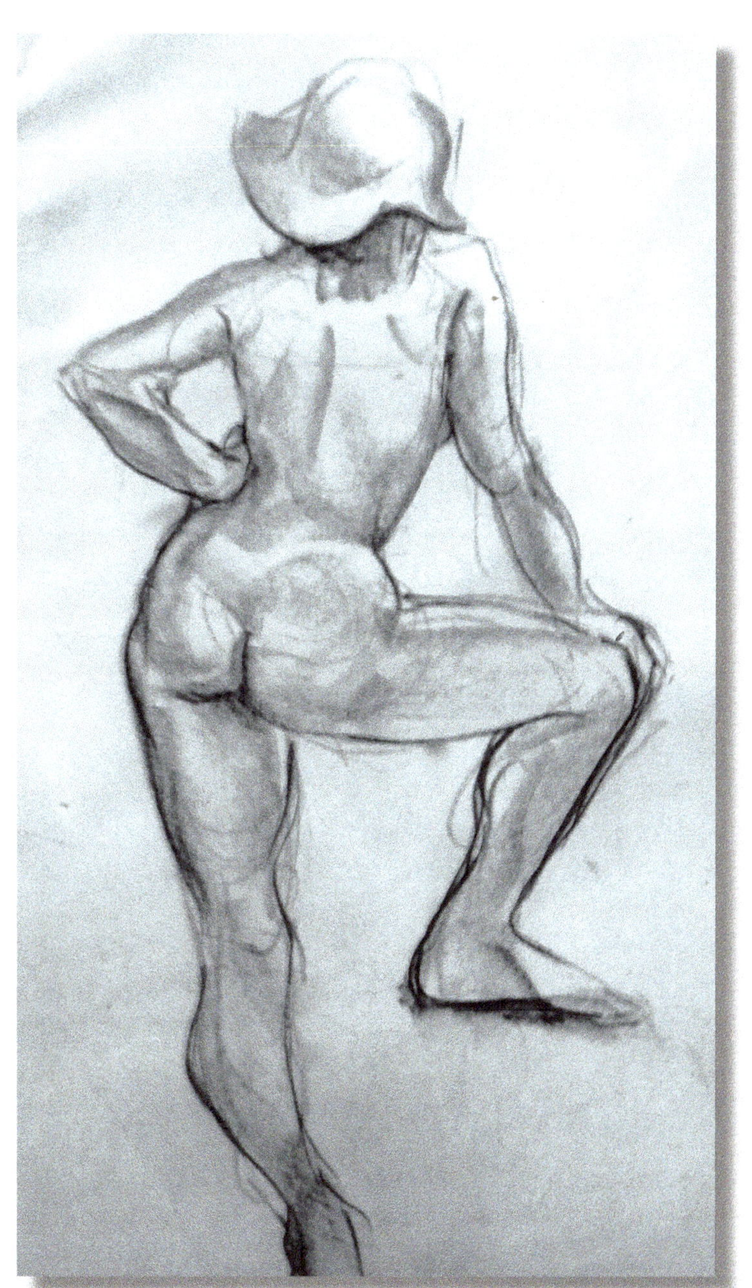

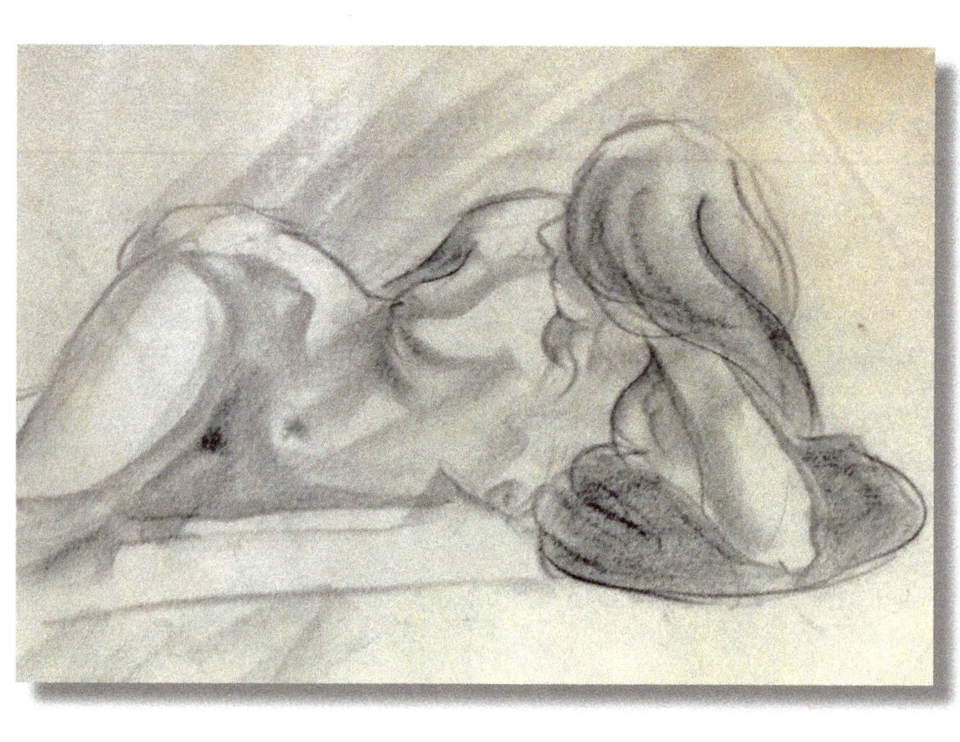

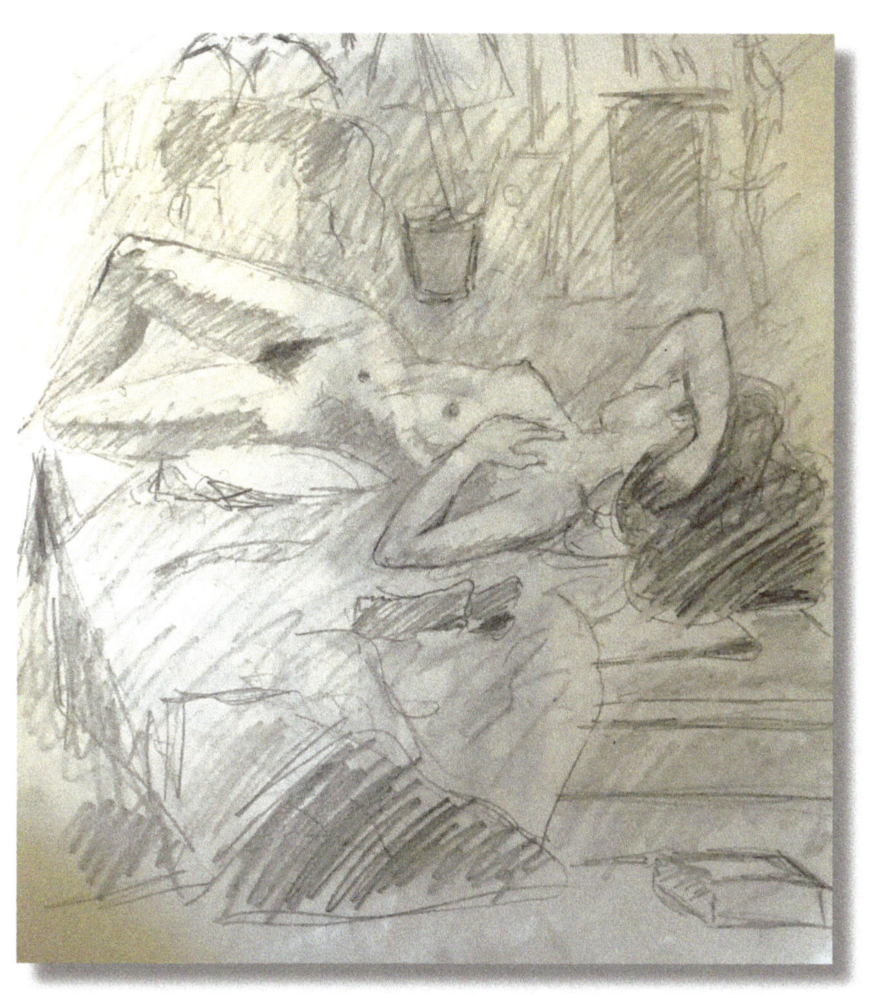

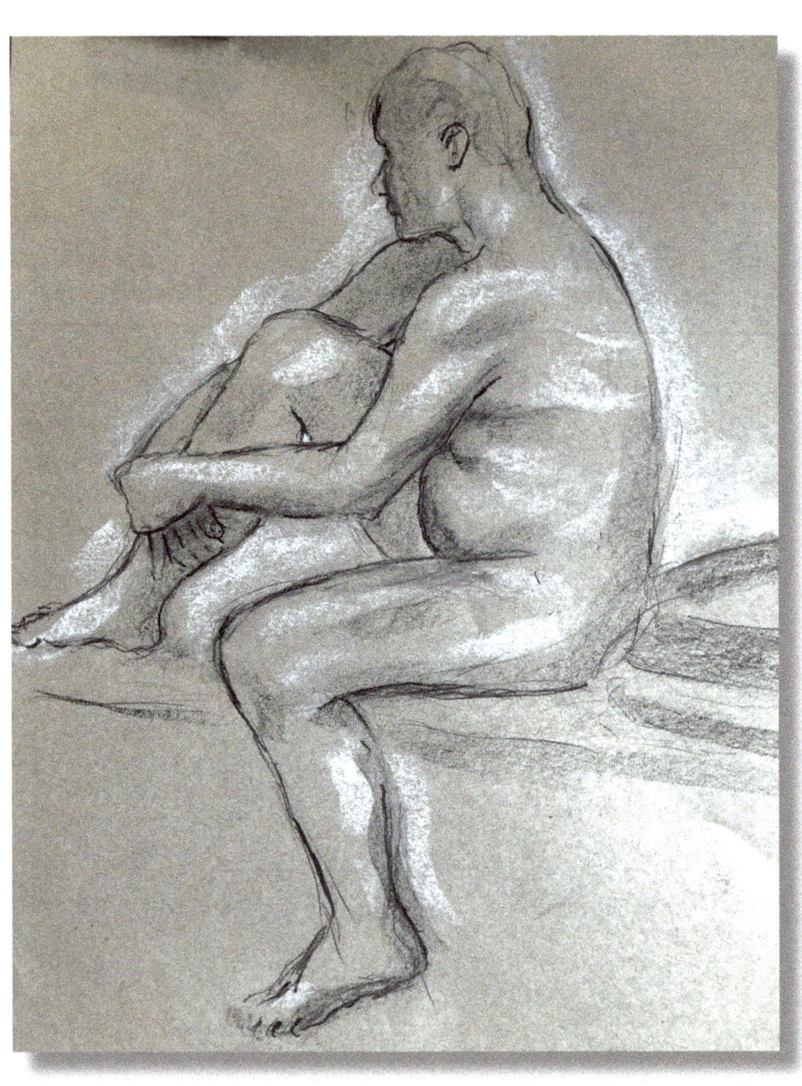

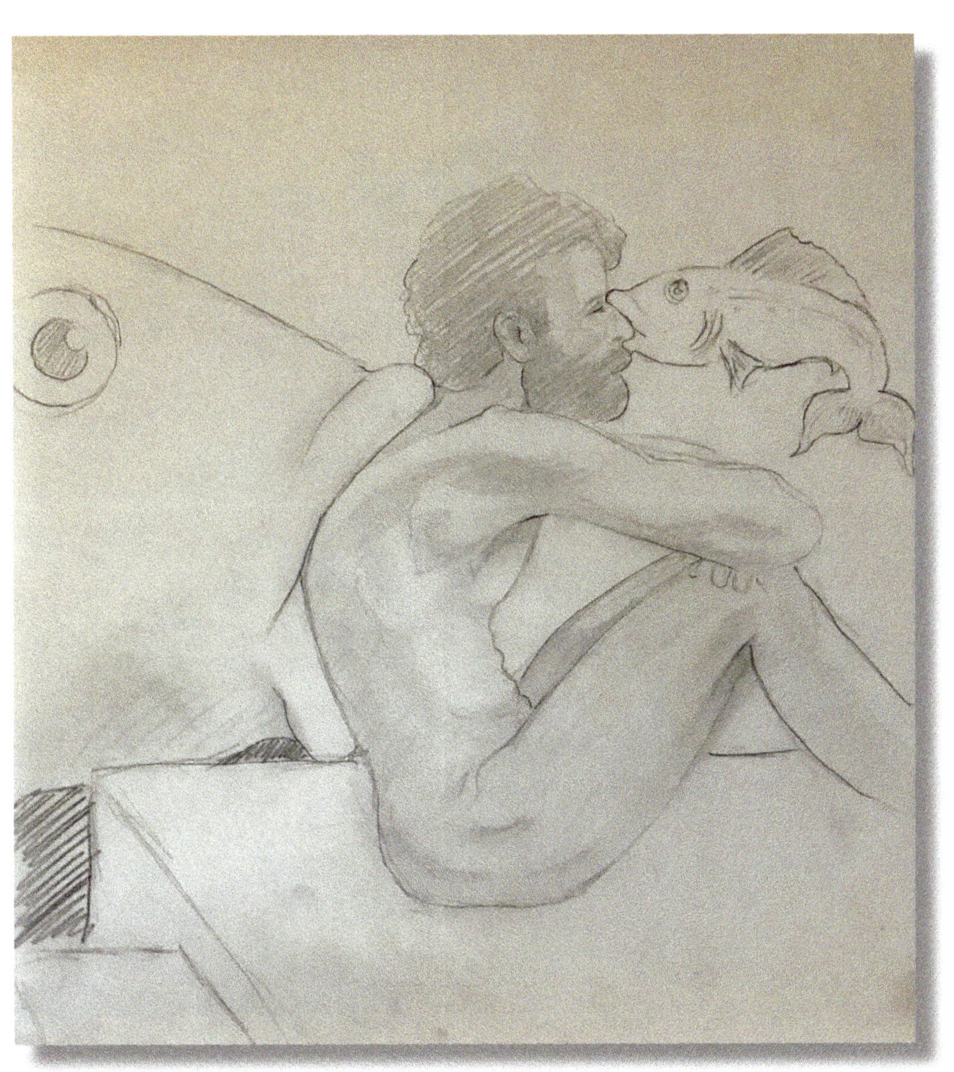

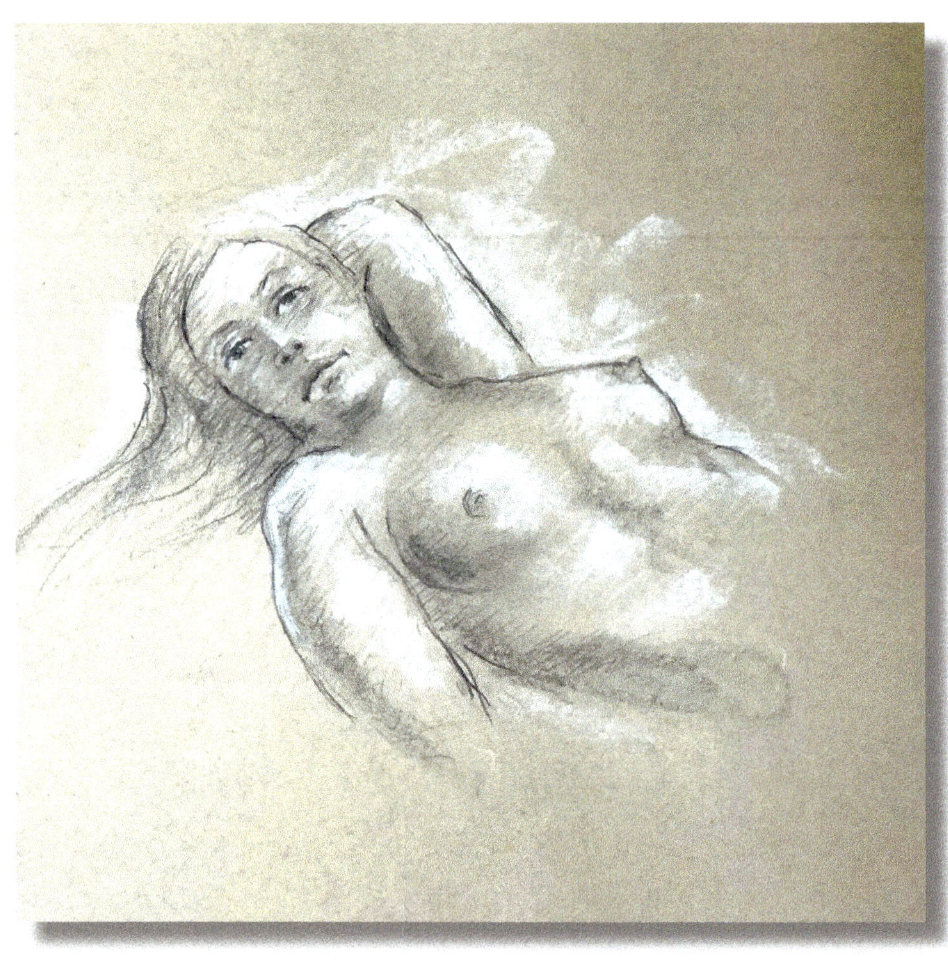

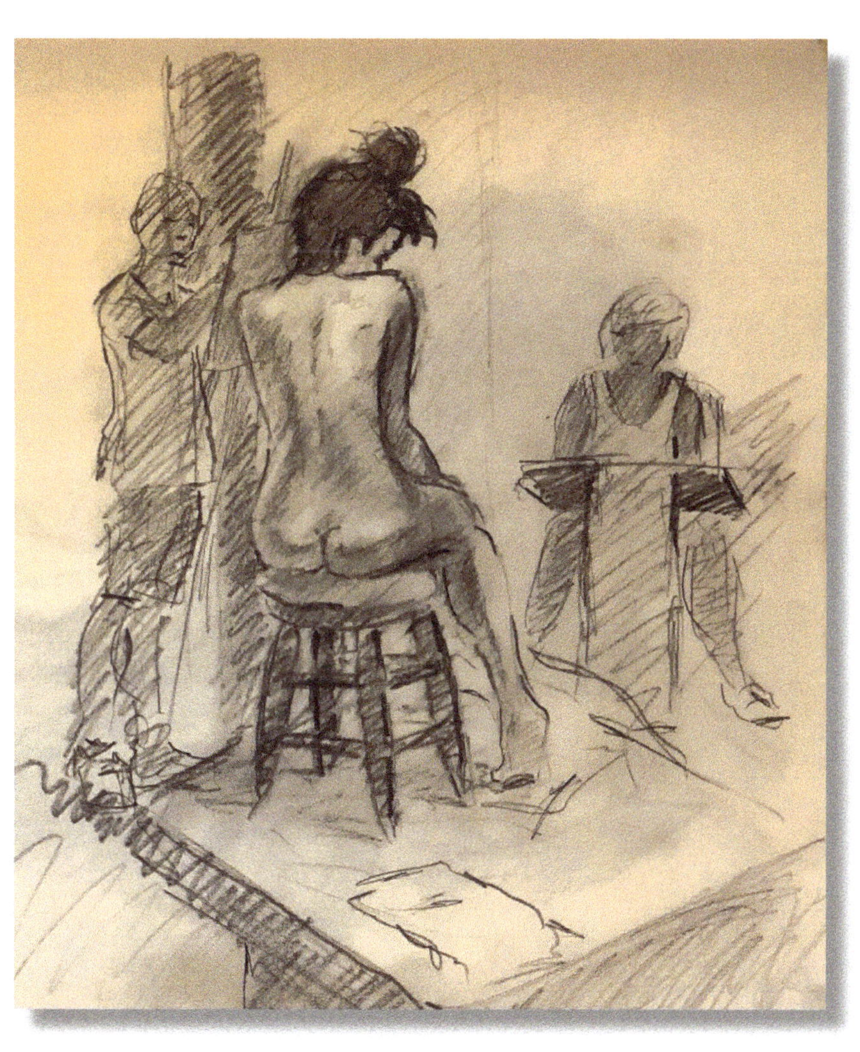

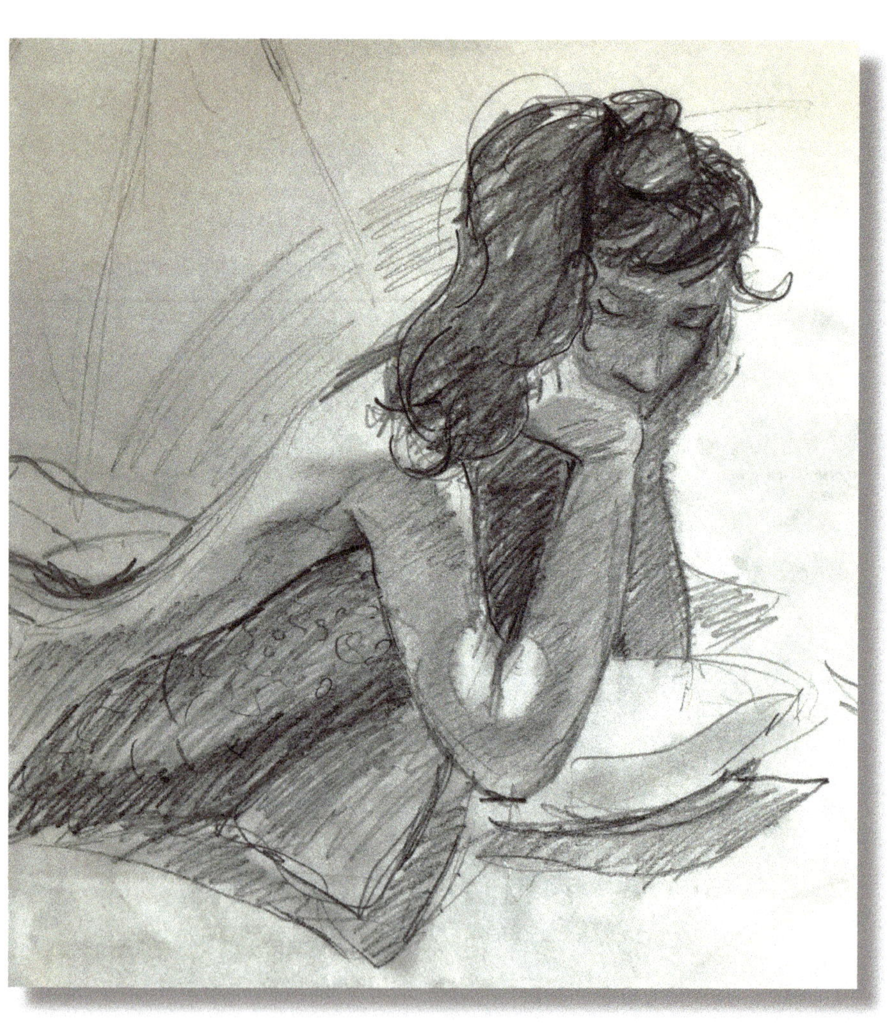

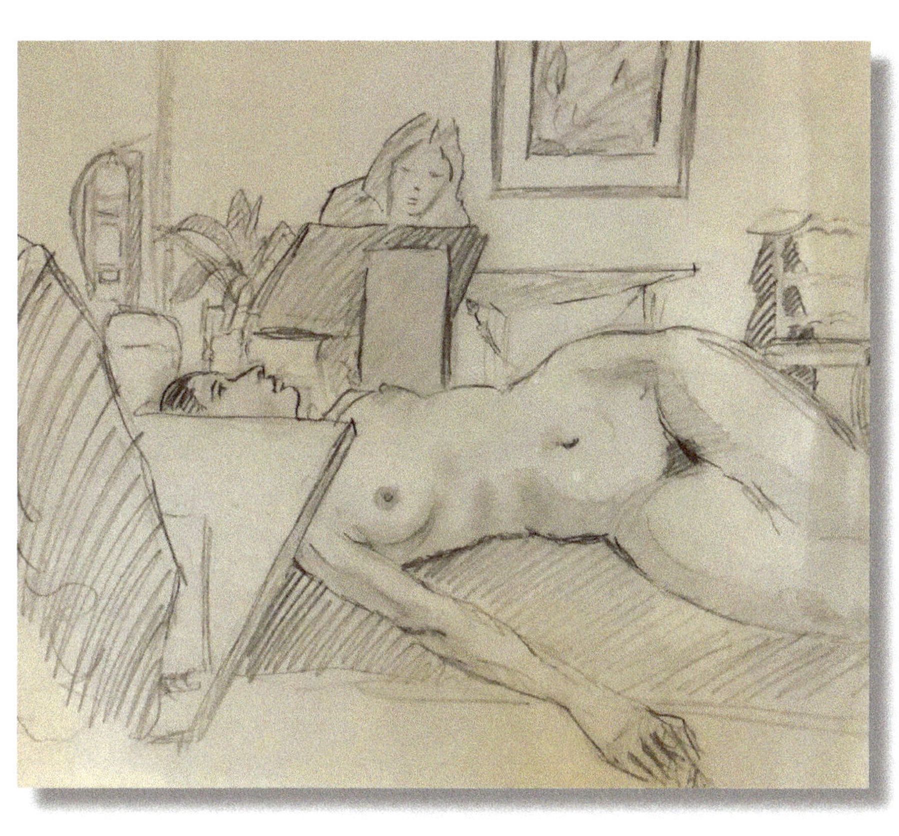

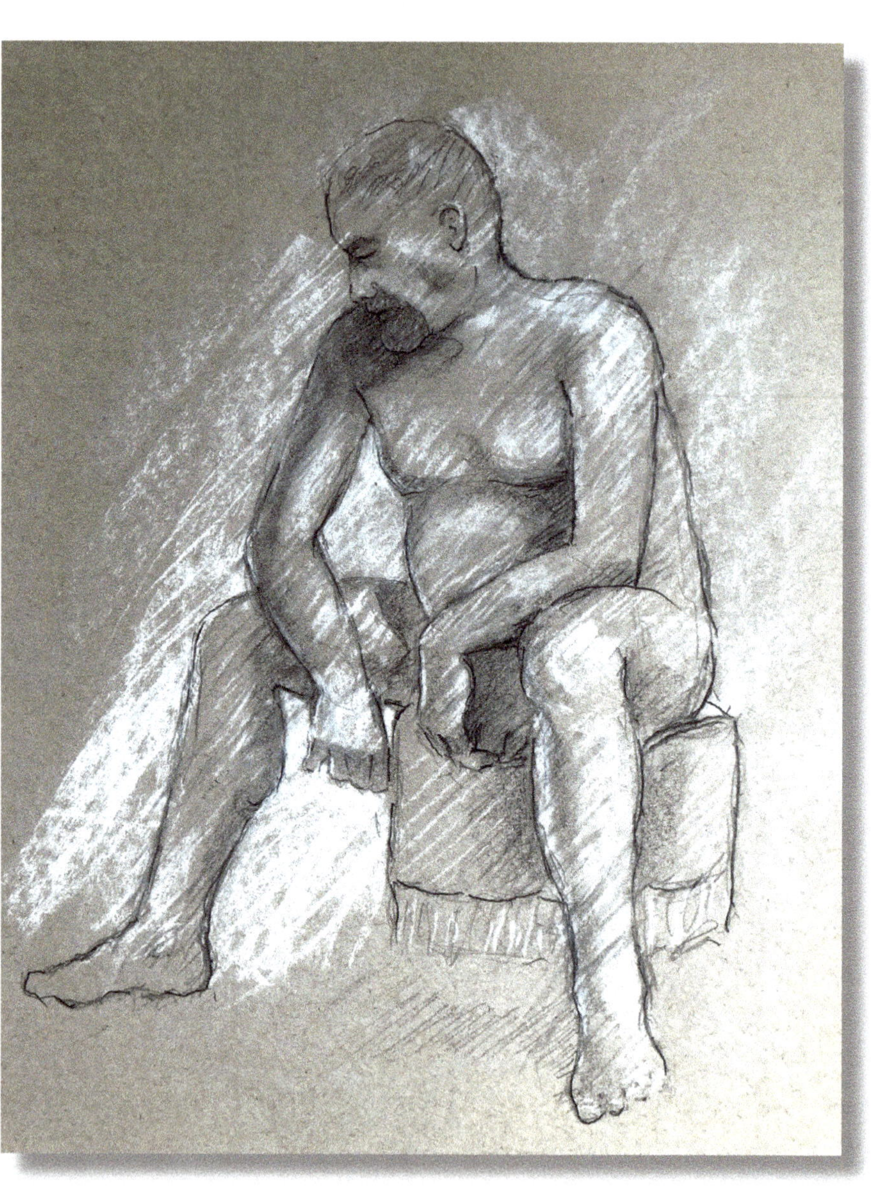

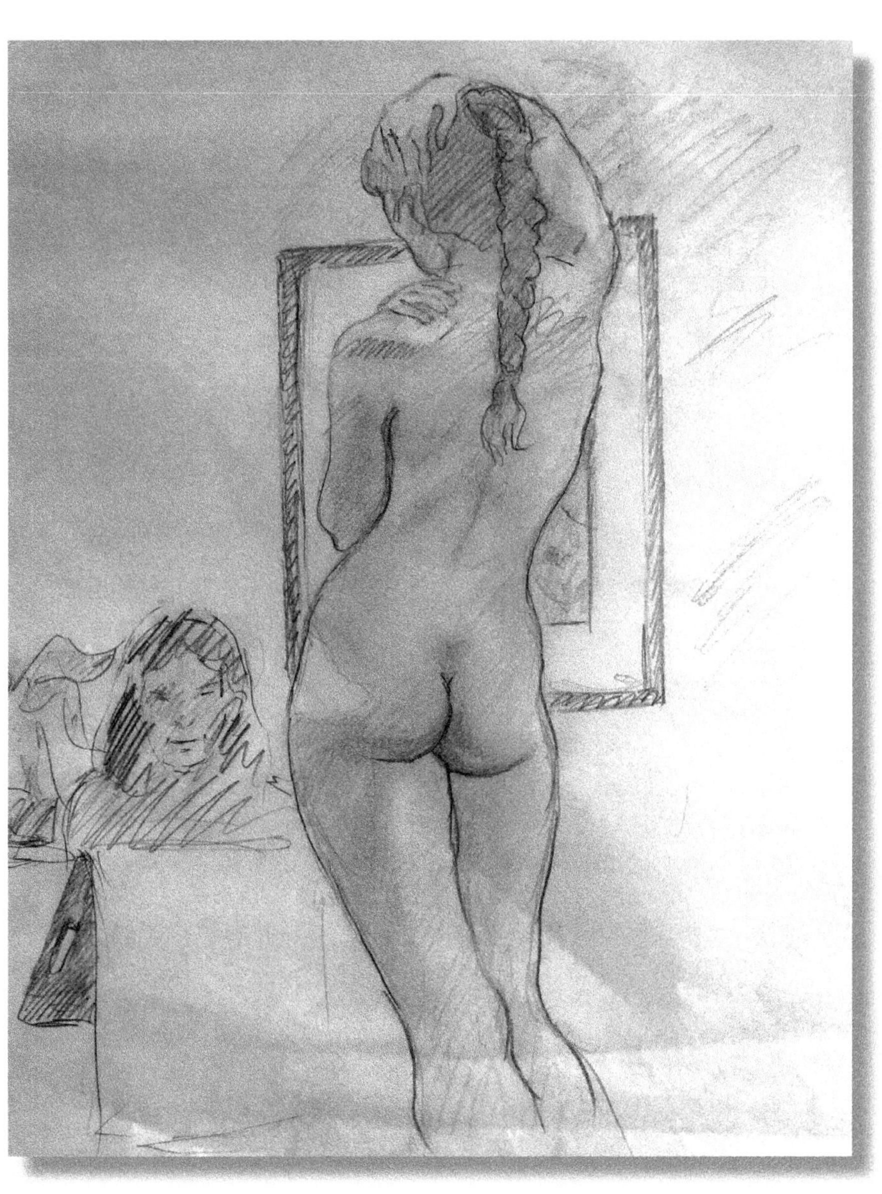

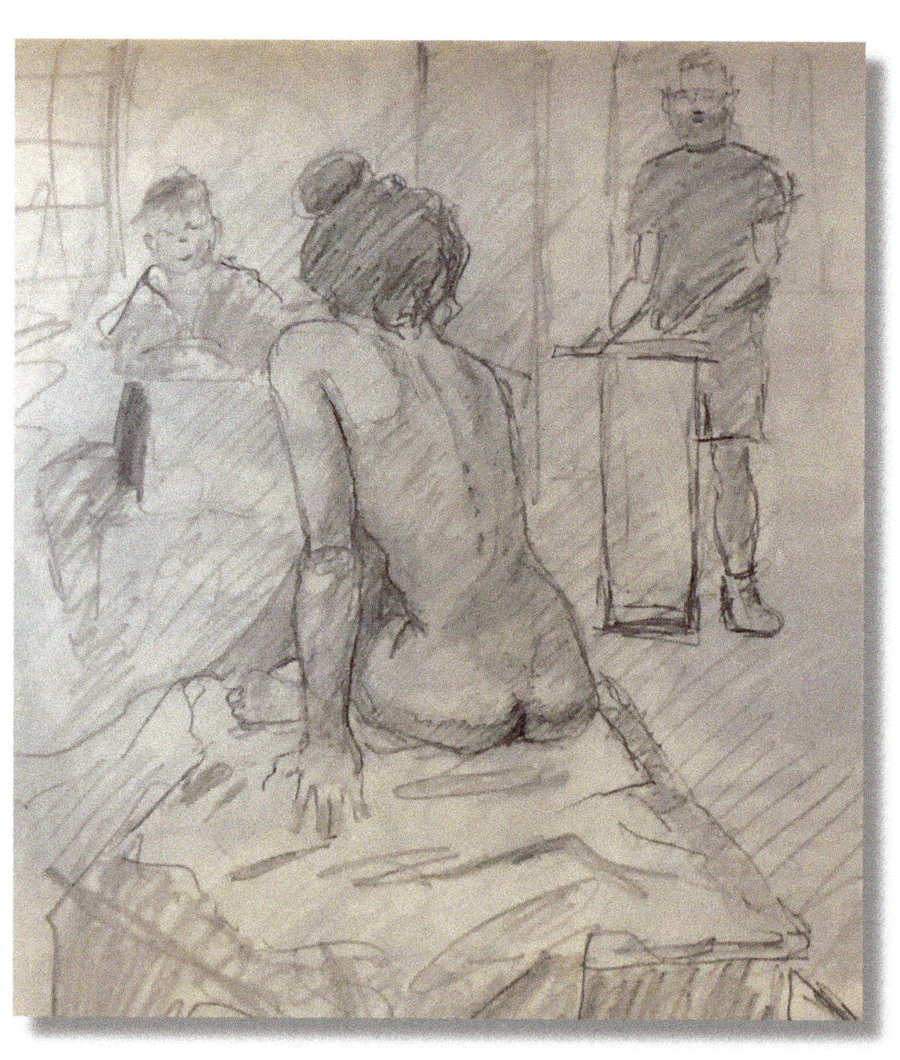

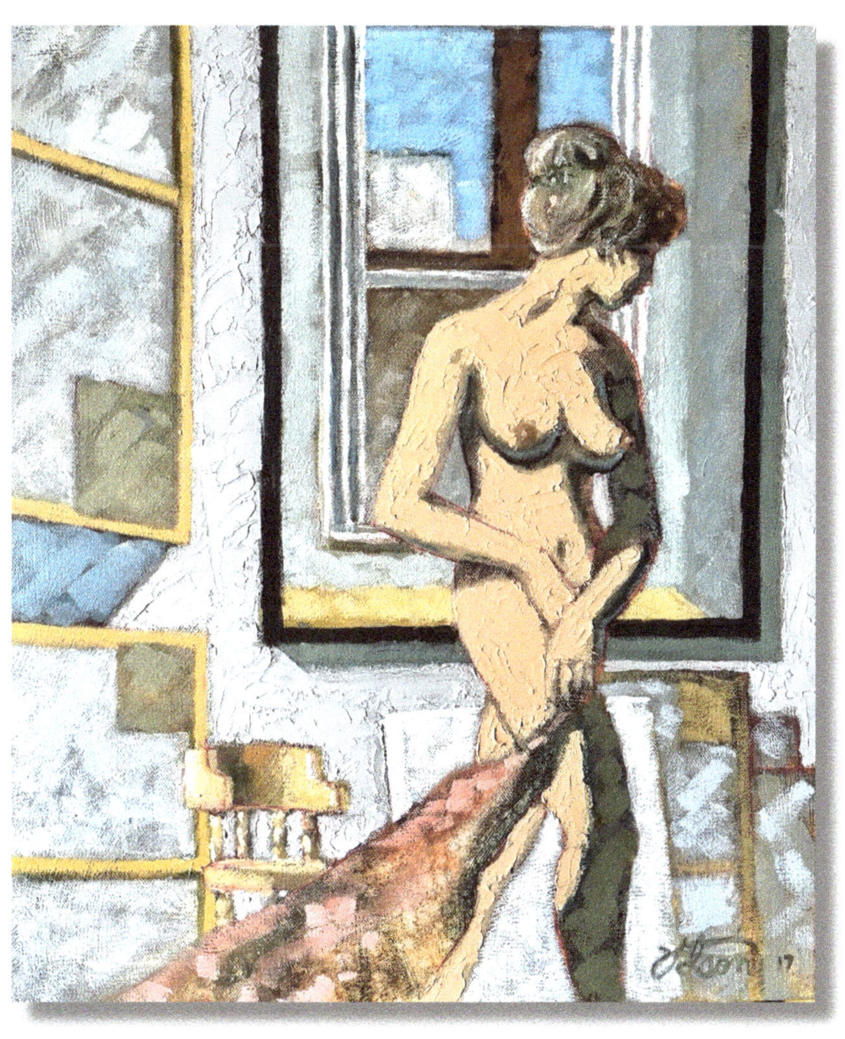

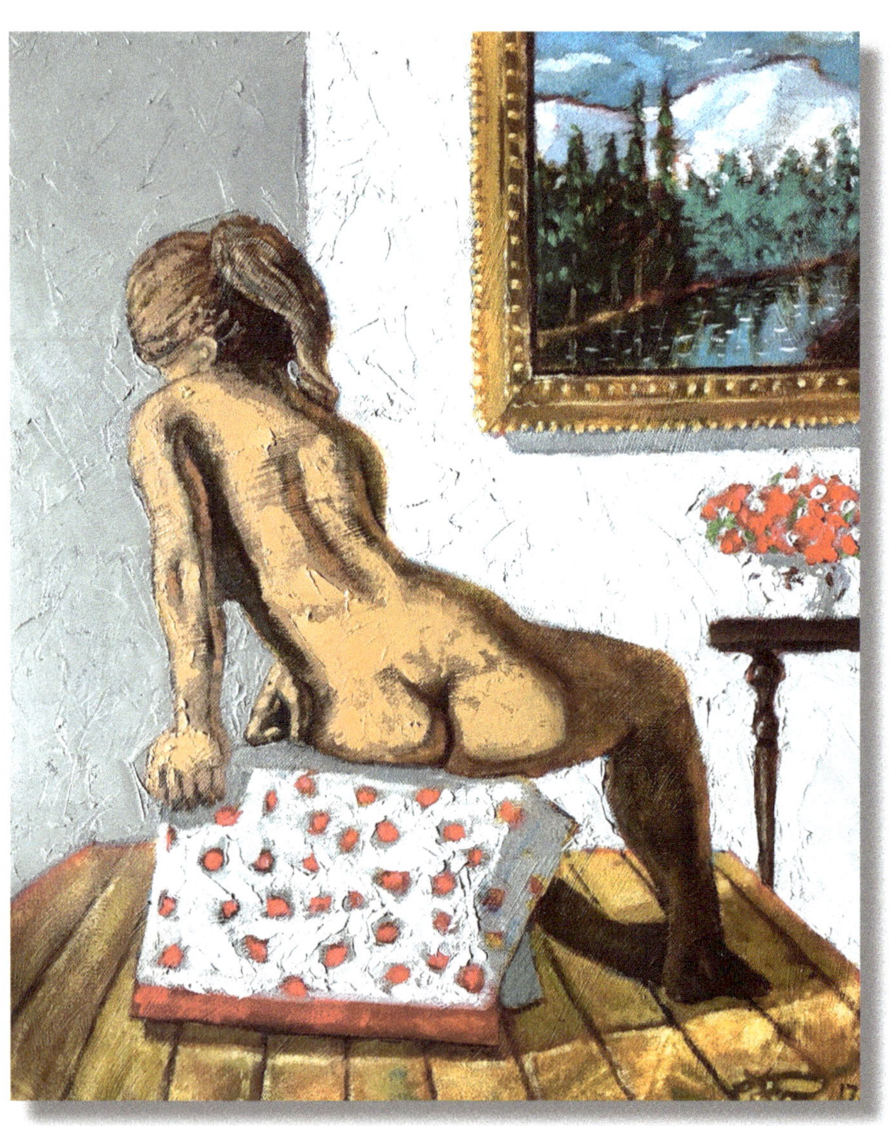

14

PAUL'S OPENING

It's **art walk time**, and the doors are open to Paul's exhibit in the most beautiful building in the area. The streets are busy, and it didn't take long for a decent-sized crowd to fill the space.

The sun had set, but there is still a glow in the western sky. The streetlights are bright, and the street people seemed to have diminished, making room for the art scene.

Many of Paul's friends and acquaintances showed up. Strangers arrived who had been taking in the other shows on Fifth Avenue. Maybe they read about his show in the paper or received an invitation. The galleries and exhibits are listed in several publications.

Paul's paintings are well scattered—not too close to one another. Each can be viewed without being crowded by other work.

All the work is unique in that it isn't consistent as other galleries would have expected.

Paul's whole process of painting resists uniformity. Each painting has its own space and time, depending on what he wanted to try and his motive for each piece. There are still consistencies in the paintings, just not as narrow as most shows. Some galleries present work that is so similar that once you see one painting, you have seen them all. It's the same thing, just rearranged.

There are many comments and questions—each shows respect for the quality of Paul's work. They are unanswered mysteries that make the viewers think and look inside themselves for meaning.

But what's a show without its quirks? There are stories to be told afterward and lessons to be learned.

"Hey Paul," said Martin as he strolled over with his sly grin. "A guy is pacing back and forth in front of one of your large paintings. He seems to be mumbling and complaining to other viewers."

"Alright!" Paul said. "A little interaction." He loves it when he affects people—it brings out the worst and the best in a person.

Martin is right about the animated character in front of Paul's painting. The man is about five feet, eight inches tall, and appeared to be about forty years old. He's wearing a red and black plaid shirt (un-tucked), worn jeans, and dirty tennis shoes. His "almost" beard looks like it had existed for three days at the most.

Paul wouldn't expect him to be a critic, but he could be. Maybe he's a disgruntled artist who felt he knows it all and has a valid complaint "why won't people listen" or perhaps a university professor. Maybe he taught abstract expressionism at San Diego State and felt that all other art is irrelevant.

The painting is nine feet tall and twelve feet wide.

Paul spent lots of time and detail on this work. There are two prominent people, a man and a woman in the foreground, and behind them are stairs and a parapet surrounding a platform. The railings are supported by sculpted nude figures instead of small columns. There is a forest of trees with towers of tall buildings rising behind them. Vertical lines abstractly divide sections of the painting.

Oh, and a sad overweight girl is sitting on the steps looking rejected.

Some areas consisted of loose brushstrokes that played well with solid color areas.

All in all, it is a pretty complicated painting but composed well—Paul thought. Overall, regardless of its complexity, it looked simple.

This man immediately proclaimed his objection. It is the red negative space he used in certain areas. He might have a point. Paul seems to use a lot of red in his paintings—even today. It would have been easier on the eye if a gray or earthy color was used instead.

"Are you the artist?" he challenged.

"Why, yes I am," Paul said confidently, looking at this cartoon of a man while he sipped on a cabernet.

He is good at flinging his arms like an Italian trying desperately to get his point across.

"What possessed you to put spaghetti sauce all over your painting?" he said as if finally blurting the words helped him relax.

He put his hands on his hips, tilted his head, and awaited Paul's profound answer.

Since he approached Paul with an absurd question, he felt that it needed an absurd answer. He could have said, "What possessed you to use this color in your painting?" That could have led to an actual logical discussion.

"I'm delighted that you asked," Paul said, "You're the only one who has picked up on that aspect of my painting. It wasn't as easy as it looks. My first attempts failed since the first coat dried out and flaked off. Digging into the techniques that the old masters used, I scraped off what was left and ground it into a powder. I mixed the powder with linseed oil to get the proper consistency of oil paint. But as long as I was experimenting, I first tried *Ragu* but found that *Prego* worked better because of the olive oil they used during its original manufacturing."

Paul continued, "I am a little disappointed that you didn't catch how I made the other colors. If you smell each color, you can get a faint whiff of what I used. The darker earth colors are made from Hostess cupcakes, and the sweet white filling worked well for the whites."

That's where Paul lost him. The man turned around and stomped out the door.

It did make him wonder if he actually could make oil paint from spaghetti sauce.

At that point, a beautiful slim Latino woman walked up to Paul, complimented him on his show, and pointed out her favorite paintings. Paul had met her before but couldn't quite remember where.

She had a little too much wine as she seemed a bit unsteady and sloshed a little of the contents of her glass on the floor.

Geoff, a friend of David's, immediately broke into the conversation with his English accent, a bit slurred from his own enjoyment of the great selections of wine Paul had provided for the opening.

"Back off, you whore!" he loudly spouted. "Paul has no interest in you. Go find someone else to slobber on, you cunt!"

She abruptly turned and walked away.

Geoff patted him on the back. "There, I got rid of that nuisance for ya," he said, proud that he saved him from a fate worse than death.

I silently thought to myself, "Damn you, Geoff, she is gorgeous!"

Martin quickly picked up on this Latino woman, and it turned into a two-year live-in relationship. Thinking back on Martin's last few relationships, each lasted about two or three years. At work, he filled Paul in on his exploits. Cooped up in one room together framing pictures all day, they talked a lot like a couple of women. But that's okay, that's our feminine side expressing itself—according to C.G. Jung.

In general, Paul had some great conversations with the viewers and many compliments.

Paul talked a lot about his overall work. There are techniques that some people will say, "That looks like Impressionism" or "This part of your painting looks smooth and detailed with vibrant colors, Like Maxfield Parrish." Maybe it's "this is so earthy and subdued!"

That's Paul's goal—to use what he has learned and make it work on one canvas, not take what he has learned and express it on twenty canvases so they all would work together. Each work is a universe unto itself, and he can't put "everything" he has learned on each canvas. He picks the elements that work well together. Each painting has its own components. The goal is to make it work.

The most common response is that Paul's show is different from any other show they have experienced.

Paul had other interesting conversations as the evening wore on. The traffic remained consistent. Some people Paul talked to said that while they were at other gallery shows, they were told to check out his opening.

One young gentleman seemed particularly interested and spent a lot of time looking at each painting. He eventually walked over to Paul.

"You know," he said. "Your art is really good, but you will never make it as an artist."

"Why is that?" Paul asked.

"You're not rich.'"

"What does rich have to do with being an artist?" Paul asked. (He then wondered how he knew that he wasn't rich.)

"Any artist that became famous came from rich families," said the man in all seriousness.

"I've never heard that before," Paul said. "Does the goal of an artist need to be a pursuit of money and fame?"

"Isn't that what art is about?" he said.

"I don't think so. Ask a caveman; they started it," Paul said, "I want more than fame even though you're right in the respect that I would like to share my insight with the world *if* I have something to say, and I don't think I need money or fame to do that. That insight comes from internal growth and a personal, almost self-centered act of creation. Saying it relates just to fame and money devalues it."

The man said, "You need money to go to the best art schools with the best connections. With the responsibilities of life, the normal person needs to work jobs to survive or feel like they should have families. It doesn't even matter if you're good at art or not. You just need the money to do your work and the words to describe it. You can be obsessive with any behavior."

This guy has a warped sense of art as far as Paul is concerned. Each to their own, but Paul continued with his reasoning, "I choose to think of it like being a monk or a guru. It is a religious journey that requires the absence of material goods or riches. It requires a humbleness to gain the insight of being an artist in the first place—an awareness of life and a pursuit of the Holy Grail."

Paul could tell that he isn't convincing him and that he isn't convincing Paul. Their talk is a stalemate. It is stubbornness with no compromise. Each to his own; thus, the communication ended like two opposite political parties or two opposing religions that knows the other is wrong and would burn in hell.

— ✳ —

Paul viewed the opening as a fabulous success. He didn't get a write-up, but the exhibit's experience filled his heart with joy and encouragement.

Paul had been to a hundred openings, and this one was unique. It is beyond sales and write-ups. He believes that.

His work would continue to be exhibited for a month. Since Paul has work to do in his studio, he put his name and phone number on the door. Several friends told him that people are trying to get in. Maybe he should have sat in the improvised gallery during regular hours or even hired someone to watch the exhibit, just in case people were interested in buying or viewing his work.

Okay, Paul isn't a businessman.

15

JACKALOPES

It is mid-May on a Friday night. Paul's been working on a canvas all evening. The prior week, he stretched and primed a new batch of *"ready to paint on"* canvases. He began the first one earlier this morning.

The atmosphere of the studio turned to the better, mainly because Richard moved out. Regardless of what games he played, it did not interfere with Paul's work. It made him focus on it all the more.

Paul thinks that Richard finally gave up and left. He isn't very productive like he was before his show.

Paul expanded his studio into Richard's space; he now had the whole west third of the ballroom for $150 more.

It is a few minutes after 9:00 PM. Paul is wound up and energized by his painting. Nobody else is in the studio, and he felt like getting out for a while.

He had heard of a theater bar on Market Street. Market crosses Fifth Avenue and the bar, *Uncle Bills,* is just half a block west of the intersection, still considered to be in the Gaslamp. This bar is a take-off from a famous New York theater bar named *Playbills.* There are two theaters in this part of the city.

As Paul walked into Uncle Bills, he noticed that the walls are covered with framed black and white photos of the actors and actresses who had once performed in the neighborhood theaters and the ones who perform here now. They are like wallpaper, covering every available space.

Uncle Bills is almost empty. He heard it is usually packed with theatergoers as well as performers. There are two people at the bar and only one table of three.

As Paul looked behind the bar, his jaw dropped in surprise. There stood Steve, the Cockney bartender from *Ten Downing*.

Steve looked in Paul's direction with a huge grin as he approached a barstool.

"Hey, Paul!" he said. "What a pleasan' surprise!" He reached over the bar and shook hands. "Cognac fer ya?"

"Sounds good," Paul said as he returned the grin and seated himself. "Still working in empty dives, I see."

"Not 'ardly," he said. "This place explodes wiv partiers on a regular basis—usually befawer an' after rehearsals an' perfawmances. We should get 'i' wiv da after-theater crowd in abaaaht ten minutes."

"I heard it gets busy here," Paul said as Steve prepared the Cognac in his usual fashion.

"They're not gon'a believe dis," he said. "The first time yew came ter *Ten Downin'* was me first day there. It just so 'appens what today's me first day 'ere."

"No way," Paul said. "You look right at home."

"This is 'ow I like ter work," he said. "It gets crazy in 'ere. I arrived at faaahr dis afternoon an' I've 'ad two madhouse theater crowds so far. The next'll last until abaaaht two in da morning."

"Speakin' ov 'ome, did yew say yew was from Wyoming? Most ov da people I talk ter in America are from somewhere else, especially Southern California."

"Yes, Wyoming, the home of the jackalope. I don't miss it at all."

"What's a jackalope?" he asked.

"It's a cross between a jackrabbit and an antelope."

"Whats a an'elope?"

"It's like a deer. Antelopes are really fast, tan, and white in color and have horns. You can find their cousins in Africa and Asia."

"So, 'ow did a jackalope come about? Interbreeding?

"Yea," Paul said. "Something like that. We lived next to a rancher that breeds and raises jackalope. Some get so big you can throw a saddle on them and ride em."

"Lawd above! Thee're kiddin' me."

"No, really. Next time I go to Wyoming, I'll send you a photo."

"Yea, do 'at will ya'?"

True to his word, after about ten minutes, people began to enter the establishment. Within a half-hour, every table and seat at the bar was taken. Three waitresses took care of the tables.

It is a delight to watch a professional work. Nobody waited for a drink. Steve is fast and efficient.

He even sat a Keoke coffee in front of Paul as he took the last sip of his Cognac.

"This one's on me," he said.

He also kept the waitresses drink orders ready and waiting for pick up. The second someone pulled out a cigarette, Steve is there with a lighter.

And conversations! He kept lighthearted conversations going with each person at the bar, including the waitresses.

Steve is like a well-oiled machine. He can even spot trouble—inappropriate behavior, raised voices, and would dampen it before it became an issue.

He ruined every relationship Paul could have with any future bartender or waitress he would meet. No one compared.

Paul was sure he wasn't kidding when he said he had awards and trophies from bartender competitions.

The tips flowed from the well-taken care of customers. What a professional!

It is close to midnight when Paul left *Uncle Bills* and began his stroll back to his studio. Being a Friday night, the Gaslamp is hopping. Every form of nefarious creature indigenous to this street life is out and active.

As Paul nears his studio, two large—and he means *Large* African Americans are walking toward him. They looked like they should be playing the offensive line for the San Diego Chargers.

Paul moved to the right as they began to walk past each other when the nearest one grabbed Paul by the front of his shirt and dragged him over to the curb between two cars. Paul is helpless. He is a big man.

Immediately, his friend grabbed him by the back of his collar and pulled him away.

"Hey, man, he's one of the artists."

"Oh, sorry, man," he said as he released his grip and threw his arms in the air.

They continued down the street. The door to Paul's studio is just a couple of doorways further.

As Paul stated before, the street people and the artists had a bond, as did the building owners and the artists. He wasn't sure how it became the law of the street, but it did.

16

MASTERS DEGREE

A lot had transpired in the void between my two studios—the ideal dream studio at Pacific Beach to the Ballroom in the Gaslamp. It wasn't really a void, and it isn't just a move to the excitement of downtown to live the life of a serious artist.

Paul went through his only aging crises.

This crisis didn't threaten his passion for the arts. It is a decision of how to pursue or use this discovery of creative energy he found flowing from somewhere within the universe. What is most important to him? What did he want to do with this gold mine?

"Oh, my God! I'm turning thirty."

Most people, Paul's age, have secure homes and families. They also have the trappings of materialism that parallels the American success story.

Even if they aren't successful, most people seem to be grasping at the toys in life to at least look or feel like they are successful. These people need to develop more practical survival techniques to make their lives easier, like not falling in debt and spending the rest of their lives paying it back.

Paul decided that he should get a Masters of Fine Arts degree.

The summer of 1978 was approaching. At the end of the summer, Paul would turn thirty, so he decided to go back to his old alma mater—The University of Wyoming.

Paul moved out of his Pacific Beach studio and loaded his Ford Econoline for the trip.

He followed his familiar route. He visited his parents who had just moved to Las Vegas, his mother's hometown. She met Paul's father in Vegas, a young Wyoming man during the Second World War. He was stationed at Nellis Air force base—a navigator in a bomber who picked the lucky straw of staying in the states protecting our borders and coastlines.

He followed Highway 15 to Provo Utah and across the Wasatch Mountains to Evanston Wyoming. Memories flowed into his mind from his upbringing in this state.

Evanston is the birthplace of his daughter. At that time, he worked at the Wyoming State Hospital. After being relieved of active duty in the Army, his marriage failed, and Evanston became his springboard to California to pursue the arts.

Then there was the small town of Granger Wyoming where he took the school bus thirty miles a day to attend high school in Green River.

After a 300-mile trip across a desolate high desert and plains, Paul ended up in Laramie Wyoming, his birthplace. Laramie is also where he married and had a son. All of these are left behind now from the choices he had made.

Paul's younger brother Don is living in Laramie with his wife, Leslie. He teaches at the College of Engineering and graduated in structural engineering; he decided to stay and continue toward his Masters. Don planted his roots there, as opposed to him, taking on the identity of a tumbling tumbleweed, bouncing along to wherever life took him.

His brother welcomed him to his home.

Paul only took one class. It was an independent study class, and he would paint at the UW art department with the tutoring of the painter and professor he most admired, Richard Evans.

Paul touched bases with Evans who directed him to his work area. He just needed to begin painting.

Walking into the past, Paul found himself standing in a large space filled with skylights and large easels scattered throughout the area. This studio space isn't the same art department he experienced ten years earlier. It is new and beautiful.

Paul wasted no time building three large stretcher bars. Then, he stretched canvases over them as if he is in his own studio. Paul then applies two coats of acrylic gesso in a criss-cross pattern. He purchases brushes, paints, and turpentine at the UW bookstore where he bought a lot of his supplies.

He began one painting after the other. Eventually, all three were underway and being worked on.

Even though Paul showed up every day, he thought it strange that he didn't see or talk to anyone else.

He also wondered why Evans hadn't shown up. He is excited about having a conversation and critique of his paintings at different points in their development. If there is one person he thought could identify with his work and feed him constructive criticism, it would be Evans. Paul had always admired his paintings.

When Paul was an undergraduate, he would walk into Evans' studio and be awed by him standing in front of a canvas with a small brush in his hand, painting in minute details. Evans was usually painting when he entered. Paul enjoyed just standing behind him and watching him work.

It has been three weeks since he arrived, so he decided to take a walk to his office/studio and see if he is there.

Evans greeted Paul when he entered.

"Hello, Paul," he said as he swiveled in his direction from his easel.

"Hello, Mr. Evans. I was wondering if you have time to come look at the progress of my paintings?"

"Are all three of the large paintings in the classroom yours?" he asked.

"Yes."

"You know, I've been checking your progress at the end of each day. You said you are interested in getting your master's?"

"Yes, I am," Paul said.

"Are you interested in teaching at the college level?" he asked.

"Well, maybe. Actually, I would like to improve my painting and focus on my work."

"You seem to be a strongly committed painter. I can tell you have been working and developing. If I were you, I wouldn't waste my time working toward a master's degree unless you want to teach."

"Teaching isn't my priority. I just want to learn more. I was thinking that working toward a master's degree would help me do that."

"Honestly, Paul, I think that will only slow you down. When you arrived, you said you have a studio in San Diego, and you're involved in the art community?"

"Yes."

"My suggestion is that you go back to your studio. You've advanced far enough that I really can't help you. All I would be doing is telling you how I paint. You already have a direction. You just need to do your work."

Paul felt a little disappointed. He is ready to use an academic facility for his growth, and Evans is telling him it would only slow him down.

"You should go back to your studio. I don't think you realize that even art instructors dream of breaking away and doing what you're doing. That is a step up from teaching. I'll tell you what," he said as he put his hand under his chin, as if in deep thought. "Go back to your studio and get to work. Don't worry about finishing this class. I'll give you an A."

When Paul decided to pursue a higher degree, he moved out of his Pacific Beach studio. He knew that his landlady wouldn't think twice about letting him move back in. After all, Xavier had recommended him, and she knew he is there to work—to do his art.

Paul actually felt good, not disappointed. The talk with Evans, and being away from his studio for a month, made him realize that going back to San Diego is the best move. He missed it already and felt even more empowered.

Before Paul left his studio to go to Wyoming, he became involved with a woman he worked with at the Fine Art Store, Marcia.

Karen was involved with other things at the time. He heard that she met the man that she would eventually marry. She also knew about his recent involvement with Marcia and backed off.

Marcia lived up a short flight of stairs from the La Jolla Cove in a tiny apartment. She said Paul could move in with her until he leaves for Wyoming. It was like a vacation at a beautiful resort. They got along great.

So when Paul left for Wyoming to pursue his master's degree, Marcia and Paul made plans for her to visit him. As it worked out, she flew into Denver, and he picked her up a day after Evans and Paul had their discussion about what he needed to do.

Marcia stayed with him at his brother's house for a couple of days. They decided that this would be a great time to take a vacation. Consulting a map, they plotted a route back to Southern California that would take them through the Tetons, Yellowstone, and then west to Northern California. They reached the Pacific Ocean well north of San Francisco and followed the coast down to San Diego.

It was a wonderful trip.

When they returned to Marcia's apartment, as fate would have it, Paul heard about available studio space in the Gaslamp Quarter in Downtown San Diego.

So, these were the events that took place between his PB studio and his Ballroom studio. It wasn't a void at all, and his aging crisis is resolved.

— * ✹ * —

After Paul's near-miss, being mugged on the streets of the Gas Lamp Quarter, he walked up the steps to his studio. He is actually calm, considering his ordeal.

Memorics and good thoughts permeated his mind—undoubtedly encouraged by a couple of drinks and the discovery of a fun bar.

Paul had good conversations, but not only with Steve. The crowd is friendly and intelligent. Uncle Bills is invigorating.

Paul sat in his contemplation chair and examined his painting. There is still work he needs to do to bring it together, and he wants to throw some elements into it that will make it more of a challenge as well as visually exciting.

This particular evening, his thoughts kept him distracted from his usual focus. The trip to Wyoming almost two years ago was on his mind. He is thankful that he knows an old college professor who could help him see the reality of where he was going.

His life couldn't be better. He could live like this forever.

As happy as he is about his artistic life, Paul realizes that he lives in a forever-changing world. To hold up in his studio and be satisfied with his routines would eventually lead to stagnation.

Carl Jung would describe it as *Synchronicity and Human Destiny*. Life experiences can be slowed but not stifled by limiting his experiences. Even if he has a routine life, he could not avoid walking down a city street and being mugged by a couple of black men or the coincidence of "*not*" being mugged because of an underlying collective unconscious that permeated the Gaslamp District.

His job at Reuter Gallery has an element of stability, both financially and socially.

Haunting his favorite art or intellectual bars, where he enjoys conversations over a self-imposed euphoric drug (alcohol), allows him to lower his barriers and have a constructive interactive confrontation with others.

Visiting other artists in their studios and discussing their work and motivations is a fabulous experience. Also, inviting other artists to his studio to bare his inner world and share his myth gives him the feedback that he needs.

Exposing one's art to the public is another matter. It doesn't matter how much artists enjoy their artwork; there are elements of responsibility in presenting their creations to the public.

To be involved with the public, you can have a gallery represent you, join a coop, or get accepted in juried shows.

Having a one-person show is an excellent moment for an artist. It helps to present your work professionally and gauge the public's reaction. It is essential that your creations evolve to the point of the work *itself being* justifiable by its quality, which is important.

Unfortunately, verbal justifications, your philosophy, and intelligent explanations can help. You will always have a viewer say, "What is that? What does it mean? Why did you use that color? Etc."

You need to know your art and believe in it. You need to respond with confidence and be able to spout convincing and understandable rhetoric.

The more you are involved in the arts, the more involved it gets.

17

JURIED SHOWS

When Paul first became a member of the San Diego Art Institute, he entered the monthly juried shows on a regular basis. He also volunteered to help at the gallery during jury decisions. There are usually three jurors. Paul's job, along with other volunteers, is to separate the artwork that is not accepted and hang the accepted pieces.

Paul is accepted most of the time, but he learned not to be disappointed if his work didn't make the cut. The shows are generally quality exhibits, and he still considers himself a young upstart with a lot to learn.

To be honest, if you are a volunteer, your chances of being accepted are higher.

Paul was spoiled the first year as a member in 1973. He had just arrived in San Diego from Wyoming. Paul painted on Masonite, and after sanding the panels, he applied two coats of gesso with a cross stroke for textural purposes.

His work is surrealistic and detailed. When he arrived in San Diego, he had an amazing amount of patience, and his work turned out better than he could have imagined.

When Paul enters his first painting in the monthly exhibit, he is accepted and the painting is sold. The next month is a Southern California juried exhibit. Again, he is accepted and received a purchase award. This painting sold as well, and the gallery asked him to bring in another piece. They had a customer who wanted to purchase it—sight unseen.

After a year of success, he began stretching canvases instead of painting on wood panels. Paul struggled a bit with the new surface but felt it was necessary for archival purposes. Masonite is prone to weaken and get brittle due to the acid content.

When Paul did convert to canvas, he didn't have as many paintings accepted in juried shows. Still, he eventually became more proficient with canvas, and he settled down to a consistent technique.

———— * ✺ * ————

Since moving into the ballroom studio, Paul focused on new work and the exciting dynamics of downtown life. As a result, he had ignored the monthly shows at the San Diego Art Institute for the last couple of years.

He eventually received a *Call for Artists* letter, stating that the annual Southern California Juried Art Exhibit at the art institute would be the following month. Artists needed to deliver their work sometime in the next week.

Paul finished a lot of new work since he last exhibited at the art institute and thought he would enter this year. He picked three pieces that met the size requirements and represented his later work.

Unfortunately, none of his paintings were selected.

Paul decided to attend the opening of the show. The rejection did not bother him much. As a sensitive artist, it is a letdown, but one needs to realize that maybe one in five pieces of artwork are selected, and the juror, or jurors, are all biased toward their genre or philosophy even if they try to be objective.

Art is a personal endeavor, and a creator of art should not let a competitive art exhibit affect their direction and beliefs. Many artists see juried competitions for what they are—comparing different artists and making a judgment that again cannot help but be biased.

You cannot compare an artist's work with other artists. All art is unique. The term comparing apples to oranges comes to mind.

Some juried shows have up to three jurors to minimize this bias. This show has one juror.

During the opening, Paul saw what he considered to be many naïve pieces that, frankly, didn't seem to show much talent. The work did not appear to be done by artists who understood the basics of art.

When he saw the piece that took the first place cash award, he could only shake his head.

When a person puts a model car together or an airplane, you lay a piece of paper on a table and paint each piece with spray paint or a small brush. When they dry, you assemble the pieces to complete your model. The paper is left with images of the parts that had been painted. This entry was framed under glass and entered in the show.

Viola! First place.

Sure enough, there is a juror's statement that proudly applauded himself for pulling a fast one on all the serious artists by rejecting the good art and accepting the work with no skill or experience.

"Take that!" he seemed to say. "I showed you!"

Another juried show Paul entered had one juror who painted on canvases 10" X 14". His work was very good—he produced beautiful realistic paintings. To him, though, if you have seen one, you've seen them all. He had his technique down so well that it became absent of creativity. It was just copying and enhancing what he saw. It became a craft (not meant to be derogatory).

Reading his biography, he spent twenty-five years as an illustrator. Some artists like him, as well as airbrush artists, assume that their work is above and beyond any other artistic technique. Many look down on artists that don't paint the way they do. To them, the best artist is the one who can make his or her art the most realistic.

Again, Paul's paintings are not accepted. He did believe the ability to paint realistically is an excellent talent to have, but Paul feels a need to add impressions from his mind. Whether they are surrealistic, abstract, or objects that don't belong, it's like a dream. When you have a visual dream experience, like walking down a street with odd buildings and then finding yourself underwater and unable to breathe, he needs to add these dynamics.

This realistic juror also has a bias toward large paintings as if a person's reason to paint large is to get attention when viewed. Paul's reason for painting large is because of the act of painting. He likes a large field in front of him so he can paint with his arm and shoulder, even his whole body. He could never restrict his work to just his fingers and wrist. Paul is not against painting small; he paints small when he needs to work in small areas with more detail to coincide with the bigger brush strokes. The larger strokes show more action in prominent areas of the painting and offer more viewing dynamics alongside the smaller detail.

He is also rejected from a couple of shows where he probably should have been denied acceptance.

In two of these cases, he received a letter explaining that his work was good enough to be accepted, maybe even better than some of the other work, but because of the size, color, or images, they didn't work with the rest of the show. If there were other works like his in the exhibit, it would have worked. They had to have a complete, uniform presentation.

In another case, a large painting Paul had entered (even though it was under the acceptable size) took up the space they could have used to show three other artists who did smaller work. However, if a painting is rejected when the artist follows the exhibit's guidelines, they should change the maximum size allowed so he won't be wasting his time. He could have entered smaller pieces.

Paul is grateful that they gave him a reason. They can't provide reasons for the rejection of every artist.

* ❋ *

The arts in the Gaslamp cannot be discussed without the topic of performance art.

Sushi, the performance stage, is a drop in the bucket compared to what is really happening. Not that *Sushi* lacked cutting-edge creative shows, it's just that there is one small room with weekly performances for any artist who put their name on the schedule, no auditions.

There are several locations where avant-garde experimentalists did their artistic performances—some taking up full floors of buildings. There are performance artists who gathered in the Gaslamp from New York, Chicago, and San Francisco, to name a few.

In one instance, word got around that a building in the area is hosting several simultaneous performances on the second floor. It reminded Paul of Cirque du Soleil, in that wherever you looked, something is going on.

One fellow walked from one end of the floor to the opposite end "so slowly" that he looked as if he is standing still at any point in time. If you looked back at him after fifteen minutes, he had gained about three feet, even though he looked rigid and unmoving.

In another situation, a small area is enclosed in walls made of hanging sheets—a long line formed outside the space with only five observers allowed in at a time. When you entered the tiny area, the small group stood around a bed. A nude woman is covered with a sheet. She thrashed and rolled around, revealing her body as she talked in her sleep, verbally describing horrible events she is experiencing in her semi-conscious state.

✳

The Reutter Gallery is doing well. So well, that after a few years, David found an even better spot to locate his business.

It is a storefront in the middle of Fifth Avenue. No more upstairs or being on the fringes of the Gaslamp. They are in the middle of all the action.

When David dropped the news on Martin and Paul, again, they are surprised at the sudden move. Their present location is a fantastic place. Why leave?

They still needed to prepare for a show the following month. After that exhibit, the gallery would move the three blocks to the new location.

Phillip Dimitri Galas was with David when he told them the news. Phillip was doing performance art in the area.

Phillip pulled Paul aside, "I have a question about your space." He had been there before. "Could my performance partner and I use it next month? Your stage would be perfect!"

"Sure," Paul said.

"Can we come over and check out the logistics? We would need to practice there as well. It will be a big show, and we have a large following."

"You can practice there whenever you need to," said, Paul.

"Like tomorrow evening?"

"Sure, I'll be there."

On show night, Phillip is a little concerned since the surface of the stage hadn't been maintained, and they are worried about slivers. The room is packed.

After the performance started, Paul is the one who is concerned. He realizes that some people are sitting on a long plank of scaffolding (used outside of windows on huge buildings). Ten people are sitting on it. One end is supported by a built-in bench and is holding fine, and the other end is supported by one step of a wooden A-frame ladder. That means there are at least 1,500 pounds of viewers sitting on it. Paul quickly scampered to his woodpile and found some lengths of wood that would fit underneath. Sneaking behind the scaffolding, he propped it up from underneath with several vertical boards. Most of the viewers didn't notice him, but some did understand what he is doing.

Paul missed out on most of the show since he spent a lot of time observing the crowd, but in the end, the audience roared and clapped with approval.

18

INFLATABLE SCULPTURE

Paul made a quick trip to Wyoming** in his Ford Econoline to pick up the three paintings he left with his brother a couple of years early—the ones he had mostly finished during his temporary quest for a master's degree at the University of Wyoming.

It feels good to break away from the routines of life. There is something about taking a trip. It's like meditation, seeing the white and yellow lines on the road coming at him with landscapes sliding by on either side for hundreds of miles. He can look back at his life and the decisions he made. Is being a painter what he wants to do?

Arriving in Laramie, Paul made a point of finding a postcard of a jackalope to send to Steve, the bartender. There are no problems finding postcards of this elusive animal. He picks one that shows a cowboy throwing a saddle on the back of an eight-foot jackalope. Surely, he would guess the humor in this gesture.

Paul returned to San Diego and immediately finished the three paintings he had rescued from Wyoming. It is easy to bring them to fruition, though it felt odd to be away from them for so long. He knew what he needed to do.

After a chat with the other three artists in the space, they all decided to build a large gallery in front of the ballroom and enclose each artist's space. It ruined the open space feeling, but they had more privacy.

The *ballroom four* began to prepare for a four-person art exhibit. They plan to show their creations in the monthly art walk. No hurry, though, maybe in a couple of months. It will give them time to finish the gallery, do more work, and spread the word.

After the group show, the artists will each take turns having their own solo show.

It is incredible how fast time flies when one finds themselves in the environment and lifestyle they have always longed to obtain. Paul feels good about this experience and about what he has learned during this journey. The people he meets, his friends and relationships, are all part of his life—a time that he will always remember and cherish.

Paul has lived here for almost nine years, and the experience has offered a better art education than the best schools.

This artist's wonderland in San Diego is winding *"down"* here in the old Gaslamp Quarter. The owners received help from the city to bring their buildings up to the new earthquake code. The city is winding *"up"* to clear the riff-raff (and the artists) from Fifth Avenue. The *well-to-do* will take over the now expensive apartments—once artist studios—to be in a newly revitalized downtown, finally dragging the energy of San Diego from the beaches and valleys to the middle of the city with its colorful history.

Artists are moving out. Paul and the ballroom artists are luckier than most. The ballroom is on the third floor of a stable icon of Fifth Avenue, San Diego Hardware. Even though that bought one more year, they eventually followed on the tails of the other artists.

Since returning from Wyoming, Paul decided it's time to visit Uncle Bills. He enjoys the chats with his favorite bartender. The stroll down Fifth is always an adventure. The sun had just disappeared below the western horizon; it is six in the evening. The streets are busy, and the energy seems to infect his mood with anxiety. He just wants to sit at the bar and talk to his friend. The surroundings are always magical at Uncle Bills, with people around him who are consumed by theater and love to talk.

Paul walks into a small crowd of diners and drinkers. He sits on his favorite barstool as he notices Steve at the far end of the bar chatting with a light-hearted group of revelers.

He waits to be noticed, but Steve stayed at that end of the bar to serve others in need of drinks and conversation.

"This is weird," Paul thinks. Steve always notices him and delights in their usual banter. He is now acting like I don't exist. Steve walks to where Paul is sitting, grabs some glasses, and returns to the other end of the bar. He didn't even look up.

"Excuse me, Steve?" Paul said in a slightly raised voice.

Steve looked in his direction. With his head down, he walks to where Paul was sitting.

"Are you okay?"

"Actually, no. Yu embarrassed me in funt uf du whole restaurant. I's excited to show der pos card yer sent me, eveyone broke ot in laughin."

"Oh, no!" Paul covered his face with both hands. "I didn't mean to embarrass you. I picked out the most ridiculous card I could find. I was hoping you would realize it and have a good laugh. I am so sorry!"

Paul then explained the myth and legend of a Wyoming joke, backed by photos and mounted heads that are displayed in bars to invite ridiculous conversations with the gullible. It is something you pull on friends who are new to the west—not meant to embarrass, but to say "I gotchya!" as you slap them on the back and buy them a drink.

Steve understood. He swallowed his pride and, with a half-smile, looked at him and said, "Keoke coffee?"

"That sounds perfect!" Paul said.

"So, aur yur trip to Wyomin?" Steve asked.

"It is always a nice drive and good to see family, but it also reminds me of why I moved here and how lucky I am."

During the walk back to the studio, Paul is in a contemplative mood. When he arrives, he grabs a bottle of red wine, walks the full length of the room, and continues up the rickety ladder outside the building. When Paul reaches the top, he looks back at the bustling street below—the noise, the lights, and the mayhem, then climbs over the roof edge to an eerie silence. It is dark and quiet with high-rise buildings surrounding him. A few windows and floors are lit, making an uncanny pattern of squares and rectangles.

Sitting next to one of the skylights above the ballroom, Paul can see the studios below—little workstations to create art. What goes on in the mind of an artist? Is it creating good art or finding out what they are about?

———— ✳ ————

Paul's opening went as expected. There are lots of people—friends, other artists, and the curious.

One person stood out, Bob Thompson, my former roommate at Ocean Beach and co-worker from the Fine Art Store. Paul hadn't seen him for years since he moved downtown.

Bob looked a little less hippie and more corporate as he strolled around the gallery checking out the work.

Paul walked up and shook his hand. "Hey, Bob! It's nice to see you. What have you been up to?"

"Hey, nice show!" Bob said as he gazed around the ballroom. "I see you've been busy."

"I have!"

"This is your studio?"

"Yes, pretty amazing, huh? I work part-time at a gallery a couple of blocks away."

"Nice!" Bob countered. "I landed a great job! I'm the art director of Robert Keith & Company."

"Sounds impressive, what's that?"

"We make giant inflatable shapes—like huge balloons."

Paul became a little less impressed when he said the word "balloons."

"We have some big jobs coming up," he said. "I wanted to see what you were doing. We need help. We're looking for someone to make clay sculptures. That's how we start each project."

"Sounds cool, but I'm enjoying my situation at the moment."

"I think you should come check us out. You can drop by anytime. I'll introduce you to everyone. I think you'll be impressed."

Paul smiled and gave him a semi-enthusiastic reply. "Yeah, I think I can do that."

He showed Bob around and introduced him to a few people. As usual, the opening is during the monthly art walk. There is a great turnout. Bob stayed through the opening, and afterward, went to Uncle Bills for a few drinks.

When he left, Bob put his arm around Paul's shoulder and said, "Really. Come see what we do."

He likes Bob; he has always been a good friend. At first, Paul didn't follow up with the visit, but Bob didn't give up. He received a call about ten days later.

"So do I need to twist your arm?" asked Bob.

"OK. Where is this place again?"

"Kearny Mesa."

During the opening, Bob handed Paul a Robert Keith & Company card confirming its location with his *"Art Director"* title prominently displayed.

"I gave you a card. Do you still have it?"

"Yes, I do."

"How about tomorrow?" Bob said. "I've already built you up, and they are anxious to meet you."

"Okay, Bob, I'll be there."

— ⁕ —

Walking into a *"company"* is a whole new world for Paul.
First comes the reception desk.
"Hello, can I help you?"

"Uuuuh. Yeah! I have an appointment to see Bob Thompson."

"Oh yes, Paul!" said an awake and beautiful receptionist.

She picked up the phone, punched a couple of buttons, and said, "Hey, Bob, Paul's here!"

Paul is awed by the beautiful smile.

"He'll be right here."

Bob walked in less than a minute later with a smile on his face and a firm handshake.

"Come on; I'll show you around."

As it turned out, it is much more than a balloon factory. At the time, there were about fifty employees. Bob introduced Paul to the owners—Robert Keith himself and his wife, Ann Wawer.

They had a great sales staff, but what impressed him is the warehouse. Twenty-foot tall inflatable characters, beer cans, and numerous other projects fill the enormous space. Huge sewing tables lined the walls. Painters did the artwork from tall ladders, and silk screeners worked on twenty-foot screens.

The big project that Robert Keith is gearing up to fabricate is a seventy-foot inflatable King Kong to put on top of the Empire State building for the 50th anniversary of the movie and the 50th anniversary of the Empire State building.

For Paul, this is the beginning of a thirty-three-year involvement with inflatable sculpture. But, he is also determined to continue his painting.

The good thing about making inflatable art is that it uses all of his art skills and refines his algebra and geometry abilities.

The bad thing is that it lacks the inner creative source that Paul has always depended on for his artistic ambitions.

Not only would Paul make the original sculpture for each project, but he is also asked to do a technical drawing on grid velum, showing all views. Paul had little experience with technical drawings. (This is before personal computers, and design software are common.) But he did pick it up fast. He enjoys hanging over a drawing table, doing detailed work, and figuring out mathematical solutions for the shapes.

19

KING KONG

The ballroom artists are given their notice to vacate, but it wasn't a rush. They still had a while before they needed to leave. It was Paul's turn to have his show this next month. His focus is working on an Earth theme, mostly Earth as seen from space, somewhere around 50 inches square.

As stated earlier, change is happening; in fact, it seems that everything is changing.

One is obvious. Paul needs to find a new studio.

Another change is sad but all too real. David became ill, and he seems to be getting worse. Martin and Paul are left to run the gallery. David is confined to his bed as his condition is getting worse. No one knows what is wrong. David didn't know either.

Martin left for another job. He disappeared. The gallery is closed.

David eventually passed away, and his illness soon became known. He was diagnosed with AIDS. Phillip soon followed.

Paul found an old church for a studio three blocks away, on Sixth Avenue and Market.

Other artists found it. Paul didn't know them, but it's another great space. His studio had a high ceiling. There's a split-level riser, like a stage, where he placed his easel, and two other large rooms adjoined the stage. Paul plans to use one room as a sculpting studio, and the separate room is perfect for making stretcher bars, stretching canvas, and picture framing.

Okay, now for the domestic side. There is an actual bedroom! The building has a "huge" shower and restroom, with a mirror running the length of the longest wall. The room is thirty-five by twenty-five feet. There is also a high ceiling about fourteen feet.

Paul looks at this studio in a whole different light. It's time to reflect on the direction he wants to go. He plans to map a new course of habits and routines. When change happens, it's an excellent time to take advantage of the options he is given.

Paul turned his paintings to face the wall, put a new canvas on his easel, and started anew.

He began, as usual, making stretcher bars and stretching canvases. The beginning washes immediately brought him home. It was Paul and the canvas—a relationship he has had for at least two decades. It is a relationship with its ups and downs, gives and takes, and is comparable to an actual human partner. You let it have its say, and the relationship becomes stronger. It's a compromise that works with your conscious intent. It can be like oil and water, or it can blend perfectly together. The result is always a pleasant surprise, working together to create a newborn that will have a life of its own.

Art becomes a window to the soul, the melding of the anima and animus, an expression of the personal unconscious with the collective unconscious.

So, in truth, the artist doesn't need to control or understand his work. He knows it comes from somewhere deep within the universe and is one with creation.

Of course, you don't turn off the world around you and just allow the unconscious to function. You need to soak in the beauties and challenges of living on this planet. You need to experience life.

Develop your physical abilities and understand the world around you. You need to learn painting techniques, experiment with color, and paint from life—still lifes, landscapes, and the figure. You should always be drawing.

The more you understand the world and life's experiences, the better you will be at drawing and painting. The stronger the work of art becomes, the more the unconscious is revealed.

These are the elements at work with Paul when he accepts the job at Robert Keith and Company. He is working with a group of people who are mostly naïve to art—what art does, why it is here, and basically, what it is. After all, history shows us that art has been deeply rooted in human existence from the beginning.

So, Paul's work at Robert Keith is the creative and artistic side of the company. He thought he would never work for a company, let alone use his artistic ability to be part of the machinery.

Robert Keith, as a whole, is a creative company. The amount of work and research required for the development of these inflatable shapes are groundbreaking.

There are many aspects and elements for the construction of an inflatable.

Blowers to inflate the shapes are not something that you order from a catalog. You needed to order the parts and experiment with them.

There are fan blades used for different functions. The same goes for the specs on the motor to power the blades. You try them out and conclude what works and why it works. The size of the intake and exhaust will vary depending on how you want it to function. The casing needs to be developed to work for its intended purpose. The electrical system needs to be developed as to the size and type of cord required to supply the correct amps and voltage.

There is so much to learn!

The fabric is hunted down at awning shops, sail shops, hot air balloon manufacturers, and banner supply businesses.

The kind of industrial sewing machine to use is essential, along with the thread size and strength.

What types of paint, inks, or dyes are best? The colors need to be flexible and durable, and in many cases, fire-retarded.

As the inflatable industry grows, suppliers eventually develop and manufacture these materials and tools specifically for the inflatable builders.

Paul is enthusiastic about the potential of this medium. Every day is a challenge.

The best part of this job is that at 5:00 PM, he can go back to his studio and work on his painting.

<hr>

When Paul started at Robert Keith, it was time to begin creating the seventy-foot-high King Kong that would grace the Empire State Building. Several other projects that are being worked on are still in progress at the time, but King Kong is the priority.

When it came time to install King Kong in New York, the crew found themselves working late nights to iron out the final details. The winds are expected to be high, so the production crew made a webbing system that crossed his back in several places. The inflatable needs to be firmly attached to the building.

The Robert Keith crew took the inflatable as far up in the Empire State Building as possible via the elevator. Then it had to be spread out and rolled into a long thin shape to be snaked up the final stairs to the appropriate spot.

Now, how did we get it outside the building? The solution: The riggers had to break a window.

From this point, it was the riggers' responsibility. The process is well planned, but of course, there is always the unexpected. For starters, the inflatable needs to be stretched out and tied down before inflation. A five-horsepower blower is standing by, awaiting its grand entry to inflate King Kong to its final shape.

One detail of how this inflatable functions is the continual running blower used for inflation because the seams are not sealed.

When the rigging crew secures King Kong to the building, it will be ready to inflate. The blower is then attached and turned on.

Oops! The inflatable is twisted. It had to be detached from the building, brought back inside, and untwisted. The winds made it all but impossible to untwist while outside the building.

The second try went much better. King Kong was spread out and attached securely to the building.

Okay, now for the second snag. It is time for lunch. The riggers are required to come back inside and take their lunch—union rules. When they returned, the fabric had ripped from the intense winds. Once the balloon is inflated, that won't be a problem. The strapped-down shape will be much more stable and secure.

So, for the second time, the King needs to be unstrapped and brought back inside. Great forethought then prevailed. A sewing machine had already been made available, and within a couple of hours, the sewing is finished.

Keep in mind that struggling with this inflation with the high winds took days—maybe even a week. I don't recall. News crews and helicopters are ready to report the inflation when it happens—if it happens. Nationwide, the news channels are continually updating the progress.

Ta-da! Finally, King Kong stood out in its full glory, and the images are splashed across the world. It is up for only a couple of hours—enough time for the photo ops—and then removed. Why tempt fate any longer?

Installing King Kong is a great coup for Robert Keith. The amount of time it took to install King Kong on the Empire State building didn't matter; the exposure did. The daily struggle kept it in the news cycle longer than had been anticipated.

Robert Keith enjoyed the flood of orders that poured in after the publicity.

The company had to move to a larger facility. The employees referred to this building as Darth Vader's Castle because of its size, black windows, and structure. It had twice the necessary space. More employees are hired, and the company began producing on a massive scale.

20

OUTHOUSE

A couple of years earlier, when Paul lived in the Gaslamp studio, he had become tired of improvising last-minute costumes for Halloween. The artist community came up with fabulous parties, so he finally decided to make something that took a little effort.

Finding a tall, thin cardboard box, Paul turned it into an outhouse. It had no door. He pulled it over his head so that his real legs stuck out the bottom while fake legs made it look like he was sitting on the crapper.

The fake legs are made from Styrofoam, and he dressed them in old jeans and underwear. Paul nailed a pair of tennis shoes on the floor of the outhouse and fit the legs into them.

Pulling out a black Magic Marker, he drew wood grain with knotholes on the outside. For ventilation, he cut a crescent moon above the door and made a stovepipe with a cone head coming out the top.

This costume is hilarious. Paul equipped it with a *Penthouse* magazine and a roll of toilet paper. The party he went to that year is not a contest, but the costume blew people's minds. It is embarrassing to look at—like you are invading someone's privacy. It produced endless remarks and jokes.

"What a crappy costume!"

"Where does the line start?"

"Are you constipated? You've been sitting there for a long time." The remarks are continual.

Several people made this same comment: "What are you doing here? You should be at a Halloween contest. That's a sure winner!"

The following year, Paul went to his next party. This one isn't a contest either. It is a Robert Keith company party.

Lo and behold—Suzy from the painting/visual effects department was dressed in her sandwich costume.

She came up to Paul and said, "Hey, I'm going to two contests tonight. Want to join me?"

"Sure!" Paul said.

That Friday, the two of them loaded their costumes into Paul's van and went to two Halloween contests. Paul placed first at the first party—a trip for two to Mazatlan—and Suzy took second place.

At the next party, Paul got first again—five hundred dollars— and Suzy got third.

The next night, Saturday, Paul went to another costume party by himself and won again. Going to these costume contests is the beginning of a ten-year run that netted him sixteen first places. After a while, it isn't so much fun. It's like going to work, and the way the costume hung around his hips made him fart all night after he took it off.

* ❋ *

Robert Keith grew to over one hundred employees and is mobbed by clients wanting to buy an inflatable. They made giant product samples and did work for world expos, sports events, and theater—just as a start.

The list grew much more extensive. RK did work for the US electrical exhibit at the World's Expo in New Orleans, The Olympics in LA in 1984, and many other exciting projects.

It is a grand adventure to be involved in these projects with a fantastic crew, many of who became great friends.

After three years, Paul is ready to move to Seattle, find a studio, and get back to his painting.

When Paul put in his notice to leave, fate jumped in. He is pulled aside by Robert Keith's accountant Andy and Mark the production manager. They took him out for dinner when they heard he was leaving.

"So, I see that you put in your notice to leave the company," Andy said, as we settled into our booth.

"Yeah, I've been planning this for years. I really want to move to Seattle."

Not beating around the bush, Mark chimed in.

"We're starting a new inflatable company. Do you want to be a part owner? You're the only one who understands all of the production aspects of the business and can do the whole process."

Their proposal is a surprise to Paul. He likes Andy a lot but isn't sure about Mark. He's pretty naive. Paul worked well with him—or so he thought.

His thoughts were on Seattle, but helping start a new inflatable business would be an adventure.

"Are you asking me to be a part owner because of my merits, or do you need money?"

Andy replied, "We know your abilities and need them, but we also need funding. Can you raise any money? Any amount would work; your investment would get you a percentage of ownership, depending on what you can contribute."

"I'm not your guy," Paul said. "I don't have access to large funds."

"Any rich relatives? Can you get a loan?" said Mark, "This will work. I know it will."

"The money I could contribute would be a drop in the bucket compared to what you would need."

Andy looked a little disappointed.

"We're just hesitant, not knowing the real risks of our other options. We understand your position. It would be nice if the owners were actually participating in the company and not just investors."

"So, could you still help us get started?" asked Mark. "We can make you art director and pay you more than you're making now."

Paul did like the opportunity to see how this would go. It would be no risk on his part. He could leave at any time.

"OK, this is what I can do. I gave my two-week notice. When I leave, I'll take a three-week vacation in Seattle. That will get the place temporarily out of my system. If you get your funding figured out by the time, I'll return. I'll work for a couple of years and we can see how things look at that time."

"Fair enough," said Andy. "Can you make a list of who you think would be the best people to hire? It is easy to approach you since you are leaving anyway."

Paul responded with a slight shrug, "Sure, I can do that."

* ❋ *

Paul's trip is fantastic, as usual. He felt the security of returning to a job and the adventure of helping start another inflatable company.

The drive up the coast to Seattle was amazingly beautiful. He visited his friend Mark Zingarelli in Ballard for a couple of days. Mark worked at the Fine Art Store when Paul was there. He is a fantastic cartoonist. He moved to Seattle a few years ago and is smothered in jobs, not only in the Seattle area but nationally.

Paul spent the rest of his stay in the Northwest camping, painting, and hiking the Olympic Peninsula.

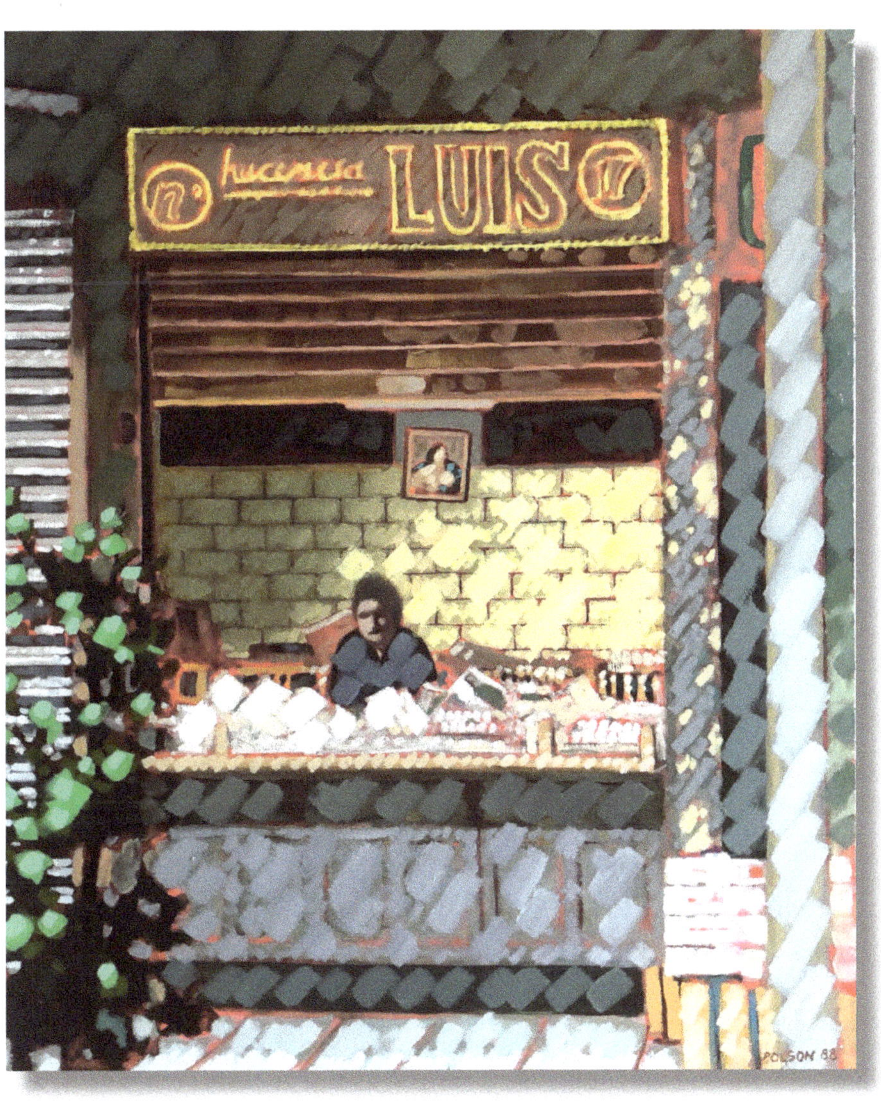

nº huevería LUIS 17

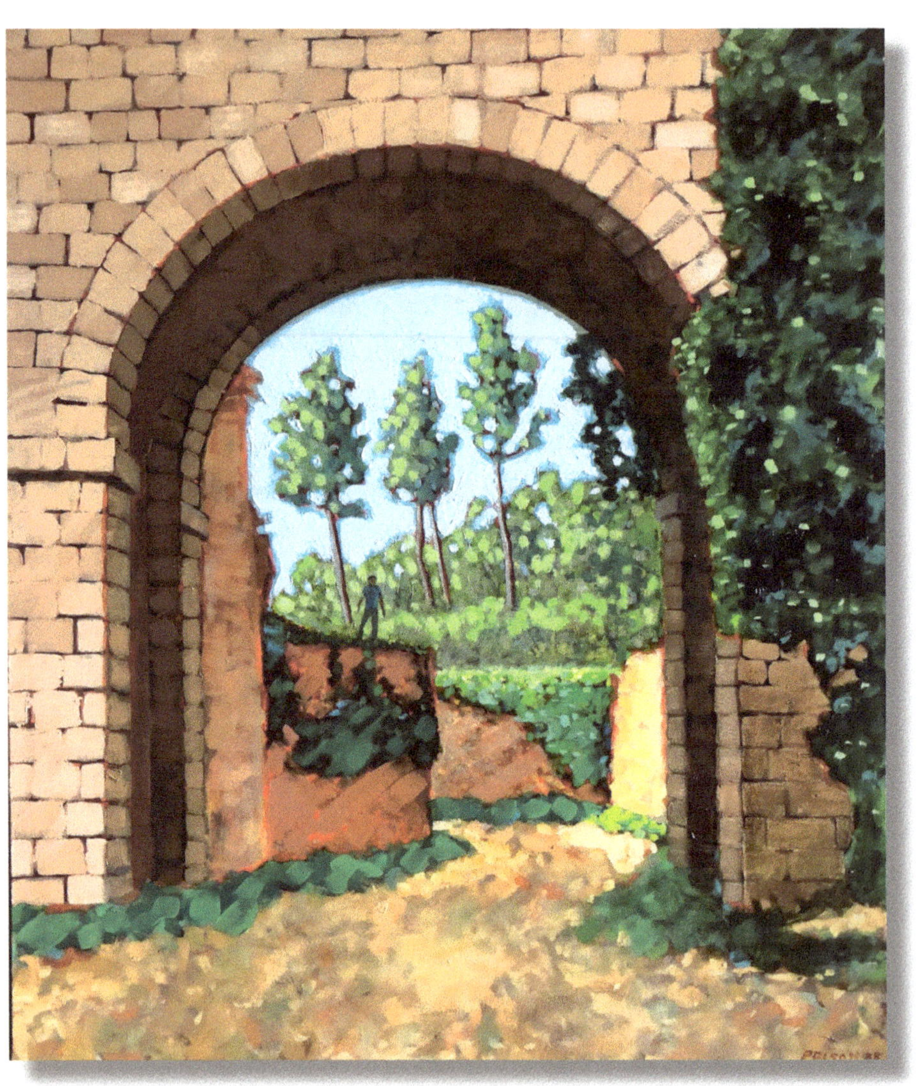

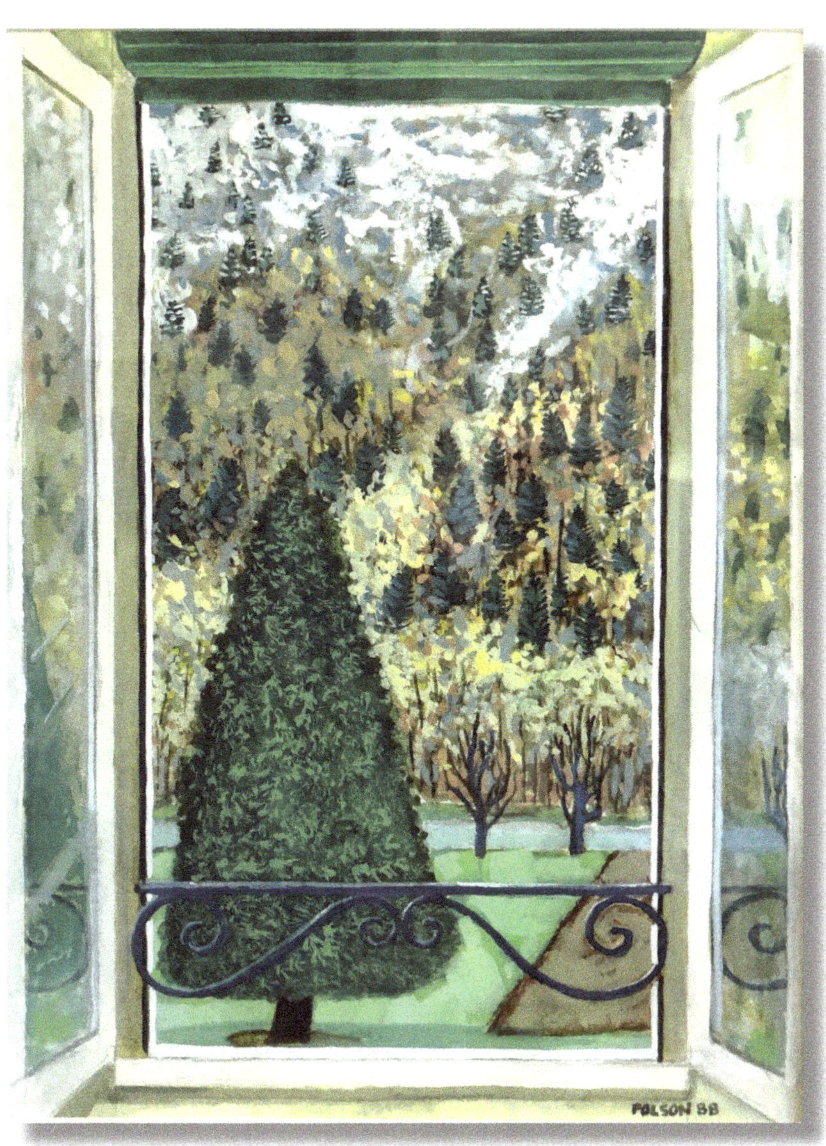

FOLSON 88

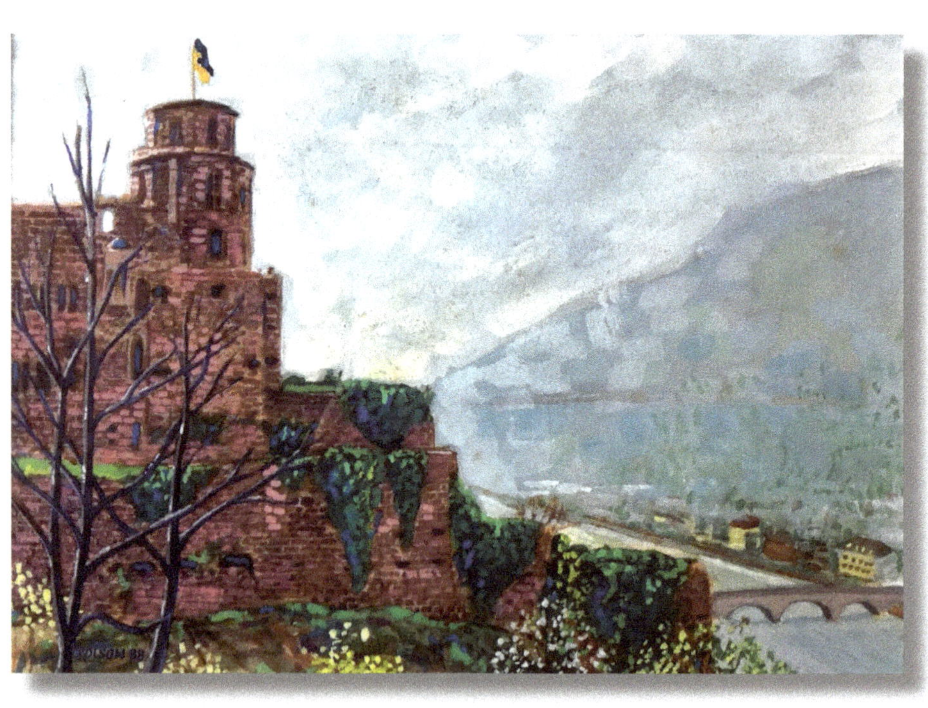

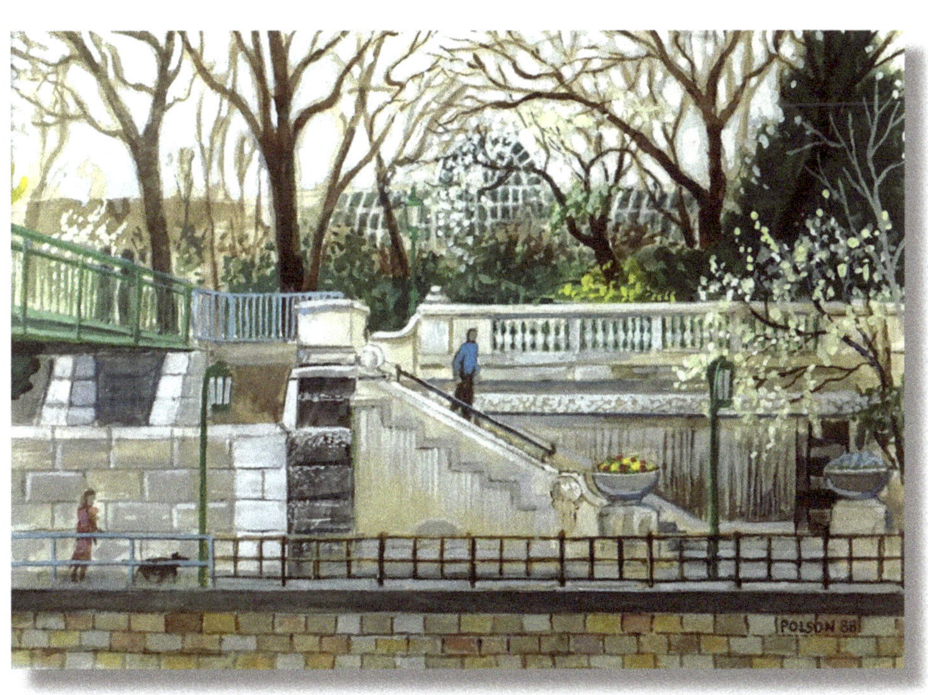

POLSON 88

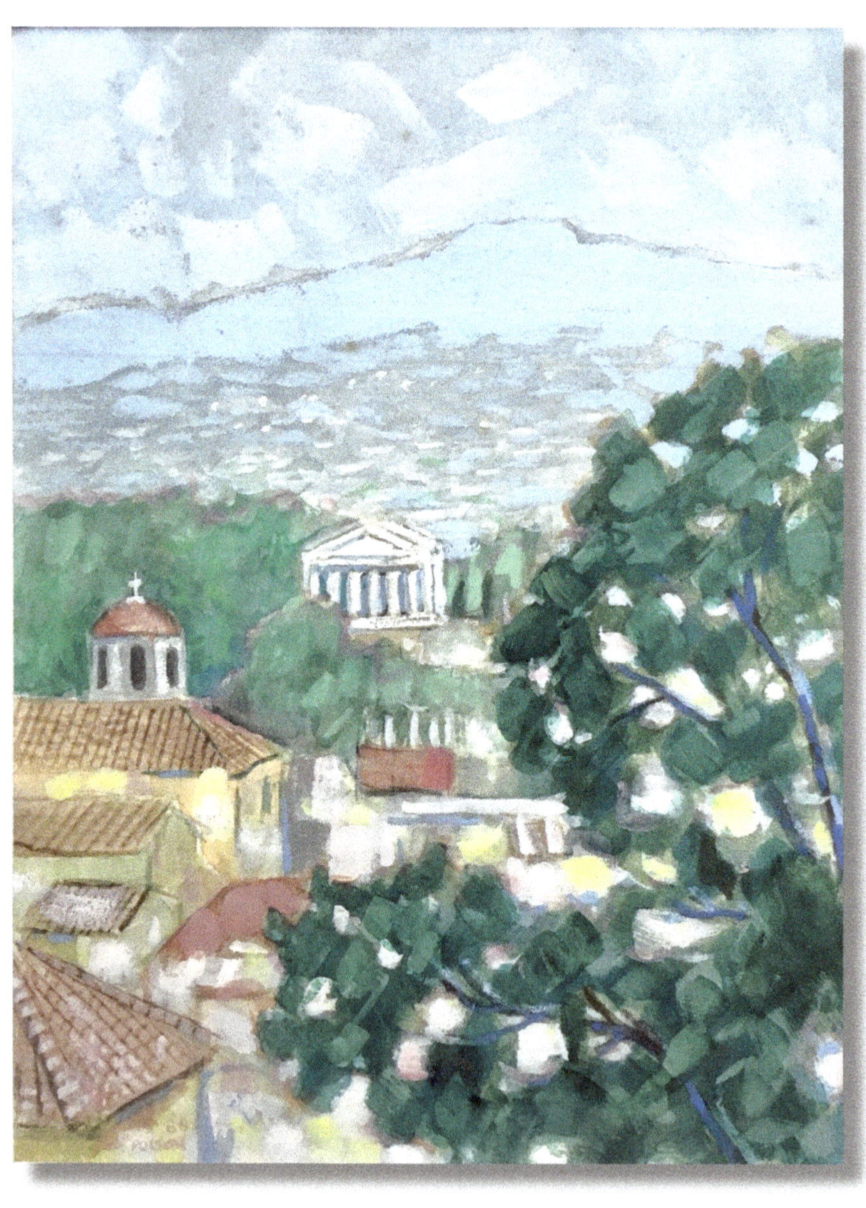

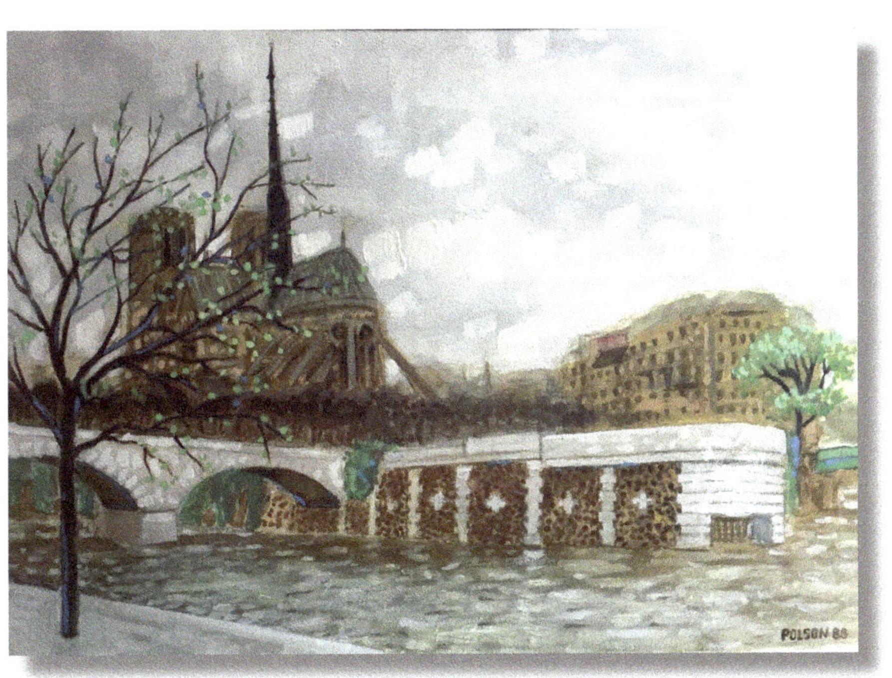

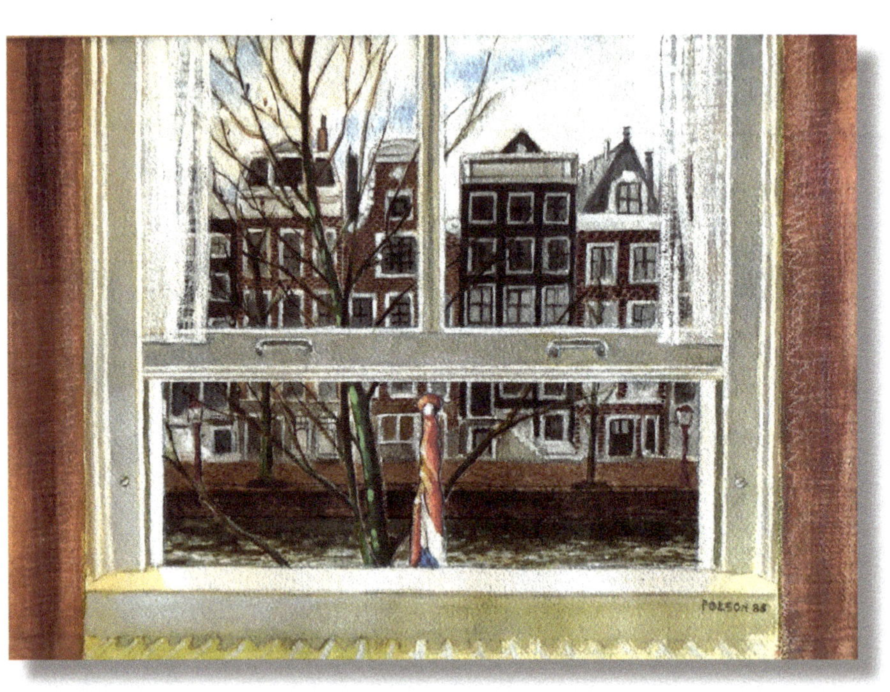

21

BTL

When Paul returned to San Diego, he called Andy. Things didn't quite go as planned.

"I decided not to get involved," said Andy. "Mark ran into Dick who was excited about becoming a partner." Dick was once the head of the sales team at Robert Keith. "I wasn't interested after I heard the details."

Dick had just returned from a year stint in prison for some white-collar crime. While serving his time, he met a fellow inmate from Mexico who was there on drug-related charges. This friend of Dick's is interested in investing and had the financial ability to fund the start of "Bigger Than Life" the name that they decided on for the new company.

Paul called Mark who is still excited about Paul coming on board. They even found a facility in El Cajon. Through Dick, they coerced the better salesmen from Robert Keith to join them. Many of the employees did just that.

Bigger Than Life made a million dollars in sales in the first three months.

As it was at Robert Keith, so it is with BTL.

It turns out that RK is having financial difficulties. They have plenty of sales but decided they only want to take on the higher-paying jobs. Because of the size and cost of their "Darth Vader" building, and their generosity with their employees, RK is slowly going bankrupt. Employees are asked if they could wait longer for their paychecks. Andy saw this since he is the accountant; hence his interest in starting a new business.

Paul began work at BTL immediately. Everyone is glad to see him, and they all brought their happy faces. He had a list of clay sculptures that needed to be done, and he began each project with a technical drawing. The rumors about the owners didn't bother him, and he is treated well. They appreciated his work and the artistic ability he put into it. That changed after a couple of years.

The immediate success of Bigger Than Life is due to the unmatched sales team they had assembled. Fortunately for BTL, these salesmen had already been working on inflatable sales at RK, and they knew their clients personally. They just carried on where they left off.

Not just any salesman could work there. Their sales abilities are way beyond any used car salesmen. They are dealing with savvy, intelligent clients who wouldn't put up with any bullshit.

When they started work at Bigger Than Life, they received twelve dollars an hour for three months. After that, it is just a commission. If they didn't have their act together by then, it was goodbye. They made million-dollar sales. A talented salesperson made damn good money at ten percent commission.

As salesmen, they wanted potential buyers to understand the advantages of using inflatables for advertising and events. It is common for them to call Paul to their office to talk with the clients who wanted to know the details. How are inflatables made? What are the advantages of using inflatables over solid work? What special effects could BTL offer that other 3D materials could not?

The differences between Robert Keith and Bigger Than Life quickly became apparent.

Robert and Ann, the owners of Robert Keith, had built their business around unique energy and artistic ability. They are on the ground floor of developing the technology and materials needed to make a quality product. They also like having a good relationship with their employees, and in their meetings, they encourage working together, doing their part, and helping each other.

When they created a high-profile job, they contacted the employee's hometown media, giving them credit for their work.

Just wanting to accept the highest-paying jobs is a mistake. Becoming successful quickly added to their illusion that the cornucopia of riches pouring into the company is endless. This attitude, along with their national (and in many cases international) popularity, did go to their heads. That isn't surprising, since the jobs they landed are the best clients you could imagine.

Bigger Than Life is a company run by salesmen. They see the potential in what Robert Keith offered. The problem is that, if the employees disappeared, they would have no idea how to build an inflatable. Well, that's not exactly true. They knew how to make an inflatable, but none of them had the talent or artistic ability to create one. They lacked artistic input—you know—creative thinking. They depended on the employees to supply that aspect of the business.

———➤ ✳ ◄———

Paul's transition from Robert Keith to BTL was seamless. He immediately bonded with the owners, the salesmen, and the employees.

The jobs are plentiful and high profile. The most exciting project that year is the half-time show for Super Bowl XX in New Orleans. They fabricated a futuristic city that is 100 feet in diameter. Along with this, they made a fifty-foot diameter Earth and other giant planets ranging from twenty to forty feet that hung from the ceiling.

BTL made hundreds of product samples ranging from twenty-foot beer bottles and cans of Pepsi and Coke products to potato chip bags and chewing tobacco packages, all ranging from twenty to forty feet in diameter. These are substantial quantity orders and also moneymakers; in some cases, they made hundreds of each, if not more.

Absorbed in his daily routines, Paul follows each project down the production line. The sewing machine operators like his interest in their work and enjoy it when he visits them. They are proud of the part they played in the projects. Many of the pieces are huge. It is hard to know what part to sew first—where it starts and where it ends. Having designed the project, Paul would take one end and pin it at the starting point. They are impressed by how much he knew about each project. They even taught him how to sew.

Suzie and Buzz from the RK painting department are there, and it is fun to visit them while they worked. They are good at what they do and maintained the humor they had at Robert Keith. It always brought a smile to everyone's face.

Suzie became Paul's favorite sushi buddy. Paul took her to his favorite sushi bar, and she is immediately hooked. The chefs loved her. Suzie had the whole restaurant laughing uncontrollably at times. It helped that she did stand-up comedy on the side. She told Paul of one successful performance but didn't show much enthusiasm for continuing. It is just a daily thing for her. She entertains whoever is around her at the time.

The wood and metal shop make the blowers from scratch. They also found that carpet dryers worked well. Each job is custom-made for the particular inflatable they are producing. Some fans are internal.

The silkscreen department also has its own uniqueness developed by Robert Keith.

* ✳ *

Paul's euphoria over his great job and friends didn't continue for the full three years he worked at BTL. As it turned out, Mark is having difficulty with him. He didn't pick up on that at first, but it began to sink in as the years progressed. He is young—somewhere in his early twenties.

At Robert Keith, they got along great, but as BTL's owner, he seemed to act strangely toward Paul. The rest of the company respected what he had to offer. The employees saw him as the person who made things happen since he started each project. Paul didn't think he was different from anyone else. They all had their duties. A couple of other employees asked him why he didn't start his own company. It's because he isn't a businessman and loves what his job entails. He didn't have to deal with the problems that the owners and managers had. Mark still perceived Paul as a threat.

Paul thought he was on his side—helping him make a quality product.

Management decided that they needed to choose an actual production manager. Paul isn't sure exactly what that means, except maybe being able to boss employees around and getting a pay raise.

A company meeting is called after a few days of this subject floating in the air.

There must have been over one hundred employees at the time.

The big announcement came during a special meeting. Dave Rodriquez is to be the new production manager. The employees just sat there with maybe a couple of claps from a couple of people. Paul noticed Dave looking at him with a big smile on his face.

It seems that each department ran itself pretty well. They had production meetings to discuss everyone's part and what needs to be done. However, Paul did understand that the company is getting bigger, and there probably is a need for that position. Each department has to work together in a coordinated way.

After the meeting, Dave came to Paul's sculpting room.

"Hey, man," he said. "I know you wanted to be production manager. I just wanted to say good try, but I think my qualifications are better."

Paul looked at him in astonishment. "What?"

"I know, I know. You thought you worked well with everyone, and the employees would listen to you."

"Sorry to disappoint you, Dave, but the last job I want is production manager. The reason I'm here is that I love to design and make inflatable shapes. I couldn't do that if I had to manage people. To your credit, they need someone who can organize and manage people. That's not me."

"Oh," he said with a confused look on his face. "I just thought you wanted to be the production manager."

"Nope. I'm happy where I'm at."

Dave turned and walked out.

Little did Paul realize how this conversation would affect the rest of his stay at "Bigger Than Life."

22

NY ANNE

Paul is excited about a new project for Honda. The client wants a thirty-foot-high inflatable Honda four-wheeler. At the production meeting, he received the concept art and a brochure. There is also a spec sheet for the four-wheeler. It shows the sizes and different views.

Taking the info to his drafting table, Paul did a to-scale drawing showing all sides and a view from the top. He drew out the lettering and art that they need to project, including the tread for the tires. He drew a section of the tire that provided a continual tread around the circumference when placed end to end. The tread pattern will be silk-screened, using six pieces per tire. When sewn, the ends would match up to make a continual tread.

The next step is for Paul to make a clay sculpture to scale. Clay isn't needed to create most of the patterns, but for specific areas like the handlebars and other details, it is easier to work from. He kept an eye on the production and helped where he could.

Several weeks later, one of the production people came to his workspace and told him they are doing the first inflation.

Alright, they will finally get to see this monster! It still needs to be painted, so if changes are made, they need to do that before the painting department gets to it.

When Paul walks into the painting area, the blowers are turned on, and the inflatable starts to rise. Employees are arriving from the different departments to see the first inflation. It is always fun to get the first glimpse of a new project.

As it took shape, there are *oohs* and *aahs*. Mark and Dave walked in and stood next to it.

"Beautiful job, gang. Boy, that bugger is big!" said Dave. "What do you think, Mark?"

"I like it. It looks like we're ready to paint."

"Ah, excuse me," Paul said. "I see a big problem."

"Huh? What's that?" asked Dave.

Paul pointed at the tires. "The front tires are touching the back tires."

Dave looked at the tires. "I think it looks good that way. The pattern maker and I decided to move them in. It will be more stable."

"There is a whole engine that is supposed to fit between them," I said. "How can you leave out the engine? The client will flip out."

Dave looked around and yelled, "Hey, Buzz, come here."

Buzz walked over, and Dave said, "Do you think we need to show the engine?"

"Uh, yeah?"

"Do you think you can paint it above the tires?"

"I'll do whatever you want, Dave," said Buzz.

"Just a minute," Paul said as he left for his drawing table. He grabbed his technical drawing along with the client's art and brochure.

Paul returned and put a photo of the Honda in front of them. "Look—the engine—between the two tires. I figured this out to scale; it is exact. You need eight feet between the tires, so there is room to paint the engine."

Mark was standing behind them as they talked.

"So, Mark, what do you think?" Dave asked.

Mark paused, then said, "I'll tell you what . . . let's compromise. Make it four feet apart."

"Hey, Buzz," Dave said, "Could you put that engine in a four-foot space?"

"Sure, we can do anything. We can paint it on top of the tires if you want." He shook his head and walked off.

"Four feet it is," said Dave as everyone filed back to their workstations.

Paul can't understand what just happened. As time went on, he realized that Mark, Dave, and the pattern person wanted to be involved in some design decisions. Paul is up for that, but why make a product different from what the client wanted?

— * ✳ * —

A couple of months later, Mark called Paul to his office.

When he walked in, Mark sat at his desk with a young woman sitting across from him. Dick is also there.

"Have a seat, Paul," Dick said. "This is Ann. She's an artist from New York and needs to have an inflatable built. She's looking for someone to fabricate it."

"Hello, Ann," Paul said as he sat down.

"Hi, Paul. So what is your job here?" Her tone was a little uptight—almost angry.

"I start with the artwork provided by the client. The first thing I do is a technical drawing, and then I make an armature for the clay. I scale the drawing to the size of the clay to make sure they are the exact size to scale. We then pattern it so we can project it to the actual size for the cutters."

"What kind of clay do you use?"

"Plasticine. It's a clay with an oil and wax base."

Ann glared at Mark and Dick. "Was that so hard? Why didn't you ask him to come here in the first place?"

She stood up and added, "Can I go see where he works? I would like to see his process."

Mark and Dick looked peevishly at each other and said, "Sure."

Paul took Ann to his drawing table first and showed her the drawings he is doing that day. Then they went to the sculpture room, which is filled with old cut-up clays, and one that is almost finished.

He explained the process. Ann had calmed down from her experience with Mark and Dick.

"I don't care much for the owners of this place."

"Why? What happened?"

"Can we have dinner tonight? We can talk then."

"Sure," Paul said. "Do you like sushi?"

"I love sushi."

Paul gave her the address. "Great. See you at six o'clock?"

"I'll be there."

That evening, Ann is waiting at the door of his favorite sushi bar, the one where he and Suzie frequent.

They are seated at the bar, and she begins speaking. "I need a giant pair of legs to put on a theater in New York. I've searched the country. Robert Keith and BTL are the only ones I found who can make what I want."

"So," she said. "Who should make it, BTL or Robert Keith?"

Paul took a drink of sake to wash down the *uni* he had just devoured. "Well, I would say that the patterning is better at Robert Keith and the art department is better at Bigger Than Life."

Ann gripped a piece of yellowtail sashimi with her chopsticks. As she brought it to her mouth, she glanced at him. "Why don't you start your own company?"

Paul was a little taken aback. He had never had the desire.

"I don't consider myself a businessman. I like what I'm doing, and it's fun to make inflatables. I would enjoy doing what you're doing more, I guess."

Paul continued, "I've been painting most of my life, and I want to pursue that. I can probably do the same with an inflatable—make one that came from my own mind and heart. I like doing these projects for the company; it's a challenge. I guess it would be nicer to build an inflatable the way I would prefer to make it—especially when I can do it better without all the bad decisions from people who don't know what they're talking about."

Changing the subject, Paul asked her, "So, what happened in Mark's office?"

With a slight expression of disgust, she said, "I already visited Robert Keith, and it was a good experience. I called and made an appointment with BTL to compare the two and decide which company I would prefer."

"When I walked into Mark's office, he called Dick in. I sat down and asked if I could speak to the artist who designs the inflatables. Mark said he is the guy. I asked a couple of simple questions like how do you make these? What kind of clay do you use? Did you go to school in art?"

"I could tell right away that he isn't the one doing the design or artwork. So I said, 'Who really designs these?'"

"He stammered and picked up the phone. A short while later, a guy named Dave walked in. I asked what his job was, and he said he was the production manager. I told him I wanted to see the person who designs the inflatables."

"He said that he did. I asked him similar questions and got similar responses."

"I started getting mad and asked them why I couldn't talk to the person who designs the inflatables. That's when they called you in."

Ann later called me and said that she asked Robert Keith to pattern and sew her project. She wanted to design it and do the painting herself.

23

DELMAR

hat's the way things are changing. It's time to move on. Paul's stint at BTL is just short of three years. Not being the impulsive type, he begins to plan his move to Seattle. He already has money in the bank for the move but wants to concentrate on saving more.

It is the end of October 1987. Paul's looking for one final Halloween party before quitting BTL and moving to Seattle.

In previous years, he attended parties with contests sponsored by radio stations. They had the best prizes. When he heard there is a huge costume party every year, alternating locations from Sea World to the Del Mar Fairgrounds, Paul decides to go for it. The Halloween party this year is at the Del Mar Fair Grounds.

When Paul arrives at the fairground facility, he is blown away. The building is enormous, and the crowd packs the place. Three popular bands are playing that night, but Paul's not sure what bands they are. He's focused on other matters.

Halfway through the event, someone came over and gave Paul a number.

"You're one of the finalists," she yelled over the music and crowd noise. "When the band finishes this set, they will ask you to come up on stage."

There are some fantastic costumes. One guy is in a large ultra-realistic shell covered with thousands of beads. The beads are iridescent, and the whole shell shimmers with changing colors depending on how the light hits it.

One prize is the "People's Choice Award." All the finalists stepped forward one at a time. As they worked down the line, the applause is moderate and, in some cases, quiet. When Paul stepped forward, the whole place erupted.

So that's the prize Paul received.

Then there are first, second, and third prizes. First prize is a motorcycle. Paul can't remember the other prizes—something like a weekend at a resort or dinner for two at an expensive restaurant?

Anyway, Paul received a ten-day round trip for two to London at a five-star hotel (next to Hyde Park). Also included are two tickets to a theater to see the production of *Cats*.

When Paul returned to work on Monday, the phone in his sculpture area rang. It's Mark.

"Did you go to a contest over the weekend?"

"Yes, I did," said Paul, wondering why Mark was interested. "I went to the Del Mar Fairgrounds."

"How did you do?" he asked.

"Great! I got the People's Choice Award." Paul explained the details.

"Darn!" he said. "I went to one and was picked as a finalist."

"What costume did you wear?"

"I used an inflatable elephant costume we made for a client. When they called us to select the winners, the battery died, so they excluded me."

"Wow! Sorry, Mark. You probably would have placed first." Paul is honored that he chose to share that with him.

— * ❋ * —

Paul set a date for his London trip—March 1, 1988—four months away.

He spent those months doing his regular duties at BTL while organizing his thoughts to prepare for the trip.

Paul needs someone to watch his studio while he is away.

Doug Anderson is one of the painters in the art department at BTL and he's excited about starting a picture-framing business. Paul knows the trade and wants to help Doug learn the process. At the same time, he thought he should keep up with his ability to frame artwork. Not wanting that knowledge to be wasted, he shows Doug the ropes, and Doug loves it.

Doug also said he would stay in Paul's studio while he is in Europe.

Paul finally came to the ultimate decision concerning his trip. He has money saved for his move to Seattle, but he can't resist using the money to travel to Europe for three months. When Paul returns, his money will be gone, but so what? This situation has presented itself before. Things always work out, and moving to the Northwest is still an option when he returns.

Paul usually prefers to travel alone, but he didn't want to waste the other ticket. Whoever he finds can go with him until the trip's ten-day gift portion is over, but he plans to travel alone for the remainder of his journey.

There are a couple of options, but one is an obvious choice. Karen at the time had married, and she lined Paul up with a friend of hers a couple of months earlier. Her name is Anellina, and they had dated a few times.

Anellina is excited about going, and she offered to store his van in her garage. Paul is comfortable around Anellina. She is a therapist and has a charming home in the Mount Helix area. The trip will give him a chance to know her better. Paul isn't sure, but it seems like a relationship that could work out. It's a matter of learning more about each other. Paul is still dead set on moving to the Northwest, and she just settled in a new house in a beautiful area. He's not sure she will give that up.

— * ❈ * —

Halfway through February, Paul did the deed and put in his notice at BTL. More than a few co-workers seem concerned about his job, and they don't think it's possible to replace him. Paul doesn't think the owners feel that way. They don't seem to care about the quality end of things—just the profits. To them, everyone is replaceable—like the pieces of a machine. If something broke, you just pick up a catalog and order a new one.

On the last day of work, Paul plans to get together with a couple of close friends at a local bar to celebrate. He cleans out his personal items and makes the rounds to say his goodbyes. There are lots of hugs. Paul will miss them, and he will miss his job. He loved what he was able to do there, but he needs to control his own life and get back into the arts.

When Paul arrives at the bar, a few other employees are already waiting for him. There seems to be a continual flow of co-workers coming through the door. It looks like the whole company is here. The owners didn't show up. Dave is here, and that surprises him. He actually sat in the seat next to him.

The art department crew walked over, carrying a large poster board. They had cut around the edges to shape it into a large artist's palette. The paint on the palette consists of colored construction paper, one color for each of the departments. They all signed their names and wished him luck, saying they would miss him. Green is the painting department; blue is the silk screeners; and on it went— the sewing department, the wood and metal shop, the sales staff, the office workers, the shipping department, etc.

Paul looks over at Dave, and there are tears in his eyes—actually flowing. He picked up his napkin to wipe his face.

"How nice," Paul thought. He didn't know Dave cared.

Paul heard that after he left, the owners gave each employee a $500 bonus, thinking that would keep them from deserting. Since they had taken the employees from Robert Keith, they are sure that Paul will do the same to them.

That is not Paul's motivation at all. He's excited to travel to Europe and see great art. The business life is not appealing to him. He enjoys designing and making inflatables.

Paul has some ideas for making an inflatable or two that he is interested in pursuing. Other than that, Paul has no goals after Europe except to move to Seattle and pursue his passion for fine arts.

24

LONDON

Since Paul has finally put Bigger Than Life behind him, he begins preparing for the trip to London. He starts by making lists and thinking about what he wants to do while traveling Europe.

Paul has three objectives:

> ➤ Do watercolors paintings of the trip.
> Bring two watercolor blocks—twelve inches by sixteen inches and the other eight inches by twelve inches.

> ➤ Go to the major museums of each city and see each museum more than once. Paul wants to see the sights and meet the people. He plans to stay at each location for a while so he can relax and get the feel of each place.

> ➤ Eat well!
> Each country has its unique menu and flavor. He wants to experience each country through its food.

Anellina and Paul connected for dinner and spent the night together on a few occasions talking about the trip. She has a sister going to London at the same time they were, and Anellina wants to see her. They also made plans to rent a car and drive around southern England.

Paul has a close friend, Betty Rose, the best salesperson Robert Keith ever had. Unfortunately, she was so good that the company wanted to reduce her commission. Betty was making more than they were, and the owners couldn't allow that. She quit and decided to sell real estate.

They go out for sushi together often. Betty took him out in exchange for giving her son drum lessons.

Her family had often traveled to Europe, and she did a great job helping Paul prepare for the trip. One thing he needs to get is a Dolt bag. It's easy to carry with comfortable shoulder and waist straps. It holds a lot of stuff. She told him to get a line with clamps on each end to hang clothes to dry after he does laundry. Dramamine is high on her list. The list went on. Her advice and recommendations all turned out to be useful. Unfortunately, he didn't take some of her advice but wishes he had.

There are a few minor hassles Paul needs to take care of before he leaves. When he attempts to drive his van into Anellina's garage, he finds that it is too high to fit in the door. Getting it into the garage is an easy fix. He let the air out of the tires—not entirely though, just enough to lower it and not be riding on the rims.

———⋆✳⋆———

LONDON

Anellina and Paul fly out of San Diego at five o'clock in the evening on February 29. They connected with a flight at LAX airport and took a 747 jet to London. It is an eleven-hour flight. The movie *Surrender* passed some of the time, but other than that, Paul didn't get much sleep.

Arriving in London at noon on March 1, they went through customs and exchanged their money for English currency—$1.86 for one pound.

They take the underground to the Marble Arch in Central London, next to Hyde Park, and found the hotel a block away—the Mount Royal.

Needless to say, they both took a nap for a couple of hours.

Anellina contacted her sister Marina and arranged to meet her and her boss Fred at their hotel for a drink.

That evening, they went out to a high-class French restaurant. The meal cost over 140 pounds for the two of them, but it is excellent. Paul is not a white-wine drinker, but the bottle they share is the best wine he has ever tasted. They order escargot and duck, and the desserts are incredible. They each had their own waiter serve them in unison, lifting the lids on the dishes while revealing the courses they are serving. This meal is a great way to kick off their vacation.

The following morning, they have a continental breakfast in their room, followed by a walk and a visit to the Tate gallery.

Paul is finally seeing the great works of the old artists—in real life—for the first time. Even before arriving, he is anxious to see Joseph Turner's paintings and is not disappointed. They are large pieces that photos in books cannot compare. They are borderline abstract with amazing colors. He was definitely an influence on the impressionist movement.

They took a lunch break at one-thirty at an English pub, and then back to the Tate to see the work of another artist, David Hockney. Again, photos could not do them justice.

Paul finds himself saying that about every artist he has experienced for the first time, not surprising since he hadn't seen most artists except in books.

When they returned to the hotel, Anellina freshened up and left to visit her sister.

Anellina must have had a great time since she didn't arrive back at the hotel until 2:00 in the morning. After confirming her fantastic night with her sister, she immediately fell into a deep sleep.

They slept until noon. Anellina is not feeling well when she wakes.

She asked if Paul is upset with her.

"No, of course not. Why would I be upset?"

"We didn't have sex last night. I just thought you were mad."

"I didn't think you were up for it."

Paul let her go back to sleep. He is wide-awake and decides to visit the same English tavern they were at the day before. He then went back to the Tate Museum to see the rest of what he had missed.

Seeing this artwork is like an injection of energy. Paul found himself in a contemplative mood when he left the museum and walked north along the Thames River. When he reached the House of Commons and Big Ben—lo and behold—there is Rodin's *Burghers of Calais*! He had seen photos of it, as well as detail shots. It is magnificent!

When he returns to the hotel, Anellina is feeling better. They dressed up and went to their appointed time to see *Cats*.

As it turned out, they didn't have tickets to *Cats*. Paul called Mr. R Miller of RCA when they returned.

Oops! It's the production of *Chess* they are supposed to see. Since they missed the show that night, Mr. Miller arranged seats for them the following evening at the Prince Edward Theatre. It is getting late by that time, so Anellina and Paul went to the hotel bar and drowned their sorrows in a couple of drinks.

The next morning, Paul had the usual continental breakfast. Anellina is still not wholly recovered from two nights ago, so she stayed in bed. Paul walked to Hyde Park in the early morning and painted. The clear air is a bit nippy, but it feels good. It feels good to be in London, and it feels good to paint.

Anellina felt much better when he returned, and she is ready to do something. They walked through the park to the Victoria and Albert Museum and spent a lot of time viewing paintings, the majority by Constable. Then it is back to the hotel to nap and prepare themselves for the theater that evening. The napping is not all because of drinking. They are wrestling with a bit of jet lag.

Tickets are waiting at the door this time. *Chess* is a wonderful play—great sets, singing, and acting.

Italian food is next on their list. The restaurant is in the SOHO district, and they both love that part of town. Not only are there interesting places to eat, but there are also more theaters, galleries, and pubs. The streets are narrow and cobblestoned, adding to the old European atmosphere.

Waking up a little later than usual the following morning, they took the Underground back to the SOHO district. Paul took his thirty-five-millimeter camera and shot some black and white photos. His friend Doug wanted a tee shirt at the London Hard Rock Cafe. That is the next thing on the agenda.

Both Anellina and Paul are disappointed that they didn't get to see *Cats* the other night, so they decided to see if they could get tickets at the door—no problem! The scenery awed Paul with its detail, and he fantasized about actually making a set like that.

25

STONEHENGE

On their last day at the hotel, Anellina and Paul split up so they could do the things they personally wanted to do before leaving London. Anellina wants to go to Harrods department store. Paul wants to explore parts of the city he hasn't seen and shoot some black and white photography. There are also more museums that interest him. He walks toward Trafalgar Square and spends some time at London's National Gallery. He didn't come close to seeing it all—maybe on his return trip.

According to their plans, it is time to find a car to rent so they can explore southern England. The best tactic is to take a cab to Heathrow Airport and rent one there. When they return, he would take Anellina straight to the airport, turn in the car, and start his solo trip to mainland Europe.

They headed west from London. It felt odd driving on the opposite side of the road. Paul had a latent fear that he might space out and just start driving in the wrong lane. Finally, he got used to it. The cars on the freeway zoomed past them at what seemed like incredible speeds. Paul accelerated and got in the flow.

There are things they want to see, but they just relaxed and drove for the time being. They would hit those places on the way back. Somewhere along the way, he took a wrong turn, and they ended up in Wales.

It is starting to get late. Anellina brought a book on bed and breakfasts, and she began taking notice of their location. She is checking to see what is in the area.

Anellina found a place in a small town—Newport—just as the sun was setting. Climbing the stairs, they knocked on the door only to find out that they are full. They are pleasant people, and they referred them to the house next door.

They climbed the stairs to the neighbor's house and knocked on the door. A woman answered with a big smile.

"We're looking for a place to stay tonight," Anellina said. "Your neighbors suggested we see if you have a vacancy."

"Yes, we do," she said in some sort of British accent. "They just called us and said you are coming over. Come in."

"Go ahead," Paul told Anellina. "I'll grab our bags and be right back."

The same lady was at the door when he returned.

"Your wife is waiting in the living room. Make yourself at home."

It's not surprising she assumed that we were married. They figured they would play along to avoid confusion.

She showed them to their room. "Dinner will be in about forty-five minutes."

They deposited their bags and walked down to the living room to chat.

Suddenly, the front door swung open, and the man of the house walked in. He is in his work clothes with scuffed boots, and from the looks of it, he has a physical job. His shirt is a little worn and a bit dirty from whatever he does for a living.

He darts upstairs as he said, "I'll be back down in a few minutes."

Our hostess herded Anellina and Paul into the dining room and showed them to their seats. A few minutes later, her children came down and joined us.

She starts bringing in plates of food.

Her husband, Harvey, came back downstairs. He looks to be about sixty-five years old and had changed his clothes to an elaborate suit with a vest and cufflinks. He sat at the head of the table.

"Wonderful, we have company!" Harvey is delighted. There is a smile on his face as he introduces his family. He looks like a very proud man and seems much respected by his wife and children.

Anellina and Paul introduced themselves and told him where they live.

The food is tasty, and there is plenty more food if they want seconds.

After dinner, Harvey stood and said, "Please excuse Paul and me. We have business to attend to."

He motioned for Paul to follow him as he opened the front door. They walk across the street, through the door of a tavern, and found a table to sit down. Harvey waved at a waitress while holding up two fingers. She brought them two pints of beer. Harvey and Paul had a fun conversation comparing their two countries and chatting about Anellina and Paul's trip.

As they drank their beers, Paul realized his drinking buddy had already finished his. Harvey waved at the waitress and along came two more beers. He looked at Paul with a dour look on his face. Paul was sipping his and had barely started.

"Drink that beer," he said. "Don't sip it."

He is talking to the right man as Paul recalled his fraternity days and downed the pint in five seconds.

"There you go!" Harvey said. "You know how to do it!"

Being in a bar across the street from his house, Paul realized that he is proud to show him off to his bar buddies.

As they downed the beers, Paul noticed that the waitress had been pacing them for about twenty minutes between beers. They are so involved in their conversation that they didn't notice the gaps.

After four pints, they staggered back across the street, up his stairs, and through the door. It had been a fun conversation, and Harvey is a hell of a nice guy.

The next morning, they had a filling breakfast, hopped in the car, and headed back to England. Anellina had her own stories to tell about the night before. This visit gave them a little insight into how these people live. They are part of their family from the moment they arrived until the moment they left.

On the drive back, Anellina and Paul stopped at the town of Bath and saw the remnants of the Roman-built bathhouses.

Stonehenge is their next stop. They spent a couple of hours gazing at the mysterious formation, then had a little picnic from the sandwiches they bought at a small store before they left Newport.

These huge, monumental stones captured the feelings of an epic history that is still not fully understood. Paul took photos as they strolled between the stones feeling the power and the history in them.

Anellina and Paul spent one more night together at a Holiday Inn. They tried to find a little British inn or a place with a bit of atmosphere but failed. It is getting dark, and they are tired. Leaving each other is sad, and they sat at the bar that evening talking about their trip. She wants Paul to call her every week. He agreed. "Well, maybe two times a week," she said.

Paul is a little reluctant but agreed. He cares for Anellina, but the calls turned out to be a mistake. He needs to stick up for what he wants. Paul is terrible that way. As it later turns out, he began to resent the two times a week calls. Paul tried to immerse himself in Europe, and after a while, felt like he is reporting home to Mom. Paul explained that to her over the phone, but it came out like he had met someone else. He hadn't.

In the morning, they drove straight to the airport and returned the car. Anellina has an early flight. That's why the hotel they stayed at was to be as close to Heathrow as possible. Paul took her as far as he could—to the departure gate—and said their goodbyes.

Early the next morning, Paul took the Underground to Central London. He bought a train ticket to Harwich by British Rail for that evening and a ferry reservation to the Hook of Holland. There are still about eight hours to kill, so Paul took the Tube to their usual pub next to the Tate Gallery, enjoyed an early lunch, and revisited the National Gallery. After getting his fill, he walks to the National Portrait Gallery and spends the rest of his time there.

26

AMSTERDAM

Paul caught the train at 7:08 p.m., and by midnight, he is in the middle of the English Channel on a boat to Holland.

That night, he took short catnaps anywhere to be comfortable, but he didn't get much sleep. The boat arrived at the Hook of Holland just before sunup. He activated his Eurail Pass and rode first class into Amsterdam.

The one thing that makes the biggest impression on his mind is how flat Holland is. Also, the number of people on bicycles is unexpected, even though he had heard of it. Seeing it looked to him like a cartoon. There are a lot of canals, even before reaching Amsterdam.

When the train arrives, he takes a tram to the Heineken brewery. This place must be a tourist attraction, more than a local hangout. Everyone there seems to be an American. Having only one beer, Paul walked the short distance to the Hotel de Moor.

He stayed in room number fourteen, which has a history of famous people of the past staying here. It is a tiny, quaint little room overlooking the Prinsengracht Canal.

Paul began painting a view out his window, framed by curtains. The buildings across the canal are very detailed. They also remind him of cartoons. A few days later, he did another "quicker" painting of a bridge going over a canal with a boat moored to the sidewall.

Paul loves these arched pedestrian bridges! The brick and stone environment with the walkways and canals had an eerie but wonderful feeling—also like a cartoon—no disrespect meant.

⚜

Paul had previously mentioned the artists that influenced him in his youth. One is Salvador Dali. The other is Vincent van Gogh.

He would like to think that he admires all artists since each has a unique view and process. Real artists learn from other artists, creative thinking, and experimentation. These are the tools needed to build their own styles.

Several artists have influenced him more than others. He saw things in their work that were eye-opening, and that transcended typical views of art.

Vincent affected Paul because of his colors—more so than other artists. Seeing his work in books did not do him justice; seeing his work in real life was astonishing.

Paul liked Van Gogh when he first saw photos of his work, but the real paintings took the surface of the canvas away, and his colors wove in and out of space as if alive. His brushstrokes made his paintings come alive.

Hence, when Paul first walked into his room, he threw his bag on the bed and left immediately to see the Van Gogh Museum. It is still early.

The Van Gogh Museum is like being in a candy store for the eyes. He spends the morning and early afternoon enjoying each painting.

Finally, after a lifetime of scouring books about his life and his work, Paul is seeing them in real life. When he was in London, he saw Vincent's work in an impressionism exhibit at the Tate. Here, the walls are filled with his paintings.

He did have a favorite. Paul liked one particular self-portrait from the several that he had seen. His earlier description of his work embodies in this painting. He did not see a surface, just the colors and brush strokes dancing around in space, like a portal into a three-dimensional world.

This exhibit isn't the last of the Van Gogh's Paul will see. Paris has some of his best paintings. The Musée d'Orsay has a remarkable permanent collection of the impressionist period.

Before heading back to the hotel, Paul stops at a grocery store for cheese, sausage, and bread. Back in the room, he has a snack and took a long nap. Paul hadn't slept well since he left England.

That evening, he walks around the area with his camera and ends up in Rembrandt Square (Rembrandtplein) where he had a couple of beers. He feels a little disabled because of the language barrier. That didn't last long. When he talked to or responded to someone who spoke to him in Dutch, they answered in perfect English with a delightful Dutch accent. All in all, they had fluent and fun conversations.

When he arrives back at the hotel, Paul hears a lot of talking and giggling. The owner is at the reception desk and tells him there is a TV in the lounge. "My daughter is in there with her friends, but don't mind them. They are used to our guests relaxing in there."

That wasn't his original plan, but Paul walks in and seats himself in the back of the room. There is a TV placed high enough to see over the heads of a group of girls. There are ten of them, and they are chatting in Dutch and laughing. They seem to be playing some game. They took turns standing and talking to the group. The TV is boring, but the girls are animated and having a blast. They are too young for his interests—maybe thirteenish. They ignore him for a while. Then one girl who is talking looks over at him, turns red (noticeable with her pale skin), and giggles. All of their heads turn to Paul, and they burst out laughing. They say a few things that sounded like an apology and then continued. Just the atmosphere they created made him want to laugh.

Paul stood and walked up to his room. Before leaving, they all waved goodbye with their happy faces and said something that he didn't understand, but it sounded friendly.

He woke up fresh the following morning and walked downstairs to try their breakfast. It was tasty and filling. Returning to his room, he worked on the painting from his window overlooking the Prinsengracht Canal. Then it is off to the Rijksmuseum.

Wow! This museum is a huge step into the past with beautiful paintings by Rembrandt, Rubens, and Vermeer. Artist's names, the portraits, the landscapes, and the human bodies fill the walls. The paintings are dark, but it allows the light that is in them to come out strong.

In the afternoon, Paul went back to his room overlooking the canal and took a long nap. He is hungry when he awoke and kept thinking of a food vendor parked close to the bridge, just down the street. Paul wants to try it since they served herring, eel, and other exotic Dutch treats. He bought an eel sandwich. It is pretty good.

Okay, time for a little bar hopping!

Paul spruced himself up, which meant trimming his mustache and putting on his last clean set of clothes. He then walked to a square called Leidseplein.

The first bar he walked into had a friendly owner, who actually sat next to him. They began talking about general topics that are common when you first meet someone. It then evolves into the reality around them.

"So, what can I get you?" he asked as he casually stood up and moved behind the bar.

"I'll have a Keoke Coffee."

"Okay. What's a Keoke Coffee?" he asked.

"It's Kahlua, brandy, and coffee. You top it with whipped cream and a cherry, then pour a bit of crème de cocoa over it."

"We don't have coffee—just espresso," he said.

"Sounds intense, but I'll try it."

The other patrons are listening and chime in with "Me, too!" and "Hey, I'll try that." The bartender served them, and—yes—it is pretty intense. It is like a thick desert with alcohol. A regular keoke Coffee is intense just as it is. Paul thought it best only to have one.

He said his goodbyes. Everyone gave him a thumbs-up and said, "Enjoy your trip" and "Stop in again" remarks.

Paul wandered around until he found a packed tavern. There didn't seem to be a place to sit until he spied a few seats at the end of the bar. As soon as Paul sits down, three gorgeous Dutch women came over and joined him. They greeted him and switched to English as soon as they realized he had no idea what they are saying.

They live north of Amsterdam, and they come here to drink and party. They kept plying Paul with drinks. As soon as he finished one, another appeared in front of him. They are regulars and knew a lot of others who frequented the place. They introduced him to their friends who also asked if they could buy him a drink.

Paul is drinking brandy. It's a Dutch brandy that is very smooth (meaning that it is a little too easy to drink). It's also half the price of the French equivalent. He realized the need to refuse their generous offers before he fell on the floor.

On the way back to the hotel, Paul walked by the first bar where he had stopped earlier and poked his head in the door.

"Hello," he called out, only to be coaxed in for another espresso Keoke Coffee. The bartender refused to charge him. Paul got into bed around two-thirty a.m.

"Oh my God" is all he could mutter when he woke that morning. He went downstairs and had breakfast. It helped to get something in his stomach.

For most of the day, he stayed in his room, recovering from the night before. He slept a lot but was still productive. He washed his clothes in the sink, then stretched his laundry cord across the room. The clothes are dry enough to wear in a couple of hours.

Paul worked on the painting of the view out his window between the napping.

Feeling hungry, he finally went out in the fresh air at five o'clock in the evening. He walked back to Leidseplein, had a nice meal at an Indian restaurant, then went to bed early.

The following morning, light rain fell that lasted all day. Paul painted and then wandered around with his camera to areas he hadn't yet seen. During this trip of discovery, he found himself on Zeedijk

Street. It is Sunday, and there is nobody on the street, but he remembered reading about this place—high crime rate, hookers, and drug dealers. It reminds him of his studio in the Gaslamp. He also sees the windows where women display their goods. The streets are narrow, but that is his vision of what most of Europe must be like.

One thing on his list is to stop at the train station. He will leave for Paris on Tuesday. Paul took the tram back to the hotel but had an odd experience. The driver kept looking at him in his mirror, and his expression seems angry. When they are close to the Prinsengracht, he stood and walked to the front, as he did the time before, taking his lead from what other passengers do. The driver drove past his stop while still glaring at Paul in the mirror. Immediately, a tiny elderly lady got up from her seat, walked upfront with her cane, and stood in front of Paul. She is glaring at the driver who immediately stops the tram and opens the door. She moved aside and motioned for him to leave. She smiled at Paul, and he thanked her.

Anne Frank's house is his last stop.

On the walk back to his room, he found a Telehouse (telephone booth). Paul made his first call to Anellina.

Paul woke to his last day in Amsterdam and finished his paintings, grabbed his thirty-five-millimeter camera, and went in a direction he hadn't been—up the Amstel Canal. It is a great walk, but it seems that he is experiencing more of the same. He has several gilders left. Hmmm, what to do?

There is a restaurant on the corner across from the canal that he likes, but a woman he met at the hotel breakfast said he should try the one on our side of the canal.

The restaurant is downstairs from street level, and Paul enjoyed a fantastic plate of ribs. It has a pleasant brick interior, and they played Cat Stevens' music the whole time. He is in heaven.

Paul walked to Leidseplein—again. He likes this place. After priming himself with a couple of beers, he walked to the center of the square. There are people playing ice hockey and a four-piece band doing their thing.

Realizing that he hadn't had a single cup of coffee since arriving in Holland, he is in the mood to just sit down and have a cup. He looked around and saw a sign that said "coffee," so he walked in that direction. The coffee shop is down about five steps, and he walked into a wide entrance. Paul hit a wall of smoke.

"Whoa! That smells like marijuana!" Paul thought—and it is.

He had always heard that weed is legal and wondered why he hadn't seen any signs of it since he arrived. Now he knew—coffee shops.

Paul walked up to the bar, and a woman with heavy eyelids casually strolled in his direction.

"I'll have a latte, please."

"Got it," she said. "The marijuana is over there." She motioned with her eyes to the corner of the café.

He looked in the direction she nodded and saw a man with several mini bags of pot from "everywhere." Paul walked over to see his goods.

"Wow," he said. "I'm from the States, and you never see anything like this!"

"I feel sorry for you, man. Land of the free?"

"Someday," Paul said. "They're working on it. Oh, yeah. I'll have some of this 'Tiberian numb tongue.'" (Paul made that up but the real names are just as good.)

Paul bought a small baggy for half what it costs in the States.

He walked back to the counter, and his latte is waiting for him. He sat down and had a sip.

An elbow nudged his left side. It's the guy sitting next to him trying to get his attention. He passed Paul a lit joint.

"Thanks!" Paul gripped it with his thumb and index finger then took a puff. He almost fell off his stool. Whatever this is, it's strong. He held on to his barstool to make sure he isn't going to tip over and then focuses on his coffee.

Looking down the bar's length, he sees people rolling joints with little piles of weed poured out on the bar.

So the stories are true: pot is legal, but smoking is contained and not anything you would experience in public.

27

PARIS

Crawling out of bed earlier than usual, Paul packed his gear in the Dolt bag, had breakfast, and made his way to the train station. He caught the 8:53 a.m. train to Paris.

He tossed the rest of the weed he bought yesterday. He heard that if you get busted in France, they will send you to the guillotine, and he didn't want to lose his head over such a small purchase.

On the train, Paul sat next to an Australian man named Barry. Barry was born in Yugoslavia. That is his destination; he is going home to see family.

There are rumors of troubles in that country. The problems are just beginning as it became evident in the news after returning to the States.

When Paul arrived in Paris, he and Barry hung together until they figured out the Metro subway system and found their hotels. Paul's is the Grand Hotel de Lima—175 francs per night.

Barry's hotel is three blocks away, and they met for a beer and dinner. They sat next to three young women and tried to have a conversation, but the language barrier hindered it. While they are there, it began pouring rain, so Paul dug in his pack and pulled out a poncho. He loaned it to Barry; he had farther to go.

Initially, there is a lot on Paul's agenda. Betty Rose has a friend named Rivian whom she introduced him to in San Diego.

Rivian is now in Paris and lives next door to the Musée d'Orsay. He called her and took the Metro to her place. They made plans, chatted until it was late, and then walked back along the Seine to his hotel, arriving at twelve-thirty that night.

Barry met Paul at his hotel the following morning. They walked to the Notre Dame Cathedral and had coffee while waiting for the Louvre Museum to open.

They entered the Louvre together but quickly realized that they needed to part and go the direction they each wanted to go—such a vast museum! Viewing artwork is a personal experience between an individual and the artist. They made plans to meet that evening.

Paul walked around, again being overwhelmed by the size, the history, and the painting techniques. He had plans to meet Rivian a couple of hours later at a café next to the opera. As it turned out, his watch was off by an hour. It was in Cairo time. He is there an hour early. Paul didn't realize it at the time, so he decided to check out some more museums.

The next item on his list is the George Pompidou Center. There are so many galleries, so much to see. He then spent most of the afternoon at the National Museum of Modern Art and then went to a Picasso show at the Grand Gallery.

Barry is at Paul's hotel at eight-thirty that evening. They went out to dinner and then went bar hopping. He returned to his room at two-thirty in the morning.

That morning is Barry's last day in Paris. He decided to go to Nice for a couple of days before moving on. They had breakfast, exchanged addresses, and said their goodbyes. Before Barry left, he invited Paul to travel with him. Paul considered the offer but preferred his own plans.

Boy! Paul hit the ground running when he arrived in Paris. He is overly occupied—meeting people, dining with others, and visiting museums. Amsterdam is slow and mellow compared to Paris. His whole visit continues at this pace until he caught the train out of town.

Rivian called and asked what happened to their meeting the day before. Paul realized the evening before that his watch had been wrong. He explained the time problem to her. Rivian had been there when she was supposed to be.

They planned to meet for dinner that evening with two Frenchmen she knew.

Paul treated himself to a long nap that afternoon. When he woke, he grabbed his camera, went to the Pompidou Center, and took detailed black and white photos of the architecture. The shots he enjoys most are from the top of the building. The view is amazing. He took panoramic shots of the skyline and rooftops.

That evening, Paul caught the Metro to Rivian's house. Her two French friends are there, and they decided to go out for Italian food.

Jean-Paul, one of her friends, lives in a small town named Angouleme—not real small—about 40,000 people. Jean-Paul asked him if he could visit his family; not just visit—he wants him to stay awhile. Paul is excited about that opportunity.

Jean-Paul is in Paris for his work. If Paul remembers correctly, he made theater sets, trade show booths, and exhibitions.

It is a unique and fun evening.

Knowing he likes Van Gogh, Rivian informed him that the Musée d'Orsay has a special exhibit that mainly focused on Van Gogh's paintings. There are samples of other impressionist artists in the show as well. Lines to get in the museum stretched around the corner. Rivian knew that, so they went early.

Up until now, this is the most awesome show Paul had seen yet. It is a "best of" selection of work that outshined the Van Gogh Museum in Amsterdam.

After a snack on the top floor, Rivian and Paul parted. He decided to stay and see the other exhibits.

What an impressive museum the Musée d'Orsay is. It used to be a train station. They built it in 1897, and after a period of decline and disuse, was transformed into the museum it is now. That was in 1986—two years before his visit. The museum's center is entirely open, and the ceiling of glass arches over the vast space. The sides of the building have smaller galleries showing both their permanent shows and their special exhibits. These galleries continue up in tiers until they reach the ceiling. The best sculptures Paul has seen since the beginning of his trip occupy its center.

The sculpture needs to be commented on since it is such a significant presence in the museum. The detailed and ultra-lifelike work almost seems to breathe.

Alexandre Schoenewerk sculpted a marble figure—*Young Tarantine*—a reclining nude stretching and twisting over a box shape covered in sculpted fabric.

A sculpture appeared as a large wall with figures and animals, larger than life, standing out from the wall in full three dimensions while the wall itself has shapes carved in deep relief. Jean-Baptiste Carpeaux sculpted the piece in marble.

Finally, one of Paul's favorites is the marble version of *The Gates of Hell* by Rodin. He saw the bronze the next day at the Rodin Museum.

Just a few months before, he had read a biography of Rodin. Paul was glued to that book until he finished it. Seeing Rodin's work in Europe is special since it is so fresh in his memory. Rodin worked on *The Gates of Hell* for thirty-seven years, and it is still said to be unfinished. He did multiple sculptures of the individual parts and had them made in marble and cast bronze.

Rodin was commissioned to do *The Gates of Hell* in 1880 for a decorative arts museum that never opened. Some of Rodin's most known works, such as *The Kiss* and *The Thinker,* were originally sculpted into *The Gates of Hell.*

The sculptor died in 1917. *The Gates of Hell* was later cast in bronze, in full for the first time, eight years later.

The museum has a wide variety of European paintings, sculptures, etchings, and drawings from the distant pre-Renaissance period until now. The countries of Europe are all so different with their many unique artists and styles—from the time of dominant influence by Christianity to the modern individual artists expressing their unique visions.

Paul returned to the room and decided to go to an outdoor café close to the hotel. It is deserted but open. A waiter walked over, and like an idiot, he asked for red wine in French—or what he thought is French. He massacred it. After pointing to the menu, the waiter stomped off. Five minutes later, he brought the wine, and he never saw him the rest of the evening. Paul rocked back on his chair, rested his legs on the table, and read his book for two hours. He then put some francs on the table and went back to his room.

I've heard that some French people are insulted if you pronounce the words in their language wrong. Paul found out there is truth to that statement, but it was the only time it happened.

THE PARTY

Paul had breakfast at the hotel, and Rivian called while he was eating. She wanted to invite him to a little get-together later that afternoon. He had a full day ahead of him.

He gathered his art supplies and camera and took the Metro to the Eiffel Tower. The tower is enormous. Standing at a distance and seeing it on the horizon doesn't do it justice. Standing next to or under it makes you realize its size. You feel downright puny.

From there, he walked to the Musée Rodin. The grounds weren't open until two o'clock, and it is noon, so he found a small park with a wonderful view. The Eiffel Tower is in the distance, and the park has a white figurative sculpture in the middle of it. He removed his art supplies from his bag and painted for two hours.

Just after two o'clock, Paul returns to the grounds of the Musée Rodin. Inside the gates, there is a whole city block of grass and trees. There is a small but beautiful stone manor in the middle that houses Rodin's smaller works with descriptions of his process and history.

Rodin's large bronze sculptures cover the grounds—perfect for the presentation of his work.

Paul took the Metro to meet Rivian. She informed him that there is a party at the place where she lived.

This place is an immaculate building and owned by a prince. Entering the building, he walked up the stairs and into a large room where several groups of people are scattered about. He wanders around, listening in on the conversations. They are all talking in the language to which they are familiar.

There is a large table filled with fruits, vegetables, and cheese, arranged artistically by someone with an eye for interior decoration.

As was pointed out to him later in the evening, the people they invited are artists: visual artists, dancers, performing artists, musicians, and writers.

"Excuse me," said a voice, as a woman laid a friendly hand on his shoulder. "There is a group over there." She pointed to a group of nine people. "They are speaking English."

"Thank you," Paul said, and he walked over—sidling his way in a covert manner, trying to pick up bits of their conversation.

A woman is talking passionately about South Africa. She lives there—or did once. The people listening are enrapt in her words. They are all sitting comfortably on the floor next to a window. Paul sat just at the edge of their group.

At the first lull in the conversation, Paul chimed in as if he is knowledgeable.

"So, if I am correct, I have heard that the area has three factions: the Boers who are Dutch, the Zulus and associated native tribes, and the English. There is no possibility of their working together, and tensions are always high, correct?"

The group—all women—looked at Paul. The speaker confirmed his remarks.

"Yes, that is correct." And she changed her dialog to describe in more detail what he had contributed.

Paul is relieved and proud of himself to contribute and take his place in the group. His tactic from that point on is to say as little as possible and listen. He tries to avoid any untamed ego from baring itself, resulting in his coming across as a "know it all" asshole. He didn't know much more than what he had said, and he is genuinely interested in her dialog.

It is nice to sit with intelligent people talking about interesting things in a light and casual interchange. After a while, some of the group got up and mingled with others, or other guests joined them. Paul also needed to stand up and stretch his legs.

He walked over to the balcony doors that are wide open, revealing the Musee d'Orsay's courtyard with the Seine flowing in the background.

Even though he could have stood there enjoying the view, his eyes kept wandering to the ornate arrangement of cheeses, salads, and fruits. Paul is starving and has a great desire to walk over, pick up one of the conveniently placed knives, and politely slice off a piece of cheese. So he did just that.

He felt that familiar soft, tender touch on his shoulder from the same woman who had pointed his way to the English-speaking group.

"I'm sorry, but the cheese table is for after the meal."

"Oh, shoot," Paul responded. "I feel awful."

"It's no problem. Everyone now knows you're from the States where the appetizers and salads come first. They understand."

The problem is that he still had to look at the cheese with the slice cut out of the middle for the next hour. That's when they serve dinner.

The variety of people at the party is truly amazing. He didn't see Rivian.

Paul met a couple from the American Embassy, two Germans—one who had just returned from South Africa—a woman from Sweden, and an English actress.

The list continued. There is a Frenchman who speaks good English and talks a lot about painting. Carolyn Belko is a dancer from America and is living in Paris.

Paul wonders why they invited him. Of course, it is through Rivian. She later explained that she moved out of her room at this house to spend time in Southern California. That is when Betty introduced us. Her room is opening up again at the end of the month. She definitely had connections.

Carolyn, the American dancer, expressed an interest in doing something with him before she leaves Paris. Paul is leaving early on Tuesday, and Monday is the only available day. Unfortunately, Sarah, the English actress, had already called and invited him to accompany her to the Picasso Museum on Monday.

On Sunday morning, Paul focused on the painting he is working on. He painted until four in the afternoon then went out to dinner. When he returned to the hotel, he talked to Anellina on the phone. Doug called him right after, and it made him miss home. Paul's friends sounded like they missed him.

It is Monday morning. Paul rose early and went down to the lower level of the Seine. He walked along the river until the Notre Dame Cathedral is visible. Finding a comfortable spot, Paul painted the building with the river in the foreground. He then ascended the stairs of the cathedral and took photos from the top.

Returning to his room, he received a phone call from Sarah. She couldn't meet him for the Picasso tour but wanted him to go with her to meet friends for dinner at a Jewish restaurant. Again, typical of most restaurants during his travels, the food was fantastic. They decided to go to a movie—*House of Games,* an American film with French subtitles. They went out for a beer afterward then said their goodbyes.

Paul had a restless night trying to sleep—thinking of his next day's train ride.

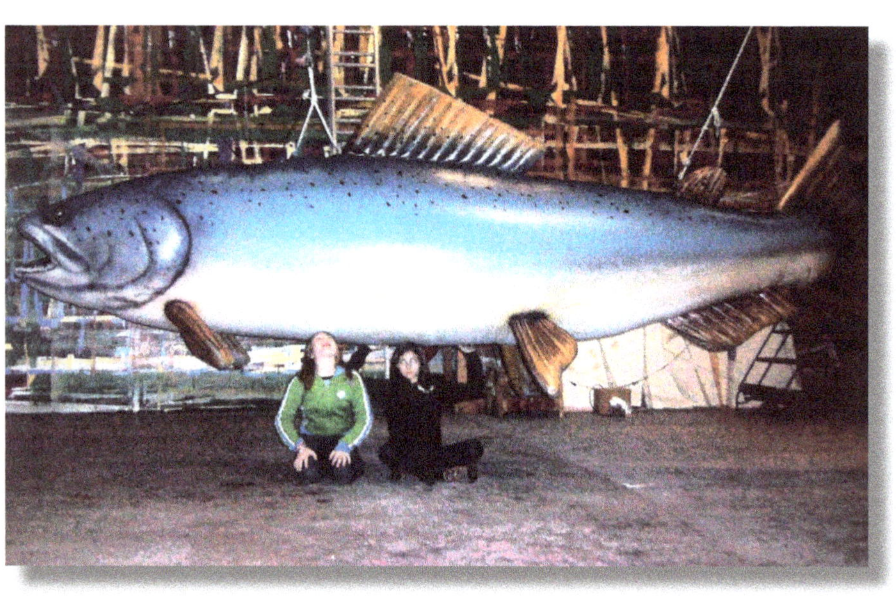

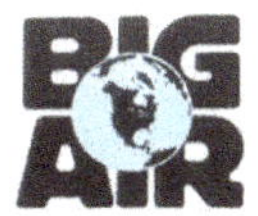

P.O. BOX 475
INDIANOLA
WASHINGTON
98342-0475
tel 360-779-9157
fax 360-779-6299

BILLBOARDS

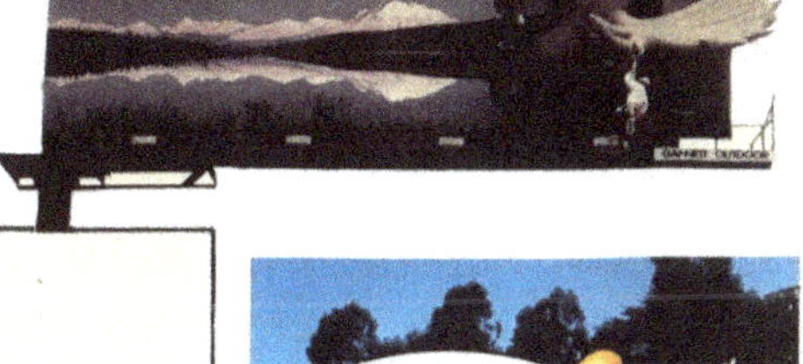

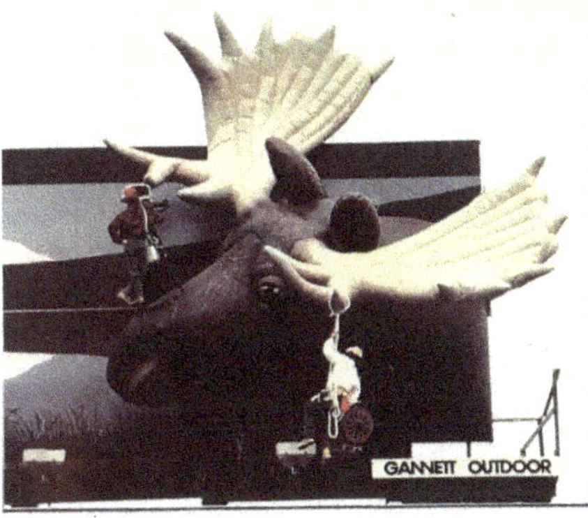

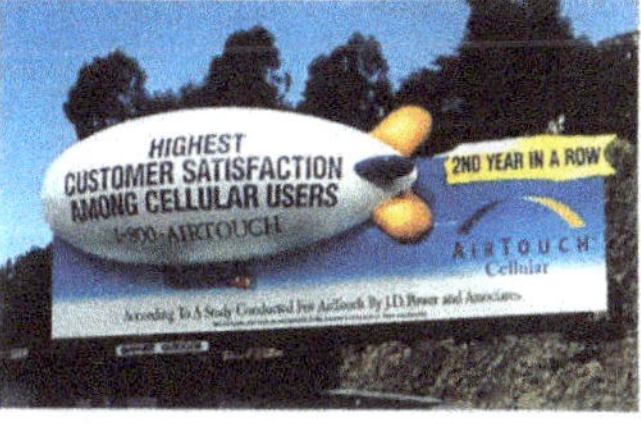

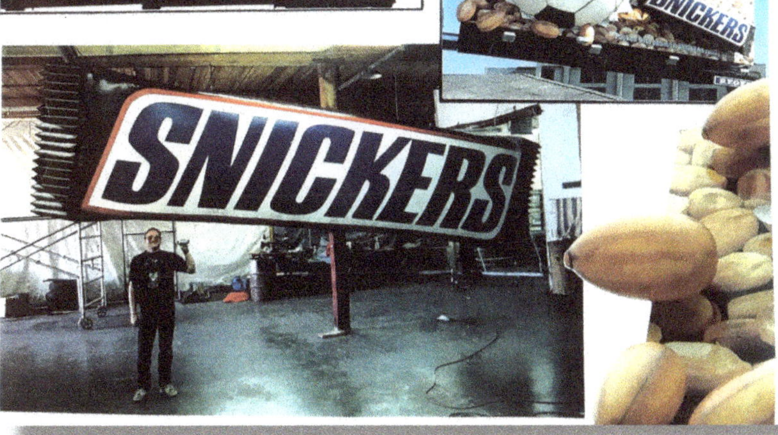

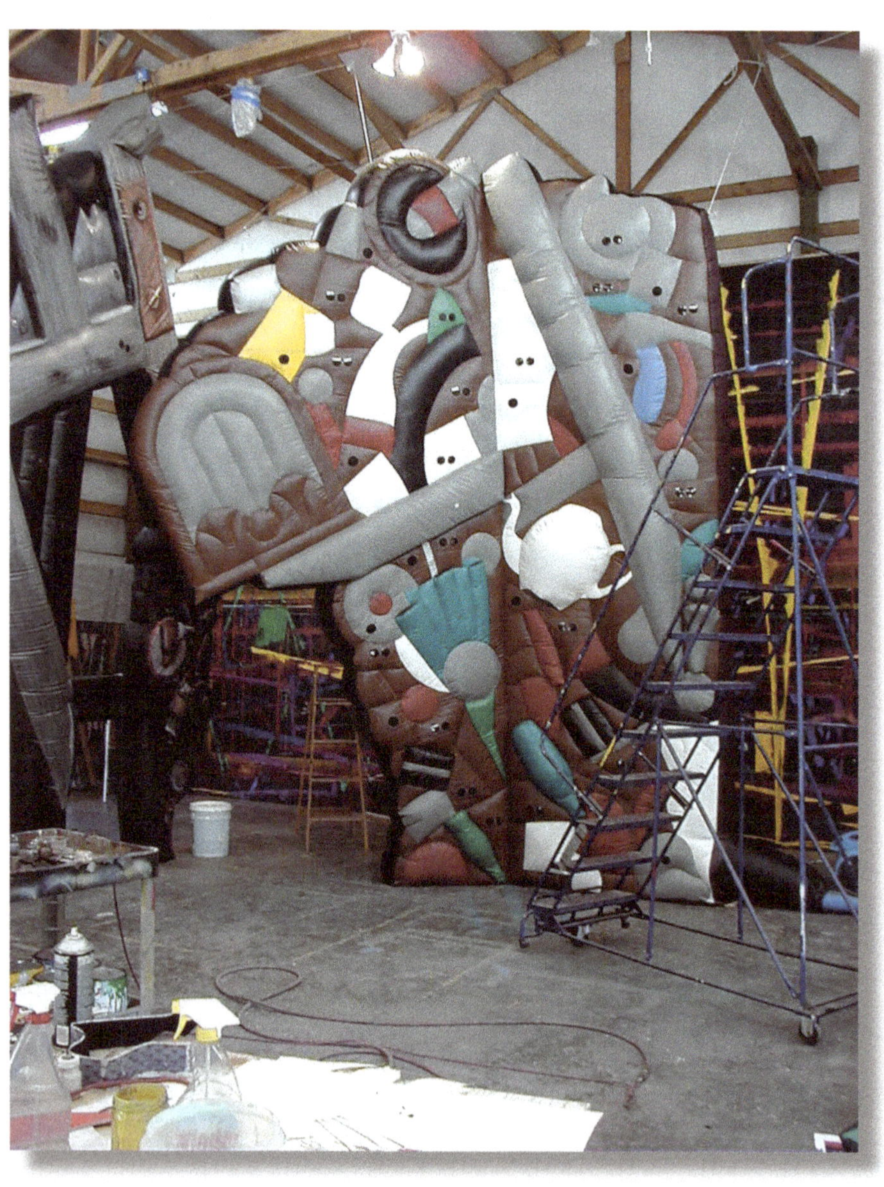

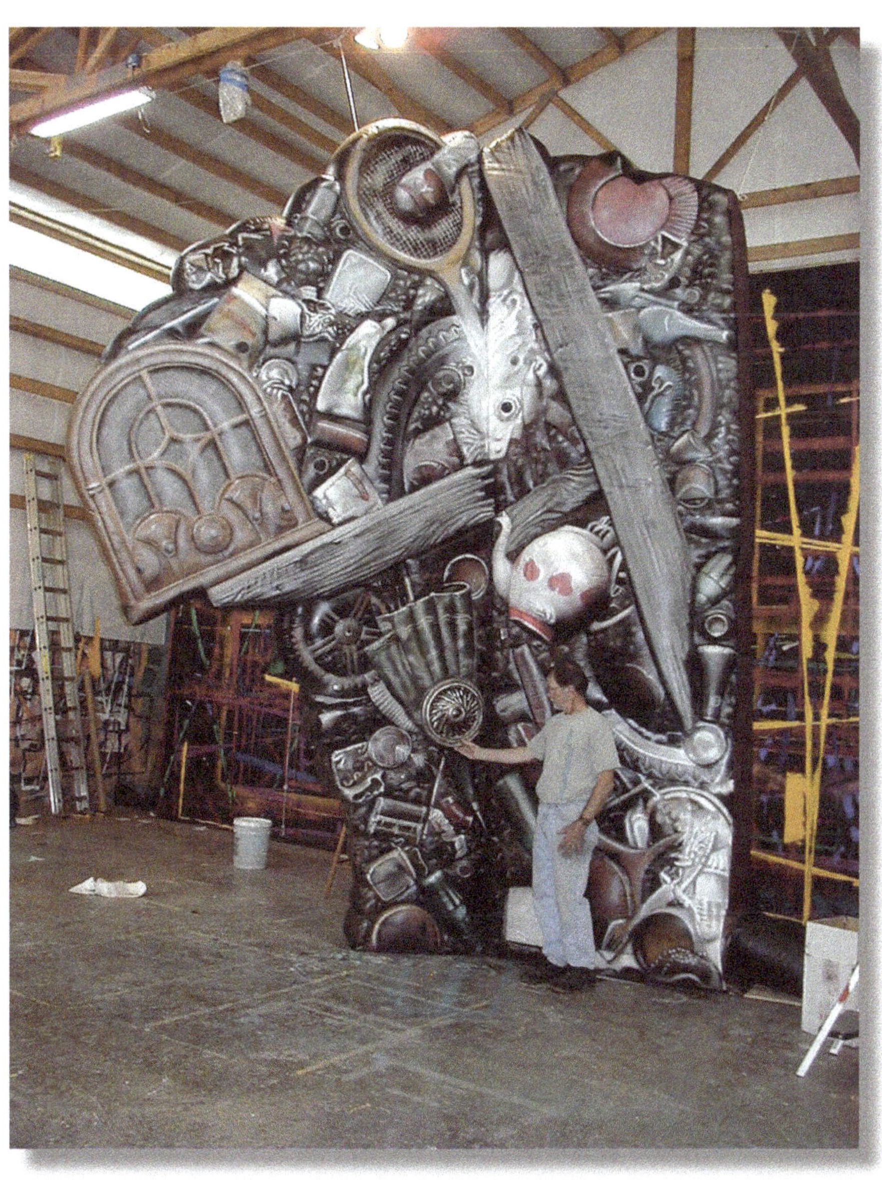

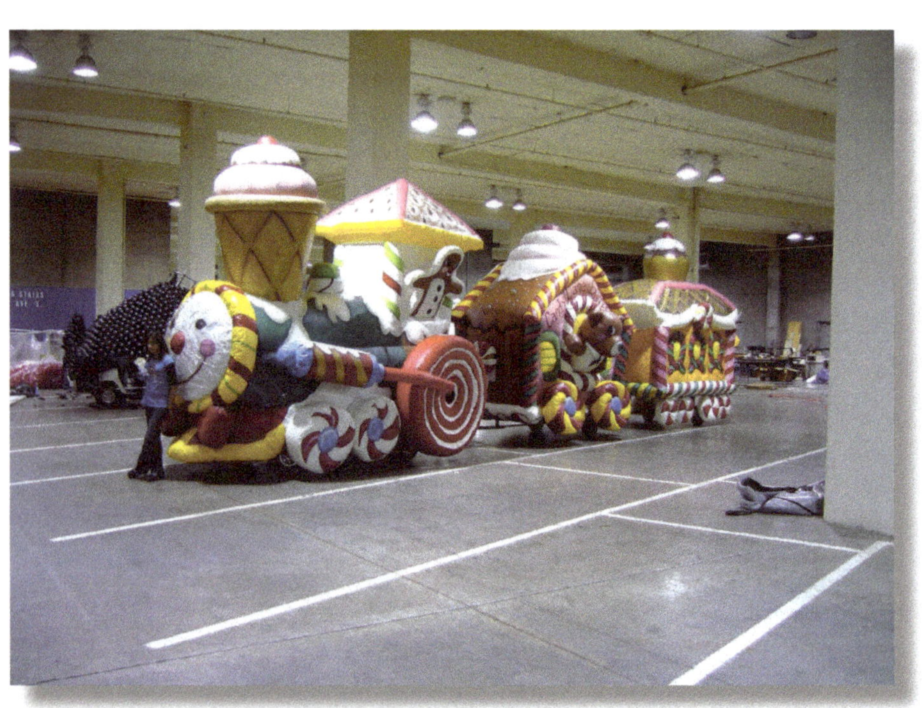

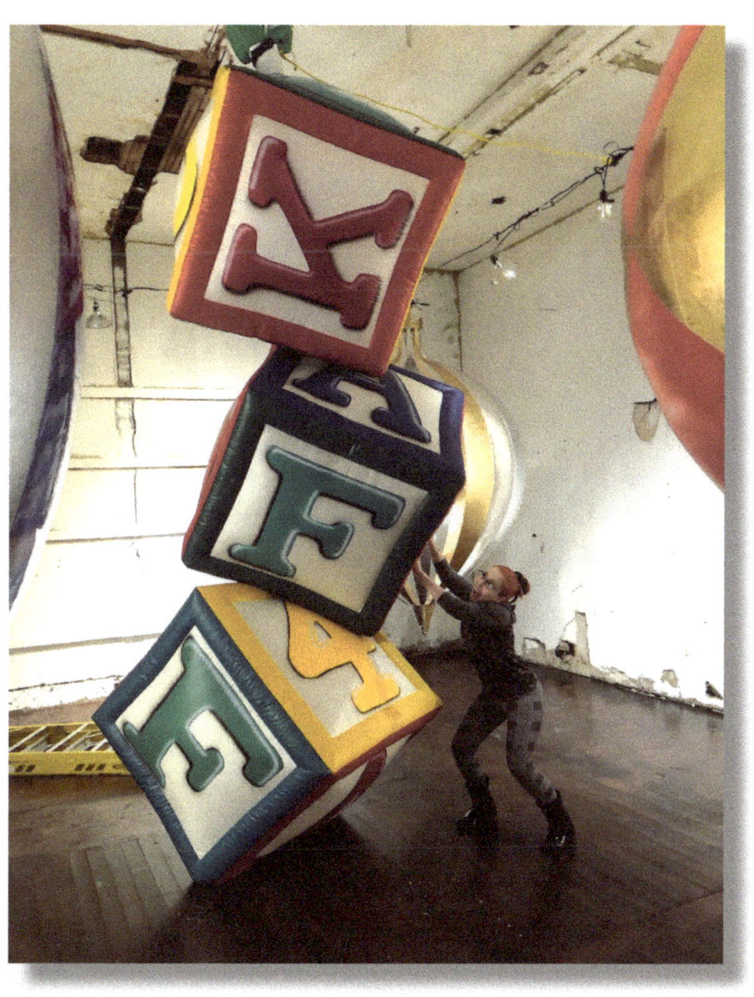

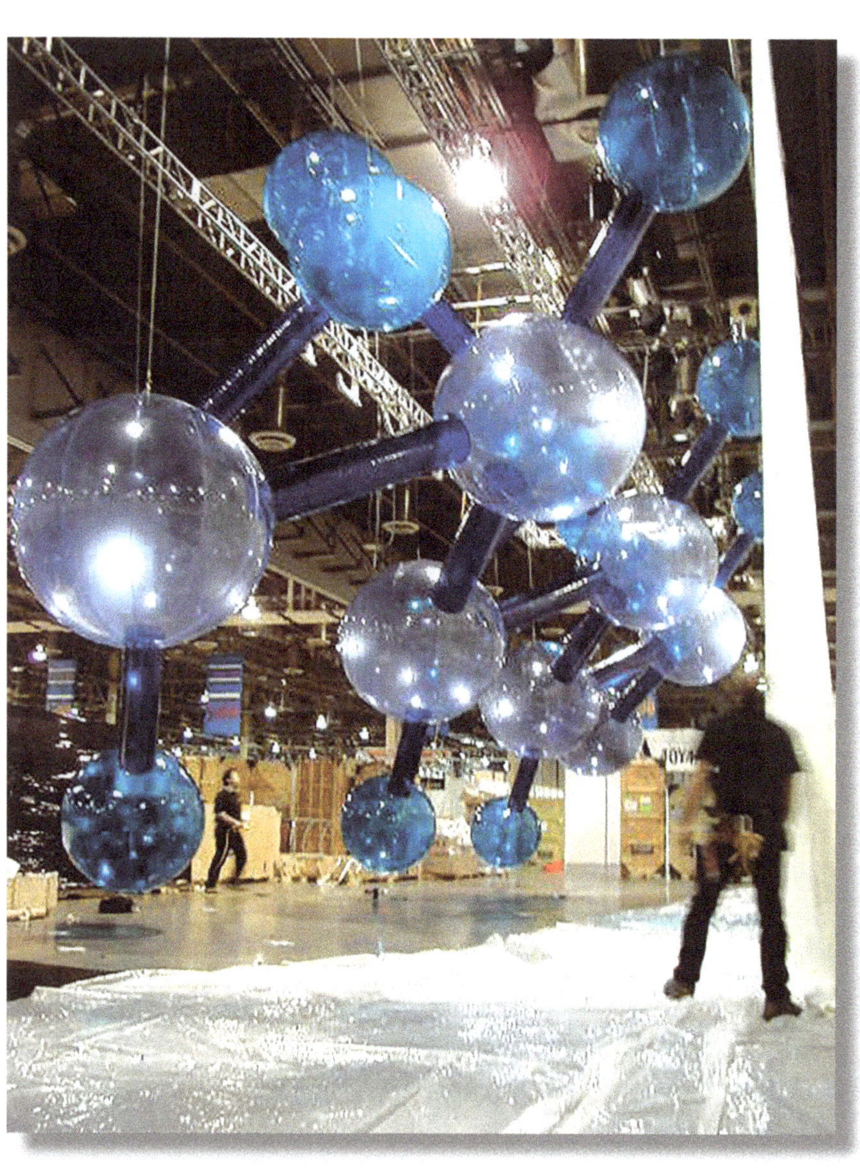

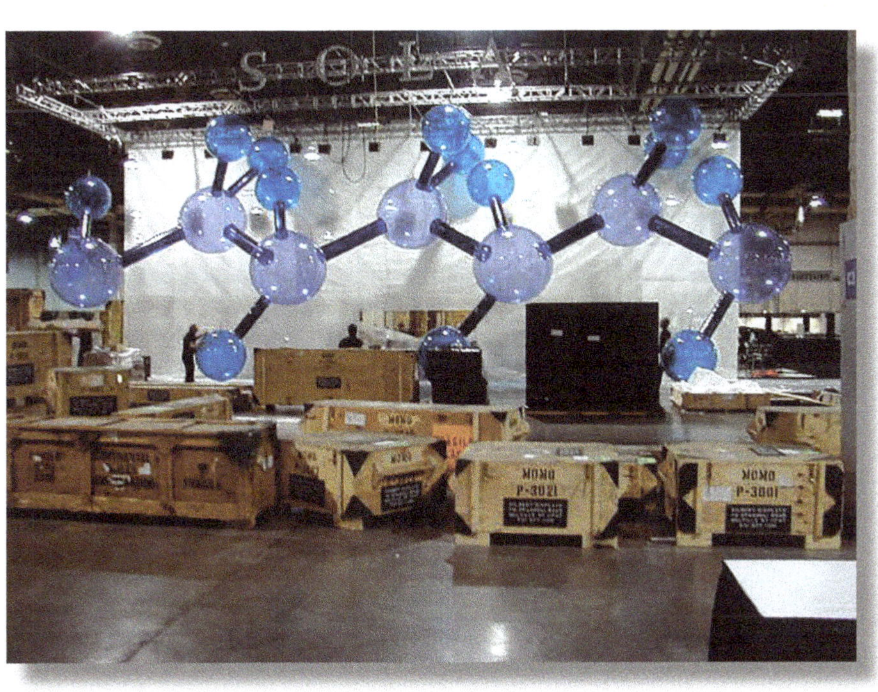
MOMO
P-3021
MOMO
P-3001

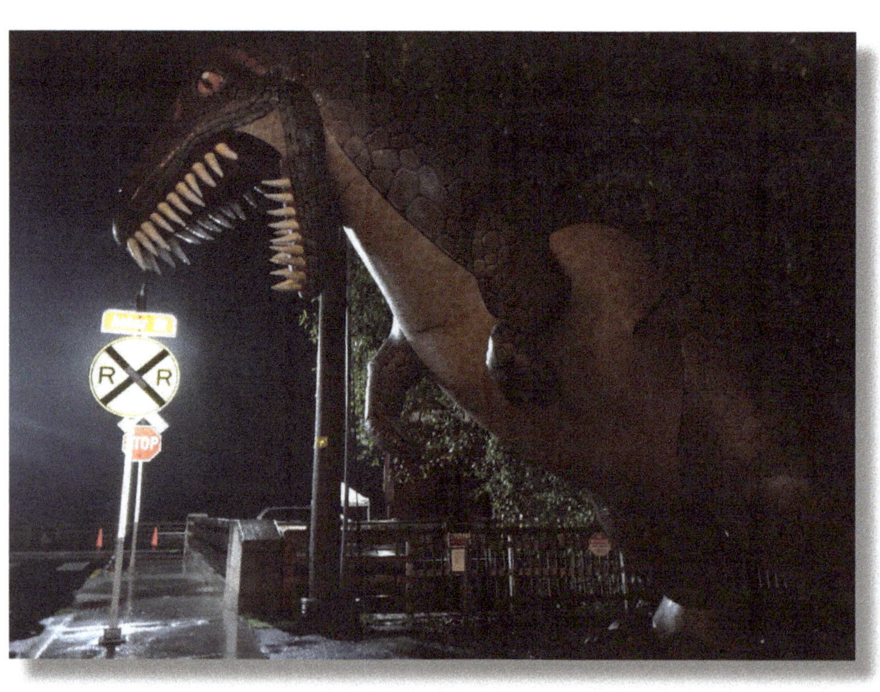

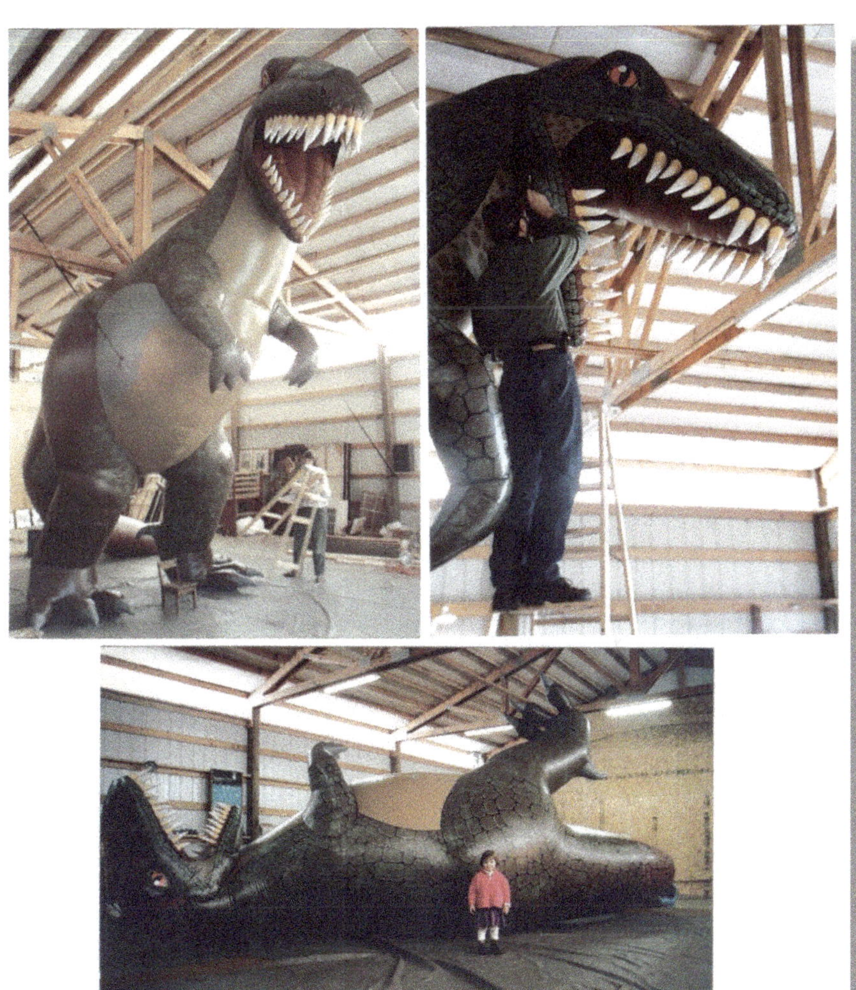

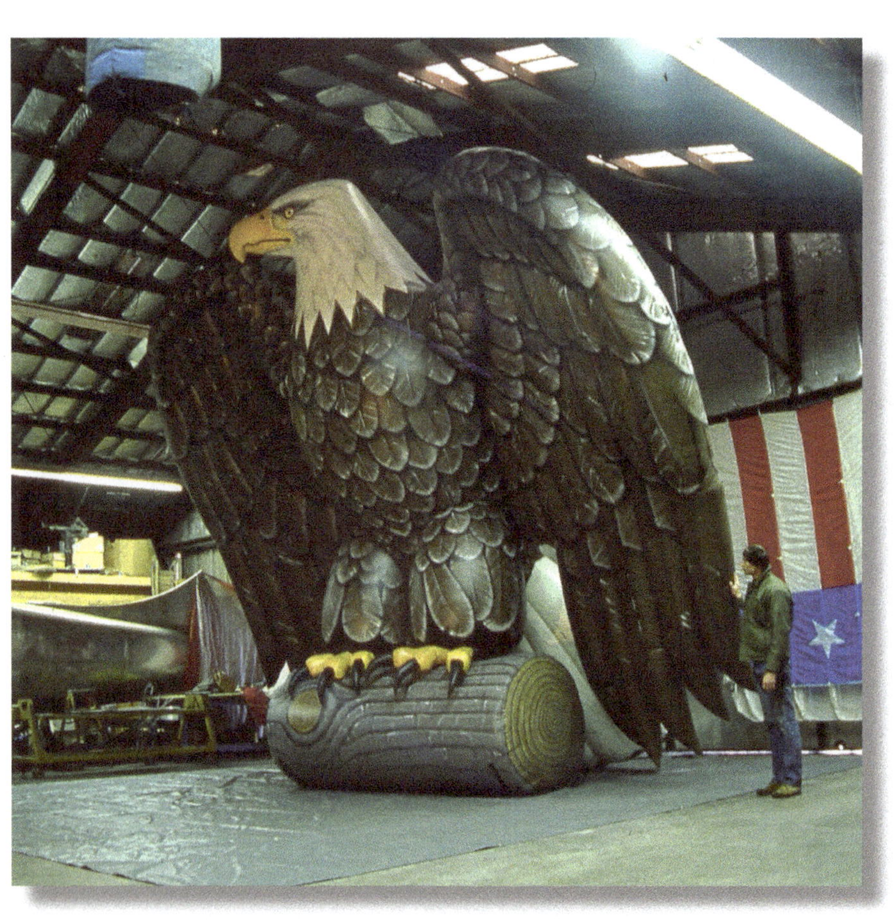

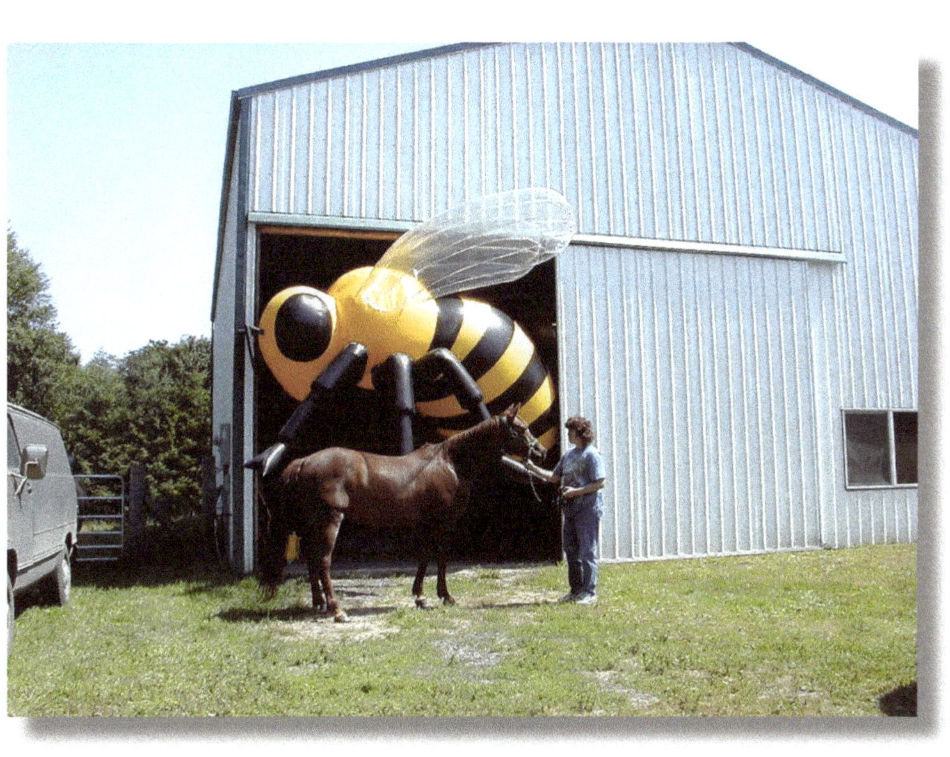

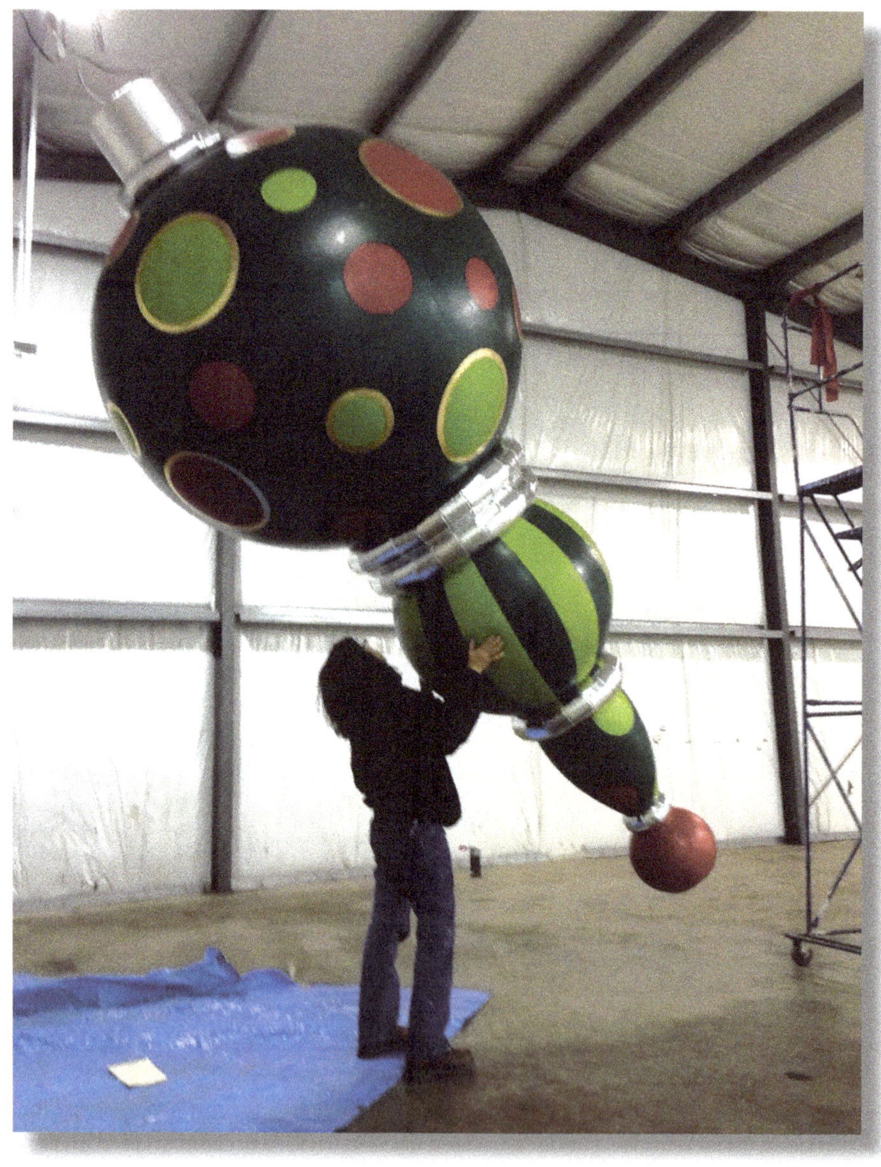

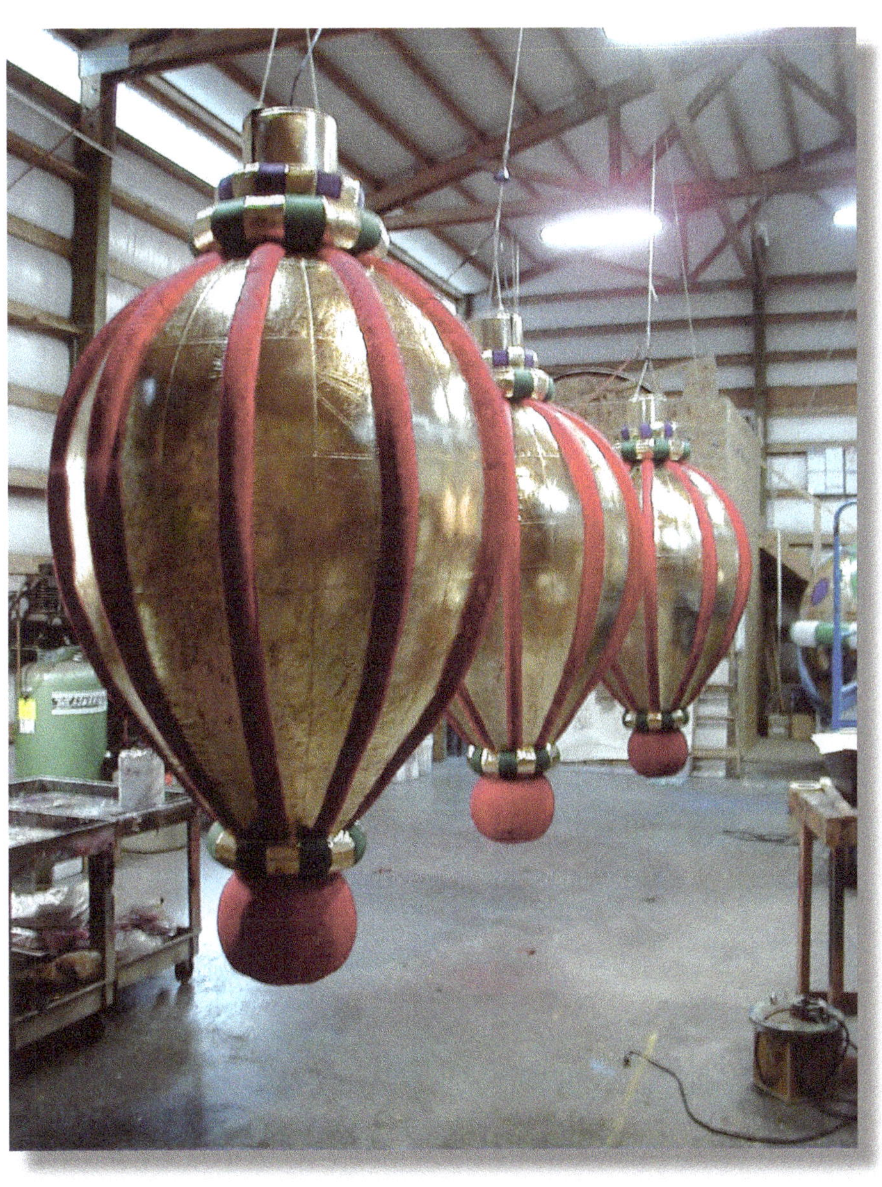

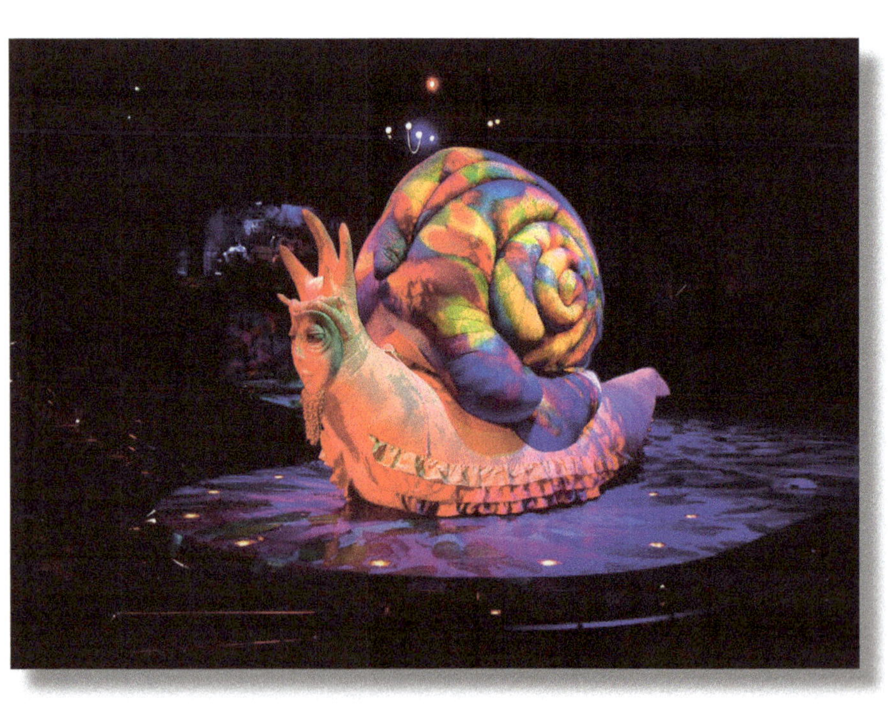

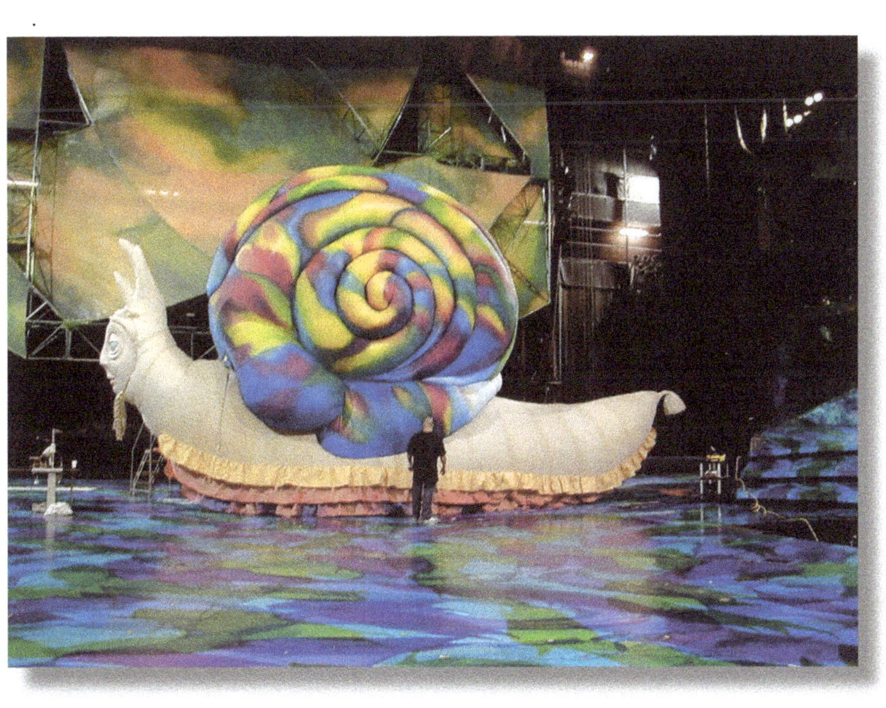

28

SWITZERLAND

THE LONG TRAIN RIDE

The rail system in Europe is pretty amazing compared to what we have in the States. Paul bought a Eurail pass and is quickly getting used to the ins and outs of the process. It requires that he travel first class since he is over twenty-one. Travelers under that age travel second class.

Up to this point, Paul has only traveled in northern Europe, and the trains are modern, clean, and on time. The Eurail pass is for three months and costs 300 dollars.

Paul isn't quite sure where he is going, only that he is heading south from Paris. This route will take him through Angouleme where Jean-Paul lives. Jean-Paul is still in Paris as far as he knows, so he might not be there yet. It has been a week since they met.

It's a short walk to the train station. Bordeaux is his first destination, but he will go through Angouleme to get there. When he arrived at Angouleme, Paul got off the train and called Jean-Paul's residence to see if he had returned. He hadn't, so he hopped back on the train. He would pass through Angoulême at least once more.

When he arrived at Bordeaux, Paul had a choice to make—east to Italy or south to Spain.

Paul has a good friend in Spain. Linda worked as a waitress at Yakitori II, his favorite sushi bar in San Diego, and she majored in Spanish. As a senior, Linda needs to spend a year living in Spain. She also had to attend classes at the local university in Granada.

Linda and Paul talked about the best time to visit before he left on his trip. It didn't matter much to Linda, but they did settle on a date, and he would be arriving about a month early if he visited there now.

So, east to Italy, it was.

Paul had a five-hour layover in Bordeaux, so he strolled through the city looking for a good restaurant. The skyline of the town encompassed a large old church with a spire reaching to the sky to a sharp point. Paul headed straight toward the church, but the streets wouldn't cooperate. The character of the place is intriguing, even though it seems gray and drab. The roads are thin and wound around in what appeared to be directionless curves. The stone walls seem to close in around you. There are no signs or lights. It is mid-day, so he isn't sure how lit up it would be at night. He hasn't seen a soul.

He finally found what his psychic self thought was a good restaurant.

The food he could only describe as strange, but the red wine is excellent. He didn't understand what he ordered, just a stab in the dark. He still didn't know what he ordered after eating it.

As Paul is finishing his meal, a young lady came in, asking for an English menu. The staff looked a bit dumbfounded, probably because they couldn't understand her. She sat at the table next to Paul, and they fell into an instant conversation.

He moved to her table, and they talked until he had to catch the train. She is from New Orleans, had worked in London for six months, and is doing a quick tour of Europe with a friend before going home.

The first-class sleeping car Paul had reserved is a welcome sight. He has it all to himself.

He awoke in Lyon. It is early, and he had four eggs and ham breakfast at the train station. Then it's back on board to Geneva.

The country is changing from the beautiful French countryside to foothills and mountains. The Alps are gorgeous with turquoise lakes at their base.

From Geneva, the train traveled to Lausanne, then on to Bern, and from Bern to Interlaken.

Interlaken is a place he picked on the map to take a break from the train and find a hotel. It turns out that it's pretty touristy. The weather is rainy, and the trains going to the high Alps aren't running. He decided to leave the next day. His original plan to stay awhile is cut short.

Paul found a fantastic Swiss restaurant with local food and slept in a comfortable bed back at the hotel without the motion of the train beneath him.

He called Anellina. Checking in—it was nice to hear a voice from home.

In the morning, Paul did a painting of the view out his window. It is a beautiful view except it seems manicured, as if gardeners worked full time to maintain its pristine condition.

The train he originally wanted to catch was going to Florence, but avalanches had closed the route between Interlaken and Milan. Instead, he took the train to Lucerne, a gorgeous town, and headed south through beautiful snow-covered mountains.

KB, a salesman at BTL, told him to stay at Lugano. He said it's the best time he ever had. When Paul arrived, it didn't look like much, so he decided not to stop. As the train continued, the town's view revealed a steep drop with tiers of houses and buildings dropping down to a beautiful lake at its foot.

Paul realized he made a mistake by not stopping. Especially when his arrival in Florence dropped him in the middle of a madhouse of Italians and tourists. It's Easter week.

With the Lugano option behind him, he continued to Milan and then transferred to Florence, arriving at eleven that night.

The Hotel Fedora is the place he plans to stay, but they are full. All the other hotels and inns he tried are full also, but he finally found one dingy *pensione* for that night.

Paul didn't have a chance to exchange his money for Italian lira. Trying to communicate with the older man behind the desk of his pensione is difficult. They finally agreed to have Paul give him his passport and pay him the next day. He seems like a charming man. He took his time trying to communicate.

Early the next morning, Paul went to a bank to change his Swiss francs to Italian lira. He wandered the streets looking for a place to stay, but they are all filled with groups. He found one that would take a credit card, but it is hectic with people running all over the place. Paul isn't ready for the craziness. He left and found a higher-class hotel with a large, quiet room and a big bed. It is also clean. A bit more expensive, but at the moment, he has no choice. He would have to flounder in decadence.

Paul retrieved his bags and passport from the previous night's *pensione* and paid the bill.

The number of people packing the city confused Paul. That's when he realized it is Easter week—a big thing in Florence. This whole week will be crazy. If he had figured that out sooner—or realized it is such a big deal—he would have stayed in Lugano for the week.

Paul took a couple of hours to relax in his room at the Hotel Arianna and then started wandering around Florence. He had pizza and beer for lunch then bought a map and some postcards. The streets are typically "old European," being narrow and made of stone.

Paul brought his camera, but that made it too easy to view the scenery with it attached to his eye. Sometimes, he purposely doesn't take his camera with him so he can just look and let his brain flow and absorb the images. Tourists are everywhere, crowding the shops and alleyways; galleries and museums too, probably.

When Paul returns to his room, he addresses postcards and marks all the museums on the map for the next day's schedule.

He spent the rest of the evening finishing the Swiss "out the window" painting.

That night, Paul has a dream. When he dreams, he usually remembers them. But this one is especially ultra-vivid and realistic.

The dream

He was in San Diego. The last he remembered he was in Florence.

He doesn't know what happened in between or how he ended up in San Diego. He thought this should be a dream, but it seemed too real—like he had completely lost his memory of what happened on the rest of his Europe tour.

He asked people if they could fill him in on what had happened to the rest of his trip, but no one responded.

He was several people lying in a bed.

There was a huge wheel with a large dowel sticking out of the bed. He began to climb the dowel, and that makes the wheel turn. He's going nowhere, but not trying very hard to get anywhere.

Then he found himself sitting at a sushi bar. Two Japanese chefs are talking to each other. One glanced in his direction and said, "He's too nice."

When Paul woke, he has no idea where he is. It shocks him to see the strange room surrounding him as if this were the dream. It took about a minute to realize that he is in his hotel room in Florence. A minute can be a long time.

29

FLORENCE

The epitome of the craziness of people in Florence during Easter is during his visit the next day at the Uffizi Gallery. Even though Paul went early, the lines are long. They are so long; they are worse than a security check on a busy day at the airport.

You know—roped off in a zigzag, covering the whole courtyard in front of the entrance.

Paul waited an hour as Italians continually crowded in front of the tourists. The line isn't moving at all. He is still close to the back of the line. There is an older American couple in front of him.

The good thing is that there are two muscle-bound Italian guards in tight tee shirts at the museum's entrance. They are also smart and aware of what is happening. When a person who crowded in line made it to the entrance, they muscled him to the side to let others pass. He eventually gave up and left.

There is a shrill whistle, and Paul looked around until he saw that one of the entrance guards is pointing at him.

"How many?" he yelled.

"Who, me?" Paul yelled back.

"Yes. How many?"

Paul held up three fingers to include the couple ahead of him. The bouncer waved them up to the door.

"Enjoy," he said, as he opened the door for them.

When Paul walked inside, he is delighted to find that each gallery inside the Uffizi has only three or four people viewing the artwork. When people left, the guard allowed the same number to enter. Paul could relax and enjoy at his own pace without fighting the crowds.

The work at the Uffizi mostly ranges from the thirteenth century to the seventeenth century.

The earlier paintings are with tempera on wood panels. You can see the use of oil paint on canvas growing in the next two centuries.

A well-known painting for those who have any interest in art history is *The Birth of Venus*, painted in the 1480s by Sandro Botticelli with tempera on canvas. Venus is depicted nude and standing on a shell.

There is a beautiful collection of works painted by Leonardo da Vinci in the late fifteenth and early sixteenth century. DaVinci's work included his *Annunciation* that has received some attention because of the type of paint he used on the kneeling angel. The figure of the angel disappears when x-rayed.

Also displayed at the Uffizi is The Adoration of the Magi. This painting was left unfinished but is incredible in its sketched-out form in sepia colors.

Titian's work of a controversial nude, *Venus of Urbino*, has been shown in many art history books. It is beautiful in real life.

But most of all, Paul loved the work of Rembrandt van Rijn. Two of his portraits—*Portrait of the Artist as a Young Man* and *Portrait of an Old Man*—are his favorites.

Leaving the museum, Paul walked around the area and found himself behind the Pitti Palace. He is in the middle of a lush garden—well-tended and immaculate.

From there, he climbed to Forte Belvedere. When he reached the top, he is looking at a fabulous view of the city. This place is ideal for his next painting. It is quiet and shaded. He plans to do that the next day, along with taking photos.

Searching for a place with as few people as possible, Paul walked through a back street and found a small restaurant and had another fantastic meal.

When he returned to his room, he requested another two nights—no problem.

He called Anellina. The hotel did not have a phone, so Paul walked to the train station and called from there. They talked for a long time.

After breakfast the next morning, he made the walk to Forte Belvedere and began painting. This work depicted Florence's city with the Cathedral rising above the rooftops in the center of town.

Paul then began investigating the neighborhood taking photos.

Returning to the hotel, Paul read up on Rome and took a long nap. It is Sunday, and the museums are all closed. He painted until late, refining the Cathedral painting.

He also found time to do his laundry, hoping it would dry by morning.

ROME

Paul paid his hotel bill and walked directly to the train station. It took a little over two hours to get to Rome. The train is packed.

He imagined Rome to be filled with beautiful art and architecture and is one of his long-awaited cities to visit.

Rome is old and filled with Roman art and architecture. It will take weeks to enjoy its history and accomplishments if that is his focus. Frankly, he tired of Italians and Italy. A little too harsh, Paul supposed. He hasn't seen southern Italy, and he hasn't yet seen Rome for that matter—so why jump to conclusions? Paul will stay and learn. But instead of lingering to feel the character of the place, he plans to see what he came to see and do a painting or two. He plans to do it all in two days.

Paul felt the character and aura of Rome. He thought so, anyway. It wasn't that he didn't like the place. It would consume him to appreciate what Rome had to offer.

To begin this process, he grabbed the first hotel he saw, close to the train station.

He immediately took his watercolors and camera to the Colosseum and the Roman Forum and started to paint.

Wow! What an empire this must have been. Imagine what it would be like to live in ancient Rome as a citizen, soldier, or artist. How about a gladiator, an actor, or a politician? Paul imagined wearing a toga and seeing beautiful women in tunics with belts around their waists, or just loose folds of fabric.

He admired Rome's innovative water system. What was it like to be the conquerors of the known world? How about soaking in the baths in Britain like the ones he saw a month ago, or what was it like to march into ancient Egypt?

Did the ordinary citizen go to work like they do today? Go to bars and dine on foods imported from ancient lands? What was it like going to the theater or watching Christians as they are thrown to the lions and ripped apart in front of roaring crowds?

All of this history, and then watched—disheartened—as an Italian took a pee on a beautiful marble column.

Paul stopped at a small restaurant and had lasagna and a salad. The rest of the evening, he worked on the painting he started while at the Colosseum.

All of these revelations, and he was still calling Anellina regularly. Oh yeah, she is Italian.

When Paul crawls out of bed the next morning, he feels like he has a cold. He packed his bag, readying himself for a full day's jaunt through the city.

Visiting the bank is the first thing he needs to do. He cashed some travelers' checks and returned to the Colosseum. Instead of thinking about Rome's glories, he was saddened—almost disgusted— by the degradation of this society. What internal politics or strife lead to the rotting away—the falling apart—of such an empire?

There is plenty of literature on these thoughts and concerns. Paul read about them as many students have, but did they feel it? Could they, the people of today's world, feel and understand? Did they learn the lessons that came from Rome's downfall and the demise of this once-great society?

The streets are confusing and going every which way; they seem like utter chaos. He is looking for the Pantheon and finally found it after finding Piazza Navona, a landmark he circled on the map to know when he had arrived.

The Pantheon was quite the sight. At first glance, it seemed small and unimpressive. When he moved closer and entered, it is pretty amazing. The massive dome spans 142 feet and is made of concrete. It was built in 27 to 25 BC and later burned down. They rebuilt it in 125 AD. Paul is transfixed; the whole interior is beautiful.

Next stop: the Vatican. On his way there, he decided he needed a friend for the rest of the trip, so he walked into a store and bought a Sony Walkman. He also bought two tapes: Cat Sevens and Jarre.

The Vatican is inundated with decorations and art: frescos, sculptures, and fantastic murals.

Paul walked around, enjoying the ornate place. He went downstairs and saw the tombs.

The Sistine Chapel is a must-see. The art is the best he has seen in Vatican City, with the ceiling and wall fresco of *The Last Judgment* by Michelangelo. There are also works by Botticelli and tapestries by Raphael. The ceiling is being restored, so it has scaffolding covering a large section. You can see the difference between the older dark areas of the painting and the restored section.

The sculpture of the Pietà is also on view, but you can't get close because of the day it was attacked with a hammer. Paul is close enough to see how well the restoration is going. The statue is so life-like it seems to breathe.

Paul moved on to the Vatican Museum. The modern art is not impressive, but the busts and statues are very impressive—dating from before Christ.

Not being Catholic, Paul didn't understand the rituals or the riches, but the religion has lasted through the centuries and is still strong and powerful in countries throughout the world.

Born and raised in the LDS church, he could not understand the guilt thing or the confession.

If Paul understands this correctly, Catholics are born guilty. You confess and ask for forgiveness for the rest of your life.

The Mormons are born innocent. You become ultimately responsible for your actions at the age of eight when you are baptized.

When Paul left, he had pizza and a beer across the street and followed the Tiber River to an island. He crossed the river and found that he is completely lost. Paul didn't care. He walked for hours before finally asking someone for directions to the train station. Once there, he found his bearings; his hotel is within a block.

By this time, it is six-thirty in the evening. Paul found a bookstore with books in English and bought *Poland* by Michener. He found a place where he could relax and have a beer, and then retire to his hotel room.

Paul filled out postcards, kicked back, and prepared for his trip. Tomorrow, he is going to Greece.

30

ATHENS

THE LONG TRAIN AND FERRY RIDE

The train left at 9:05 a.m. for Bari, Italy.

Paul decides to stop depending on the train schedule for departures and arrivals.

The trains in Italy are not like those in northern Europe. They can be late—sometimes hours late. The trains are older and not as comfortable as the trains he has experienced to this point. There is no first-class, and the passengers are crammed together in a rickety coach.

The train ride seems to take forever. The good part is the view of the southern Italian countryside. The landscape is lush with olives, grapes, and other crops.

The Sony Walkman and Paul became fast friends—as he thought they would.

When they finally arrive at Bari after a half day's travel, there is a two-hour layover.

Paul is thirsty and walks to a little shop that has food items.

There is no one in the shop—he thought—until a high-pitched voice said something Italian.

A young boy's head popped above the counter and repeated what he said before.

Paul asked in English, "What do you have to drink?"

The boy couldn't understand him.

Paul looks on the counter and sees some juice cans—obviously warm. He picked one up and said, "How much?" He has no idea what the exchange rate is.

He took out his Italian lire and showed them to the boy who pointed at a couple of coins. Paul picked them up and reached out to pay.

Suddenly, the door to the backroom swung open, and an older lady charged in, ranting in Italian.

Paul showed her the can of juice and the lire.

The woman glares at him with angry eyes, grabs the lire Paul is holding out, then reaches down and grabs a few more. She gripped the boy roughly by the upper arm and marched him back through the door with an angry glance back at Paul as she is exiting.

"Wow! What was that about?" Paul left the store, opened his small can of warm juice, and downs it in a couple of gulps.

That's three times now that someone has shown Paul such livid anger: the tram driver in Amsterdam, the waiter in Paris, and the elderly lady in her shop in Bari.

It seems they are responding to Paul being from America. He wonders if this is latent anger from World War II. Out of all the people he had talked to or met, only three responded that way. Big deal? It shouldn't, but something hurt inside him with each encounter; he had done nothing to deserve it.

Paul caught an even older train to Brindisi.

When the train arrives, he walks a little less than a mile to the port, acquired his boarding pass, and reserved a seat on the ferry to Greece. By the end of the boat ride, he regretted not booking a cabin. The seats are comfortable—like being in a movie theater—but after a night of windy, rough seas, it becomes increasingly uncomfortable, to the point of not being able to sleep.

The good part is the people he meets on either side of him. One is a Mormon missionary from Provo, Utah. He had just served his mission in Italy, so he spoke the language quite well. He is also a painter. He majored in art at Brigham Young University.

To the right of Paul is a young student named Michelle. She is on spring break from a school in Germany. After a night of traveling through the Strait of Otranto, they arrive at the island of Corfu in Greece. It is a beautiful early morning. The missionary disembarked at this point.

As they follow the west coast of Greece, Paul couldn't help being awed by the beauty of the islands and the snow-capped mountains. There is a bitter wind, but he sits on the deck and enjoys a break from the stuffy, packed interior.

They traveled all day and arrived at Patras at seven-thirty that evening.

Paul checked the train station schedule and found that the next train leaves at two the next morning.

Patras is crazy with people, but Michelle and Paul manage to find a quiet authentic Greek restaurant. They had an amazing and inexpensive fish dinner—two beers each. Communicating is difficult with the waitress until Michelle found out that she spoke German. Michelle carried on from there. They are both fluent in German, enough to joke and carry on about their travels and tell stories. Paul is left out but is caught up with the ease and happiness of the moment. Michelle translated as they talk.

They returned to the train station and watched an old American Western movie with Greek subtitles. It is still too early for their departure, so they played rummy until it was time to leave. She kicked his butt.

ATHENS

Paul arrives in Athens at 7:30 a.m., April 1, 1988.

Being a little bit on the hungry side, Michelle and Paul found a small café for coffee and donuts. Michelle accompanies him until he finds his hotel, close to the Greek ruins—the Attalos Hotel, room 310.

Paul stays with her until she gets a taxi. She is lucky to have a friend and her friend's family where she can stay. She will be able to experience the Greek side of life.

Paul went to his room, took a hot bath, and slept until two in the afternoon —the first real sleep he has had in three days. Just being horizontal is nice.

After Paul recovers from his stupor, he explored the surrounding area. Athens impressed him. He found a store where he can buy some art supplies. The streets have open markets with fruit, meats, vegetables, clothes, cheese, etc. and many of the vendors use carts to wheel their goods home by the end of the day.

The negative side is that it reminds him of Tijuana, Mexico, meaning it seems unclean with flies buzzing around the stands.

Returning to his hotel, he climbs the stairs to the roof and takes photos of the view—fantastic!

Paul walks back to his room, calls Anellina, looks over the info on places to visit in Athens, and then hits the sack.

Paul went to the lobby the next morning and asked if he could stay more nights, but all of their bookings had arrived. There are no rooms available. They did recommend a hotel that was close by—the Hotel Carolina. When he finds the place, he is not excited about staying there. The room is small and didn't feel clean. The bed is lumpy, but his biggest concern is the other guests. Paul didn't trust them. They seem shady, and they look at him in weird ways. It made his skin crawl.

Paul hadn't checked out of the first hotel yet, so he returned and packed the rest of his stuff. While he is there, Michelle called, and they met a couple of blocks away.

He dropped his pack off at the new digs, then the two of them walked to the Acropolis. The crowds are horrible—almost bad enough to go back to the hotel and return later, but they persevered and finally hiked to the top.

It is worth the visit. The Parthenon is more amazing than he thought. Again, his mind ran wild, imagining how it must have looked and what life must have been like two and a half centuries ago. He found other ancient structures at the Acropolis: the temple of Athena Nike, the Propylaia, and the Erechtheion. There isn't a lot to see other than that. However, what they did see is impressive. Oh, yeah, the view of Athens is spectacular!

They descended from the Acropolis and found a place for lunch. Michelle suggested they take the Metro to Piraeus—a port not far from the center of Athens.

They made the trip and strolled around, gazing at the harbor and the yachts. There are also fishing boats and large ships anchored in the bay. Other than a beautiful port, there doesn't seem to be much to do. They don't need to be entertained. Why not just relax and enjoy the beautiful harbor?

They decided to head back.

When you visit Athens, taking a two-week tour of the islands makes it all worth it. One company is selling an island tour on a large yacht. They can take up to twenty people. The journey is for two weeks, and they stop at each island for the passengers to see the sights, party, and sleep in a comfortable bed.

On their return, Paul kept his eyes open for a better hotel. When they did arrive at his dive, Michelle pulled out a book, *Let's Go Europe*. They go through it, pointing out the exciting and not-so-exciting places to visit.

Michelle returned to her friend's place, but not for long. Within an hour, she called and wanted to go to a late movie. Paul took the Metro to the other side of Athens and met her. After the movie, they had a midnight meal and parted. The Metro isn't running, so he walks back. It took about an hour.

Paul had to admit; he had been standoffish that night. Sitting together at the movie would have been an ideal time to put an arm around Michelle. She would have responded. It would then be hard not to continue; he would have gone with it.

He is beginning to feel troubled about Michelle. She suggested they travel together, and she is interested in having a closer relationship.

Paul is enjoying having her around. What is wrong with him? He should have been taking advantage of this. What man wouldn't want to travel Europe and meet a young woman to travel with, make love with, and support each other?

When Paul thinks of past opportunities to get involved with women, his record isn't good. He had shunned a vast majority of women who opened up to him, even though he liked them and felt comfortable around them.

Paul didn't know what it was. He's a loner and probably always will be.

When he asked Anellina to go with him to London, it's because he had tickets for two, and Karen prompted him. He wasn't sure if they were going to be an item but knows she likes him and is willing to get involved to see what would happen. Paul cared for her too, and she is a great traveling companion. He felt comfortable with her. They had gone out several times before leaving for London.

It bothers Paul that Anellina expects him to check in with her at least once a week. He wants to immerse himself in Europe. It has nothing to do with Anellina. Even though he had enjoyed London with her, he couldn't wait to get away and be by himself.

That is how he is feeling about Michelle.

Paul knows that about himself because he has never had a one-night stand or picked anyone up at a bar. He always became involved with a woman after a long time in a working environment, in school, or after hanging with them through groups of friends. That allowed them to flirt and joke with each other. It allowed time to understand what the other person is really like—a little mating dance, as it were.

⟶ * ✳ * ⟵

It is a quiet Sunday morning when he wakes. The electricity went out for an hour. He packed, went down to the lobby, and checked out. He searched the area for a better place to stay and ran across a more modern touristy place called Hotel Electra.

Paul got a super room. He read, relaxed, and watched TV. It is a bit expensive, but he deserved it. Treat yourself good when you can.

That afternoon, Paul walked around Athens for a while and picked a quiet restaurant where he could eat and read his book.

When he returned, he called Anellina, and they had a long talk. Then Doug called and filled him in on the continuing drama and farce of Bigger Than Life.

Paul worked on an Athens painting and then called Michelle. She had asked him to call her earlier, but he kept putting it off. By the time he did call, she had left to do something with her friend. Just as well.

Greek food is *so* good! He found another great restaurant for dinner and then tried the hotel bar when he returned to the Electra. It was dead.

He soaked in a hot bubble bath and dried himself off after spending too long reading *Poland*—too long because the bathtub drained his energy and turned him into a prune. Before he retired, he booked a full-day cruise to three islands for Tuesday.

The next morning, Paul's sinuses are killing him. He crawled out of bed and went downstairs for breakfast then returned to his room to start a new painting—another "view out the window."

Paul is pondering his next destination when he leaves Greece. Taking a train through Yugoslavia sounds like an adventure, so he caught the Metro to the train station to check the schedule. Maybe he wasn't paying attention when he arrived because it seemed like a different station. It is small and dirty with dry sand around it as if it were sitting in the middle of a desert. He saw two characters that are borderline bums with old clothes, baggier than usual, and unshaven. One is leaning against the wall of the station, hands in his pockets glaring at him. The other one—dressed the same—is next to the tracks, pacing back and forth. His head hung down, but he saw the guy glance toward him every few seconds.

For some reason, Paul felt like he was entering a Stephen King novel. Continuing on this path would lead to horror and insane confusion.

He turned around, went to the hotel, and booked a flight to Vienna for Wednesday. He will view Yugoslavia from the air.

A trip through Yugoslavia to Austria by train takes about three days. It is supposed to be a beautiful trip. More than one person had warned him about traveling alone through this country. There's a good chance of losing his passport. U.S. passports are in high demand, so he had heard. Who knows what else he could have lost? It felt wrong.

He painted until he received a call from Michelle. She's in the lobby. They walked together to the docks to pick up his island tour ticket. Paul had failed to ask her to join him. They went out to dinner, followed by dessert and coffee at a different restaurant.

They said their goodbyes with a hug, wished each other well and parted.

Returning to his room, he dove back into his paintings. He finished his Athens work, then did some final retouches on his Interlaken and Rome paintings. He spread all of his paintings around the room to see how they looked as a group.

The tour boat leaves the following morning when the sun is rising. It's a comfortable and relaxing cruise, and the islands are beautiful!

What was he thinking, spending so much time hanging in Athens? That two-week tour on a yacht would have been heaven.

They stopped at Paros first and then on to Hydra—beautiful!

He walked up a steep-winding road through whitewashed homes. The higher he walks, the more beautiful the view—looking out across the Aegean Sea, dotted with islands among the turquoise water. He could live the rest of his life here.

Their final stop is the island of Aegina. It is more populated and flat compared to the other two.

They arrive back in Athens as the sun is setting.

Paul met some people from San Diego at the end of the tour, and they had dinner together that night.

31

VIENNA

It's a little too early to go to the airport, so Paul took his time packing. He felt anxious to move on. The taxi Paul called will be here in fifteen minutes. He could have relaxed in his room another hour—maybe two.

Paul arrived at the airport three hours before his flight, and the time in the air takes two hours. He has never flown in Europe, so being early will relieve the stress of rushing through ticketing and security.

The most remarkable thing about this flight is the meal. Flights in the States are pretty lame in the food department. Sometimes, it's only a snack. If you served a meal, it's because you're on a much longer flight, and that's usually a quick meal in a box.

The meal on Paul's flight to Vienna is like being in a restaurant. He is served a three-course meal—served one at a time on actual plates and real silverware. The food is excellent.

The skies are clear, and the view below is of the mountains Paul probably would have traversed if he had taken a train. It is beautiful and rugged, and he's sure he would have had stories to tell. Would he have made it alive?

Maybe he would have been abducted into a rebel army and given a uniform and a rifle.

This fantasy is more of a reality than he realizes at the time. After returning to the States, he read about the turmoil Yugoslavia is experiencing. Maybe if he had traveled with companions, it could have worked.

When Paul arrived at the Vienna airport, he took the bus to the city center and found a peaceful park. There are good vibes in this place. Everyone he talked to speaks English fluently.

What a shock Vienna is after southern Italy and Athens.

The city is spit-shine clean with architecture that impresses him more than the United States or many parts of Europe. It has that European feel with cobblestone streets and narrow alleyways yet has broader, more modern roads and buildings.

The strangest thing about Vienna is that Paul didn't see many people on the streets. Maybe it's the time of day. Or perhaps this is the old historical part of the city, and the mad rush is in other more commercial areas.

Anyway, this is all conjecture and first impressions. Paul's primary goal is to find a hotel. He eventually came upon Hotel Pension Nossek. They have no single rooms, so he took a room with two beds for one night. The room was large with high ceilings.

Paul walked around the city to see if he could find a suitable room that isn't so expensive and found one. He will change hotels tomorrow.

Returning to his hotel, Paul is gearing up for a late meal and a little bar hopping but didn't make it. He flopped on the bed and is out for the night.

A good night's sleep is all he needs. After packing his bag, he moved to the new hotel. It was nice—Hotel Post, room 311.

He takes a stroll to the Museum of Fine Art. This museum is definitely on par with the better museums he has seen thus far. Paul recognized the paintings of several masters—Rembrandt, Titian, Peter Bruegel, etc. It's smaller than most museums, but it's big enough to wander through and not feel worn out when finished.

The rest of the evening, he spends eating food and checking out a few pubs. He then retired to his hotel and made phone calls.

Anellina has another friend of a friend—Diane and her family—who lives in Heidelberg, Germany. They are expecting him.

Gathering his painting supplies, Paul walks to the park he initially saw when he first arrived. He does a detailed painting overlooking a canal with stairs leading up to a park.

Paul's subway experience is odd. It's like stepping into the future. The station is empty, modern, and again, spit-shined like the rest of the city. He goes to a machine, buys ten tickets, and waits for his ride. When the train quietly zooms into the station, he noticed that it is ultra-modern—sleek and futuristic.

The doors hiss open; there is no one inside. Paul looks around for someone to take his ticket; there is no one.

Stepping cautiously inside a car, in case alarm bells go off, he takes his seat next to nobody—heading for a destination he knew not where, on an empty train.

Is he in that damn Stephen King novel again?

Paul took the subway to the river Danube. He is still waving his ticket around when he disembarks, expecting someone to say, "Hey, idiot, over here!"

Finding himself across the river from UNO City, a building complex that hosts the United Nations offices, he sits under a bridge and does his second painting of the day. He then returns to his neck of the woods and has another excellent meal.

At the hotel, he has to pay to take a bath; it's worth it.

The next day, Paul spends his time focusing on finishing the two paintings he started the day before. It is enjoyable walking the streets of this city. The shops are closed—strange for a Saturday. He wants to buy some souvenirs, and he also wants to get something for Anellina. Instead, he relaxes over some lasagna, a glass of red wine, and reads his book.

Venice is high on his list to visit. While going through the Swiss Alps, he checks the route, thinking seriously about making that his next stay. Unfortunately, there is a railroad strike in the area.

Thinking the strike will be over, Paul hops on the subway to the train station. A sleeper car sounds perfect for this leg of his journey. When he arrives, he found that the railroad employees in Venice are still on strike.

He calls Anellina's friend Diane to see if he could arrive at her place early the next night. She agrees.

Heidelberg

Paul checked out of the hotel and took the subway to the train station. Unfortunately, this station has connections to Venice but not to Germany. There is another train station with a destination to Germany. He catches a taxi and found the right station.

There is a first-class cabin available—thank God.

Shortly after departure, it starts to snow. What can Paul say other than it is beautiful and contemplative?

It reminded him of a small snow cave when he was a child—sneaking out of his window in a snowstorm to escape going to church.

It's a pleasant trip.

Paul changed trains in Munich and arrived in Heidelberg at 5:15 p.m. Diane and a young German fellow, Frank, are waiting for him. They went to Diane's house, played cards, drank, and watched TV. She didn't live in Heidelberg; her home is next to a military base a few miles away. They gave Paul some tourist info, and he retired to a cozy room with a bed and three skylights.

It's not often that he sleeps in, but the next morning, he did. Shuffling into the living room, he ran into Richard, Diane's son, who watched TV and studied the bible. He has the day off from school. Diane showed up at eleven-thirty and escorted Paul on base to cash a travelers' check.

From there, Paul caught the OEG (the local train) to Heidelberg.

Wow! What a neat place. It's in a valley with the Neckar River running through it. There are locks for barges and small ships to pass. He stood on the bridge for a while, watching a cargo boat enter and depart one of the locks. A small building that he supposed was a little energy plant stood on one side.

Paul crossed the locks, walked around town, and climbed a hill to the town's historic castle that sits on top of the hill overlooking the whole scene; then, it's back down to a restaurant to feast on German food and red wine. The waitress is friendly. He must have stayed there for at least two hours.

He caught the OEG back to Diane's house with a little difficulty since he isn't familiar with the trains yet. It was nine-thirty that evening when he walked in the front door. Diane and Paul talked a while, and then he went to bed.

The next morning, Paul took a shower, downed some Raisin Bran, and caught the OEG back to Heidelberg.

He crossed the locks, climbed back up to the castle, and paints.

The weather is cloudy and drizzly today, but Heidelberg maintained its charm.

Back in town, Paul found another restaurant and spent a couple of hours reading, eating, and drinking wine. When finished, he crossed back over the river and climbed up to the Philosopher's Walk—a long paved trail high on a hill overlooking Heidelberg—a breathtaking view! The walk up to this trail is a narrow cobblestone passageway with eight-foot rock walls on either side.

The Philosopher's Walk extends the town's length and follows the valley, high above the river.

Paul returned at six that evening. Diane and Richard arrive shortly afterward. They kick back, watch the Oscars, and go to bed.

The next day is rainy and stormy. Paul finishes the castle painting and takes the train to Mannheim twelve miles away. He decides to see the Kunsthalle Mannheim Museum—small but nice—with paintings by Francis Bacon, Manet, Cezanne, Van Gogh, Lieberman, etc.

Noticing a needle-like structure—called the Fernmeldeturm—Paul takes the elevator to its rotating restaurant and has a meal, taking in the view. Initially, it was a concrete telecommunications tower.

He returned to Diane's and met Gary, an old friend of hers. They had a fun social evening. Gary did a good job of talking Paul into going to Berlin—well, almost a good job, anyway.

Paul is confused as to his next destination, and Berlin sounds like an adventure.

Something is nagging at him, though. It's called Venice. When he was in Mannheim earlier in the day, he asked at the rail station if the strike is still on. They didn't know a thing about it.

Thinking that's a good sign, he packs up and sets out for Venice.

Paul's time at Diane's has been comfortable, and he has thoughts of using her place as a home base. He could do a tour of Germany and hit a list of cities with nice museums. It's the list that Gary had given him.

There are too many places he wants to experience other than what is on the list, so he decides to exit Germany.

He barely caught the train to Munich. Paul could travel on to Venice from there.

When he arrives in Munich, he tried to transfer to the Venice train, but he's met with the usual news.

Damn. Still on strike!

He thought of going back to Diane's.

Nah, he needs to move on.

Should he go north to Sweden or west to Spain? He decides to get a room in a hotel, relax, and make some decisions.

After dumping his pack in a hotel across the street from the train station, he wanders the city. Munich looks like a gigantic shopping mall—both at ground level and underground.

He escaped the area and ran into a fabulous museum. The Alte Pinakothek has world-famous paintings from all the old masters.

Instead of running down the list of painters whose work he had seen during this trip, there is one, in particular, he needs to mention: Peter Paul Rubens.

Rubens is a Flemish painter with a Baroque style. His work is noted for its movement, color, and sensuality. It's his color that drew Paul's attention.

He has seen a lot of his work in the Louvre and the Uffizi. They seemed different. As he discovered, old paintings cannot be stripped of their varnish or restored because of the damage risk. The paintings appear dark. The Vatican is an exception since there is restoration work going on there.

It's also different in Germany. One large painting of a nude by Rubens has intense color—*really* intense!

Could they have embellished it? I don't think so. It would be a sin to have changed this painting to something that it had never been. It is absolutely brilliant. It gave him more of an understanding and appreciation of the work of the old masters.

Returning from Europe, Paul found that they are beginning to do restoration work in Italy and France. There must have recently been some significant inroads made in restoration techniques.

32

BARCELONA

Paul **made his decision.** Spain it is.

The view out the train window is gorgeous as he travels through Switzerland—a beautiful fairy-tale land of Alpine peaks covered in snow with turquoise lakes and quaint villages.

He changes trains in Zurich and proceeds to Geneva. After a five-hour layover, he takes a *couchette* to Barcelona, sharing it with a German man who works for the railroad. He is an amusing and animated man.

He makes sure that Paul's head is next to the window and his feet next to the door. It's common for thieves to quietly slide the door open and render the passenger unconscious from a nitrous-oxide-soaked rag. The passenger would wake up with a headache and the absence of his money and travel documents—if he woke up.

Then came more stories in his heavy Germanic accent—while he occasionally hung his head over the side of his top bunk—smiling to see how Paul responded to his unusual tales.

They had a lengthy stop at the Spanish border. My German companion explained that they had to change the wheels on the train since the track size in Spain is different from that of the rest of Europe.

Barcelona

Experiencing the Spanish railway system takes a lot of patience. Compared to the rest of Europe, this system is a disaster. Forget times of arrival or departure. Since crossing the border into Spain at five in the morning, the train continually broke down for hours.

Once there was a two-hour stoppage inside a tunnel. Many passengers grabbed their luggage and got off to look for other modes of transportation. One group of young travelers asked Paul if he would like to join them. He politely refuses, deciding instead to curl up in his seat—read and take naps—putting the thought of reaching a destination out of his mind. He thinks that's called the art of Zen.

The train finally arrived in Barcelona at 11:45 a.m. He located a locker for his belongings and found a place to stay—The Hotel Transient. Finding a main street, he hailed a cab and had the driver take him to the Picasso Museum.

Picasso is a painter known for his cubistic style. Few have understood where cubism originated. In most of his exhibits, you see his style in full force—the colors, deformed shapes, and the use of the flat surface with the depth of space. Analytic cubism began with very little color and later developed into a more colorful abstract style.

But could he draw? Did he learn the basics? Could he paint a landscape or realistic figure?

The answer is "yes"—and the Picasso Museum shows the artist's progression from the age of ten (as a child prodigy) to his death.

At the age of fifteen, his work was amazing and realistic.

The Picasso paintings Paul loves the most don't depict his known style. These are paintings of doves on a windowsill. There are three, four, or five-foot square—wonderfully realistic and painterly. I've looked for reproductions of these paintings and have yet to find them.

As Paul walked into a beautiful plaza with the museum behind him, he felt elation and excitement about Picasso's work. The energy inside him makes him want to be back in his studio.

His reverie is short-lived as he looked across the plaza. A middle-aged woman is walking with an elderly woman. She is a bit frail, gauging from her guarded walk across the cobblestones.

Paul's eye catches movement at the edge of the open space. A man is sprinting across the plaza toward the women, whose backs are turned, walking away.

Comprehending the gist of the situation, Paul yelled as he started running toward them. One moment later, the man grabbed the elderly lady's purse and is off running.

The woman wouldn't let go, went immediately horizontal, hit the cobblestones, and was dragged while she still maintained a fierce grip on her purse.

The man looked at Paul; he still has about twenty yards to go. The thief released the purse and darted through an alley. You can hear the crashes and bangs as he upended everything in his path; he is gone.

Paul knelt to check on the woman, as did her daughter (the middle-aged woman). They checked her condition and asked if she could stand.

"Yes, I'm OK," she said as she began to get up.

"I can't believe you held on to your purse," Paul said as he and the daughter held each arm as she rose.

"Oh, there's nothing in my purse. My money and passport are in my belt. I just didn't want the thief to get away with it."

The daughter thanked Paul and introduced her mother and herself. They are from the States. Waving goodbye with smiles, tempered by the shock of the situation, they wished each other a wonderful rest of the day.

"What a feisty woman!" Paul said to himself.

Barcelona is a one-night stand.

Before retiring, he noticed a modern structure on a hill that overlooked the city.

"What building is that?" Paul asked a vendor in the plaza.

"That's the Joan Miró museum," he said.

Paul climbed the hill. He didn't want to miss seeing his work. The structure is beautiful, reflective of his work. It didn't look busy.

"Oh, shoot! It's closed."

He did have the opportunity to look in the windows.

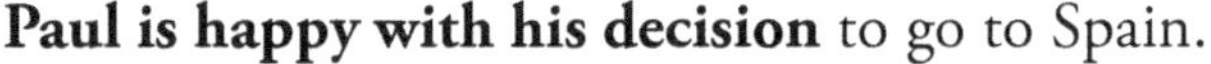

Paul is happy with his decision to go to Spain.

There is so much to see in Europe. He's sure that Berlin would have been a great experience. The wall will be torn down a little over a year from now. Of course, he didn't know that at the time.

Paul's name and the majority of his heritage are Swedish. He feels obligated to go there to experience a Nordic country, especially since it was where his grandfather was born and raised.

Then there is the elusive Venice. He would visit there one day, but it doesn't look like he will on this trip.

There is another reason for being in Spain. He wants to make sure there is time to spend with Linda in Granada. Everyone who knows her from Yakitori II was sad to see her leave for her required schooling as a Spanish major. Linda spent a lot of time convincing Paul to visit her. He didn't need convincing.

There is also Jean-Paul in Angoulême, France. His invitation to stay is an opportunity he didn't want to pass up.

Oh, yeah! He's excited to see Ireland, too.

His path to Granada is not straight. Madrid is to be his next stop. He wants to see the Prado Museum.

Before Paul left Barcelona, he walked to the corner bakery and purchased a few items for his train trip. He also wandered around the train station and bought food and liquids for his trek to Madrid.

It is an amazing trip through the Spanish countryside. Most impressive are the ruins of castles along the way. They must be scattered throughout the whole country. Many are on top of hills for obvious reasons. They seemed to be left as they were. No attempt was made to reconstruct them. He thinks that's great. Let them be what they are and don't touch them. Just learn from them.

Some of these castles have small towns at their base. Paul's knowledge of Spanish history was minimal until this visit—so much to learn!

Learning from his experiences on this trip is a good thing; having sparked his interest to know more is even better.

The train to Madrid actually has TV sets. They show movies as well as shorts—all in Spanish.

Arriving in Madrid, Paul heads straight for the Prado. It's closed. There is a sign showing the times they are open on the door. It's closed tomorrow too. Damn!

Paul will need to come back this way. He wants to see this museum. He will visit it when he leaves Spain.

He decides to catch a night train to Granada.

33

GRANADA

Paul made a reservation for a *couchette* and then took an underground train to another station for his connection to Granada.

He shared the sleeper car with a Spanish man, but he also met two young Boston women. They invited Paul to their cabin, and they talked until three in the morning.

He arrived in Granada at eight that morning and called Linda. She is excited to hear from Paul. He took a taxi to Plaza Bib-Rambla where they plan to meet. He just loves European plazas. This one has a real Spanish feel with its cobblestones and beautifully sculpted fountain.

When Linda arrives, she is "all smiles." Actually, from the time he met her, she was always "all smiles"—a great way to start a day.

She escorts Paul to her apartment, and he unloaded his pack on the foldout couch—his bed.

Linda decided to miss her first class. Instead, she took Paul on a tour of the Alhambra. The Arabs built this palace in the thirteenth and fourteenth centuries. It was their last stronghold in Spain before they lost it in 1492.

They had lunch in the Arab section, found an outside table, and talked.

There is plenty to talk about. For years, Linda had worked at Paul's favorite sushi bar in San Diego to finance her way through school. Linda and Paul had clicked immediately, and his sushi experience is made more delightful with jokes, flirts, and her smile. He had eaten there often. In fact, he was a regular.

Linda had to go to her afternoon class. Paul went back to her place, showered, and slept.

When Linda returned, she needed to give English lessons to a nine-year-old Spanish boy. She didn't want him distracted, so Paul went down to the plaza and read his book.

When Linda came down to get him, she had a friend with her. She introduced him to Jana. They took him bar hopping—he should say tapas bar hopping or tapas hopping.

Tapa bars are new for Paul. In the States, they have happy hours—half-priced drinks and appetizers. In Spain it's tapas.

It goes like this: you order a drink, and they give you a little token appetizer. Order another drink, and you get an even better appetizer. Several drinks into the evening, you are getting ten-inch slabs of fried squid.

They also serve your food on paper plates and your drinks in plastic cups. They don't bus your tables; they push everything off on the floor.

At the end of the night, you wade through knee-deep trash to get outside.

When the place is closed, the staff gets a large push broom, piles everything in a heap, and dumps it.

Okay, back to Linda and Jana who are dead set on Paul having a good time. You know it when you are around good positive people.

They had fun and amazing conversations and drinks, as they stumbled around Granada. They filled Paul in on what they are experiencing, and he told them about his travels and dreams.

He also got them hooked on his blabbering about Carl Jung. They understood exactly what he is saying.

To Paul, Jung had opened a door that allowed him to see the world differently. It applies to everything that happens every day—internally and externally.

Back to Linda and Jana. They walked Jana home and said their slurred goodbyes.

Linda and Paul still aren't finished. The two of them went to yet another bar with a pleasant atmosphere. Linda wants him to experience the differences between sweet red sherry and dry clear sherry.

Come morning, Linda and Paul went out for coffee before she went to school. When she returned, she gave him a tour of the things that might come in handy—the bank, the telephone house, and a place where he can buy stamps (a tobacco stand).

Linda's private lesson didn't happen that day. Her student didn't show up.

Instead, she took me to an upscale, expensive, Arab restaurant. We had to wait until two in the afternoon—that's when lunch starts, and the siestas are over.

Yes, siestas are a real thing in Spain. Paul thinks honoring that time is brilliant. It follows human nature.

Hanging seven-year-old dead pigs in the doorway of food establishments is a real thing, too. It's supposed to be a delicacy. There is a little tin cup below its snout that catches the oils; the soon-to-be carcass is continually sliced and salted. You seriously had to turn sideways and squeeze between the pig and the doorjamb to enter.

After their sumptuous meal, Linda and Paul parted for the afternoon. Paul grabbed his painting supplies and went looking for a magical place to paint. He found one at a local cemetery. The cemetery had whitewashed walls and housed urns that were placed on shelves inside. The cemetery is merely the background. In front of the walls is an olive tree orchard. The red soil has furrows, with yellow flowers covering the foreground. This scene is one of those paintings that just fell together.

He walked back to Linda's and met two friends of hers—Yens from Sweden and Steve from Los Angeles. They hit the bar-hopping scene—again—until two in the morning. Jana and her boyfriend showed up for a while.

Paul is having a blast with these people!

Linda had trouble getting out of bed that morning and missed her first class. They made their usual morning coffee. She did go to her next class, and Paul decided to explore the Alhambra more thoroughly.

He spent most of the day at the site and started a new painting. It is a view of Granada and the surrounding terrain from the top of the palace. The parapets inside the walls are in the foreground. He worked on it the next few days and thought he captured the feeling and details. The perspective bothered him. He made some adjustments, but it has never seemed right.

Linda and Paul are planning to have lunch at a favorite place of hers when he returns. But when they meet, she said she couldn't go. Linda needs to meet with a friend. She told him where the restaurant is and said she would meet him there later. Paul took his time, read his book, and placed his order, savoring every bite. He relaxed, ate slowly, and continued reading. He finally paid the tab and left; no Linda.

They later met at the plaza in front of her house. She said she showed up at the restaurant, but it was after he left.

Linda explained to Paul what happened with her friend. She is having a relationship with him. It sounds like it's over.

They did the usual tapas thing that evening but retired from the bar scene earlier than usual. Yens and Paul played chess and had chicken soup with Linda and Steve. The evening evolved into a fun discussion that had them laughing most of the evening. Paul needed that; Linda did too.

During their coffee the following morning, Linda placed her elbow on the table, her chin on her hand, and asked, "Can you stay longer? Like until school's over. We can travel together before we go back to the States."

Gazing back at her, Paul said, "I would enjoy that. The problem is that I have some commitments. My flight leaves in a couple of weeks. My van is stored in a friend's garage, and I'm sure it's an inconvenience."

Linda stated the obvious. "You can change your return flight. Call a friend to move your van?"

Paul adored that about Linda. She had solutions for problems, and she was up-front about wanting to be with him. They could travel together—spend time together, understand each other, and develop a real relationship. She is up for that.

"I need to think about it," Paul said.

"For now, I would like to visit a family in France. They are expecting me. I also want to visit Ireland. How about you concentrate on finishing school? I will call you. I'll use this travel time to decide."

Linda actually went to all her classes. When she returned, she asked Paul if he would join her for a couple of errands.

The first stop is to her bank to make a deposit. The second stop is a travel agent. They found that it would cost a hundred dollars to change his departure date. The agent also said that if Paul misses the flight—even if I don't notify them—it would still only be a hundred dollars.

So, I didn't need to worry about leaving on my departure date.

"There's a place I would like to take you," Linda said as she grabbed Paul's hand and led him up a thin, winding road.

They walked through an alleyway—a street made of cobblestones. The walls on either side are about ten feet high, made of stone and brick. Occasionally, Paul sees plastered and painted areas. There are few doors and no windows. He didn't see any numbers or signs.

Linda stopped at a large dark metal door, highlighted with reddish-brown rust.

She opened the door for him.

Walking in, Paul immediately stopped in astonishment. "What a cool place!"

The room is large and rectangular, made of stone and brick. Stairs led down to the floor from the doorway—about four feet. A few dark brown, varnished, picnic tables are arranged in order. Against the wall, there are kegs stacked atop each other, with spigots protruding from them.

"Have a seat," she said. "This is my favorite place."

Linda and Paul are the only ones there.

She walked over to the kegs and picked up two small glasses. She filled them to the rim and returned to their table.

"This is the best sherry you'll find in Granada," she said, as we clanked glasses in a toast. "Here's to you canceling your flight."

"Now just a minute," Paul said. "I do like your proposal, but I still need to decide. Things are a little more complicated."

"I do understand—I'm just hoping out loud. I won't pressure you."

Their conversation wandered. Linda talked of school and missing Yakitori II, and Paul is excited about the next couple of weeks.

Paul has had a great trip, but it's all going too fast. He can visualize being a constant traveler, seeing new things, and meeting more people.

Linda took his glass, walked back to the keg, and refilled both of their drinks.

They continued their conversation, and for the third time, Linda stood and refilled their glasses. "Are you hungry?"

"Yes, I am!" Paul looked around at the empty cavern.

She set both full glasses on the table and disappeared into a back room.

A few moments later, she returned with a smile on her face.

"It'll be about twenty minutes."

The conversation continued as if they are bottomless pits of information, humor, and trivia.

Twenty minutes later, Linda walked into the back room and reappeared with two salads. She placed them on the table, disappeared again, and returned with an incredible pizza—the best he's had, *really*!

One sherry refill later, Linda grabbed Paul by the hand and pulled him into her secret back room. There stood a little old man with a smile on his face. Linda introduced him and gave him a list of what they had consumed, then paid him.

Paul added a super tip, but he refused.

It was Saturday, and Linda had the day off. They strolled around Granada, and she took him to places he hadn't seen.

Paul pulled out his Walkman and let Linda listen to it.

"Oh, man! I need to get one of these."

They found a place that sold them. Walkmans are expensive in Spain, so she put it on her wish list.

Paul bought a Suzanne Vega tape, and they returned to Linda's place.

As they approached Linda's doorway, Paul excused himself and walked to the telephone house to call Anellina. He felt depressed after they talked. If Paul didn't have his truck in her garage, he might decide to stay with Linda or pursue other options that would allow him to stay here longer. Paul is concerned about Anellina's feelings.

Anellina and Paul hadn't known each other that long—just a few months before going to London. He mentioned that the calls every week are becoming more of a distraction than attempting to stay in touch. She is a little disturbed by that. She's a therapist for Christ's sake, and she should understand and appreciate his honesty.

Paul had felt this way for over a month; it isn't about Linda.

All that day, he wrestled with his options. Come evening, he is close to convincing himself that he should stay in Granada for three months, learn Spanish, and develop his relationship with Linda. He could still go to France and Ireland.

It is Monday, and it is Paul's last day in Granada. He took his camera, walked around, took photos, spent a lot of time in the Arab districts, relaxed in a couple of parks, and read his book. He is still reading *Poland* by Michener. It is a big book. He's not a fast reader, but he is a continual one. He reads at the same speed he talks. He doesn't like speed-reading.

Back in the apartment, Paul packed his bags. The train is leaving for Madrid tonight. Linda made pasta with asparagus and mushrooms, and they drank wine.

Steve met them at ten that evening. They walked over and picked up Yens, then made their way to the train station.

These three beautiful people are not into quick goodbyes. They got on the train with Paul and sat down in his *couchette*. They talked and joked. Paul told them he might come back in a couple of weeks; he needs time to think. He wants to return.

They stayed until the train lurched; they quickly hugged and said their goodbyes. Paul looked out the window as he was leaving the station. They are still waving and blowing kisses.

34

MADRID

MADRID

Arriving **early** in Madrid, Paul found a café close to the Prado, munched on rolls, drank coffee, and waited for the museum to open. He wants to be there before the crowds.

He expected a museum the size of the Louvre; it's not even close but most impressive. Most of the work is Spanish—as Paul would expect—realistic, figurative, and landscapes. El Greco, Goya, and Hieronymus Bosch have lots of work with a smattering of other Spanish painters.

Then came Picasso's *Guernica*! Wow! What history in this piece! It depicts the ruthless slaughter of the people in this Spanish town by the Germans—practicing their aerial bombing for the war. This painting is huge and painted in black and white.

The work is placed behind bulletproof glass, displayed alongside many original sketches drawn before and during the painting's creation.

It is also extremely political. The Spanish moved Guernica out of the country until the death of Francisco Franco in 1975. The painting was then moved back to Madrid. It needs to be protected. There are still strong political feelings about it that remain alive today.

Paul especially enjoyed the beautiful portraits by Madrazo. He had not heard of him until he visited The Prado.

The Prado is the only place he wanted to go while in Madrid, so afterward, he caught the subway to Chamartin, the other major railway station in the city.

He wants to time his trip to see the Pyrenees mountain range during the day and still have time to make it to Angoulême, France, before nightfall.

The train route didn't accommodate him as he hoped. His destination took him to Hendaye, a port on the southwest coast of France on the Spanish border. They skirted the western edge of the mountains.

Just before reaching Hendaye, the train came to a stop—for hours.

Someone said the Spanish railway workers are on strike. They are responsible for changing the gauge of the Spanish wheels to fit the French tracks.

Paul's not sure what that means, but it's a time-consuming process.

Because of the delay, they made it to Angoulême at three-thirty in the morning. Paul was dead tired and didn't want to wake up Jean-Paul's family at that hour. Instead, he stretched out over three seats and slept, arriving in Paris as the sun rose. His idea is to sleep until he arrives in Paris and then take the train back to Angoulême so he will arrive at a decent hour.

By the time he arrives in Paris, the train had worn out its welcome. The thought of going back to Angoulême didn't entice him anymore.

He decides to move on.

It's a quick two-hour train ride to Le Havre from Paris. From there, he can board a ferry to Ireland. At first, the information he received said the boat is leaving that day, but when he arrived at Le Havre, he found out that it leaves the next day at six in the evening. Paul found a comfortable hotel and retired early.

When Paul made his ferry reservation, he thought ahead and reserved a cabin.

—— * ✻ * ——

TRIP FROM MADRID TO IRELAND

It was ten in the morning when Paul awoke.

As he wandered around Le Havre, he found a grocery store and bought French wine (two dollars a bottle), bread, cheese, and French mustard.

When the checker finished tallying up the total, Paul paid and stood at the check stand like an idiot. Finally, one of the other customers told him it was his responsibility to bag the groceries.

That is the only English he heard in this small town. No one wanted to speak English.

The bus arrived at the train station at 2:45 p.m. This is his transport to the ferry.

Everyone on the bus speaks English, and Paul made immediate friends.

He boarded the ferry and unloaded his gear in the cabin. Wow, nice cabin! He met Daniel from Montreal, Paul's cabin mate. There are two sets of bunk beds against opposing walls—room for four. Daniel and Paul are the only ones in that cabin—or so I thought.

Paul contacted the crew and told them the door wouldn't lock. They said they would get someone to check it out.

All the workers on the boat spoke in an Irish accent. He loves that sound.

Later that evening, Daniel and Paul went to the bar and met Pat from Indianapolis, and two other Americans, Brian and Joe.

We talked and drank until after midnight, then retired to our rooms.

Later that night, the ferry is rocking and rolling, and Paul is jarred awake. The ferry is going through an intense storm.

He reached for his pack and found the Dramamine his friend Betty insisted Paul takes with him. He downed one with his bottle of water and noticed Daniel was awake.

"Hey, man, take this."

"What is it?" he asked.

"It's Dramamine—a seasick pill."

"No, I'm feeling fine. I don't need it."

"You will," I said. "It won't work if you're already sick."

"No. I'm fine."

Paul crawled back in bed, hanging on to what he could to keep from falling on the floor.

The sun had just risen. Daniel was sitting on the edge of Paul's bed, his hand on his shoulder, shaking him.

"Hey, can I have one of those seasick pills? I'm really sick."

Looking up at him with tired eyes, Paul said, "If you're already sick, it won't work."

"I don't care. Can I please have one?"

"Sure." He sat up at the edge of the bed, retrieved some Dramamine, and gave Daniel one.

Grabbing his clothes, Paul dressed and thought, "Boy, am I hungry!"

When he walks into the hall, there are lines of people trying to get into the bathroom. The maids and crew are mopping up vomit.

Paul walks to the restaurant for breakfast; the place is empty. There are people serving food, so he ate and walked up on deck. The waves are much smaller. The sun is shining, and he felt pretty good. Thank you, Betty!

When Paul returns to his cabin, an elderly man is sleeping on the top bunk.

"Damn!" he thought. "They still haven't fixed the lock."

Paul puts his hand on the shoulder of the older guy and gives him a gentle push.

"Excuse me; this is my cabin. I think you're in the wrong place."

The man groaned and turned his face to the wall.

"Excuse me," Paul repeated. "You're in the wrong cabin."

He mumbled something about it being his cabin and went back to sleep.

Paul walked into the hall and eventually found a member of the crew.

"Excuse me, miss, I have been trying to get the lock fixed on my door, and now a man is sleeping on one of the bunks. I don't know who he is. I can't wake him."

"What's your cabin number?"

"Cabin 213, on the second deck."

She walked in that direction. Paul followed.

She walked into the room and shook the guy's shoulder.

"Hello, sir. Do you have your ticket?"

No response.

"Excuse me, sir. I need to see your ticket."

The man reached into his pants pocket while still lying prone, eyes shut. He pulled out his ticket and handed it to the woman.

"Oh. Cabin 213, second deck." She looked at Paul and said, "I guess it's his cabin, too."

"Oh, he just showed up. He didn't sleep here last night."

As the crewmember left, the guy sat up on his bed. He is an older gentleman, about seventy years old.

"I'm awfully sorry, sir," Paul said with some embarrassment.

"That's OK," the guy said. "I would have done the same thing. My car is downstairs. I always reserve a cabin but usually sleep in my car. It was a rough night last night."

They introduced themselves; his name is HG Dawe.

HG stretched out on his bunk and is, again, snoozing away.

Grabbing his book, Paul read until his eyelids drooped, and he went to sleep as well.

Waking to calm seas, Paul sat by the window and placed his bottle of wine, cheese, and bread on a small table. As he is opening the wine, HG leaned over and addressed him.

"Did you buy more than one bottle?" he asked.

"No, just the one. Would you like a glass?"

"No," he said. "It's just that you should have bought more. The wine isn't nearly as good in Ireland."

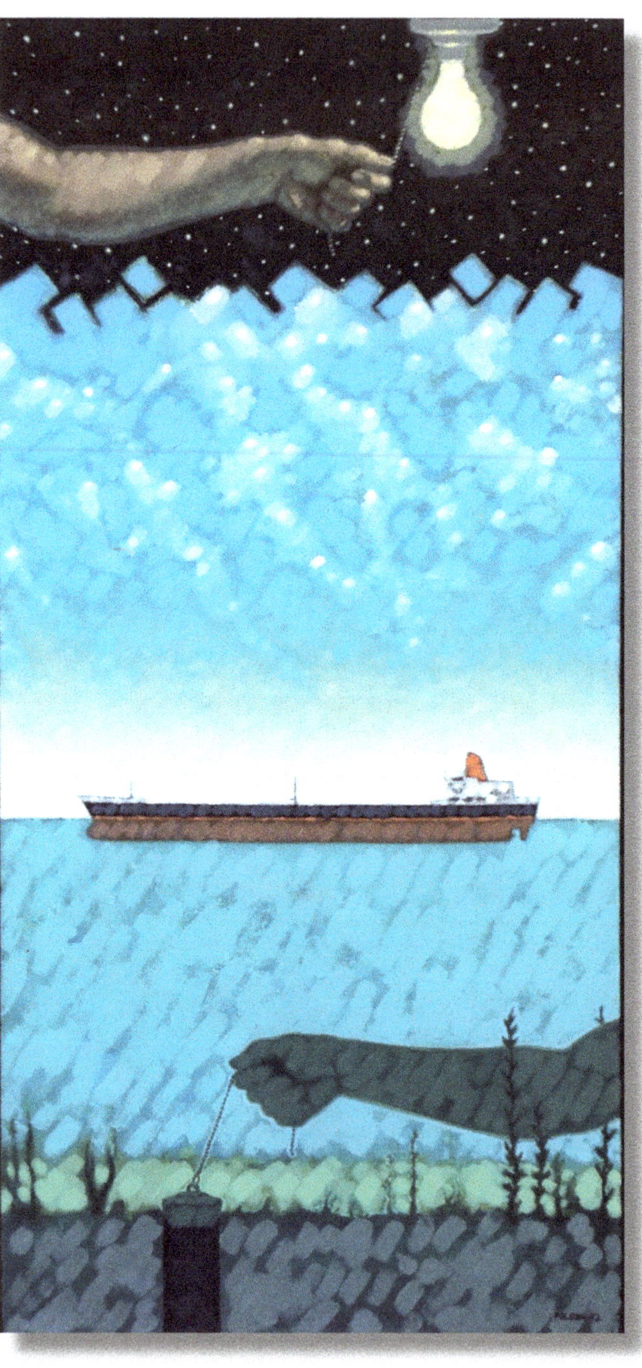

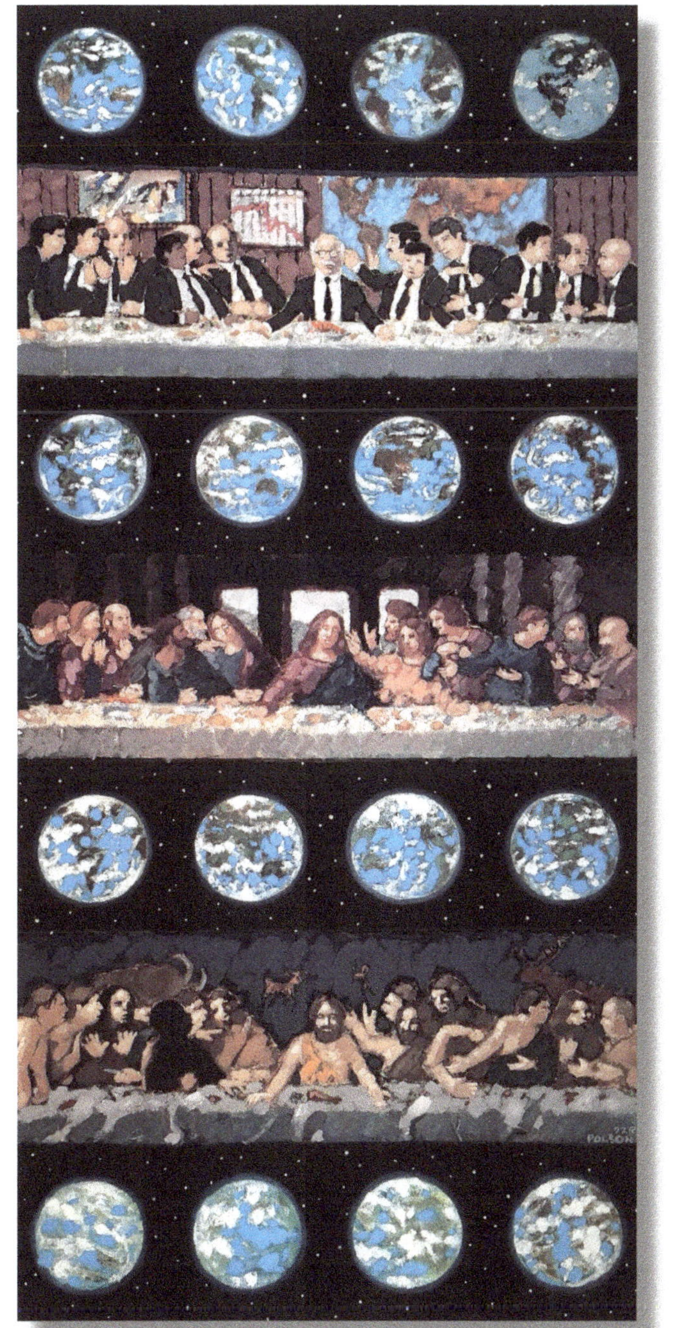

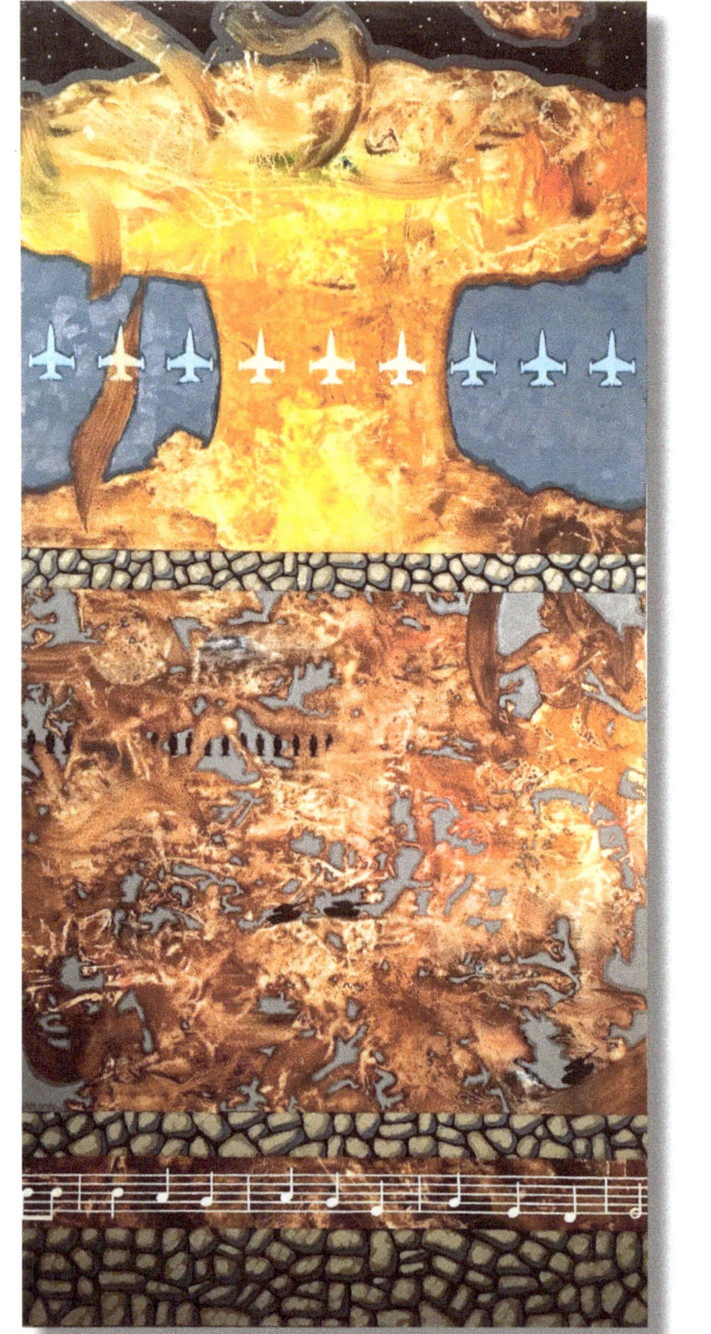

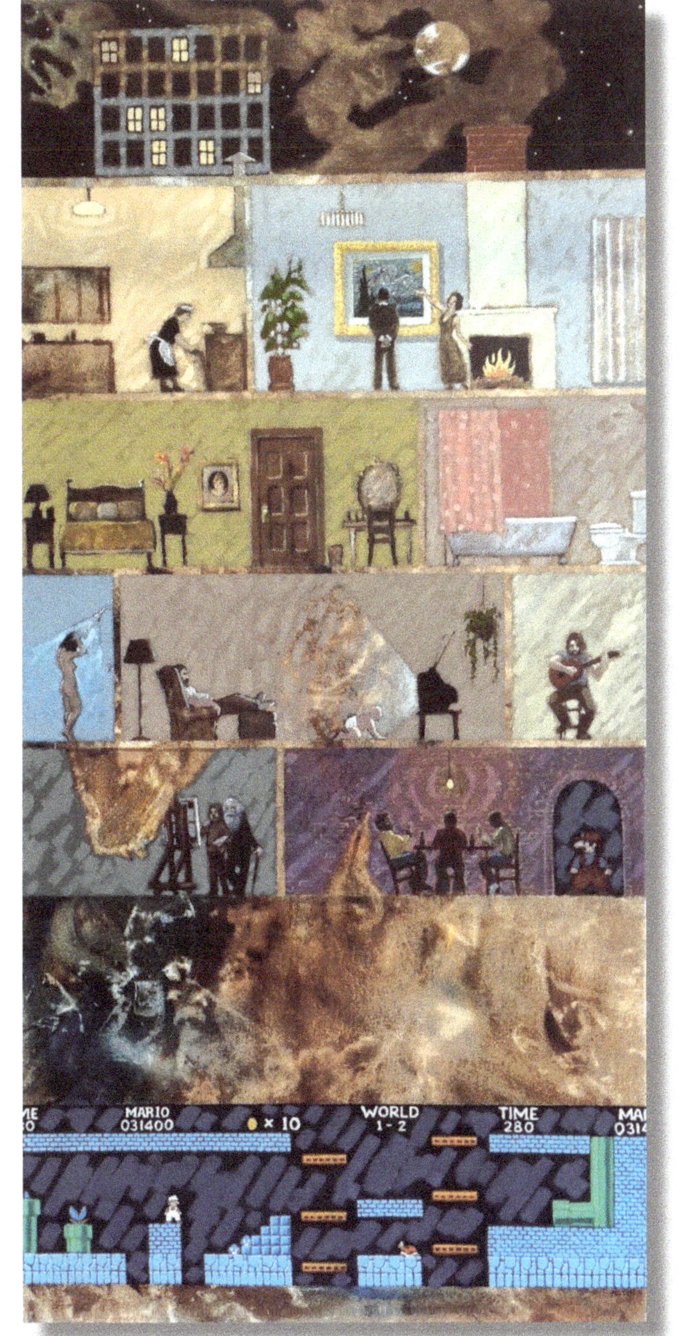
ME   MARIO   ● x 10   WORLD   TIME   MAR
0   031400   1-2   280   0314

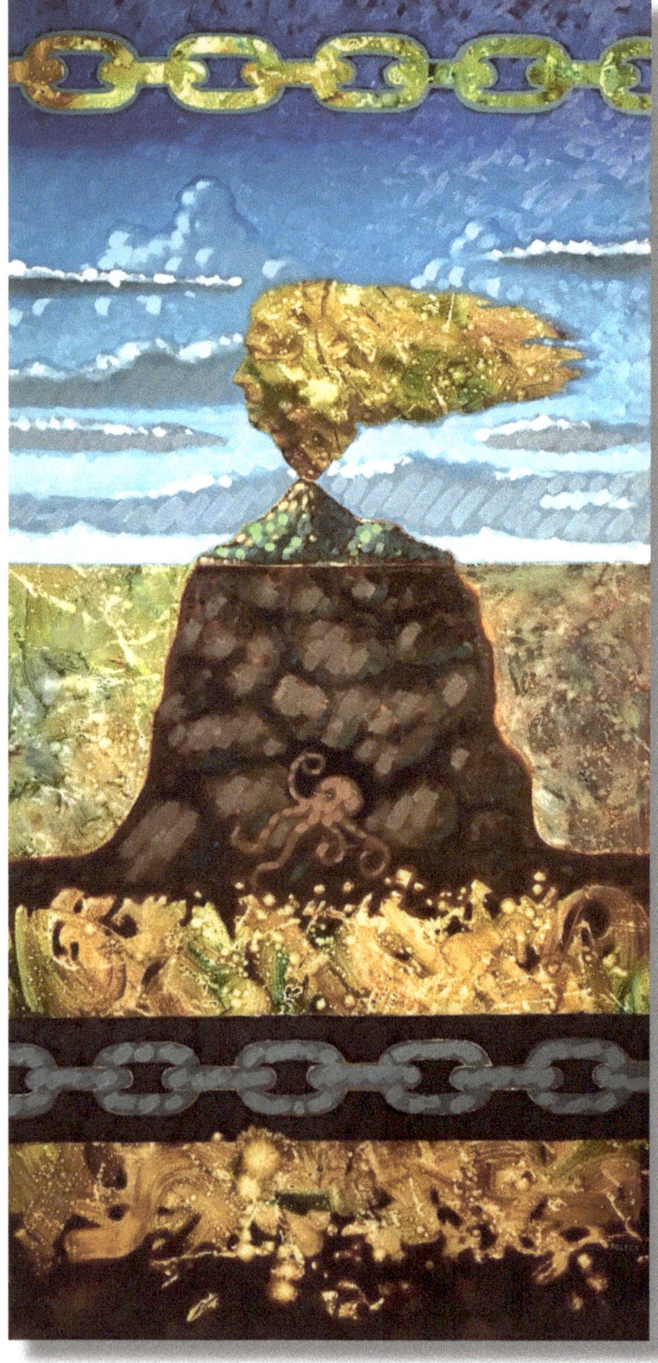

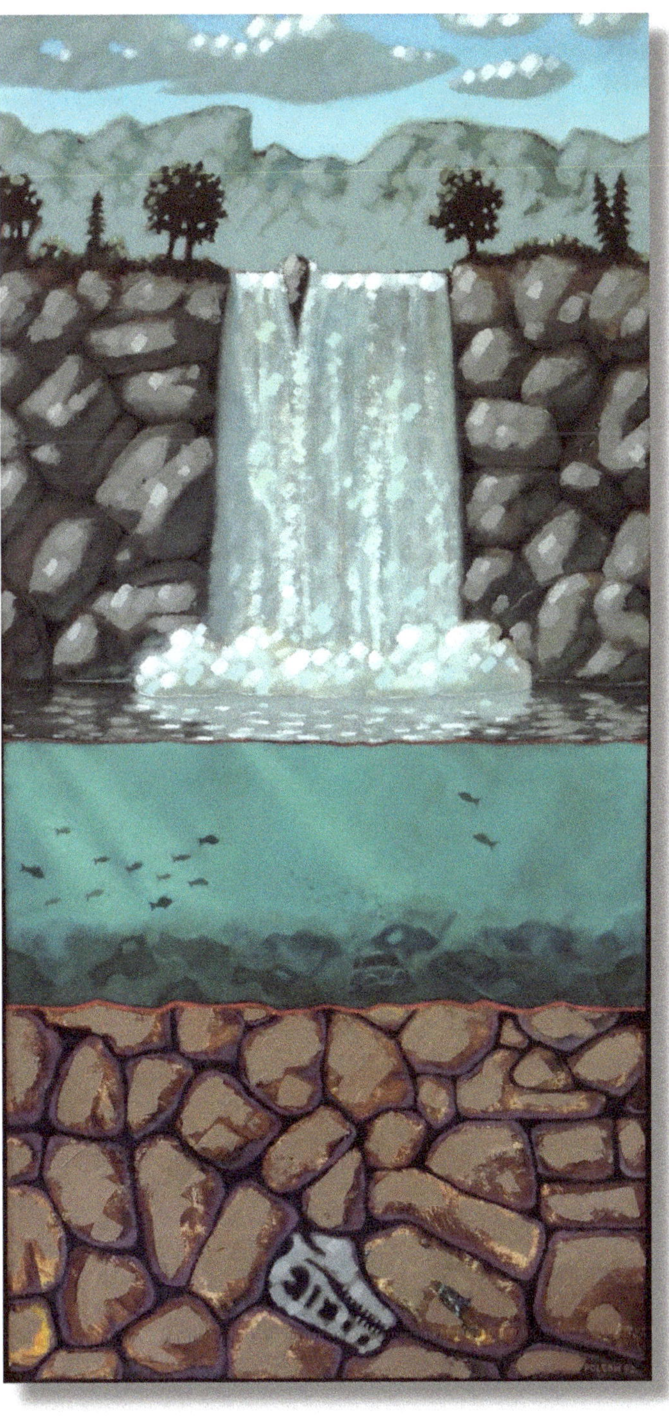

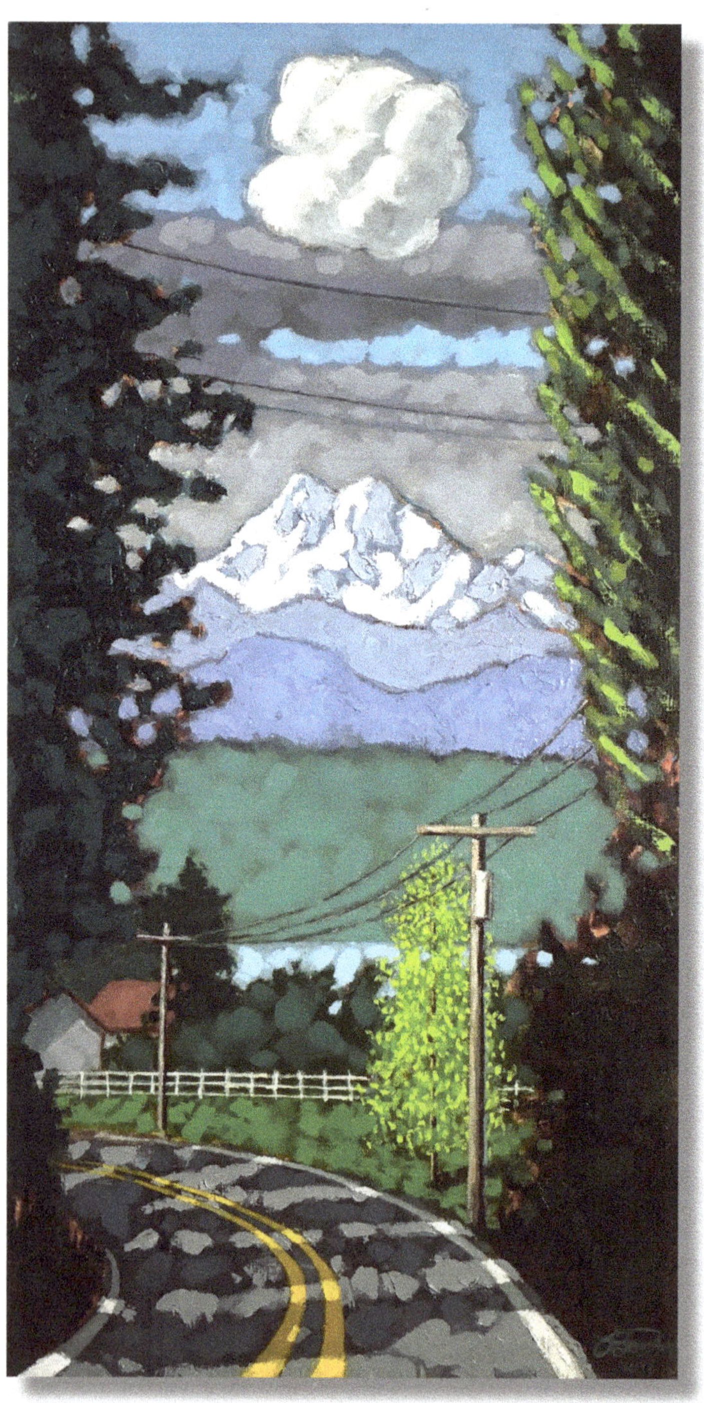

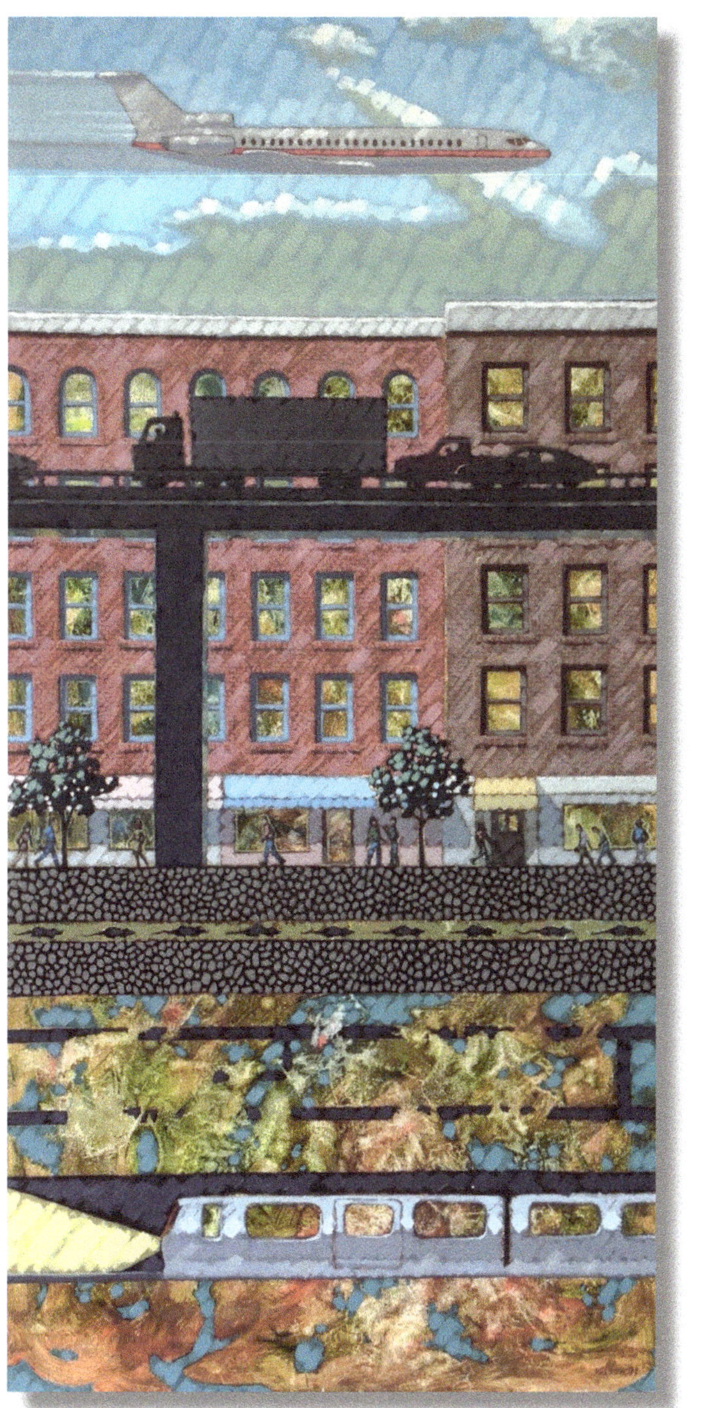

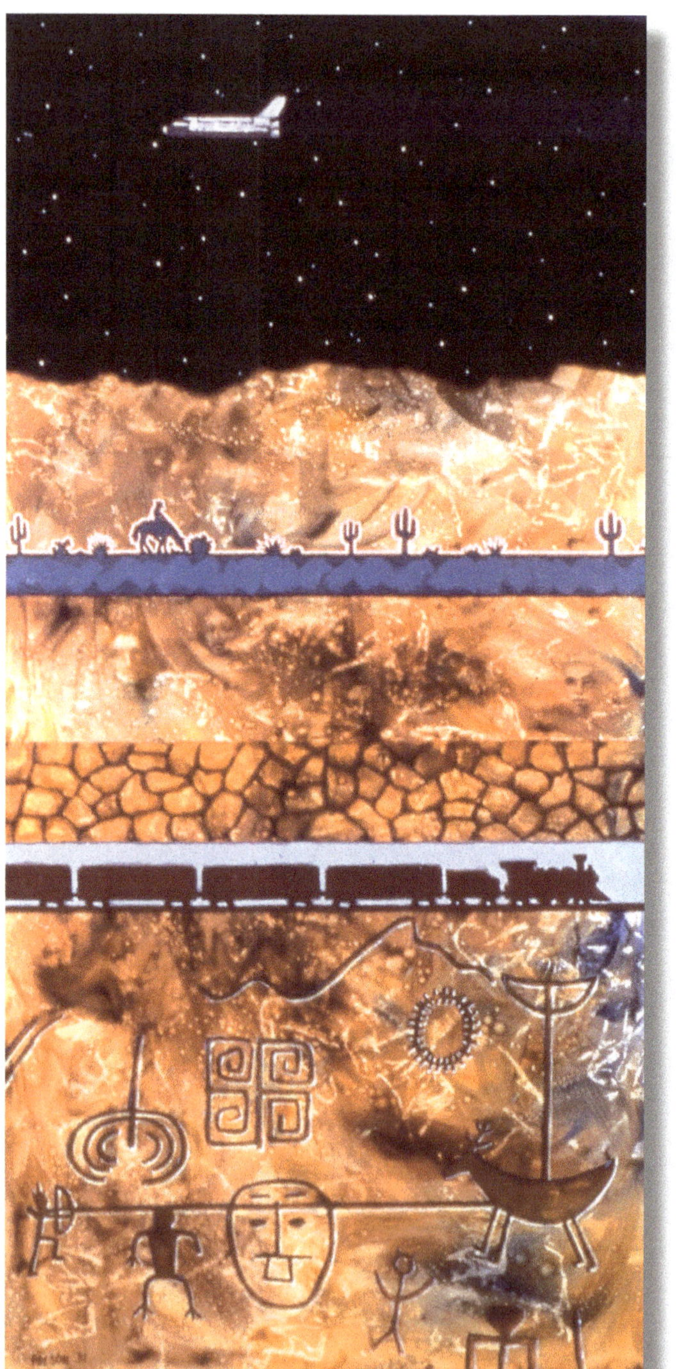

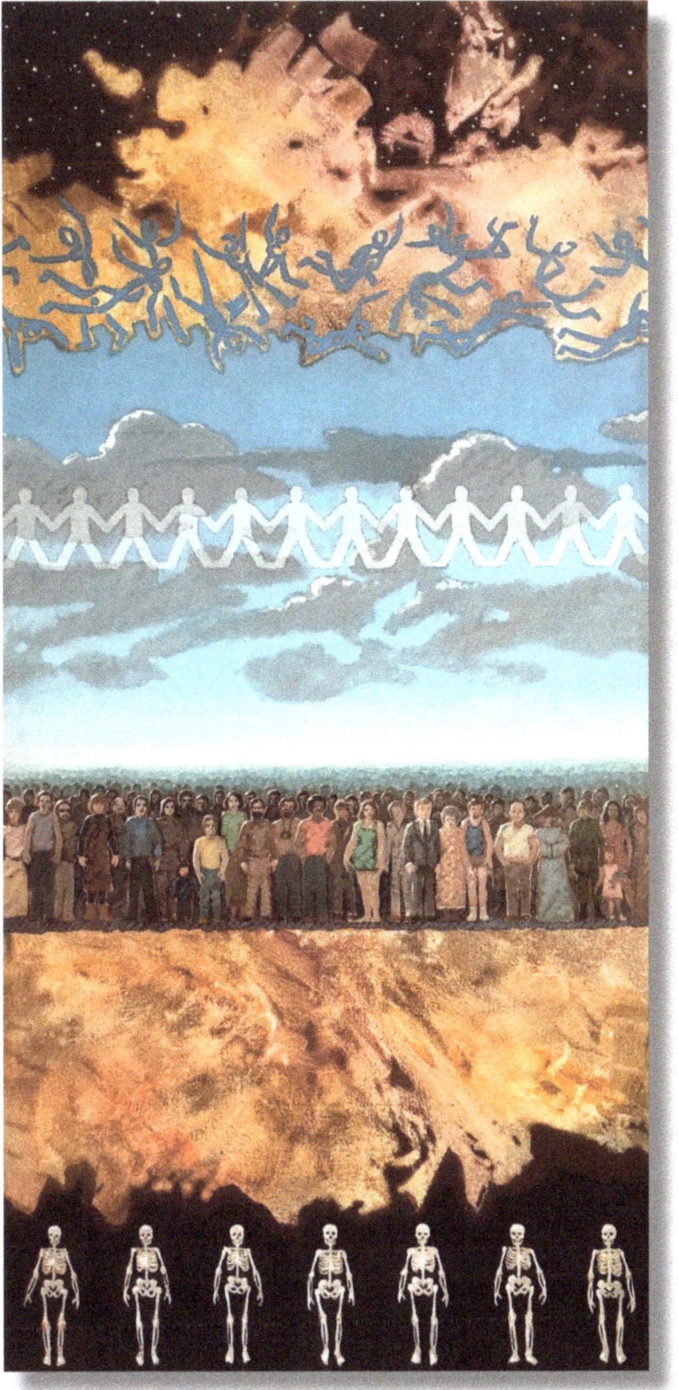

35

HG DAWE

IRELAND

The ferry arrived in Ireland shortly after the sun rose. It's raining when they disembark.

Daniel invited Paul to join him on his journey up the coast to Dublin. His friends are going with him; they are a fun group of guys.

The thing is, he had a more enticing invitation. HG lives in southwest Ireland in County Kerry, and he asked Paul to join him.

They went to the car deck, found his car, and headed west.

HG is by far the most interesting person Paul has met on this trip.

His wife recently had a stroke, and HG had taken her to a rehab facility in Germany. He didn't trust the Irish medical system—or the English, for that matter. He had made several trips between Ireland and Germany to check on her.

HG moved to Ireland from Germany. Even though he loves Ireland, he isn't that crazy about the Irish people. He's convinced that the Irish are primitive and don't have any interest in learning anything. They just want to frequent pubs and drink their lives away.

It's pouring rain during the drive to his home. HG is an architect and built his house when he and his wife moved there two years ago.

Raising sheep is his main focus now, and he is anxious to see the twin lambs that were born the day he took his wife to Germany. He is concerned about them, hoping they are okay. His Irish neighbors are not excited about HG moving here, so they often harass him and his wife, thus his concern for the lambs.

When they arrive, Paul is blown away by the beautiful countryside and how well the house fits the landscape. His home is impressive, with windows taking in his 360-degree view. Sheep roam his land, but he didn't see any lambs.

HG lives on a finger of land that protrudes into the Atlantic Ocean.

"It's the most beautiful place in Ireland," he said.

HG showed Paul around his house and where his bedroom is located. He placed his bag next to the bed and joined HG in the living room.

"I want to show you this," he said. "I had this book published seven years ago."

Paul took the book and sat down. It is filled with fantastic photography and is titled *TAIWAN: The Republic of China*, published in 1981.

This book of HGs is a professional publication. He didn't know what to say. "Wow" didn't do it justice. He just gazed at the book, page by page, scanning the descriptions of a trip HG had taken to Asia.

"You did the photography, too?" Paul asked.

"Yes, I did, and I also had the opportunity to work for the United Nations. They sent me all over the world. My camera was always with me."

He then led Paul to his study. HG is in the process of finishing a new book on Ireland. Paul had the privilege of seeing his layout and the photos he planned to use.

HG had a few errands to run, so he told Paul that he would be back soon.

"Please make yourself at home."

Paul went to his bedroom and unpacked the necessities. A nap sounded good, so he flopped on the bed and immediately fell asleep.

That evening, HG poured them both a glass of scotch. They sat in his living room and talked more about Ireland and the Irish people.

The talk about the Irish people fades away, and HG began talking about his fascination with the island. Paul thinks he expresses his view clearly and has a lot of knowledge.

HG changed the subject to the lambs; Paul hadn't seen any since he arrived.

"Where are your twin lambs?" he asked.

HG smiled and said, "They're at a neighbor's farm. I was going to get them this evening, but I thought I would wait until tomorrow. Maybe the weather will cooperate."

HG poured another round of scotch.

"Can I help you?"

"I don't need help, but if the weather is good, I want you to come. I'll give you a tour. If you think this place is nice, you should see the coast."

When he woke the next morning, HG had breakfast waiting. The interesting thing is how he presented it. A hardboiled egg is served in a tall ornate silver eggcup. He has the finest silverware and napkins, rolled and bound with a silver band. The rest of the meal would have been typical if not for its presentation—potatoes, toast, and bacon. They were in small portions on expensive china.

"It's better not to stuff yourself; it's healthier," said HG.

The weather did not cooperate this morning; in fact, it is worse. Rain is pouring down in sheets.

HG is clad in a raincoat and a water-resistant large-brimmed hat.

"Will you help me move my sheep to another pasture?"

"Sure!" Paul said. He put on a hooded poncho, and they walked out into the rain. HG opened a gate, and they herded the sheep through the opening. He secured the gate, and they returned to the house to dry off—Paul did anyway. HG left his coat and hat on.

"I'm going to meet my neighbor; I'll be back with my lambs in a few hours."

"I can help!" Paul said.

"I would prefer you to stay. If you come down with anything, it'll ruin your trip. You won't be able to see the sights in this weather anyway."

"Keep an eye out for those pesky Irish," he said. "Don't worry, they don't know you, so they won't bother you."

Raining or not, Paul pulled out his watercolor block, brushes, and paints. He found a dry place under a tree and started a painting of the property with sheep scattered over the landscape, munching on the lush grass.

When he was ready to head back to the house, he saw a figure walking towards him.

I've never seen a happier person than HG Dawe as he walked toward the house holding his two tiny baby lambs. He let Paul hold one.

Paul's no stranger to sheep being from Wyoming farm country. He had a ewe and a lamb in the 4-H Club; that was a long time ago. Lambs are beautiful and playful creatures.

Paul finished his painting that afternoon and early evening in the shelter of his room.

When Paul finally emerged from his room, HG is setting the table for dinner. That man could do anything, including cook. They had pork chops, potatoes, and peas. After the meal, they retired to the living room and continued our talk, sipping on an excellent brandy. They stayed up well past midnight as Paul continued to learn about this amazing person.

They began by talking about world affairs as they are now. HG is more knowledgeable about the States than Paul will ever be. He not only talked about what was going on in America but also their relationship with other countries.

The Arab countries are a significant issue for him. He couldn't understand why other countries ever bothered with them. If the rest of the world had left them alone, the Arab factions would have continually fought each other. The western world had given them the means and know-how to amass modern military arsenals, so the Arabs now focus on their hatred toward the west instead of each other.

HG had been in the military during World War II on the German side. He has a different view than the Americans do. He blames Churchill for the war.

"The British are a sneaky lot," he said.

According to him, Germany's beef was with the Soviet Union. And if Britain and the west had allowed them to take over Russia, we would never have had problems with them today.

He said the German attack on Poland was a defensive action.

Before this happened, Britain signed an agreement with Poland and pledged to come to their aid if attacked by Germany.

Germany first annexed Austria and Czechoslovakia without hostilities. They thought they could do the same with Poland. When France and Britain declared war on Germany, Germany was forced to protect its rear by taking France and keeping Britain at bay.

If the United States had stayed out of it, Germany's original plan to conquer Russia would have worked for everyone.

Paul failed to bring up the German atrocities and death camps. It's on his mind as they talked.

HG said, "There are three countries in the world that are unique and different from the rest—Germany, the United States, and Japan. Their innovations have led the world in most of the strides and progress of the human race."

The last point that he recalled from their conversations was when they talked about the world's history. Paul mentioned the Dark Ages.

HG looked at Paul and said, "What Dark Ages?"

His response surprised Paul since he thought it was common knowledge.

Paul felt naïve spouting out things he thought he knew but should know more about if he wanted to talk with authority.

"It's a period of time when past civilizations have faded away, and all knowledge was lost. Things fell into disrepair; the populace was unable to maintain their structured society. They resorted back to a more primitive existence. Prior knowledge was destroyed or lost."

"You know, like the period after the Roman Empire," Paul said.

"I have never heard of the Dark Ages," HG said. "The fall of Rome did not affect Germany, and we retained the knowledge we learned during that period—including what we had learned from Rome and other civilizations. Would you send me a book about that period when you get back to the States?"

Having pursued this, later on, Paul realized that HG was correct about the fall of Rome. The Romans could not defeat the Germanic people, and they were not dependent on them when Rome fell.

"Sure," Paul said. "I'll see what I can find."

It is still raining the following morning. Paul has concluded that he needs to move on and see the rest of Ireland. HG would be happier if he stayed. They enjoyed each other's company. Paul knew that HG is lonely without his wife, and his presence tempered the threat from his Irish neighbors.

Paul packed his bag. Leaving it on his bed, he walked outside his room. HG had placed a table with a red tablecloth under a window.

Displayed and perfectly organized is an astonishing gun collection, unlike one in the States where our gun people are proud of their AK-47 assault rifles, automatic pistols, and multi-ammo clips that showed their awesome mass-killing ability.

This collection is like the one you would see in a museum—single-shot miniature pistols with redwood handles. They had ornately carved barrels and grips. Some must have been dated to the seventeenth century or earlier. They are in perfect condition.

Again, HG made a beautifully prepared breakfast. Paul sat down and complimented him on his gun collection. He beamed with pride. After they ate, he went over to the display and described the guns' origins and ages.

HG's excitement over sharing things about his life made it more difficult to drop the news that he is leaving. He wants to show Paul the coast. I'm sure it's incredible—my loss.

When Paul told him he had to move on, he looked disappointed but immediately took his raincoat and hat off the hook. He understood.

Paul felt bad—like he is deserting him. He would have enjoyed staying here longer.

36

IRELAND

DUBLIN

The trains did not run in this isolated part of the country. Paul had to hitchhike to Tralee. HG drove him to a spot where he would get a quick ride. Before leaving, HG handed Paul his phone number and said to call if he needs help.

Paul thanked him for the excellent hospitality and conversation.

Within five minutes, an elderly local couple picked Paul up. Unfortunately, they dropped him off at an intersection a couple of miles away. He didn't see a car for two hours. It is raining hard, and he is getting a bit chilly.

Finally, off in the distance, Paul sees a cloud of smoke and hears the rattling of an old, out-of-tune vehicle with an occasional backfire. It's a '59 Chevy—yellow.

The car stops next to Paul and offers him a ride.

Paul felt like he stepped into a cartoon.

The driver looks like the perfect caricature of an Irishman. He has such a heavy Cork accent that Paul continually had to say, "What?"

He had orange-red hair with freckled skin, but his most noticeable feature was his bright red nose. The smell of tobacco fills the car.

The driver asked Paul where he is coming from, and Paul said he is traveling Europe from the States. He just stayed with a person he met on the ferry.

The driver asked if he was staying with that old German on the hill.

Paul says, "yes." (He is sure this is one of the Irishmen that is bugging HG. He hopes that HG will be okay.)

He took Paul to another spot where, again, he immediately gets a ride.

This time, Paul is picked up by a middle-aged English couple on vacation. They are really religious. You can tell by their constant referral to the Catholic Church and the iconic symbols inside their car.

"Would you like to join us on a trip around the Ring of Kerry?"

"Sure!" Paul said. He might as well see the sights and get out of his point A to point B mode.

It is a pleasant tour. When finished, they looked back at Paul and said, "We're planning to stop at Tralee for the night, but we can take you to Killarney first so you can catch the train."

"That won't be necessary," Paul said. "The train route starts at Tralee. I can leave from there."

They had a referral to a particular bed and breakfast. Paul found a room there as well, and the train station is only a ten-minute walk away.

That evening, he decides to do what the Irish do and hit the pubs. Paul will just do a smaller portion of that "drinking your life away" thing.

He visited three pubs. The people are friendly and eager to talk.

Paul is pleased to say the Irish people rolled out the red carpet. They treated him better than he had by any other country; the smiles are endless. This gaiety is especially true with a pub he entered. People packed the room, enjoying the Irish band that is playing. The group is fantastic, and the crowd is 100 percent involved.

His comprehension of their accent is a struggle at the start, but by the end of the evening, he perfectly understands them.

He caught the train early so that he could be in Dublin well before nightfall. It's an old rickety train to Mallow. At that point, he transferred to a modern smooth train for the remainder of the trip to Dublin.

When he arrived in Dublin, Paul isn't sure where he is going, so he checked his duffel bag at the station and took the small backpack that housed his essentials.

On the ferry to Ireland, Paul met several people. They had all sat together, drinking and talking. They decided to meet in a few days at the oldest pub in Dublin, The Brazen Head. Arriving much earlier than he thought, Paul searched for the place and quickly found it.

He hadn't eaten since early that morning, so he went to a different pub and had a meal. Digging into his bag, he found a map of Dublin that showed the bed and breakfasts in the area. The Sinclair House comes highly recommended, so he found his way there and obtained a room. It is a decent room for very little money.

Paul called Anellina and filled her in on his travels. She is upset and convinced he is ignoring her. He is just tired of checking in.

That evening, he went to The Brazen Head at the prearranged time. Only one person showed—Joanne from Philadelphia. They wandered around Dublin, talking and drinking beer. It turned out that her bed and breakfast is next to mine. They walked there together and said goodbye.

There is a fun group of people at breakfast the following morning. Everyone is animated and happy. It is a great way to start his day.

Paul decided to go home on his initially reserved flight to San Diego. That would be in two days. He was running low on money.

He thought about looking for a job. If he went back to France and visited Jean-Paul, he might be able to work at Jean Paul's business. Or there is Linda in Spain.

Paul can do anything. Maybe he can move to a small island in Greece—live a simple life, paint, and find a menial job to get food and a studio.

He quickly vetoed those ideas. He wants to get his van out of Anellina's garage. Seattle is beckoning him, and he is getting a bit tired of traveling. When Paul returns to San Diego, he can cash in his 401(k) plan from BTL and have enough money to move to Seattle.

Paul plans to spend the day at the Dublin Museums. There are two that he wants to see—The Irish Museum of Modern Art and The National Gallery of Ireland.

Today would be the end of his museum visits. Seeing the art around Europe has been fantastic. He had grown as a person, and his art knowledge had soared. This trip inspired him; there is a fire blazing in his heart, and he needs to do something with it.

The Irish Museum of Modern Art is a little disappointing. Paul is not familiar with the paintings he is viewing. There is a Russian exhibit upstairs, and he is curious about that. Paul had a little difficulty understanding Russian work. It seems dark and morbid but has its story to tell. Later, when Paul thought back on it, the diversity is refreshing. It makes him think. He thinks he likes it after all.

The odd thing about this visit is that he is the only one viewing the work. The museum is empty.

There is one guard who follows Paul from gallery to gallery. When Paul enters another room, the guard walks in and stands by the door with his arms folded and his headset on. When Paul moved to the next room, the guard moved with him and assumed the same position.

Paul reached the end of his viewing and started toward the exit; the guard stepped in front of him.

"So, what do you think about that Ronald Reagan?" he asked, as his serious demeanor dissolved into a smile.

And so the conversation started. The two of them talked about politics, art, and recent events for forty-five minutes.

He finally said, "Well, I'll leave you alone. I've taken enough of your time. Enjoy your stay."

Paul enjoyed that conversation, especially since his Irish accent accompanies it. His interest in what is happening in the States and knowledge of world events impressed Paul.

The first thing Paul did after leaving the museum is to check the ferry departure times to England. As often happens, the ferry workers were striking.

So, he bought an airline ticket to England.

Realizing he is hungry, he found a pub just down the street. He had soup and a sandwich and then headed for the National Gallery of Ireland.

The National Gallery has an excellent collection—a lot of paintings by Jean-Baptiste-Camille Corot. These are beautiful paintings! Another artist he is just getting to know.

Paul hopped on a green double-decker bus to get back to the train station and retrieve his duffel bag, then headed back to the bed and breakfast. He went out for dinner and hit the sack early. The next day, he will be flying to England.

37

ANELLINA

HOME—SAN DIEGO

It's a quick flight to London Luton Airport. When Paul left the airport, he caught a bus to the train station. The train connects with the Underground, and the Underground took him to Heathrow Airport where he deposited his duffel bag and backpack in a storage locker.

A friend of Doug's, Karen Koppelman, had given him the phone number of her cousin in London and wanted him to contact her if he had time.

"Might as well," Paul thought.

Paul called the number, and Karen's cousin Gale Churney answered the phone. She is happy to hear from him, saying that Karen contacted her and said he might call. Her couch is available if he wants to spend the night.

Hopping back on the Underground, it took over an hour to get to her house on the other side of London.

Gale met him at the door. She is going to a concert, and her roommate Anita had invited a friend over for dinner. That fell through, so Paul took Anita out for dinner. They had a pleasant chat, and it made for an enjoyable evening.

The next morning, Anita woke Paul up and offered to make him tea before she left for work.

"No, thanks. How about an aspirin?" Paul had a headache from whatever he drank the night before.

Leaving a thank you note for Gale, he took the long trip back to Heathrow, grabbed his bags, and headed to his gate. Paul has never been searched so much while going through security—three times.

It is a long flight to LAX. He had a three-hour layover, then flew to San Diego.

* ❋ *

Anellina picked Paul up from the San Diego Airport. They talked a bit about his travels and flight as they drove to her house in La Mesa. It felt good to be back home. She said he was welcome to stay with her until he decided what to do.

The first thought he had was to remove his van from her garage. Anellina must have felt relieved to have her unwanted guest out of there. She didn't say that, but Paul would have felt that way if he had been her. Three months can be a long time.

Paul backed the van out on his mostly flat tires and used a hand pump to inflate them a bit more—enough to make it to a local gas station. Then he drove back to Anellina's house.

"I'm dead tired, Anellina. Is it okay if I take a nap?"

"Of course, you can," she said, smiling. "Want to go out for dinner this evening?"

"Oh, yeah! Sushi?"

Doug met Anellina and Paul at Yakitori II. He had been eating there for fifteen years. He introduced many friends to this fantastic restaurant, and it had been a hangout for all of them since. Yakitori II is the place where it all started.

The chefs and half the clientele knew him. They gave him a great welcome back. Even the owner came out to talk.

They are excited that he had visited Linda in Granada, and he filled them in on some of the high points. Linda had worked at Yakitori II for at least three years. They had great times and great sushi, and the chefs were hilarious.

Even though Paul knows what his plans are, he feels unsettled—not grounded. Doug is living in his studio, and that is good. Paul has the lease, and Doug is willing to take it over.

Anellina was particularly gracious for letting Paul stay there. She still has hopes of a potential relationship. She is ready to settle down with him, but maybe she just needs somebody. Anellina and Paul haven't known each other for that long, and they talked about their plans before he left.

Paul had bad insomnia—probably due to jet lag. In the middle of the night, he asked Anellina if he could go to her living room and watch TV—something Paul had been deprived of, not just in the last three months, but because he had been living in studios with no TV for fifteen years. He is amazed by the technological advancement of the information and entertainment that came from this box.

His anxiety is building up. He is preparing his mind to go on the adventure he has looked forward to for fifteen years.

Paul visited BTL. He needed to cash in his 401(k) plan, but that turned out to be a sideshow compared to the delight he felt when he walked around to the different departments to see all the people he used to work with around. Paul is greeted with warm smiles and hugs.

The only negative part is when he poked his nose in Mark's office to say "hi."

"I'm not hiring you back," he said.

You just can't be nice to some people.

His biggest problem is how to take his belongings to Seattle. The personal items are few, but he has many paintings—way too many to fit in his van.

But as fate would have it (probably due to that guardian angel that has been paving the way for him his whole life), there is a couple in the process of moving to San Diego from Seattle; they are friends of Doug. They already moved some of their belongings and planned to take an empty truck back to Seattle to pick up the rest of their stuff.

They offered to take the rest of his paintings to Seattle, and they had family who will store them until he arrived. The girl's mother is on the Seattle Arts Commission, and since Paul would be a new artist to Seattle, she is interested in seeing his work.

After a week, Anellina decided that he should move out. Paul kind of wanted to also.

Doug's friends brought their truck over, and they loaded it with paintings. They planned to leave for Seattle the next morning.

He left a lot behind—mostly sculpture. Paul had sculpted a life-size nude sitting on a barstool that turned out nice. He also had castings of huge faces he couldn't take.

I wonder what happened to that stuff.

———— * ✳ * ————

The *I Ching* has always interested Paul since he read Carl Jung's volume set. It is one of the world's oldest books. Also called the book of changes, it works on the concept of cause and effect and the symbols of change. A person's life follows these chance happenings in a world that is continually changing. It is surprisingly accurate. The book speaks to you in symbols, like dreams. Modern books transcribe these symbols so that western civilization can understand them. They can be personal or universal. It works on the premise that the world and our lives are constantly changing and interacting. The randomness of throwing sticks or coins creates a hexagram, then, you refer to the book to decipher what it is telling you about the changes yet to come. It is almost impossible to throw the same hexagram twice in a row due to the many possible combinations.

During his last year in San Diego, Paul threw the coins three different times. He came up with the same hexagram three times in a row. Maybe it's answering with the same hexagram because it's true. There must be something to this.

"Advantage will be found in the northwest" is the answer to the direction Paul should go. Couple that with his trips to the Seattle area over the last several years. Every time he made that trip, it felt like he was going home. He fit in perfectly. This move is meant to be.

The way things unfolded for him since his arrival in Seattle confirmed all of this.

The Northwest is his home.

38

SEATTLE

Nothing is holding Paul in San Diego now.

He spent the next week meeting with friends and saying goodbye over a meal or in a bar, discussing Seattle and the good times they had in San Diego.

Paul woke up early on the first of June and headed north. "Seattle, here I come!"

Paul followed Highway One and camped where he could. This trip is the fifth time he has traveled to Seattle, so he has his favorite spots.

His friend Mark Zingarelli is expecting him. He allowed Paul to stay until he found a place to live.

Mark introduced him to northwest ales. There are many local breweries, and they each have a unique taste.

He also introduced Paul to Kristie. She is too good for him— not her determination but his. They spent fun times together until she knew he had his feet firmly planted on the ground and settled in.

Paul's first act is to find a figure drawing workshop. He misses drawing from a model, and he found an art school, just east of downtown at the south end of Seattle by Pioneer Square. The workshops are three hours long, as is the usual. Paul has always found it easy to meet people at figure-drawing workshops. He's in his element.

There is one thing he wants to do before he dives back into his art.

At BTL, he designed a bald eagle for a client. Paul is anxious to see it as an inflatable. Before it went to production, some salesmen and the owners had nixed it. They said his design couldn't work, and it would cost too much.

It is true that the client had limited funds.

A year earlier, BTL had made an inflatable pigeon for a client. BTL's massive creative brainpower decided to use the pigeon patterns and paint it to look like an eagle.

The finished inflatable looked like a pigeon wearing an eagle costume. Paul is embarrassed to say he works there.

When he arrives in Seattle, he wants to make a twenty-five-foot-tall bald eagle.

To do this, he calls around Seattle to find shops that deal with fabrics he is familiar with and use heavy-duty industrial sewing machines. Paul contacts fabricators of awnings and banners, even businesses that make backpacks. He settled on the ideal place—a shop that makes parachutes. They also repair and fold them for use. Their hangar is at Boeing Field.

The owners, Bill and Alice, are excited about his idea. Paul told them he would teach them how to make an inflatable shape, step by step if, in return, he could make himself a huge inflatable bald eagle. They agreed.

Bill and Alice are amazing people; they are open to new and exciting projects. They are also probably the most eccentric people he has ever known.

It is at this parachute shop that he met a great friend. That friendship is alive to this day.

Rip did professional technical drawings. He did this before the computer-aided design is standard.

Rip also loves playing bass guitar. Paul brought his drum set from San Diego. They set it up in an empty hangar and jammed practically every night.

Fabricating the eagle is time-consuming, but it goes well. It is nice to be in total control and not have idiots sabotage its potential. The eagle that could not be done was a huge success. In the next eight years, Paul had numerous front-page photos and articles about it in local newspapers and publications.

During the time Paul was fabricating the eagle, he found a small place to live on Alki Point in West Seattle. This little house is temporary until he can find a studio. It is a beautiful area with beaches to the south and the north. From there, you can see Puget Sound, the ships, the ferries, and the Olympic Mountains.

Paul picked up his paintings that Doug's friend moved to Seattle. He met her mother who works for the Seattle Arts Commission. She liked Paul's work and had the paintings spread out for viewing in her living room when he arrived. She told Paul to organize some slides and send them to her. She would set up a show for him at the Smith Tower.

The Commission has a show once a month and invites the major gallery owners; he was sure to be connected to galleries who would show his work.

How lucky can he get, having these coincidences that offer him these opportunities? Something is bothering him about this, however. Moving to the Northwest, Paul wants to do all new work and go in another direction with his painting. He put the presentation of his old artwork on the back burner. When he completes his next series, he will send in slides.

It is time to get serious about a job. Paul always goes for what he wants, and he found that two custom picture frame shops are more professional than the others in Seattle. One is Artech. He stopped by and applied. They seem a little aloof as if to say, "Yeah, everyone wants to be a picture framer." Paul filled out an application.

The other one is Artform. It's in Pioneer Square, in the back of the best quality gallery in the city—Davidson Gallery.

Artform only has two people working there. One is the owner, Penny Auge, and the other is Kat, fitter, and mat-cutter extraordinaire. It didn't look like they needed anyone.

Artech is much larger, with more employees. They are the ones that should be hiring since they should have a more fluid turnover rate.

Paul talked to the owner of Artform. Penny is an open person and knows her picture framing. He filled her in on his experiences, and she hired Paul on the spot. She wanted him to come in the next day.

When he arrived for work, he entered through a door in the alley; Pioneer Square had fantastic alleys, like movie sets.

Kat is there and working; Penny usually comes in later.

She explains their system. There are three copies to each order sheet, showing the client's name, size, type of the frame, and mat size. It shows the color of the mat and the details of the frame. It has the due date and a description of the artwork—all the information needed to do the job.

Looking at the artwork, Paul realized that this is the place he wants to work. They are framing fantastic art and preparing them for shows. It's not "decorator" framing; It's museum framing—acid-free—with a white or off-white rag and acid-free mats. Every aspect is museum-quality, down to the tape and foam backing.

Kat is fast and does quality work. She cuts the mats and fits the pieces at lightning speed. She did give him "a go" on cutting a few mats to see how he did. Paul has his own mat cutter and is proud of his corners—no overcuts.

He felt it is essential to learn their techniques: the backing and ratio of the placement of the screw eyes, and the proportion of the mats, making the bottom a quarter or a half-inch wider. Visually, it looks the same as the other sides.

Before Paul arrived, Kat sanded, cut, and joined the frames. She developed her own acrylic pearlescent finishes.

That will now be Paul's primary responsibility in the shop; sand the molding, miter the corners, and join the frames. Kat would do the finishing.

Penny wants a line of frames that involve wood stains or oils to bring out the grain and character of the wood; that is my job. Paul had learned this type of framing when he worked for David at the

Reutter Gallery in San Diego and at the Fine Art Store. Paul is a perfect fit at Artform.

Paul had to prove himself, though. Penny is a tough cookie, and the tiniest mistake sends her ranting and raging for hours.

Even though Paul has his forte, they depend on him to do fitting and mat cutting along with Kat when needed, which it often is. Kat can also take a vacation now and then. Penny hated to let her go. Paul isn't quite as good, but he can handle it, and Penny feels a little better that her duties are covered when Kat is gone.

Another "blow his mind moment" is when he went downstairs to see the woodworking and finishing rooms. It's the Seattle underground. There are brick hallways and rooms that look like jail cells. He spent much of his time in this dungeon and loves every minute of it, chopping and staining frames.

When Paul goes upstairs, he is surrounded by the excellent artwork they are framing, and as mentioned before, they are working in the backroom of a top-notch gallery; they always show excellent work.

Artform frames work for a wide variety of artists in the area. They are the chosen framer for all the top photographers. They also frame the original sketches of Dale Chihuly. These are drawings and painted concepts and designs for the work he is doing. Chihuly sometimes exchanges his glass art for framing.

Another plus is getting to know the artists, collectors, and gallery owners. When these people show up, the environment brings out the best in people. Penny is good at conversation; even Kat and Paul get involved.

39

PIONEER SQUARE

One day as Kat and Paul are toiling away, Kat asked him if he wanted to go to a party the following Saturday.

"Sure!" he said. (Oh, boy. A party!)

"Here's the address. It starts at seven. You don't have to be on time."

That Saturday, Paul attended the party—not on time.

The house is packed with friendly people.

Kat saw Paul and introduced him to the hostess. She is a beautiful woman, and their short conversation seemed to indicate she is a brilliant woman. After a brief chat, they parted, and he continued to meet and talk to other partiers. Paul touched bases with Kat now and then. She seems to disappear often. That isn't too hard to figure out. She's less than five feet in height.

The following Monday at work, they chatted about the party and the interesting people who attended.

"So, your friend who hosted the party is a beautiful and smart woman."

"Don't even think about it," Kat said, as she wired and backed a frame job at record speed.

"No, I understand. She's beyond me," Paul said in defense.

"She has her own agenda."

"And what might that be?"

"She plans to find a filthy rich man, marry him, get pregnant, divorce him, acquire a new house, and collect thousands of dollars a month for eighteen years. She has always wanted to raise a child, but not with a man."

And this is how it unfolded; narration by Kat:

Three months after the party: guess who is dating a filthy rich man?

Six months after the party: guess who just married her filthy rich boyfriend?

One year after the party: guess who's pregnant?

One year six months after the party: guess who got a divorce?

Two years after the party: guess who has a brand new house? Oh, she's also getting an undisclosed amount of money, per month, for the next eighteen years.

Wow! That actually happened!

The final required element fell firmly into place. Paul found the ideal studio.

Less than half a block away from Artform and kitty-corner to Occidental Square is an old shoe factory. Artist studios are for rent on the fifth floor. Paul rented one in the northwest corner that looks out over Occidental Square, Puget Sound, and the Seattle skyline. It is less than fifty yards from where he works.

The floor also has a shared kitchen, shower, and toilet.

Building stretcher bars and stretching canvases are the first items on his list. He prepared twelve large canvases and immediately dove into painting.

There is a room in the corner with the same view Paul has; actually, it's better. It has a small stage. Perfect for a figure drawing class. Within two weeks of moving in, he organized a weekly workshop and has access to the same models used at the art schools and universities in the area. The models enjoy the three-hour sessions and the environment. They love coming down to Pioneer Square to model, and they feel comfortable with the group.

One final thing had to happen. Paul needs to find his "own" favorite sushi bar And he found it in the Asian district.

Maneki is four blocks to the east of Paul's studio. Kozo Nakayama is the chef. He introduced this place to many friends, as he had done with Yakitori II in San Diego. It is the final piece to what Paul perceives as a happy life.

Several years earlier, the fifth-floor artists transformed the center of the once open space into a gallery. They changed shows every month and opened up the floor for the monthly art walks.

Pioneer Square is ripe with art lovers during the art walks. Crowds of people climbed the five flights to see what is there.

Paul hung out with one of his studio partners, Michael Andeel. Mike is an excellent photographer, and he built a darkroom in his studio. Like Paul, Michael also lives in his studio and is devoted to his art just as much.

Mike produces unique black and white photos.

One of his things is to follow the Seattle music scene. His photos are from the most unexpected angles you could imagine. He depicts the musicians and the crowds in a professional way. Paul saw his work in local publications, but he deserved much more attention than he is getting.

They found a bar that is just a walk down the alley. It's a Mexican restaurant and bar. Taco Tuesday provides them with a warm gathering of other artists. It fits their starving-artist income—two bucks for a beer and all the tacos you can eat. Paul is doing better than most because of his job at Artform.

Paul loves to paint. It's nice having the stretched and sized canvases ready to go. He claims never to have painter's block. More ideas are bouncing around in his brain than he can keep up with.

After over twenty years of drawing from a model, he realizes that it has become an addiction—a good addiction. Sketching things from a trained eye is rewarding. It's an eye-to-brain and out-the-hand expression, spontaneous. You can train the artist's eye to be like another limb of your body.

Unfortunately, the artists on their floor are mostly "wannabes." They just want to have a studio and still live in the suburbs. It's justifiable to escape the burbs to get inside their heads by creating things.

Until recently, things had not always been this way. From what he heard, there had been a group of artists in the studio with different skills; these had been people with performance art skills and a love for the visual arts.

They had a good thing going for years. Unfortunately, the person holding the lease had some medical issues and had to hand the lease down. No one wanted it. The group that was there seemed to be dissipating and wanting to move to their next stage in life.

An artist who had just moved in said, "I'll take it!"

That turned out to be a big mistake. It had been a great co-op, splitting all costs among the artists living on the floor until it fell into the hands of Melanie, a latent capitalist. She is thinking more about the profits she can make than providing spaces for artists.

There was a time when this space had a unique energy, inundating the floor with creativity and production.

Melanie's art leaned heavily toward the satanic side. The one-piece Paul remembered was a creepy devil doll she placed on her windowsill.

Artists in the area are always looking for venues to show their work. If not at galleries, artists discovered different establishments who are willing to display their creations.

That's a good thing. These venues become places where artists can show their work in public, and the owners are more than happy to have their walls decorated. They are great supporters of the arts. It helped build the character of the crowd and the establishment.

Paul found his space to show his paintings in the Pioneer Square Saloon. They had high walls—the perfect place to display his strata series.

Evenings brought a creative crowd. The bartenders are ideal for maintaining the mood and carefree attitudes. It is a comfortable place for artists to convene and have profound conversations.

———— ❋ ————

Paul plans to focus on two different painting styles he has pursued in the past and plans to continue.

One is his pipe series—somewhat surrealistic—that involves figurative and landscape artwork. Working on a figure, he would replace an arm with a pipe, for example. Or if he painted a forest—instead of tree trunks, he uses pipes.

His purpose in doing this is purely symbolic. The rest of the work has more recognizable images.

To start a painting, Paul prepared a washy base and applied it to the surface. He textured it with splatters, towels, and brushstrokes—all in washes. This technique is an extension of how he painted in San Diego and allows unintended shapes to come through to be part of the dynamics of the painting.

The other direction is his strata paintings. Paul has always loved looking at cross-sections of the Earth in science books. It occurred to him that instead of being geographically accurate, he can make symbolic images depicting the vast unknown mysteries from the depth of the Earth to the universe above. There is no limit to what he can do.

Paul can compare these accidental shapes to the awareness of a human and the depths of his mind, the mysteries, and the symbolic nature of human existence.

He stretched canvases that are tall and thin. The first ones he painted are seventy-six inches tall and thirty-six inches wide. He later reduced the size to fifty-three inches high and twenty-five inches wide—the same proportions. He even painted a series of smaller ones fifteen inches high with water base paints.

All in all, Paul did about sixty strata paintings—probably more.

Paul also has fun combining the strata paintings with the pipes.

The techniques he describes are dependent on continual studies in landscapes and figure drawing. The more strength he has in these two areas, the better his "out of head" paintings are.

40

NEW ORLEANS

One day in the early afternoon, Paul is focused on his work when the phone rings. They only have one phone located in the shared kitchen.

Mike answered it. "Paul, it's for you!" he yelled.

A lady on the phone from a software company wants to see his work. They need to have a mural painted. Another artist had recommended him.

The next day, a couple of sharp women in business suits came to visit him. They looked around with smiles on their faces. They offer Paul the job right away.

The bummer is that he can't paint what he wants. Paul thrives on painting what he wants to paint, but these ladies already have an agenda. They want a large, three-panel mural, with a total size of twelve feet by six feet.

They want it to look like a Rousseau—a jungle scene with animals. Other than that, he can paint what he wants. It didn't need to be a copy—just a jungle.

They flew Paul to New Orleans. Megan, the woman he is working with, sat next to Paul on the plane. She is pleasant to talk with and is also drop-dead gorgeous. She explained how things would work. They would be in New Orleans for four nights. Paul would paint the panels during a trade show. They thought it would attract people.

At the end of the trade show, they would give the painting to whoever drew the lucky number.

When they arrived at the hotel, Megan handed Paul the key to his room. It turned out she had a room next to his.

That evening, the company reserved a cruise boat for a private party and a trip up the Mississippi. They served fantastic food and have an open bar.

When they returned to the hotel, she said, 'Well, I guess I'll take a bottle of wine up to my room and watch TV."

A man from the company invited Paul to join him and another guy. They were going to Bourbon Street. He accepted the offer, and they had a great time; not returning to the hotel until two in the morning.

It is fun hanging out on Bourbon Street, listening to great music, and eating good food.

The trade show went as planned, and Paul enjoyed painting on stage.

Paul feels terrible about Megan. He just couldn't flip the switch. Every evening she told him she was planning on staying in her room, and every evening, Paul went to Bourbon Street. If he could imagine the best possible scenario for a tryst with a beautiful woman—a four-day fling—this would be it.

Sometimes, Paul hates himself. As he said earlier, it's hard for him to get involved this way. Why didn't she just say, "I'm taking a bottle of wine to my room. Come join me."?

Ideally, it would have been perfect to have Megan join us on Bourbon Street. We could have easily ended up in the same room afterward. Everyone knew her. She couldn't let on that she was luring him to her room.

On the flight home, Megan again sat next to Paul. She is pissed and wouldn't talk to him.

———— * ✹ * ————

Working at Artform became routine but not lacking in the flow of excellent art. That translated into sparking his creative juices.

Penny and her lady friend met Paul at Maneki once. That evolved into more sushi get-togethers. They reserved a private room with pillows and a rectangular well under the foot high table—in case you are uncomfortable sitting cross-legged.

They left their shoes at the door—which is a sliding screen, covered in ornate Japanese art. They had many tasty feasts in this place. The food is fantastic. Their private waitress made sure that their sake stayed full, removed the trays when they finished and presented more tasty delights. They are sated to the point of not just being satisfied, but uncomfortably full.

Back at the frame shop, an international event hit the head-lines—they tore down The Berlin wall.

Shortly after that news, Artform received fifteen large paintings from the fading Soviet Union. They are oil paintings that are not stretched but rolled and put in tubes. When Paul unrolls them, he sees that there is a lot of work to be done. None of the paintings are square, and not by just a little—some stick out six inches beyond a rectangular border. The sizes ranged from eight feet by five feet down to three feet by four feet.

Paul will need to stretch them square and fit them into a floater frame. This type of frame has a thin inset frame that he places below the surface of the painting. It is usually black. Another frame is placed around that one. The result is the appearance of a painting floating inside the frame. You can see the edge of the stretched canvas.

Before placing the work inside the frame, the extra canvas carefully folds around the stretcher bars. Paul cannot cut it off; that is a no-no. He also slightly rounded the stretchers so that no sharp corners would crack the gesso or whatever the artist had used as a primer. The idea is that the artist could take them off the stretcher bars and return them to their original condition.

This Russian artist painted with loose brushstrokes that are bold and apparent.

The colors are dark, and the subject matter depressing—actually morbid.

———— * ✳ * ————

Rip contacted Paul and invited him to a party at the Ballard Locks. Rip's housemate is Dennis, a good friend of his. Dennis knows some women from the Denver area who have a fantastic house built on stilts overhanging the canal that leads to the locks in Ballard.

Their house has lots of windows and a big deck. They drank, munched on hors d'oeuvres, and watched the boats cruise in and out of the locks. You can hear the waves lapping underneath, especially when a wake from a passing boat hits the pylons and the shore.

There is one animated woman Paul ended up talking to for most of the evening. She said they had to move but were enjoying the house while they could.

Her name is Martha, and she's from Pueblo, Colorado. They had a fantastic conversation covering politics, the arts, and just general bullshit. She is intelligent and a good speaker—very entertaining.

Martha works at the Seattle Trade Center and loves her job. The Seattle Trade Center will eventually be the World Trade Center Seattle.

Paul told her that he is in the arts and works at a frame shop in Pioneer Square. His living situation is just what he's been looking for—a work studio where he can live and paint in Pioneer Square.

Speaking of Pioneer Square, a new nightclub opened underneath the viaduct, across the street from the docks—The OK Hotel.

Paul is already familiar with this place. It had been an actual old hotel that artists used for installations. The hotel itself is not fit for occupancy. It didn't meet the city's building codes.

Each artist is assigned a room. They have free rein to use it for an art installation. It became an art show where one could wander down the halls and enter each room. Each artist had his or her little cubicle of self-expression. One room had mouse traps spaced a couple of inches from each other, covering the walls and cciling—all of them cocked and ready to snap. There is incredible diversity in each room.

The building is now one of the most unusual nightclubs in the city. It has a massive bar with a greasy spoon cafe, but the highlight is the two separate stages in two different rooms. The best and the most avant-garde musicians and bands played here, including Nirvana, Flop, and Soundgarden.

There is one fantastic and genuinely unique band that Paul has heard before "The Black Cat Orchestra." They have played at several art openings. He knows some of the members. Basically, it's a neo-Jewish band that has that modern touch—a little jazz, a little rock. There are string instruments, a horn section, drums, bass guitar, keyboards—he can't remember them all, but he does remember their sound. When you start listening, you can't stop.

David Byrne, founder and lead singer/songwriter for the band 'Talking Heads," lives in the area, and he jogs around the streets. He dropped into the OK and walked into the room where "The Black Cat Orchestra" is playing.

They played their music on his next CD.

41

MARTHA

When Paul returned to his studio, there are five flights of stairs to reach their floor, and each story has approximately twelve-foot ceilings—maybe fourteen feet. He ran up the stairs—all the way—every time. That's one of the ways he stays in shape.

Panting heavily, he unlocked the door at the top of the stairs and immediately ran into Melanie—the infamous holder of the lease—as she leaves to go to her house in the suburbs.

"I found a renter for the studio next to yours," she said.

That is one of the signs of the emerging dictatorship. No one on the floor has a choice of whom they would be living around.

Thinking, "I probably should introduce myself to the new tenant or artist," Paul walked to the door and knocked.

This studio is particularly nice. It is large, and all the windows face north. The room has a full view of the Seattle skyline. It is one of two studios with a door. The rest of the studios are open to anyone roaming around the space.

The door opens.

There stood Martha, the woman Paul met at the party in Ballard a week ago.

"Oh!" She smiled. "Fancy meeting you here. Want to go out for a drink?"

"Uh, okay?"

"Do you know a good place? I'm a bit hungry, too."

"Sure," Paul said as he recovered from his surprise.

"I saw your studio, you do nice work," she said, shutting the door behind her.

They both walked down the stairs and around the corner to FX McRory's.

They each ordered a beer; this is beer heaven. Local brews on tap ran the length of the bar—over forty feet long.

"Do you like clams or oysters?" Paul asked.

"I love both."

Paul ordered Oysters Rockefeller and a large bowl of clams to share.

"I'm sorry to surprise you like that. I was thinking about what you said about your studio, and thought I would see if there are more available."

Their conversation continued from where it left off at the Ballard party. Paul enjoys intelligent conversation. He takes life seriously but feels it's important to deal with the humor in it; even sarcasm adds the ingredients to take a serious thing lightly, to him anyway. He understands that it annoys some people. Martha is good at dealing with it and throwing it back.

Martha took out a card and paid the bill.

"Tomorrow is Friday. Want to go out for coffee before work?"

"Sounds good," Paul said. "I know just the place."

They returned to FX McRory's on occasion, but instead of going into the main restaurant, they preferred the small oyster bar just outside the door. It is more intimate, and it is fun chatting with the chef as we sampled the menu.

It is Friday morning. Martha and Paul strolled through the beauty of Occidental Square and stopped at the Grand Central Bakery. He had his everyday breakfast consisting of drip coffee and one of the best cinnamon rolls he has ever had. Martha had a latte and a cinnamon roll.

"Oh, man, these are good," she said.

The interior of the Grand Central is enormous and old in its construction, fitting well with the Pioneer Square motif. There are a few businesses on the outer edges of the open space. One of them is the bakery.

After their morning treat, Martha followed the waterfront to the Seattle Trade Center, and Paul walked a block to Artform.

Having the key, he entered the back door, filled a bucket with water, and washed the filth from the steps that were left by whatever bum had used it the night before.

No one had arrived yet; Paul is there early as usual. His chop list to cut the frame molding is already organized from the day before and waiting downstairs. He replaced the blade on the circular chop saw and began his workday.

Martha is to become an everyday item, even on his walks to Maneki for sushi. Paul isn't sure if she was into sushi when he first met her, but she is now.

That evening, he was in his studio working when Martha walked in. She sat down and watched while he finished the detail on a canvas.

During their conversation the day before, Paul had told her about the OK Hotel. Since it is Friday night, she wants to check it out.

As they walk the two blocks to the OK, they almost passed Elliot Bay Books. Martha is already familiar with the place; most people in the area are.

Not being in a hurry, they independently caroused the aisles of books; the atmosphere is excellent. As Paul soon found out, Martha is an avid reader. They met downstairs and had a light meal and another coffee.

When they walked into the OK, it was still early in the evening.

A woman in leather—decked out with tattoos, a nose ring, and net leggings—played her guitar and sang. It's a solo act. Oh, yeah, you couldn't miss the turquoise hair either. She is good.

Arnis Sarma is sitting at the bar drinking whiskey. He is one of the creative photographers who live in the area. Originally, he came from some Slavic country. Paul introduced him to Martha, and they hit it off pretty well.

Martha's claim to fame is her photography and writing skills. It is nice to know that Melanie had picked someone with talent to rent the studio. You couldn't say that about a few of the others she had allowed in.

They walked into the back room where the larger bands played and watched as a group carried in their amps, guitars, and the usual performance items used to enhance their wild presentation.

It is way too early for them to play, so they returned to the bar, sat with Arnie, and ordered a drink—then another one, followed by more.

Paul knows many artists who frequent the place, and they bounced their conversation and jokes off each other as the night wore on.

The band in the back room began playing, and most of the crowd filed in to watch.

At about one in the morning, Martha and Paul staggered back to their studios. They ended up spending the night together.

Things are coming together in the art scene. The paintings he is working on grew in numbers. It's time Paul set a date for a one-person show in the studio gallery. He talked to Melanie and the rest of the renters; everyone is okay with it.

Eagle Eye Gallery on Capitol Hill also wants to show Paul's work. They scheduled a one-person show for him for the following year. It's great having something to work toward.

It's a plus that he has venues to show his work; however, his drive to paint is not affected by whether he shows or not. Being in the studio working is what he really enjoys. Exhibiting his work is like undressing in front of the world. The paintings spewed out of his thoughts and emotions without orderly intent. He feels that there is no need to have a consistent show of work that sells. His work is a visual diary of his life and experiences, and the world inside his head needs an outlet. He creates this work with symbolism and spontaneity.

Paul hung his show in the studio gallery in time for the monthly Pioneer Square art walk. More people are willing to take that five-story hike to their floor than he expected; it added to the excitement of the evening.

He had a great response, but no sales. He only showed large works, and the viewers are mostly artists themselves.

There's a lot of interest in renting his inflatable eagle, and the extra income is nice. People want it mostly for events and promotions.

Sometimes, he inflated it in unusual locations, not for money, but for exposure. Once people saw it, they were amazed at its realism.

An excellent example of this is the Fourth of July.

The Seattle Trade Center—Martha's workplace—is located on the waterfront.

One day, when meeting Martha for lunch, they walked down to Elliot Bay.

He looked back at the trade center and pointed at the roof.

"See that platform on top of the trade center?" The platform itself must have been thirty feet high and was once used to support a water tank that was no longer needed.

"Yes," she said.

"I want to put the eagle on it for the Fourth of July."

"Let's do it!" Martha exclaimed. "I'll just contact the powers that be and let them know. I'm sure it will be OK."

It's more than OK. Early on July 4th, 1990, they hauled the eagle to the top of the platform and inflated it. You can see it for miles.

The trade center people thanked Martha for the publicity.

There is one problem. There's a seagull nest on the roof, and mommy seagull kept dive-bombing the eagle, trying to scare it away. It took a while to wash the bird poop off after we took it down.

Martha enjoyed getting out of town. She loves camping and hiking, so Paul took her to his favorite spot—Shi Shi Beach.

They drove across the top of the Olympic Peninsula, passed the beautiful Lake Crescent, and continued to Lake Ozette.

They set up camp on the north edge of the lake for the night and spent the weekend walking the trails to Cape Alava and Sand

Point, then the highlight—Shi Shi Beach. They planned to stay there for the night. Martha is amazed. Even though Paul has been there twice before, he continued to be awed—so peaceful!

Martha and Paul trekked around the Northwest a lot. Paul painted on many of these trips but not in oil. His work during this time is in a variety of water-based paints on either rag board or watercolor paper.

Once, they went to the tiny town of Gold Bar in the Cascade Mountains northeast of Seattle. Some friends drove them there for dinner. When they finished eating, they told their friends to leave; they can get back to Seattle on foot. The following morning, after spending a night at the inn, they followed an old logging road and walked for most of the day. They finally came across a paved road and a bus stop. They rode the bus from there.

Paul and Martha visited Snoqualmie Falls, the Hoh Rainforest, the hills around Mount Rainier, and frequented the Ocean Crest Resort in Moclips several times. The first time they visited Moclips was because of a first-place prize from a Halloween contest.

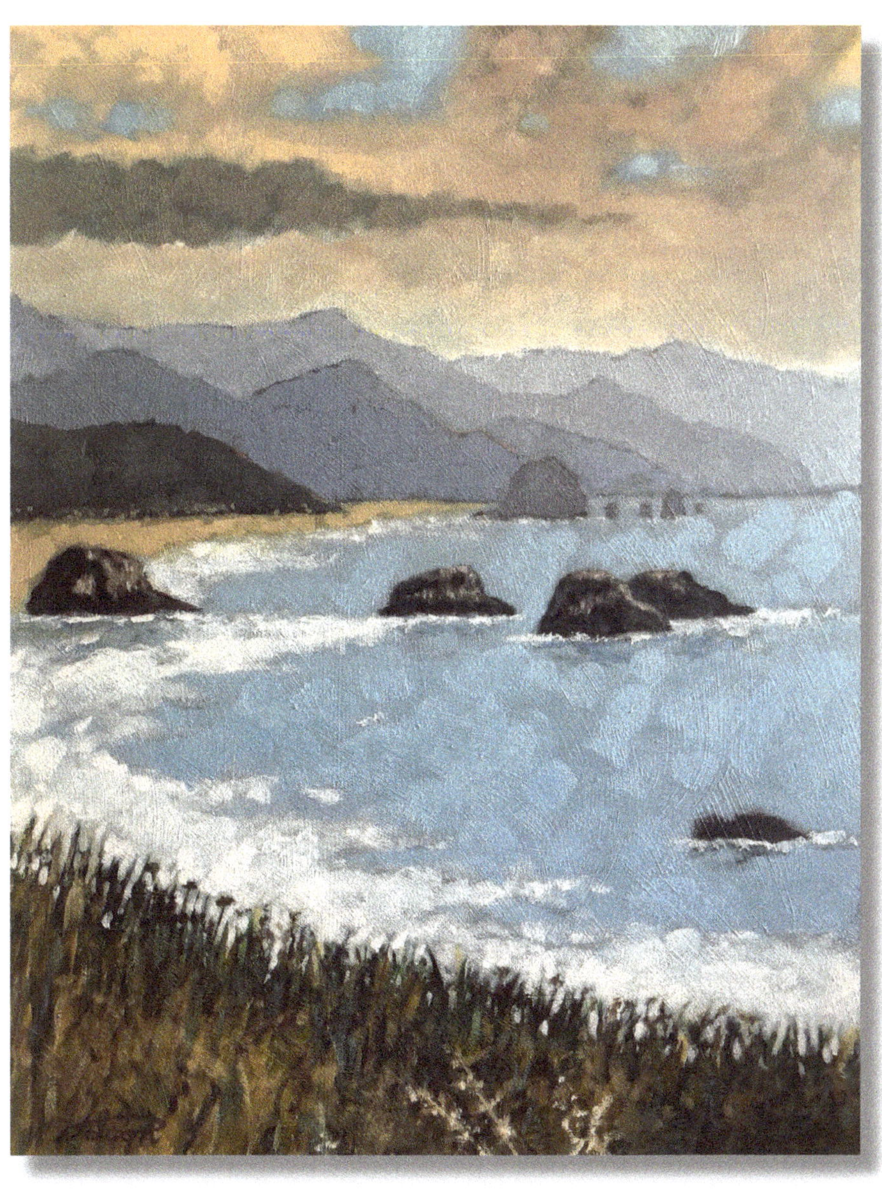

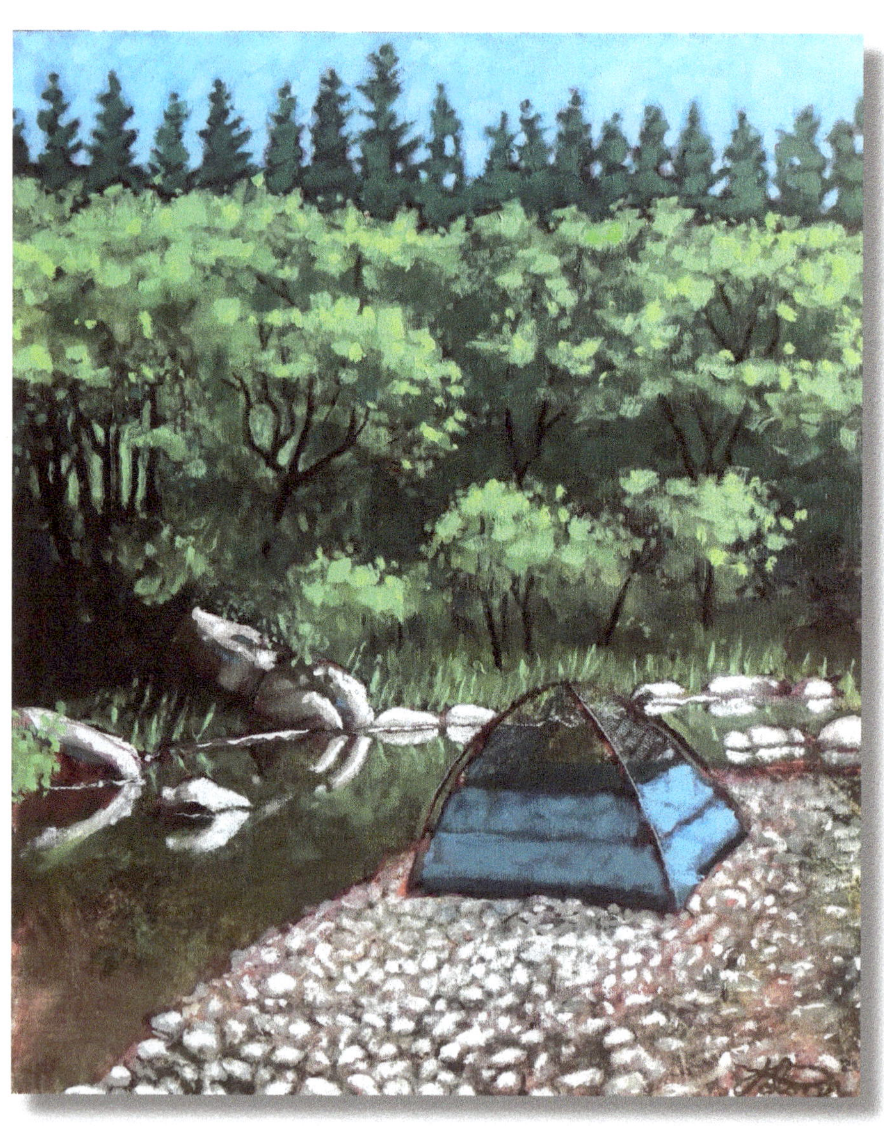

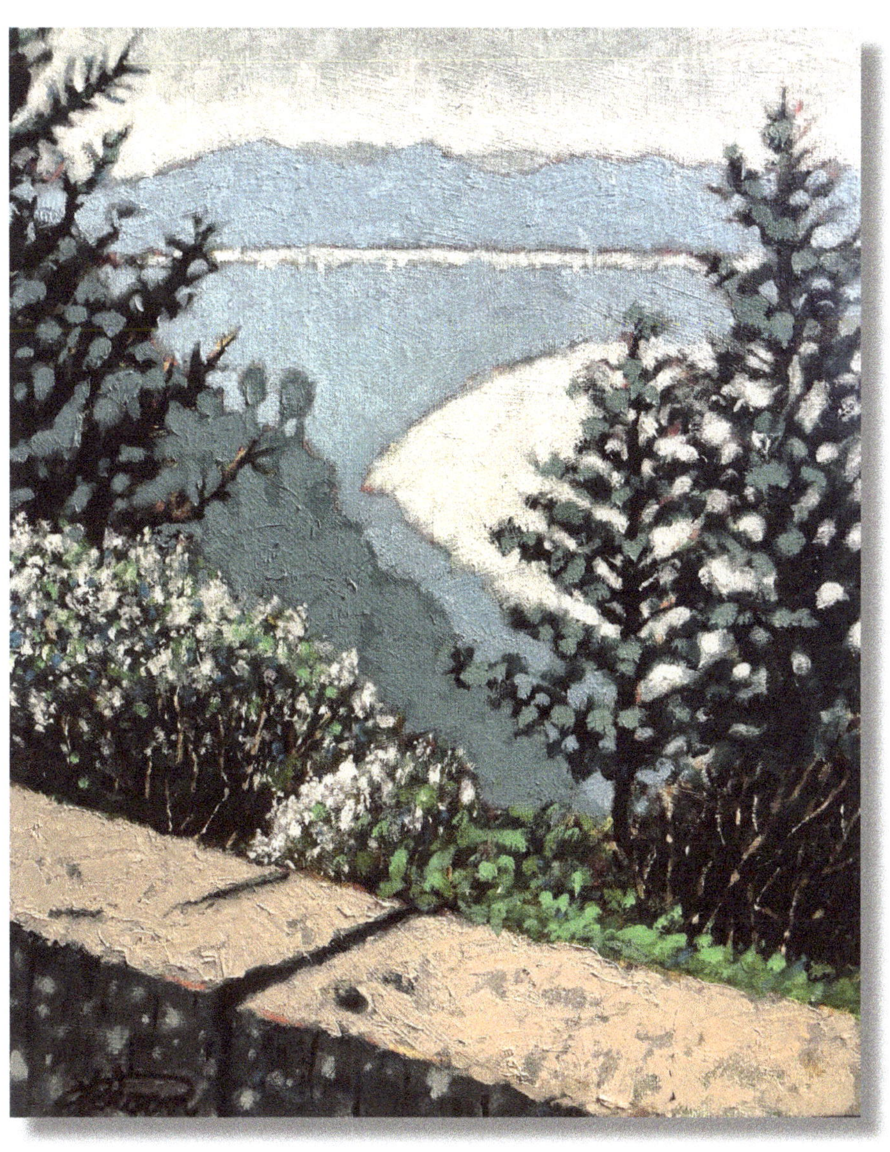

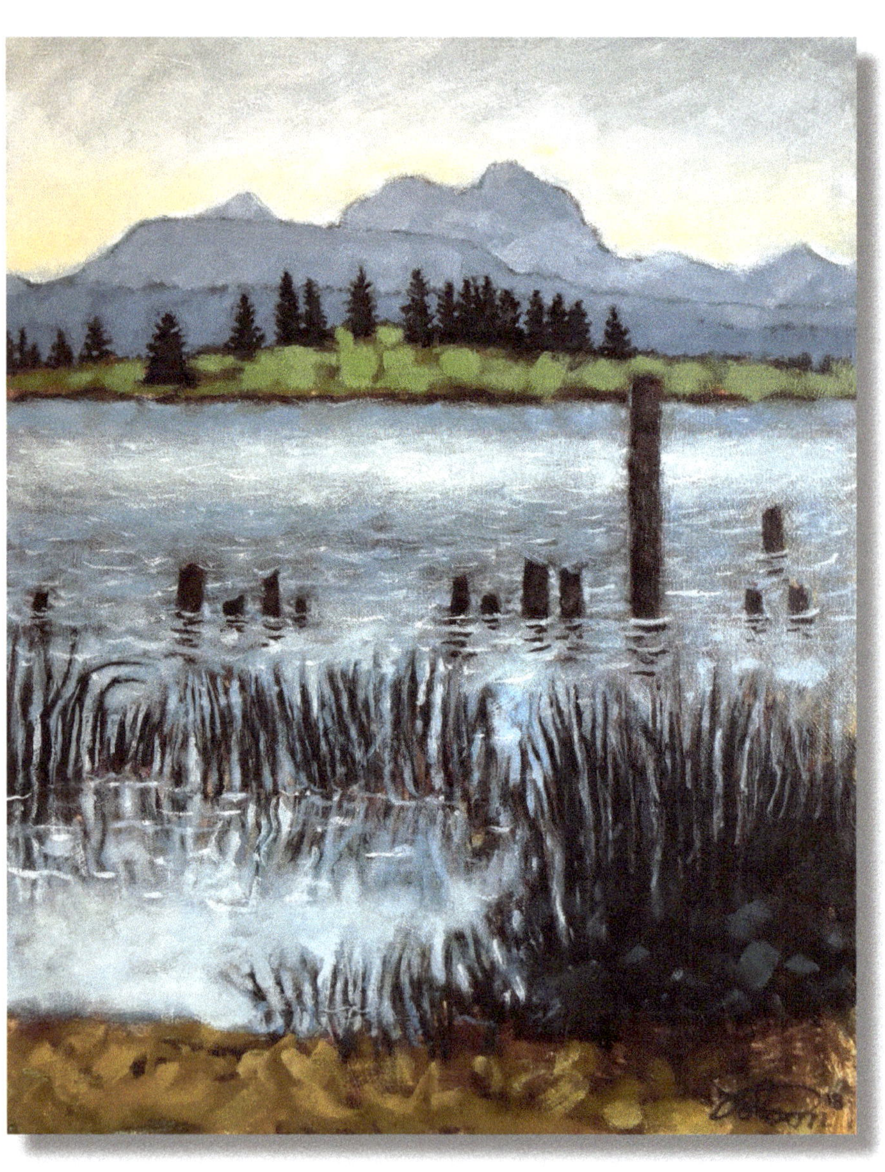

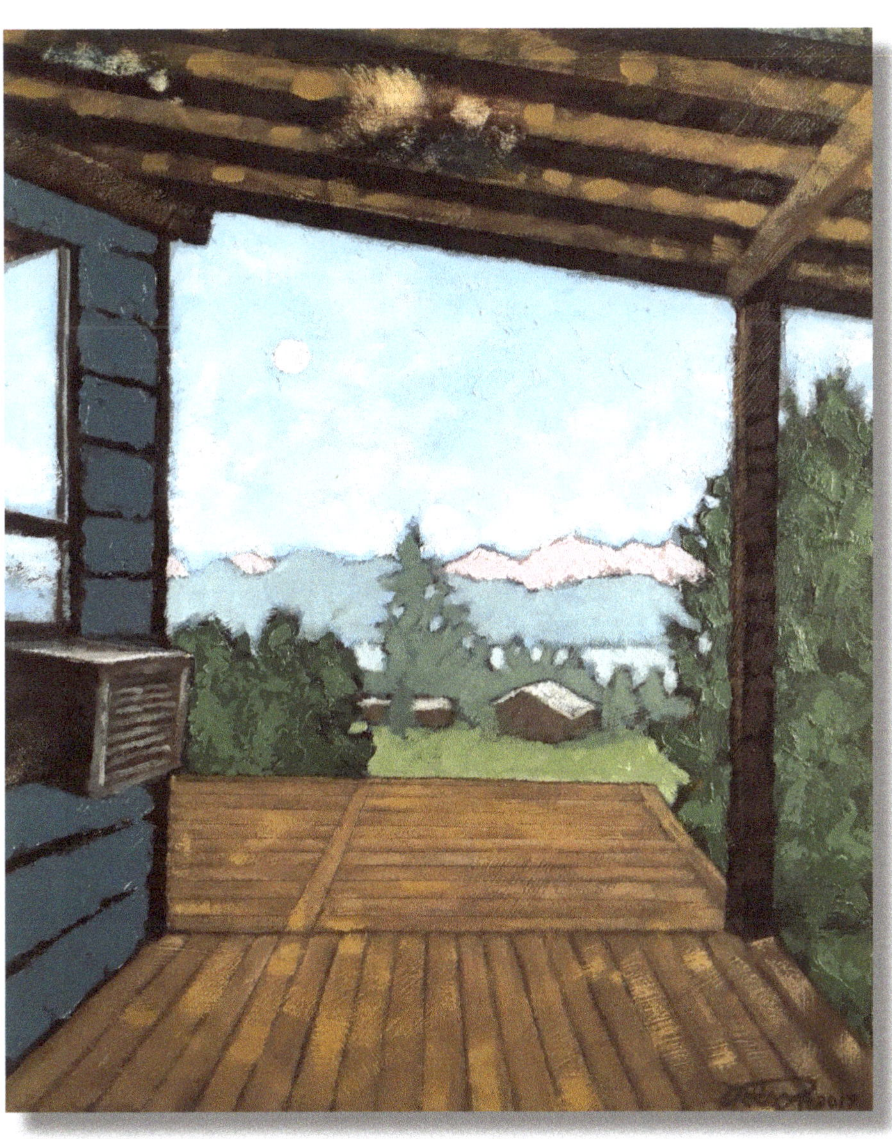

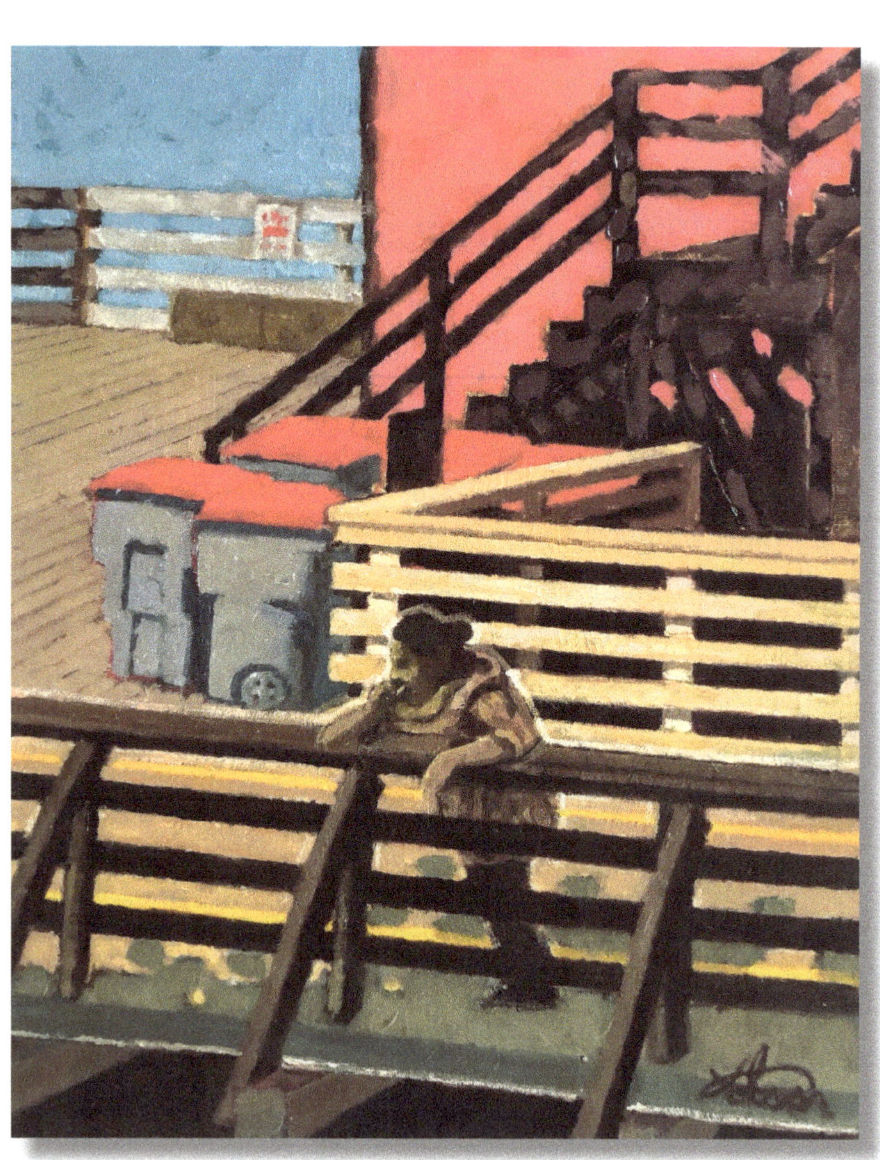

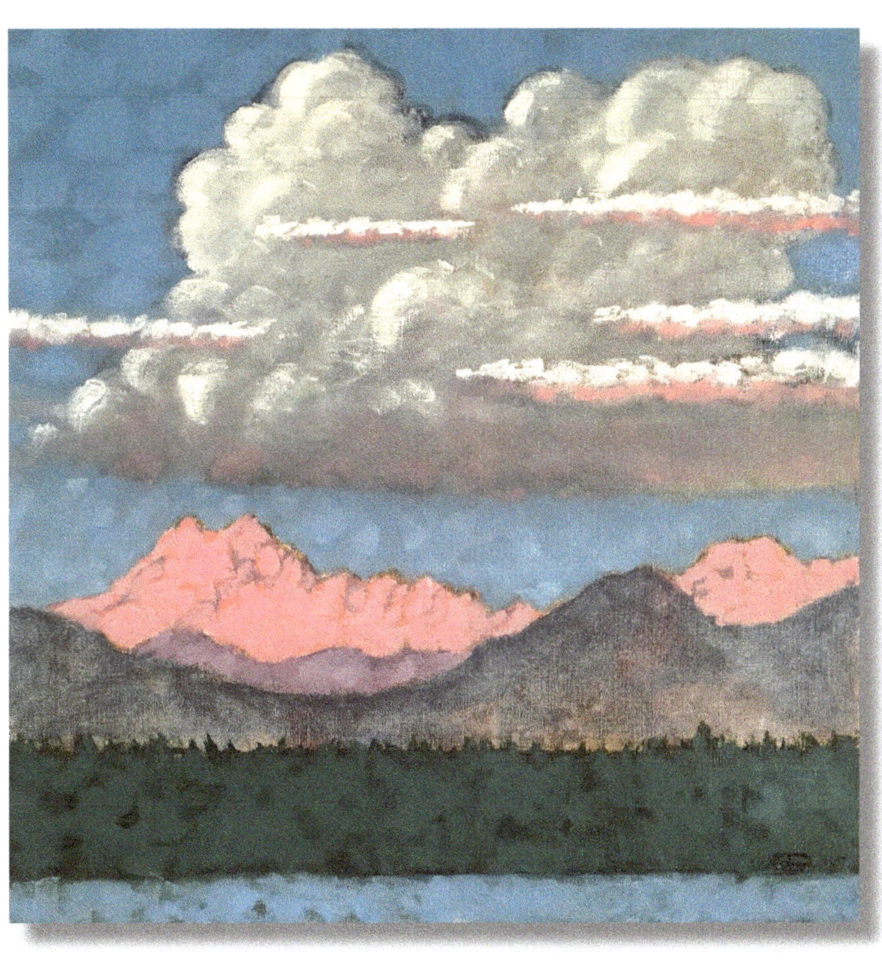

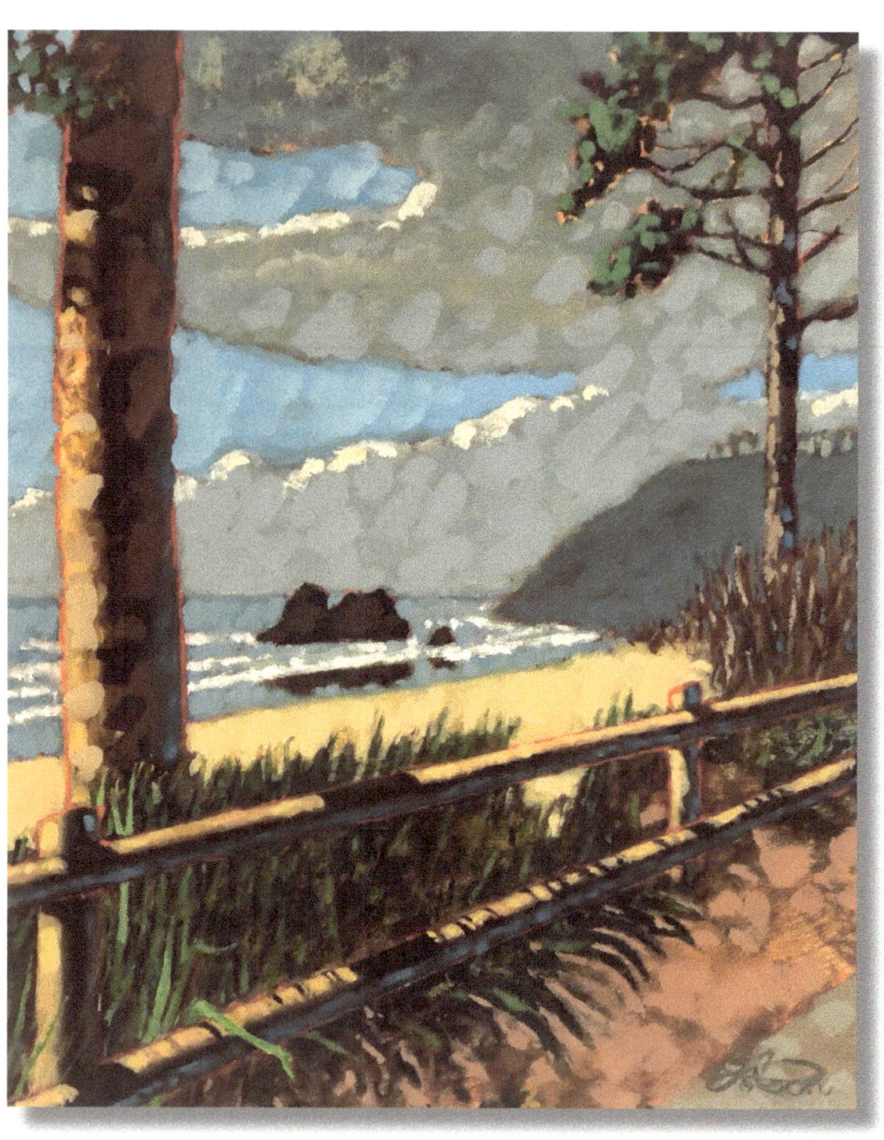

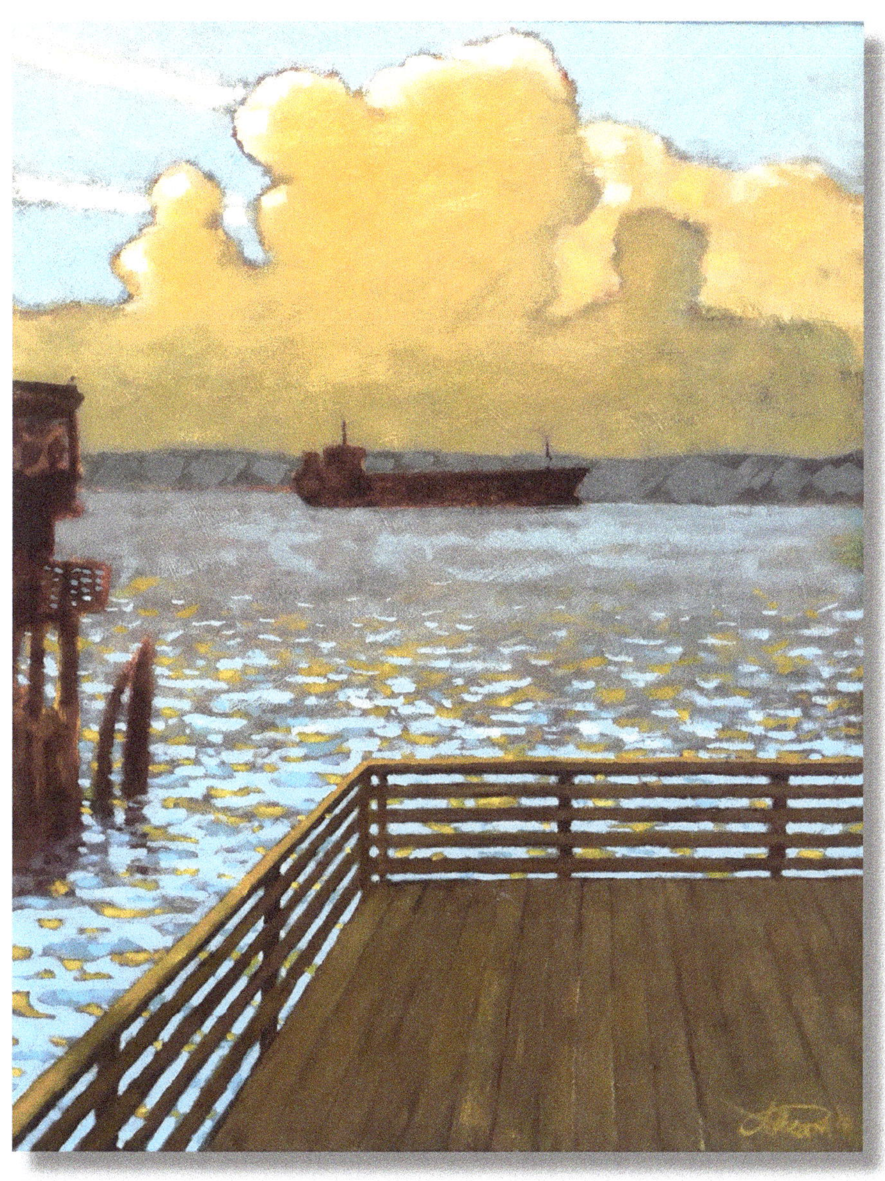

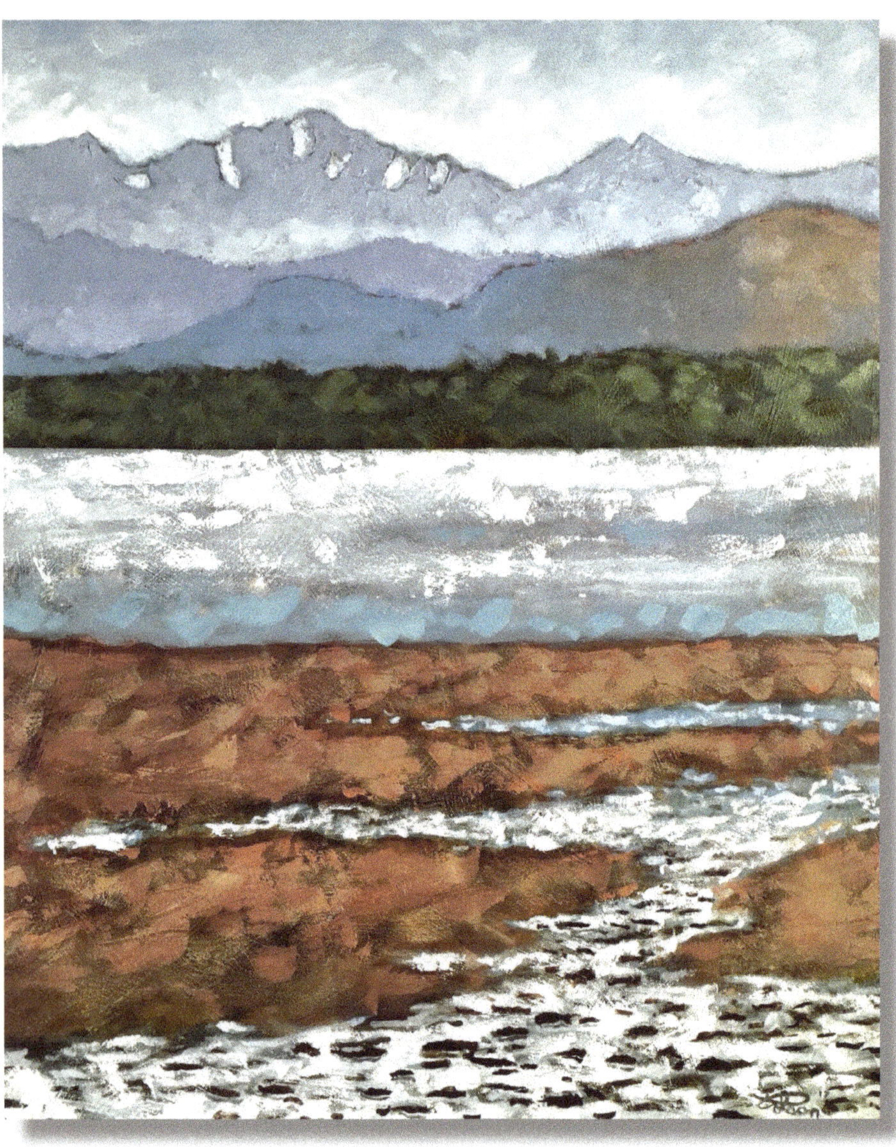

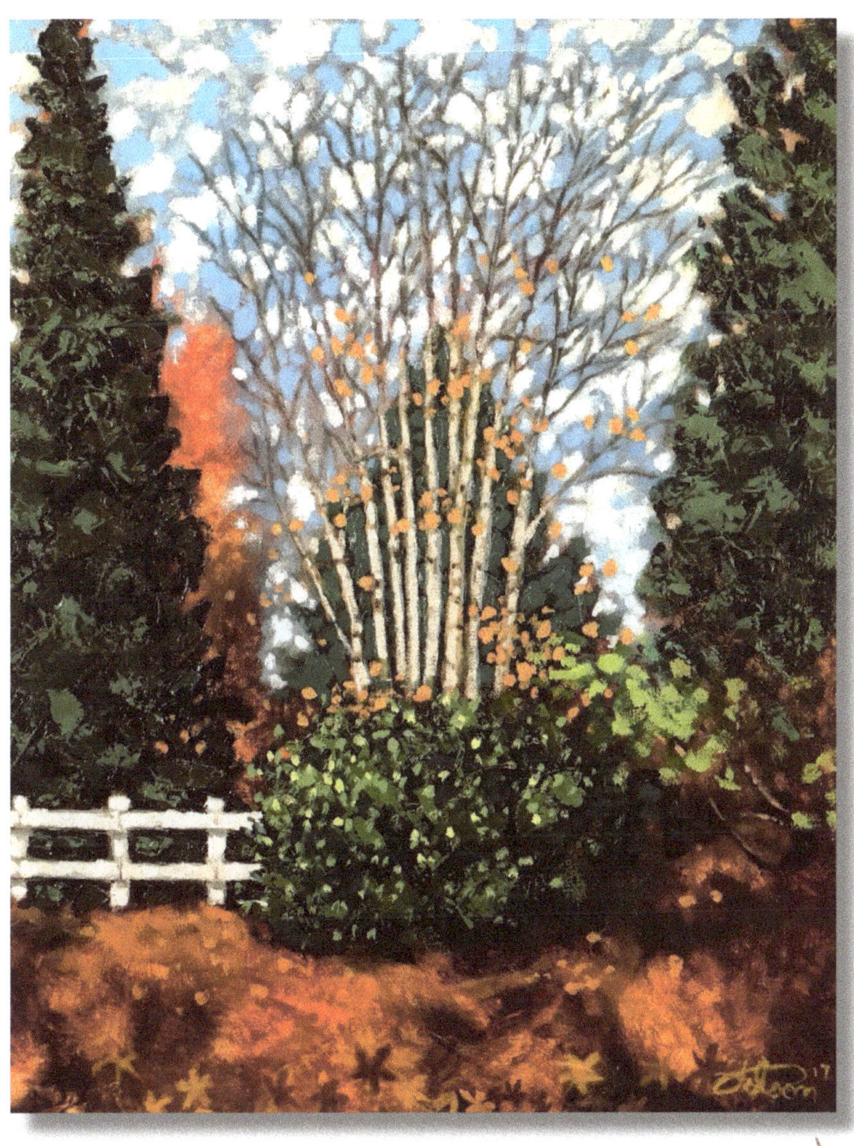

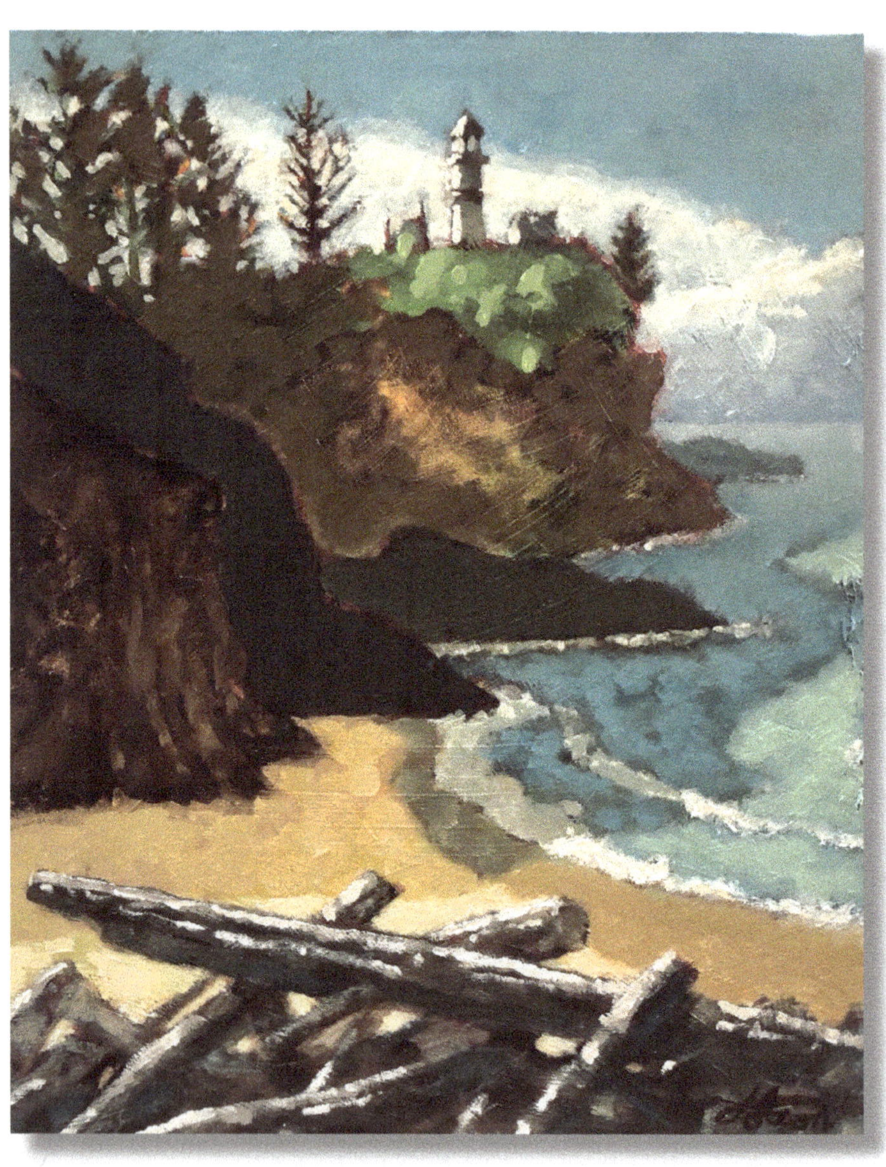

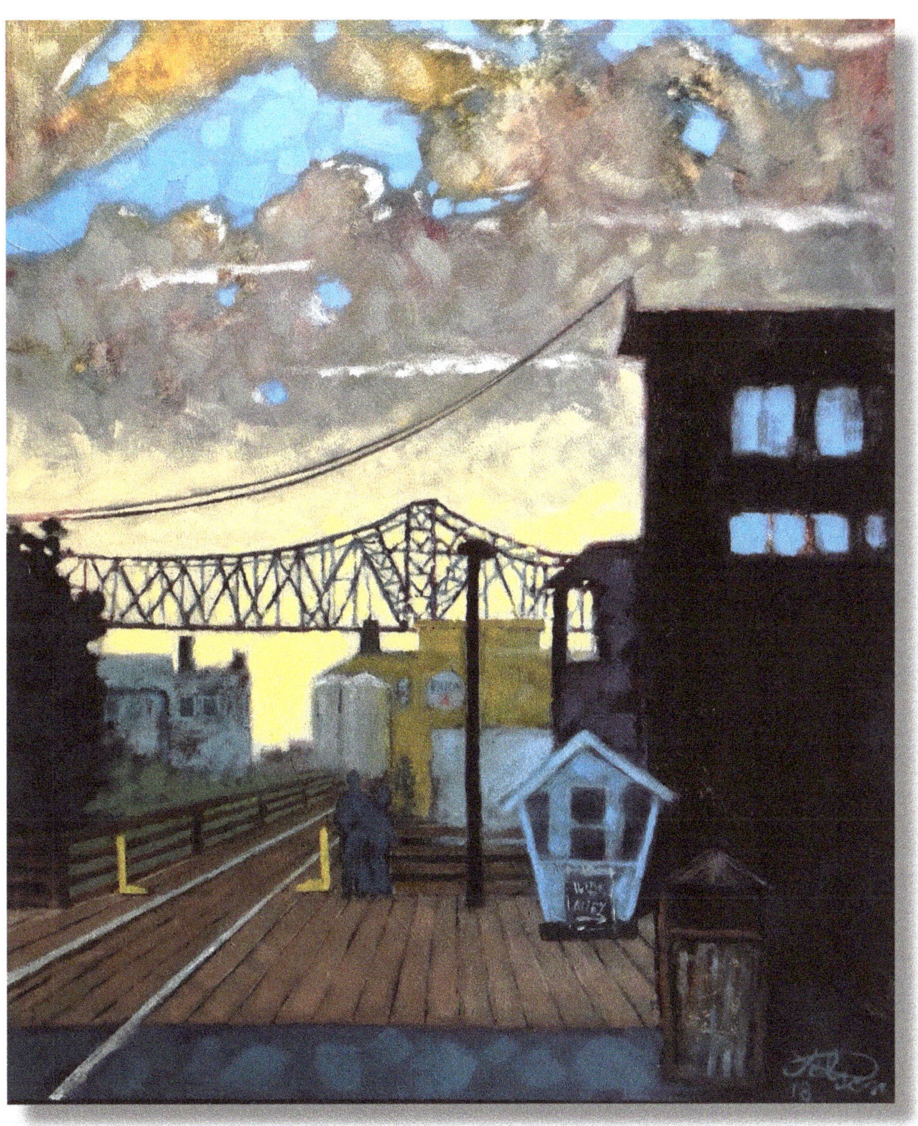

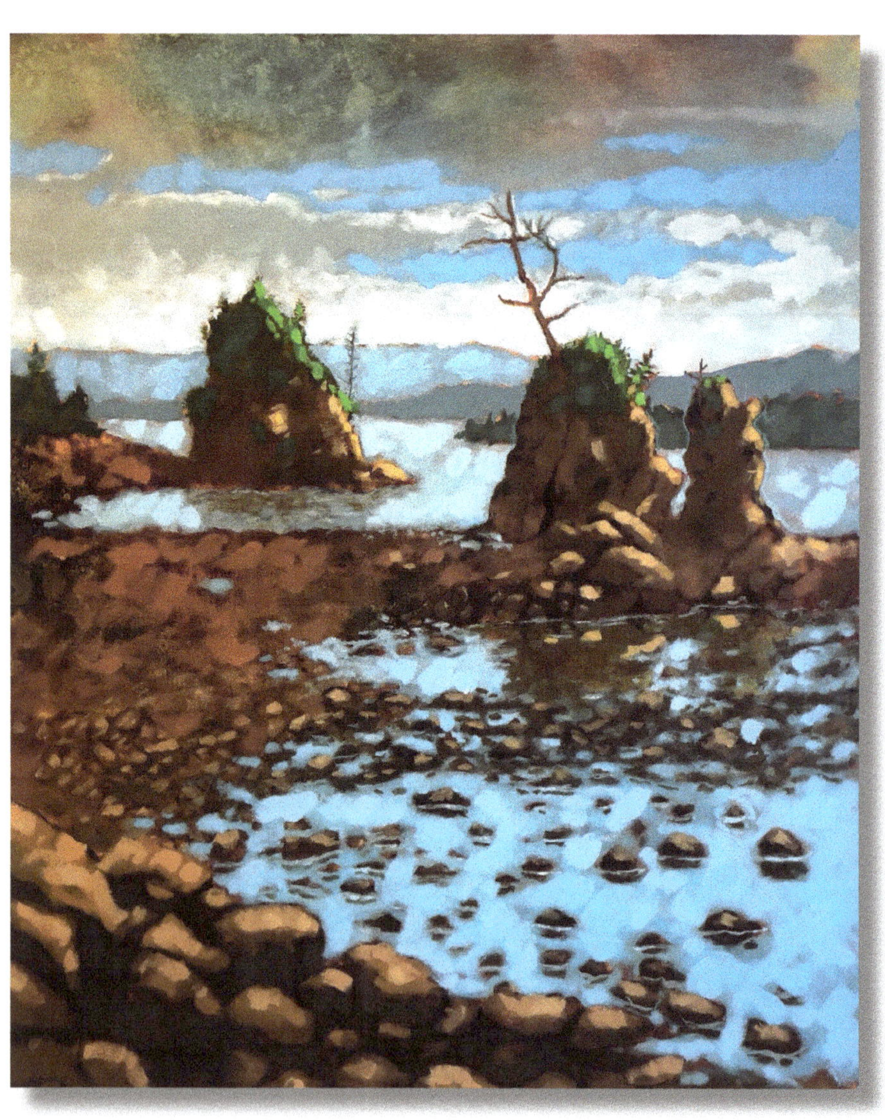

42

DEVIL DOLL

Speaking of Halloween, Paul had been tiring of the same old outhouse costume and thought he would do something different this year. There is something he wants to try that is sure to be a hit.

The next time he saw Martha, Paul asked if she wants to be involved. When he lays out the details, she's excited. Michael Andeel is up for it too. They need at least six people for this to work. Martha, Mike, and Paul will do the fabrication.

Paul bought a roll of chicken wire and formed the shapes of six tropical fish to be somewhat consistent. Each fish is thirty-six inches long with a high, exaggerated back fin and tail—you know, like real tropical fish. They covered each wire framework with Paper Mache and painted them in beautiful iridescent colors. They painted tiger stripes, polka dots, etc.—again, like real tropical fish.

Each fish is structured to act as a helmet. They would pull it over their heads, and rest it on their shoulders. The open mouth is for viewing. There are fins on the side that are attached to a stiff metal wire. Moving it up and down makes the fins flap.

Come Halloween night; they needed to find a venue that is large and packed with people. The perfect place is across the street from their studio. Paul isn't going to participate, since there is another Halloween competition two blocks away. He will wear the outhouse costume at that party.

It's easy to find friends who want to be involved with their "school of fish." Each person wore black. The idea is to walk through the crowd, and—on cue—they all change directions—then change again, as the "school of fish" makes its way through the crowd.

Paul is late arriving at the costume party he attended, but it didn't matter. They put me in with the finalists anyway. As usual, Paul got the first place—a two-night stay at the Ocean Crest Resort in Moclips.

Back at the studio, Paul can hear Martha and her crew laughing as he walked in.

"How did it go?" Paul asked.

"Great!" Martha said. "First place. It worked out just as you said."

"What's the prize?"

There's a big box on the table. It's an inflatable hot tub.

The tub is kind of lame. As it turned out, no one wants it, so they gave it away. Getting first place was award enough.

"How did you do?" Martha asked.

"First place," I said. "A trip and three days stay at some resort in Moclips."

Since meeting Martha, Paul noticed that he never saw her working on anything. She said she does photography and writing, and once showed me some photos she had taken. They are excellent.

She finally put that skill into action.

Pioneer Square decided to do a monthly publication. In the first issue—Volume One—Martha took a fantastic photo of his inflatable eagle and wrote an equally fantastic article. They not only accepted the article, but they also paid her for it. The story is on the front page.

They are excited to have her on board and asked her if she would do another article for the next publication.

"Sure!" she said. "Can I pick the topic?"

They agreed.

Martha wrote a scathing article about the Seattle police. The Pioneer Square Star refused to publish it and asked her if she would write another article or tone this one down.

"No way. If I can't write what I want, I'm not interested in writing for your paper."

At least, Martha had that rebellious, artistic attitude. She is amazingly talented. The only thing is that she didn't have the drive or passion for producing.

——— * ✳ * ———

The shit finally hit the fan. Melanie is tired of delaying her capitalist plans for the studio. Each tenant on the fifth floor has a sublease, but there is a stipulation that if she sold her lease or passed it on to another person, the leases are void.

There are rumors of a ruthless asshole, with mafia ties, on a floor below us. Melanie said she sold the lease to him.

This scam all began with Melanie gathering us together for a studio meeting. She said that there are issues with the legality of living in the studios. She asked a lawyer to come over to protect "all of their rights" and discuss their options.

This tact is a setup. Melanie wants to evict everyone and have her lawyer there when she did. The rest of the tenants didn't like Melanie, and she knew it. There are many reasons why no one likes her; you can add ruthless coward to that list.

They have a month to leave.

The evictees had a party before they left. They decided to have a potluck and invite all their friends.

There is a long table in the kitchen area, and Paul decided to do a photo of a staged *Last Supper*. Using a copy of Da Vinci's painting, he arranged the proper number of people at the table in the correct poses.

Then he placed food and drinks in front of each person. They tried to make it look as correct as possible.

Mike Andeel took the center "Christ" position, and everyone else studied the painting so they would know their poses.

Paul put his camera on a tripod and shot a few exposures. The photos turned out great!

This photo inspired Paul to do a painting: *The Last Last Supper*. It sold immediately at Eagle Eye Gallery.

The person who bought it liked the image so much; he felt like others should enjoy it. He paid to have 500 posters and 500 photo-lithographs made from the image and gave them to Paul.

"Be sure to sign and number the lithos," he said.

Shortly after getting their eviction notice, the jerk from down-stairs came up to their floor and began berating them, saying to get the hell out. He placed a butcher knife on the gallery walls and sprayed its silhouette on the wall with red spray paint.

Michael—their hero—said that if there is anything they want to throw away, even trash with old food, to put it in his room.

It just so happened that the elevator mechanisms are in Michael's studio. After the rest of them left the building, he piled all the trash on top of the gears, pulleys, and wheels used to make the old eleva-tor work and tamped it all down. The pile is at least six feet high. From the inside, he nailed the studio door shut and piled more trash against the door. He then climbed out his window and up the fire escape to the roof. He went down the main stairwell to make his escape. Paul later heard they destroyed the door to get it open.

They never knew what transpired with the transaction Melanie made, but years later, you could still see her "devil doll" in the win-dow of her studio.

— * ✳ * —

Martha and Paul found a studio, not far away on Western Avenue. The owners renovated it to provide studios for artists. The waterfront is a block away, and their studio is next to the most excel-lent restaurant ever—Wild Ginger.

There is a loft for a bed and a small, enclosed space that they turned into a dark room. Martha's brother sent her some devel-oping supplies. He is hoping it will get Martha excited about her photography.

Paul set up his easel, stretched some canvases, and started painting. The environment feels good. His work seemed like it came together more quickly than it had in the last studio.

He did some decent work in that studio. He stretched some large canvases: seventy-six inches high by thirty-six inches wide and worked on his continuing strata series—two of these paintings sold at Eagle Eye Gallery.

The New Year is coming soon. Martha and Paul decided to take a trip to San Diego. It's fun showing Martha around. He introduced her to his friends, favorite places, and old haunts. He even took her to Bigger Than Life.

The employees are excited to see him. He sent them a photo of his inflatable eagle, and they pinned it to a bulletin board in the break room.

Sunset Cliffs had been a magical place for him when he lived in San Diego. He took her to his special spot where someone had carved a profile of an Indian's face. This area of the coast is all cliffs, caves, and large rocks protruding from the surf. The waves are usually perfect for surfing, and he had taken his board there on many occasions. The sound of the waves crashing against the rocks and the swells rising and dropping reminded him of happy days. Paul used to sit there for hours watching the sunset. He also did several paintings from that site.

That's where he took Martha on New Year's Eve.

He proposed to her. The date is in September of that coming year.

43

SHI SHI

After returning to Seattle, the Gulf War is winding down. There are multiple successes, and by early February 1991, the United States claimed victory. The Iraqi army was driven from Kuwait, leaving their leadership and military beaten but intact.

Paul heard a lot of talks—some of it reflecting his thoughts—that they should have driven into Baghdad to finish the job.

As it turned out, Daddy Bush made the right move. It left the Middle East a somewhat functional area regardless of their problems.

They found out the results of what "finishing the job" meant when President Bush's son became president and decided that, if his dad wouldn't do it, he would. He blew up Iraq, killed Saddam, and disbanded the Iraqi military. The aftermath blew up the whole Middle East, leading the world on a path that helped cause the extreme instability and horror that we see today.

Winning the Gulf War developed pride in Americans, and they wanted to celebrate it.

The City of Seattle made plans to have a military parade through downtown. This parade is not something the citizens of Seattle would accept, and it is aggressively curtailed.

Somehow, the planners heard about Paul's inflatable eagle, and they wanted to put it behind the reviewing stand during the parade.

Even though Paul is disappointed that he lost the opportunity to show off his eagle—he agreed with the decision not to flaunt U.S. military power.

Thinking that this opportunity is history, Paul found out that the "powers that be" still want to honor the troops. They are pursuing different plans.

Paul is contacted by the Seattle Seahawks to be part of a tribute to their military for the halftime show at a Seahawk game. They want to see the eagle, so they invited him—and his eagle—to their training facility in Renton.

Part of boasting about the eagle is his claim that it could inflate the eagle in sixty seconds. They wanted to see if that's true.

Paul took Martha with him. They laid out the inflatable and connected it to the blower. After they found a power source, a couple of Seahawk decision-makers came out to where Paul is setting up.

"Sixty seconds, huh? We're going to walk back into the building. When we disappear inside the door, start the inflation. We'll come back out in exactly sixty seconds."

They disappeared. Precisely one minute later, they came out to the full glory of the eagle. Not only are they impressed, but they are also in awe of the detail and realism of his creation.

"Great! You've got the job."

On game day, Paul and Martha went to the Kingdome stadium early to practice with the rest of the participants.

During halftime, they unfurled a flag, almost as big as the field itself. The eagle popped up—as expected—on the fifty-yard line.

Part of their responsibility is to deflate it and remove it as quickly as possible.

They did the eagle inflation on a huge tarp. To deflate it, he had put a large deflation panel on the eagle's back. Paul yanked the rip-cord, and the eagle dropped immediately into a heap, while Martha disconnected the blower so that the air could vent out the fan tunnel.

The next step is to grab the two front corners of the tarp and pull the whole thing off the field.

Paul ran to one side and grabbed one corner. As he rushes to the other corner, there stands an Army captain who already had the corner in hand and gave it to him. Paul gave him a quick "Thank you, sir" and pulled it off the field.

Wow, the military is really on the ball! They do things as needed—even if not asked. That small act made him appreciate the armed forces even more than he already did. It's no wonder we won the war.

Martha and Paul jumped up in the air and high-fived. Success!

The Seahawks sent him a videotape of the halftime show.

Even though the eagle is twenty-four feet tall, it looks pretty small compared to the vastness of King Dome.

⎯⎯ ✳ ⎯⎯

On September 23, 1991, Paul woke to the rays of the rising sun, lighting the tent's corner. There is a chill in the quiet, damp tent where he spent the night. He can hear the sound of birds.

He opens the flap and crawls out into the crisp fresh air.

They camped on the north shore of Lake Ozette, and this is the day Martha and Paul are to be married.

Shi Shi Beach is their choice for the ceremony. Out of the few who attended, Martha and Paul are the only ones who had been there before. The rest are in for a pleasant surprise.

When they made the trek to the quiet, empty beach, the minister and attendees of the party stood in awe.

It was a magical ceremony.

When it was over, everyone but a few of Martha's friends left. Her friends camped a quarter mile down the beach and left the following morning. Martha and Paul stayed two nights.

In the middle of the first night, the night following their wedding ceremony, Martha crawled outside the tent and threw up among the ferns.

She was pregnant with their soon-to-be daughter, Shawn Claire.

⎯⎯ ✳ ⎯⎯

After returning to Seattle, Paul prepared the canvases he had recently stretched and began his initial wash to start a painting. There is something he had put on the back burner that he is anxious to pursue.

He still has several undeveloped rolls of black and white film from Europe. The darkroom is all set up, and Martha seems to have no interest in it. The room had been idle since they prepared it months earlier. Paul stayed away from it out of respect. He had brought the subject up with Martha several times, and it only annoyed her. Finally, he asked if she would mind if he used it to develop his film, and she said that would be fine.

He didn't want to be an obstacle if she wants to keep it available, just in case the bug hit her. Paul would have loved to see her shooting black and whites and developing them. It would be nice to see her driven by creativity.

Paul had developed film before, but not much; it has been a while. Martha filled him in on the process until he became comfortable with it. They had everything they needed. The darkroom is just sitting there, waiting

for Paul and his film. He is anxious to see his Europe photos.

Paul hung out developing film for hours—listening to music or not—sometimes drinking wine as he worked. The process threw him back into the past, reliving those three months. He was also learning more film-developing techniques and understood the exposure time more as he continued.

Martha is dealing with the early stages of pregnancy, and Paul is as supportive as he knows how. He rushes off to work in the morning, returns to work on his paintings, and happily caters to her needs. They usually go out for dinner. They are in the same room together, so she is used to the turpentine spell, and they seem to cohabitate well together. They cozy up in the loft every evening and watch Star Trek reruns.

With all of life's dramas going on, Paul still finds time to stretch canvases. He continues with his strata paintings and feels like he is painting better work now than ever.

The strata paintings are fun to paint and fun to look at. He has continued this theme since San Diego and lost count of how many he had painted.

They are also well received in galleries and art walks. He even sold a few.

— ✳ —

While living at the Western Avenue studio, Paul had a pleasant surprise.

His brother Don called. He is an instructor in structural engineering at UW.

Paul didn't know how he did it, but Don had arranged to have his son Kevin and his daughter Kim visit him.

The next day, Paul bought their airline tickets.

Paul met his first wife, Barbara, at the University of Wyoming. They were both too young, and they married for the wrong reasons.

Paul plans to move to a city, San Francisco, or Seattle to pursue his art. They had two children—Kevin and Kim in 1970 and 1972.

Barbara refused to go with him.

Realizing that the two of them are not a match made in heaven, they divorced.

He found out that the children always go to the mother in Wyoming, and if he leaves the state, he loses all rights to them.

Paul hadn't seen them since he was "allowed" to visit them for twenty minutes in 1975 after traveling 1,200 miles.

Even though Paul attempted to visit and stay in contact, Barbara refused to let him see or talk to them.

Kevin attended UW, and Paul's brother Don became Kevin's advisor. Kevin's major is in structural engineering, and because Don taught structural engineering, he and Kevin had developed a good relationship during his years in school.

Kim finished high school the year before her visit.

When Paul picked them up at the airport, he is thrilled, and so are they. It has been a long time.

Paul brought Kevin and Kim back to the studio. He has so much to say and show them. They are excited to tell him about their lives and experiences.

They stayed a week, and Paul gave them the grand tour of Seattle and the music scene.

It is sad to see them go, but the door has finally opened. There is now the possibility of knowing each other better and building the relationship they had been denied.

44

MOOSE

Martha's pregnancy continues. They decided that once their daughter is born, it would be nice to live in a more rural environment.

Bainbridge Island is their first choice. It is also just a ferry ride to work. When Paul disembarks from the ferry, he will be three blocks from Artform.

The ferry arrives in Seattle early. That gives him time to stop at the Grand Central Bakery for his coffee and cinnamon roll and to work on the daily crossword.

Paul and Martha found a large A-frame on the north end of the island. It has two stories and a large basement. One-half of the A-frame has the kitchen, living room, bedroom, and bathroom. The other half is entirely open. The second floor has a balcony looking out over this space. It also has a large deck looking out over trees.

This ample open space became Paul's studio.

He didn't waste any time. He set up his easel and started painting immediately.

❋

Working at Artform continues. It is a big part of Paul's life, and he loves his job, the people, and his fellow workers.

Penny is amazing. With everything going on in Paul's life, she allows him to take time off as needed.

She is the instigator of an episode that she knew would be important to him.

One day, when he arrived at work, Penny said that her sister, Andrea, worked at a prop and costume shop owned by an interesting character, Jerry Chin. Andrea wanted Paul to come to their shop and talk to her boss about a project.

When he arrived, he found himself in a most interesting place. Jerry is an intelligent, high-energy person. His warehouse is huge. It's filled with everything a movie producer could imagine. This place provides the props and costumes for movies depicting any time and place. If someone is shooting a movie, made in the 1920s, he will provide furniture, styles of dress, and knick-knacks that represented that era.

In this case, the proposal didn't have anything to do with this particular business. Jerry had unbelievable connections in Los Angeles. Jerry wants Paul to make an inflatable for a fourteen-foot by forty-eight-foot billboard on Sunset Strip in Hollywood. The Alaska Tourism Bureau wants a giant three-dimensional moose head with two life-size (fake) people—one hanging from an antler and the other filming it.

The purpose of this is to encourage the movie industry to film in Alaska. Jerry heard about Paul from Andrea and had seen his eagle. He proposed doing the moose head as an inflatable.

Jerry landed the job. After doing detailed drawings, Paul sculpted the moose head and antlers and then patterned it. He is ready to move ahead.

He still needs to buy a sewing machine.

During this time, Paul decided to attend church. Martha wasn't interested. He went for a few months, but the same thing happened as times before when he tried to be a good Mormon. The church demanded most of his time. He still hadn't advanced far enough in the priesthood, and he was put in a class with younger boys and learned things he had learned before.

As an artist, Paul needs freedom to do his work and learn about the world. To be a good Mormon, you need to tuck yourself inside the wing of the church. Each night of the week, he had duties that he could miss, but he is strongly encouraged to participate.

Paul decides again that the social side of the church is not for him; he has God's work to do through God's gifts. He truly believes that.

It is not that he didn't believe in the church; it's just that it is perfect for some people and families, but not for him. Mormons are good people.

The reason Paul brings this up is that he ran into a man at church who owns an awning shop in Seattle. He said that Paul could use his sewing machine. Better yet, they would sew the moose head for a small price.

Before sewing on the antlers, Paul needed to paint them. He used a large spray booth at the awning shop and painted each one separately.

The fabrication of the moose went flawlessly. When Paul finished the inflatable, Jerry found a warehouse where he can do the final airbrush and hand painting.

One problem is how to add support to an antler that stuck out twenty feet from the billboard. This problem can be solved with air pressure, but Paul needs to hang one of the human figures from the tip of the antler, and that adds more weight. He used PVC pipe and installed it internally for extra support along with a one-horsepower blower.

To make the figures, Paul used chicken wire wrapped around PVC pipes and used duct tape to cover the surface. He dressed them in real clothes. The faces are sculpted from clay and then cast in rubber mixed with a powdered flesh pigment. He painted the face inside the mold and strengthened it with burlap. When he peeled it out, it had a matte finish. He then painted the eyes, lips, and teeth on the outside. They came out glossy. The burlap extended beyond the edge of the face so he could sew it into the figure's head.

Jerry and Paul flew to Los Angeles to install the moose. The finished product turned out perfect. Everyone he talked to thought the figures were real.

———— * ✳ * ————

The move from Pioneer Square to Bainbridge Island offered a nice contrast—city life to country life—linked by a thirty-five-minute ferry ride.

The extra time going to work is not a problem; he saw it as a beautiful enhancement of his life.

Commuting to Seattle involved getting up early and driving his van to a park and ride. It is still dark at that hour. The bus takes him to the ferry terminal, and by that time, the sun began to show itself.

The early morning ferry ride is beautiful. Instead of sitting comfortably inside the ferry, Paul chose to climb to the top deck to feel the cool breeze.

Seattle glittered as the ferry approached, and the mountains either showed themselves or not. Sometimes, he walked aft and gazed at the wake, watching the islands recede. The Olympic Mountains are beautiful and vivid on a clear day.

When he arrived in the bustling city, he walked to the Grand Central Bakery, did his usual coffee and roll, and absorbed himself in his crossword.

Paul enjoyed the trip back to Bainbridge Island at the end of the workday too. At certain times of the year, you can see the sunset over the Olympics. He had to take a step back and realize where he is. Paul had experienced the ice-cold, windy weather of Wyoming and the heat and constant sun of the Southwest. Here, he is truly in heaven. He couldn't believe it's real.

Life became a little harder after the money from the moose billboard faded away. Martha is no longer working and is awaiting the baby. They rely on his income.

Halloween rolled around again. They are having difficulty making ends meet. Caught up in his usual routine, he didn't think of going to a Halloween contest until the day is upon him.

Martha is lying in bed.

"Why don't you find a Halloween party and make some money?"

On the one hand, he wanted to stay there with Martha; on the other hand, she gave him the okay to go out and party.

He threw the outhouse in the back of the van and headed to Seattle.

Paul returned home at one in the morning. When he walks into the bedroom, the light is still on.

"How did you do?" she asked.

He smiled and threw 500 dollars' worth of five-dollar bills up in the air. They showered down as they both grinned and relaxed. They could at least catch up on their bills and go out for dinner.

Even though financial woes continued to plague them, things kept happening, which seemed to give them an infusion of cash when needed.

Paul is still renting the eagle. He needs to install it and pack it up at the end of each event.

He inflated the dinosaur and the eagle at the local schools providing them with a lot of press—even front-page photos in many publications.

For ten years, Paul installed the eagle on Winslow Way at the Bainbridge Fourth of July celebration and parade.

Martha started working at Eagle Eye Gallery. The job is casual. She tended the gallery, allowing people to browse, and assisting them if she is needed.

Finally, the day came for Martha to take the trip to the hospital. They drove to the ferry dock, and they moved them to the front of the line for boarding.

Shawn Claire is knocking at the door. She is born on May 7, 1992, at Virginia Mason Hospital in Seattle.

45

SHOP

Then came the call from Jerry Chinn. He had landed two more inflatable billboard jobs for FIFA World Cup soccer in Los Angeles.

The sponsor is the Mars Chocolate Company. They want a giant inflatable SNICKERS candy bar next to a large inflatable soccer ball with three-dimensional peanuts scattered over the whole billboard.

This job is a dream. Paul likes starting a job from scratch. Stretching a large sheet of grid vellum on his drawing table is the most enjoyable part of his work. He loves figuring out the math and developing the patterns.

Paul enjoys every aspect of making inflatable shapes—even organizing a supply list and ordering the materials is fun.

The pay allows him to focus on the project at hand and not fret about finances.

The only part that stresses him is when the deadline approaches. That makes him shift into a higher gear. Completing a project is the ultimate highlight.

This job came off without a hitch. The inflatables are sewn at the same awning shop as the moose head had been, but he feels the need to get his own facility.

Paul began to check out possible spaces in the area and found an ideal spot. The building is in a rural area just outside of Poulsbo—a fifteen-minute drive from their home. It had 2,500 square feet and high ceilings—high enough, anyway.

He showed the space to Martha.

"This will work great!' she said. "You won't have to drive to Seattle and use someone else's business space."

Paul bought two sewing machines and built a long sewing table. The machines fit into two notches that he added to the table during construction. It is large enough to roll out lengths of fabric and do the cutting.

This facility is also big enough to set up a sculpture and woodworking area.

"I have something else I want to show you." Paul smiled at Martha in anticipation of her response.

They drove down a two-mile-long road that ended in a tiny town on the shore of Puget Sound. It had a long pier and a south-facing beach.

The town is named Indianola. It consists of a general store and a clubhouse with a dance floor and stage. It also has a post office. There is a small population of houses that spread both directions along the shoreline and into the woods.

Martha is as surprised by the town as Paul is.

She checked an information board by the post office: "Lost cat, please call," "Will do house cleaning," "Band playing at the clubhouse this Saturday," and "House available for rent."

They called the phone number for the house.

"I'm in the area. Can you meet me now?" said the voice.

They drove about three short blocks into the woods, and there stood a beautiful cabin amongst the trees. There is land around it and privacy.

The owner only lives in it while on vacation. She's from Washington, D.C., and fell in love with the house when she saw it—and with the community. She asked what Paul did for a living, and he gave her the short version.

"You're perfect!" she said. "This is an artists' community. It would be nice to keep it that way."

As it turns out, she is the senior art editor for *Smithsonian Magazine.*

"If you want it, it's yours."

The answer is, "Oh, yeah!"

We signed a one-year lease.

They lived in the Bainbridge Island A-frame for two years. It was okay, but the landlady was a tyrant.

They packed up and moved to their quaint little home in Indianola with their delightful daughter Shawn Claire. They call her Claire. She is now a little over one year old.

Shortly after moving in, Martha said, "Guess what?"

"What?"

"I'm pregnant.

Paul had his one-person show at Eagle Eye Gallery. The opening didn't draw a lot of people like the art walks in Pioneer Square had, but during the following month, there is a lot of traffic. Paul sold two more large paintings.

Jerry called again with yet another inflatable job for AirTouch Cellular. This time, he needs four billboards. The design is simple. He needs to make a forty-foot-long blimp for each billboard. The hard part is to outline the letters on each blimp with rope light. He placed grommets outlining each letter and attached the lights with pull ties.

To start this project, Paul made a list of supplies. Seattle is so close that he decides to go to his suppliers and pick out what he needs.

The fabric for the job is different. There is a specific fabric, vinyl-coated nylon that can't be substituted. There are three vendors that he uses.

His favorite is in Los Angeles. You can call in an order and give them a Pantone color. They match it exactly. It usually takes two weeks, but you can order a minimum of 100 yards. Most fabric companies demand a minimum of 1,000 yards to custom coat a fabric.

The other two fabric vendors have stock colors. They would overnight the fabric if you needed it for a project with a quick turnaround.

Paul finally had the facility he needed to do a whole inflatable by himself. Everything is ready to go.

One of the first things he did is build an actual billboard in the shop. To attach an inflatable, he made brackets with hook Velcro under a three-inch lip. When he finished a blimp, he would sew loop Velcro around the edges of the inflatable. He attached the blimp to the brackets and inflated it to make sure he had patterned it right. He then painted it while inflated.

The work is long and tedious. When Paul finished the first one, Jerry and Paul took it to Los Angeles to install it. He had packed it so tight that it damaged some of the rope light. Paul had taken extra lights to replace the ones that didn't work. Having learned his lesson, he didn't have that problem packing the other three.

Because of these billboards, *Outdoor Magazine* contacted them. At first, they wanted Big Air to buy an ad, but Paul can't afford a national ad in a magazine at the moment.

They are still intrigued by their inflatables, so they asked if they want to do an article on the work they do. Martha did most of the talking and said she could write the article.

When she finished, she sent it in with photographs.

Martha's story is their featured article eight pages with the photos of the moose (on the cover), World Cup Soccer, and the AirTouch blimp billboards.

The article also described Paul's history with Inflatables in San Diego, the process he used, and the benefits of using inflatables for outdoor advertising. Big Air Productions, Inc. became a well-known name in the inflatable industry.

Paul wanted to work on his own ideas for inflatable sculpture—things that might be rentable. Having a family, he needed to create an income.

He decided on a "*Kilroy Was Here*" character. They could put it on top of a building with Kilroy's nose and fingers hanging over the side.

This inflatable is rented out regularly and is fun.

A huge grocery store, Central Market, had just finished constructing their store while he finished Kilroy. Paul asked them if he could put it on top of their store for a photoshoot. They hadn't opened yet.

Once they saw it, they rented it regularly for at least four years. Whenever Paul installed it, they said their sales doubled.

Kilroy dates back to the early 1940s. It was a popular graffiti drawn by soldiers in World War II.

James J. Kilroy started the phrase when he was an inspector at the shipyards. During the construction of military vehicles, workers were paid for what they accomplished. Sometimes, the workers would run an item through twice to get extra credit. Kilroy noticed this, so he would label the manufactured items with the phrase "Kilroy was here."

As the war progressed, the need for more arms and ships forced these war machines to be rushed to the war theater before Kilroy's label could be painted over.

Thus "Kilroy was here" kept showing up. It became an icon used by the troops as they advanced into enemy territory.

Rumor has it that an astronaut scrawled it in the dust on the moon. "Kilroy Was Here" had been found on the underside of the Arc de Triomphe, on the Statue of Liberty, and atop Mt. Everest.

During the Potsdam Conference at the end of World War II, Truman, Stalin, and Churchill were in attendance. There was an outhouse on the premises. Stalin was the first to use it. When he came out, his first remark was, "Who is Kilroy?"

Paul also made a forty-five-foot-long dinosaur and regularly used it for school tours. The T-Rex looks like it is coming to life as he inflates it. Some kids ran away, screaming in fright.

He gave tours of his business to groups—mostly grade school classes. The dinosaur is a hit. As Paul ended the tour, he stood under the inflatable and gave his "Thank you for coming" speech as an employee turned off the fan. The dinosaur's mouth would lower and wrap around him like it had just found lunch. He had to repeat this several times, so all the children would have the chance to scream and be eaten by a dinosaur. The parents and teachers took photos.

Martha's trip to Swedish Hospital to give birth began at one o'clock in the morning after the ferries closed down. An emergency helicopter is used to take patients to a hospital in Seattle. Martha called 911, and they were told to drive to the football field at Bainbridge High School and wait for the chopper.

46

MIKE DILLON

After living in their Indianola house for a year, Paul decided they should prepare for future slow times. He had not been spending much time at Artform, and the commute is beginning to wear on him.

Since he seemed to be on his way to provide an income from his inflatable work, he thanked Penny, gave her his resignation, and told her if she ever needed help to let him know.

Paul built a loft apartment inside the shop. If they move out of the Indianola house and into the shop, they could drastically reduce their living costs.

He is pretty detail-oriented, so he bought some books and made stairs that rose to a split-level bedroom area. There are two rooms—one for the girls and one for Martha and Paul.

Next to the existing bathroom downstairs, he put in a double sink and a claw foot bathtub with a shower. They added a refrigerator, a microwave, and a hotplate. A plug-in skillet also proved useful.

Paul loves living like this. It reminds him of studios he had lived in previously. Martha is into it as well—at least she said she is. She accompanied Paul as they searched for building supplies. She found the sink and the bathtub.

There is a new addition to the office area. Martha's mother sent her a computer.

Paul's business—Big Air Productions, Inc.—suddenly had jobs flooding in. They made no sales calls; it is all word of mouth.

This required hiring people. He is unable to do it all himself.

Finding a good accountant is first on his list.

In 1995, The Becker Group took an interest in his inflatable creations. They made Christmas decorations for malls around the world.

They asked Paul if he could make an inflatable jingle bell out of gold fabric. One of the principal designers from Becker came out from Baltimore to view it.

Big Air got the job and began fabricating Christmas ornaments, snowmen, and toys for malls in Dubai, London, Paris, Rio de Janeiro, and countless places in the United States. Within fifteen years, Big Air fabricated at least 2,000 inflatable shapes for Becker. The quality of Paul's work is beyond anything else found on the market.

As jobs began coming in, Paul hired friends on occasion, but they had jobs and could only work weekends or evenings.

Finally, Paul advertised for a cutter and sewing machine operator. He ended up getting the employees who stuck with Big Air for two decades.

One is Kukiko, a Japanese woman. Paul hired her as a cutter—fast and precise. She also is competent with math. If he needs help in other areas of the business, she happily jumps in to help.

The other is Karen. Karen is a whiz at the sewing machine—also very fast, producing quality work and willing to work at home when needed.

The best thing about these talented women is that, if they were between jobs, they both agreed to take time off.

Kukiko had a family—two sons and a Navy husband. She has financial security and works on her own projects at home.

Karen has her own business and a husband, son, and daughter.

When a new job comes in, Paul calls those two immediately after he designs the work to be done.

They enjoy doing inflatable work.

When Paul moved to the Northwest, he continued hearing the name Dillon Works.

When people talked about Mike Dillon, his name is said with respect when it comes to quality fabrication.

Mike Dillon started his business in his garage. As the business grew, his company moved to an old closed motel.

Paul still tries to recall the memories of when he first saw Mike's work and met him. It was after he arrived in Seattle.

Mike asked him to do an inflatable body of a rocket needed to match the fins he had fabricated. It fit perfectly.

This job is for Sony Interactive Entertainment's PlayStation, and it led to future jobs for Big Air.

The following year, Sony wanted Big Air to make five twenty-foot-high PlayStation characters for an interactive games convention in Los Angeles. They liked them so much they ordered five more.

— ❋ —

As Big Air Productions grew, the jobs poured in. He found himself increasingly alone as far as support from his spouse.

Martha's mother sent her a computer in 1994.

Her attention was a hundred percent focused on this computer. She is a smart woman, and she picked up computer language in just a few days. Paul had no help with the kids and the business.

They tried counseling and communicating, but it became clear when she said she didn't want to be married. This decision resulted in two years in court while he raised his daughters and ran his business.

The inevitable finally occurred between Martha and Paul. Their marriage was over, and Paul became the custodial parent. The good news was that during the two years it took to resolve their divorce, his business grew by leaps and bounds.

Paul made two significant additions to his life and business. One was a person to run the office, and the other was a nanny to make sure his girls are well taken care of when he is busy. The nanny is only needed until both girls are old enough to go to elementary school, and the office manager is necessary only during busy times.

Both are essential when it comes to being able to function in a working environment.

For exercise, he played on a softball team. One of his teammates had a job as an architect. Ed is part of the team that designed the new flagship store for Nordstrom in downtown Seattle. They are looking for a spectacular event to kick off the opening celebration when they are finished.

At one of their softball games, Paul brought the inflatable eagle he made when he first arrived in Seattle. Ed asked Paul if he has a brochure or photos that he could take to work.

Paul received a call from Nordstrom eight months before the store opened. They are looking for an idea to promote the opening and want to highlight their shoes.

He suggested legs hanging over the side of their roof as if someone is sitting on the building dangling their legs over the edge.

They loved the idea; they want three pairs of legs—one for a man, one for a woman, and a pair for a child. They figured fifty-five feet in length would attract everyone's attention.

"Can you do that?"

"You bet I can!"

The opening is a grand success. Big Air inflated the legs on cue with the national press filming it. They flopped the legs over the side and inflated them all at once. It hit the front pages across the country.

They kept the legs on the roof for the whole summer—June 1 to August 31. There was only one problem. After a rainstorm, the man's legs filled with water and tore.

We repaired them and had the legs back up in a couple of hours.

A year later, Nordstrom went public. Big Air inflated the legs on the roof of the New York Stock Exchange.

The Bon Marché is two blocks from Nordstrom. Having seen the legs, they asked Paul if he would meet with them.

They had two items on their agenda.

The Bon wanted twenty-one Christmas elves to mount on the side of their building. They needed them to look like they are climbing up the side.

They also asked if he could make inflatable floats on golf carts for the MACYS holiday parade.

Paul told them he could do both.

After seeing the legs fly from the Nordstrom building, they needed little convincing. He got both jobs.

The twenty-one elves are not inflatable. Paul constructed them with chicken wire on a flexible PVC base. He ordered six five-gallon containers of "Plasti-Dip," each a different color (This is a rubbery compound used to coat the handles of tools).

Paul mixed a flesh color (with different ethnic complexions), wrapped the bodies like mummies using a loosely woven material, and painted each body with "Plasti Dip." He then sculpted elf faces from clay and cast them using the same material. They made red and green clothes and hats and then gave each elf a backpack with a wrapped gift sticking out the top.

Because the elves' substructure is flexible, the installers could change the body position to whatever they liked. Some simply hung from window-sills; others were in the act of swinging a leg up, so they could climb onto a sill, and others are standing in windows. They are all scattered across the building like an army assaulting a castle.

This event turned out to be another front-page news story in the Seattle paper. Some office workers freaked out when they walked into their offices and saw strange elfin characters staring back at them outside their windows.

47

MACY'S

The inflatable holiday floats are each powered by an internal golf cart. They became the beginning of a fifteen-year stint of fabricating floats and being in charge of driving and maintaining them. Finding drivers for the Seattle Holiday Parade is a yearly ordeal that took place on the day after Thanksgiving. Paul recruited his crew of friends and staff from his favorite haunt, "Whiskey Creek Steak House." Big Air also sent maintenance people to Portland to train the workers of another company, SCI 3.2. They were in charge of the Macy's parade in their area.

Big Air made approximately twenty-five floats for each city over those fifteen years. He also had a maintenance crew that could solve any problem on the parade route, usually within a minute.

Before Big Air arrived on the scene, the floats were made by a Texas company using tens of thousands of balloons tied across a chicken-wire frame. They are also on golf carts.

The Bon had not been getting along with the company that made these floats. That's when they asked Paul if Big Air could make them. He told them they would give it a try. Big Air took over without a problem.

As the years went by, Paul's inflatable floats replaced the tied balloon floats.

Being involved in the parade is quite the occasion for Paul's forty-five workers and volunteer drivers. Big Air provided them with hotel rooms while they labored to prepare the floats at the Washington State Convention Center. At the end of each twelve-hour workday, they transformed into party animals, but they always showed up the next day, raring to go and amazingly proficient with their duties.

Each person had his or her stories to tell. It's quite an adventure.

Oh! And Paul can't forget. Since they worked through Thanksgiving, the Bon—which later became Macy's—provided them with an excellent turkey dinner with all the fixings.

———— * ✳ * ————

Paul volunteered as an art docent at his daughter's elementary school and continued to do so for nine years. He loved teaching art and had no qualms about teaching first graders how to mix colors, learn perspective, and other basics that children should learn along with the ABCs.

The rules for a docent required twenty minutes of teaching art history. The school has a small library of large art posters depicting work from great artists—a good sampling anyway. That is a good thing. Paul had plenty to talk about with each artist he chose to present.

The school also sent some classes on field trips to the Big Air studio. He inflated his forty-five-foot-long dinosaur at the end of the tour. The students love it.

Word got around, and he gave tours to many of the elementary schools in Kitsap County, other groups as well, such as art schools and the Boy Scouts.

Paul's landlord asked if he would rent more shops if he built them.

He said he would definitely rent them. Paul ended up with four shops on four acres; each shop is 2,500 square feet with a high ceiling.

One shop contained the office and the sewing department. Paul and the girls are still living in the upstairs apartment. Another shop is for woodworking and welding. The third shop is where they paint the inflatable shapes. He stores the Macy's parade floats in the fourth building. Macy's pay rent for housing the floats.

— ❋ —

Since the first day Paul arrived in Seattle and the Puget Sound area—since breathing the fresh air with the salty and evergreen aromas, experiencing the islands, and gazing at two snow-capped mountain ranges—the thought entered his mind: "If he ever bought a house, he wanted to live in the forest with a lot of land and a view of the Olympic Mountains."

Big Air is doing well enough that he can finally look for a house. An ideal opportunity opened up.

It isn't the house so much as the property. The house is okay. It's an old farmhouse built in 1952, large enough for his daughters to have their own room. There is a lot of work that needs to be done. The deck is not there. The previous owner tore it down because it was rotten. For safety's sake, the sliding door was screwed shut so people wouldn't walk out and fall five feet to the ground. Paul had a new deck built.

The front porch was sagging and rotten. Paul had the porch rebuilt.

The repairs are capped off with a new roof.

That is the major work that needs to be done to make the place livable.

The barn is worse. It has no roof at all. It is a small barn and is filled with the remnants of chickens (hay, feathers, and poop) and a small stall for one or two cows.

Jessie is so excited about the barn that she ran into the old building and immediately fell through the floor. She is okay—whew!

Paul couldn't bear to tear the barn down—hence a new roof, new floor, and a deck with a protective overhang. He cleaned out the hay and unnecessary structures. He put up wallboard and painted everything white.

Voilà! Paul has a magnificent painting studio.

One obvious requirement is to put track lights on the ceiling above the painting area. There couldn't be enough lighting, so Paul put two rows of track lights on the sidewalls. They are attached vertically on each side with independent switches and a dimmer.

Paul then built two small studios as private painting areas for his daughters and installed a wood stove.

The house is on five and a half acres with a gorgeous view of the Olympic Mountains—not a partial view—the whole range with the Hood Canal in the foreground. The house overlooks a horse ranch; he will never lose that view.

There is a pond on the property with an island. It has an incoming stream and an outgoing stream that eventually empties into the Hood Canal.

Over half the property is dense forest, so he acquired a wildlife easement that saved on property taxes and provided an abundance of wildlife. Deer, bear, and many unusual species appeared on occasion. He saw a couple of lynxes and a tiny fox popped into view once. The deer loved to dine on the apple trees. There is a plum tree and a cherry tree, not to mention the blackberry bushes.

Oh, yeah, there are plenty of coyotes.

A snow owl made its presence known, looking for mice and filling the night with its hoots. During the day, woodpeckers knocked out their rhythm. I could go on.

The pond has its own unique visitors. There are plenty of ducks and a blue heron that makes its usual yearly visit to nest. Two river otters slept lazily on the island on a couple of occasions.

Finally, Paul can't forget the domestic inhabitants—Paul's dogs. He has had three Vizslas at different points in time. When the first one passed, she was replaced by a new pup. The dogs could run around the property without a leash but never lost sight of Paul. They won't go outside without him, even though the door is left open. They run circles around him or wait next to the open door with their heads tilted to one side.

"Come on, Dad. Let's go run around!"

Paul has never thought of himself as a businessman.
Painting and working in his studio have always been his love. He made a lot of sacrifices in his life to do that. We all live in a society where the amount of money and material items you amass in your life determines your success.

Paul has never thought of it that way. He will always be happy experiencing life and producing art, not as a tool to make money. Success to him is the internal growth and awareness you amass as you journey through life. That is what you carry with you after your death. Painting is meditation, as well as expression. His work became a visual diary of his mind with the acknowledgment that he didn't always understand what he is expressing; however, it is real, and it did emerge as a baby born to this world. Paul will leave it to others to figure it out.

That's not true for many artists. It is common for artists to paint from photographs, maybe enhancing their work to be more exciting and attractive. These artists stay on the realistic plane of life and determine their success by how much they sell. After all, we need to make a living, preferably doing something we love.

As far as fabricating inflatable sculpture, the one thing that dawned on him is that he has never made a sales call. Making inflatable sculptures is a path that life put him on—probably for a reason. He did love the challenge. It would not have been possible to make an inflatable without the knowledge and growth he acquired during his manic obsession with his art for the previous thirty-five years.

Making an inflatable began by creating concept art, making a clay sculpture, forming a shape in fabric and compressed air, and then painting it—all on a massive scale. He is still honing his art by doing this. The fact that creating an inflatable became an external process and not an internal one is the only difference; however, one did create the other. Inflatable sculpture emerged from his ability and obsession with his personal internal art. He just took the path where it led him.

48

CATS

While working on an inflatable project, Paul is interrupted by the telephone. He makes the usual mad dash to the office in time to answer it. This call is different. It's a call that became the beginning of a project that will always make him proud.

"Big Air Productions," Paul answered, slightly out of breath.

"Hello. Is this Paul?"

"Yes, it is. Can I help you?" Paul took a seat at the desk.

"I think you can. My name is Randy Buck. I'm a producer for Troika Entertainment. Are you familiar with the Broadway production of *CATS*?"

"Yes," he said. "I saw it live in London."

"Great. Do you think you can make the set as an inflatable?"

"Sure, I can!" This "can do anything" response is his usual answer to all inquiries. Paul loves challenges, but he should hear the details first.

"What's your best guess on how much it would cost?"

"I would need to see some photos or drawings of the set. It will be at least $20,000."

"I'll tell you what. I'm going to overnight our program and some photos. Call me when they arrive."

"I'll do that. Thanks."

A day later, a large envelope is delivered. Opening it revealed an eight-and-a-half-by-eleven-inch glossy brochure that they hand out to the audience before each performance. There are detailed photos, but they mostly showed the performers. You can see sections of the set but not enough to show the scope of the project.

Paul picked up the phone and called Randy. He answered immediately.

"Hello. Randy here."

"Hi, Randy. This is Paul from Big Air. I received the brochure."

"I know it doesn't show much of the set, but maybe it will give you a better idea. I don't have much more than that at the moment."

"It looks pretty detailed and complicated," Paul said, as he flipped back and forth through the program.

"It is. There are lots of lights and strobes built into the wall. There must be at least forty cats' eyes that light up. What do you think? Price-wise, I mean."

Paul stalled a few seconds—long seconds.

"Well, I feel that the price I originally gave you was really low. We could be talking $50,000."

Randy paused with his response and said, "So what are you doing this coming Friday?"

"Nothing important."

"I'll tell you what. I'll have a ticket to Boston waiting for you at the Seattle airport. It's an early flight. I'll book you a room in a hotel next to the theater and send you the details. When you arrive, check into your room and relax or see the sites. I'll meet you at the back door of the theater at eight o'clock."

"Great. I'll be there."

He hung up the phone in shock. Could this be happening?

The flight to Boston is pleasant but long. It is early February 2002, and Paul is departing from the usual drizzle and temperate weather of Seattle. He had always wanted to visit Boston. There are so many exciting things to see and do. It almost has the same lure that Seattle does.

Boston has history—old architecture and monuments. They support the arts and play a significant part in our fight for an independent nation.

During the flight, he read his book of the moment, *Passage to Juneau*, by Jonathan Rubens. The thought of the possibilities from this job distracts him from reading. On occasion, he would fade off into his thoughts only to realize he had read two pages and hadn't absorbed any of it. Instead, he is wondering how he will make this inflatable set—how would it work? Then he returned to the last part of the book he remembered and began reading again. Usually, he naps on flights, but not this time.

Paul arrives in Boston to an "all-out" snowstorm. There are huge snowflakes and no wind. A cab driver is waiting for him with his name on a rectangle of white cardboard. He drives Paul directly to the Shubert Theatre. Next to the theatre is an old hotel.

The ride has been paid, so he tipped the driver and retrieved his bag. Paul enters the hotel, and their staff directs him to his room.

Throwing his bag on the bed, he opened it and removed his winter coat, hat, and gloves.

Walking around, Boston intrigued him, and the weather reminded him of Wyoming—without the wind. Paul walked through parks and across massive bridges. There aren't many people out in this weather. He's probably the only one crazy enough to be outside.

At eight o'clock that evening, Paul knocked on the backstage door. When it opened, he asked to see Randy Buck who was expecting him. In less than a minute, he was shaking Paul's hand and inviting him in. The place is hectic, with all the performers running around half-dressed and trying to prepare for their moment. It is opening night. Randy introduces Paul to several people—mostly stagehands and managers, and a few "cats" as well.

They meandered around backstage, and Randy led him to the stage to show him its construction and characteristics. He then opened the side curtain. The place is sold out; only one seat is empty—middle front. They walked down some steps, and Randy led Paul to his seat.

"When the musical is over, meet me back on stage. We can talk," said Randy as he returned to the stage and disappeared behind the curtain.

Anybody who has seen *CATS*—especially for the first time—is usually blown away. It's a very dynamic performance. The tour is so physically taxing that Troika needs to recast most acting parts every year. The leaping and dancing are hard on the body after a year of continual performances, which are only broken up by travel from city to city.

Paul met Randy on stage after the show. As it turns out, not all parts will be inflatable. There is a massive tire that rises to heaven with cast members on it. There are doorways through large sewer pipes and an oven that the "cats" can crawl through to make a grand entrance.

The inflatable needs to fit perfectly around the solid obstacles. Cats' eyes are scattered throughout the set, and access panels need to be installed in the back of the wall so each set of eyes can be easily installed. The lights will attach with Velcro placed inside little chambers with electrical wiring passing through the back. A framework needs to be built to keep the walls firm and to support the wiring.

Randy shook Paul's hand, thanked him for coming, and said to go home and think about it. They can discuss the details later.

"By the way," said Randy. "When the opening night performance is over, we have a party. You're invited. It's in the lounge of your hotel."

Paul's flight didn't leave for a couple of days.

"Relax, and see Boston," Randy said. "Your room is taken care of."

The next day, the snow had stopped, and the chill that followed the snowstorm meant he needs to bundle up. He's glad he came prepared. He walked around Boston, had a couple of beers at the Cheers bar, and used the subway to explore. On his last night there, Paul had sushi then retired to his hotel room. It is an early flight home the next day.

The back-and-forth negotiations continue. Randy and Paul discuss ideas and concerns. Making this set will not be easy, and they both want to cover the details and resolve any problems that could come up.

Randy scheduled another trip for the opening of CATS in Baltimore.

"Can you do a prototype?" Randy asked.

"Yes, I can."

Paul took a section of the set and made an eight-foot-high and six-foot-wide inflatable wall in the technique he planned to use. He sent him photos as it progressed to see if he had any input.

Randy likes it.

So, it's off to Baltimore. When the wall deflates, it is amazingly small and fits easily into a carry bag the size of a suitcase. On this trip, Paul took his girls with him. Martha said she would watch the girls if she could accompany them. He agreed. Otherwise, he would need to leave them in the hotel while they tested the prototype.

Arriving at the venue, Paul goes to the Lyric Theatre at the Modell Performing Arts Center. The theater is immaculate. The solid set is already installed.

Paul walked out to mid-stage, took the inflatable out of the bag, inflated it, and compared it to the real set. It's a perfect likeness. They tried different lighting and are impressed. The sound of the fan isn't that noticeable. They would use bigger fans with the complete set, but the production is so loud that the audience won't notice.

That night, Paul and his family watched the Baltimore opening of CATS and went to their opening party afterward.

Claire and Jessie see the performance and are invited backstage. When they attend the party, both are given *CATS* brochures, and they excitedly ran around getting signatures from all the performers.

Randy wanted to make sure that Paul had the financing to finish the job. They finally agreed on $170,000.

"If Big Air completes the job on time, Troika will add another $10,000 as a bonus."

There is one final trip that Paul is required to take—the Queen Elizabeth Theatre in Vancouver, British Columbia.

When the production reached Vancouver, a couple of hours north of Seattle, Paul drove up to watch them unload their five—or was it seven?—semi-trucks with fifty-four-foot trailers.

As the trucks are unloading, the crew held each section of the set in front of Paul for photographs. Randy also sent him immaculate technical drawings.

The solid set took a crew of fifty workers over a week to install. When Paul finished the inflatable set, it took a team of four two days to install, and it fit in a mid-sized U-Haul truck.

When Big Air finished the CATS set six months later, four of them traveled to Biloxi, Mississippi to install it for opening night. The soft set (which it is later named) will kick off the beginning of that year's tour with a new cast and a new set. They wanted Paul to stay a few more days so Big Air could make any necessary changes. It is a great success!

Throughout the first year, Troika sent Paul and Kukiko to a few cities—including Ottawa, Canada—to go over the inflatable set to make minor changes and check for damage.

After ten years of on the road, Randy called and said that *Cats*—the longest-running show in theater history—had come to an end. The inflatable set worked great and is still in excellent condition. It made them millions. They could do one-night stands and fit it in theaters where the solid set couldn't go.

"Just to let you know," said Randy, "when I proposed the inflatable idea to Troika over ten years ago, they didn't like the idea. I searched the Internet for inflatable companies. When I found your site, I knew you could do it. I was so confident that it could be done that I used my own money.

"By the way, I'm now president of Troika Entertainment."

What a fabulous man!

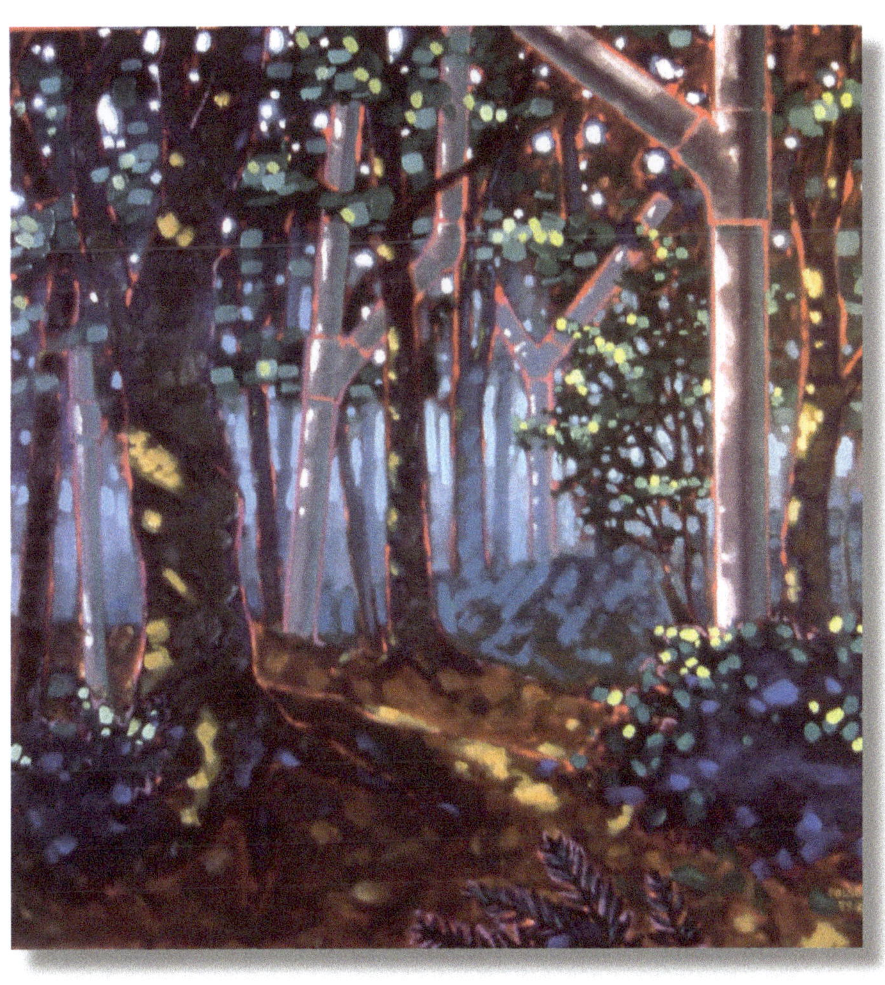

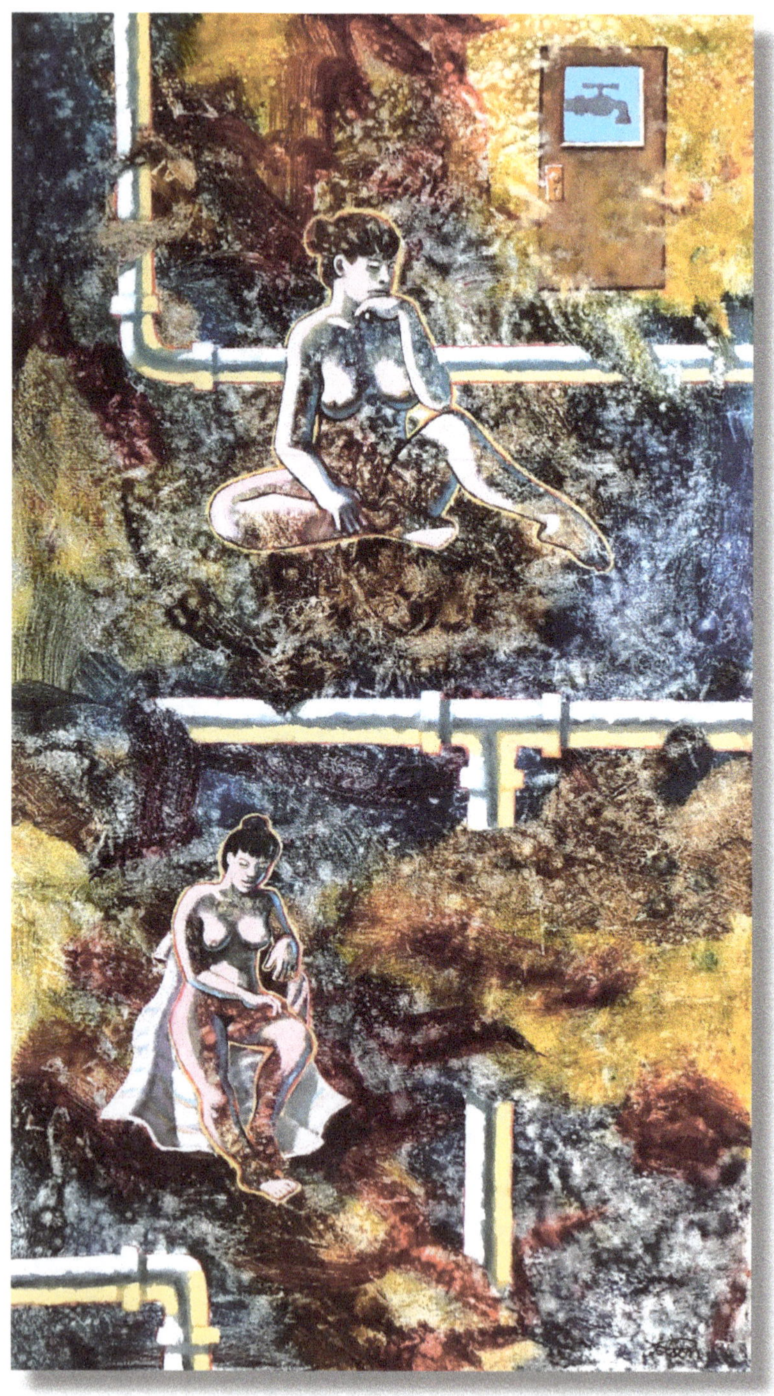

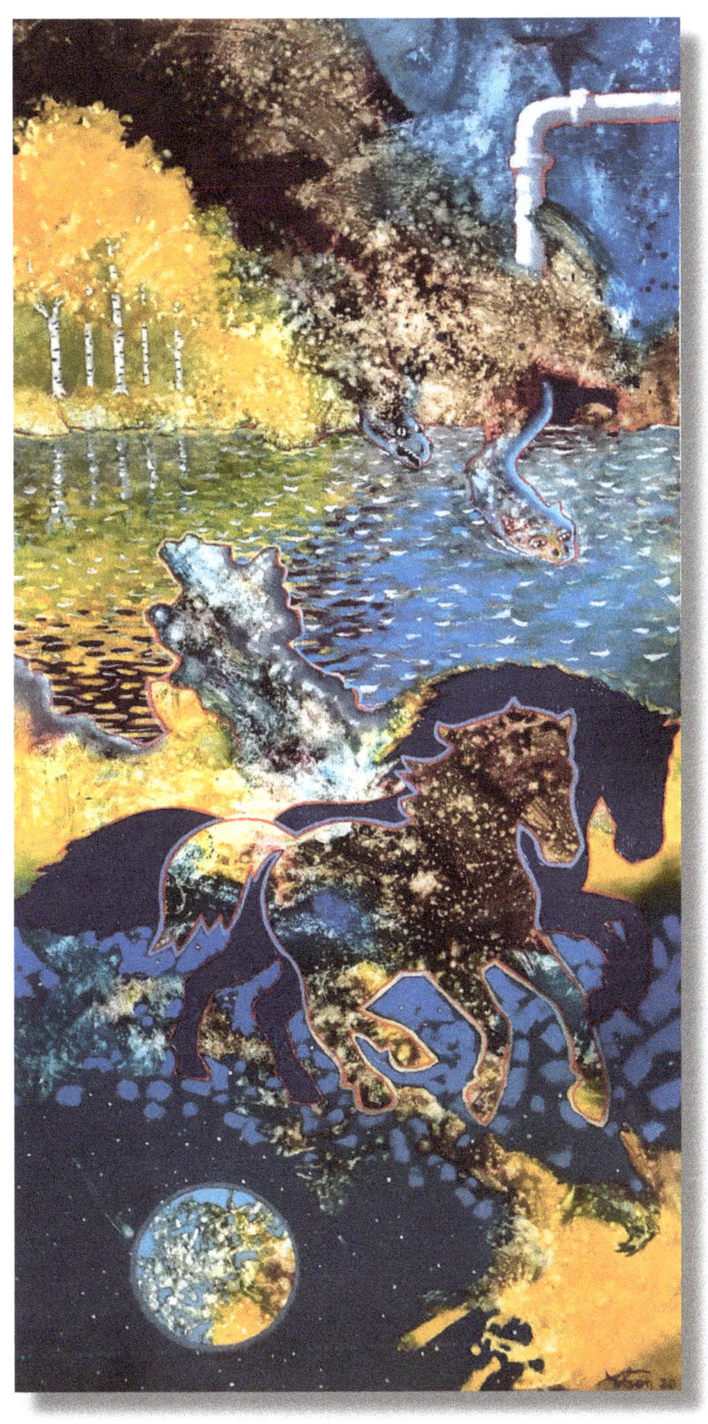

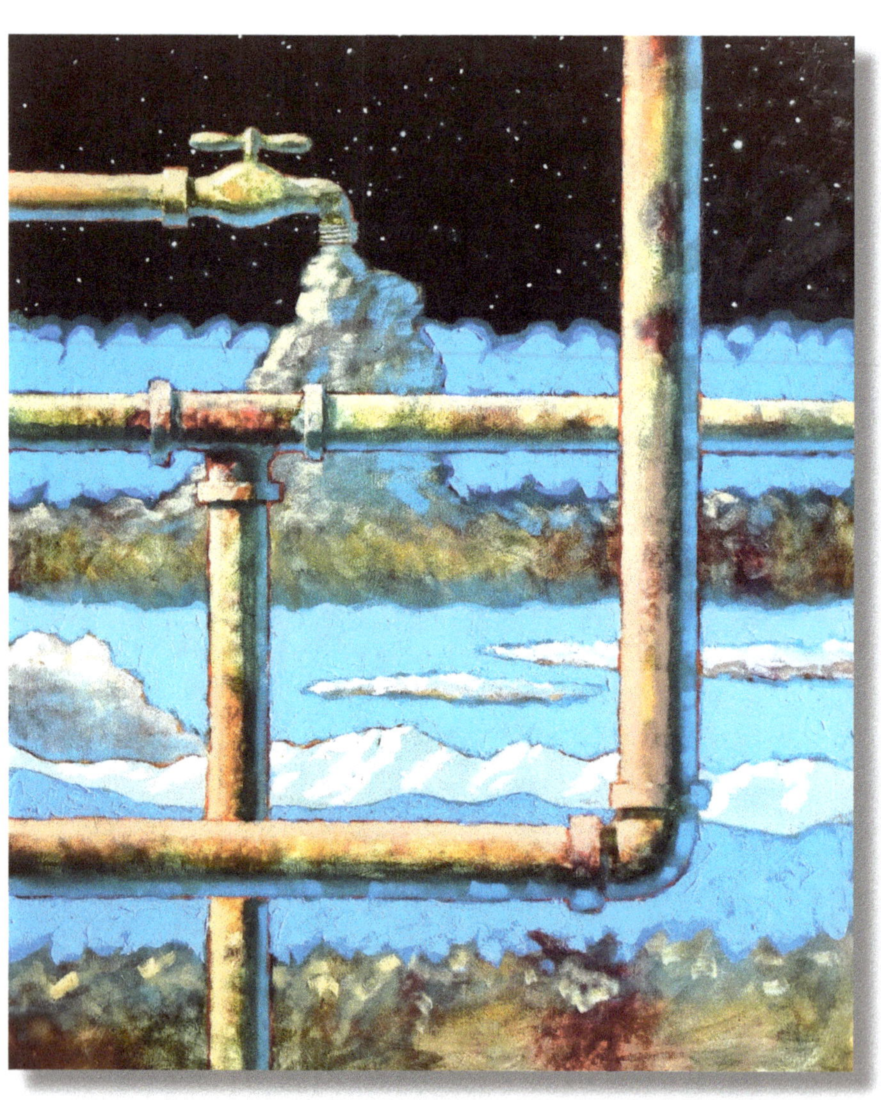

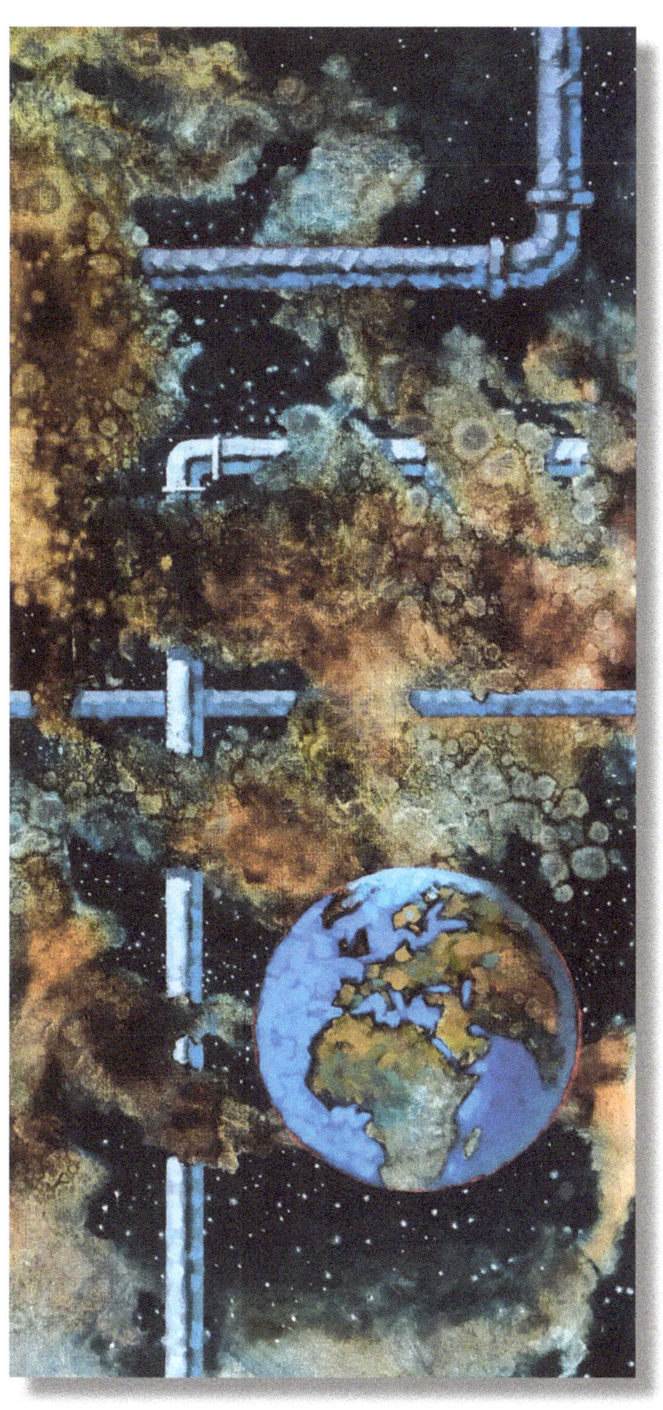

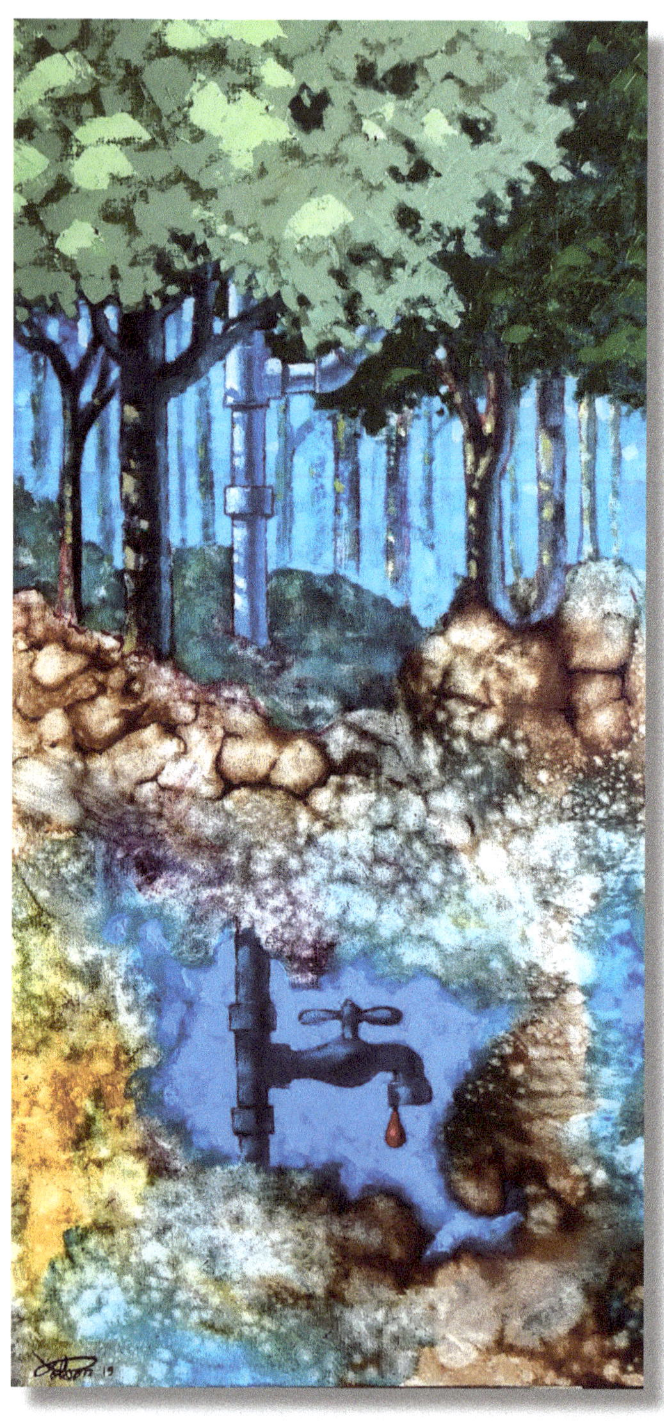

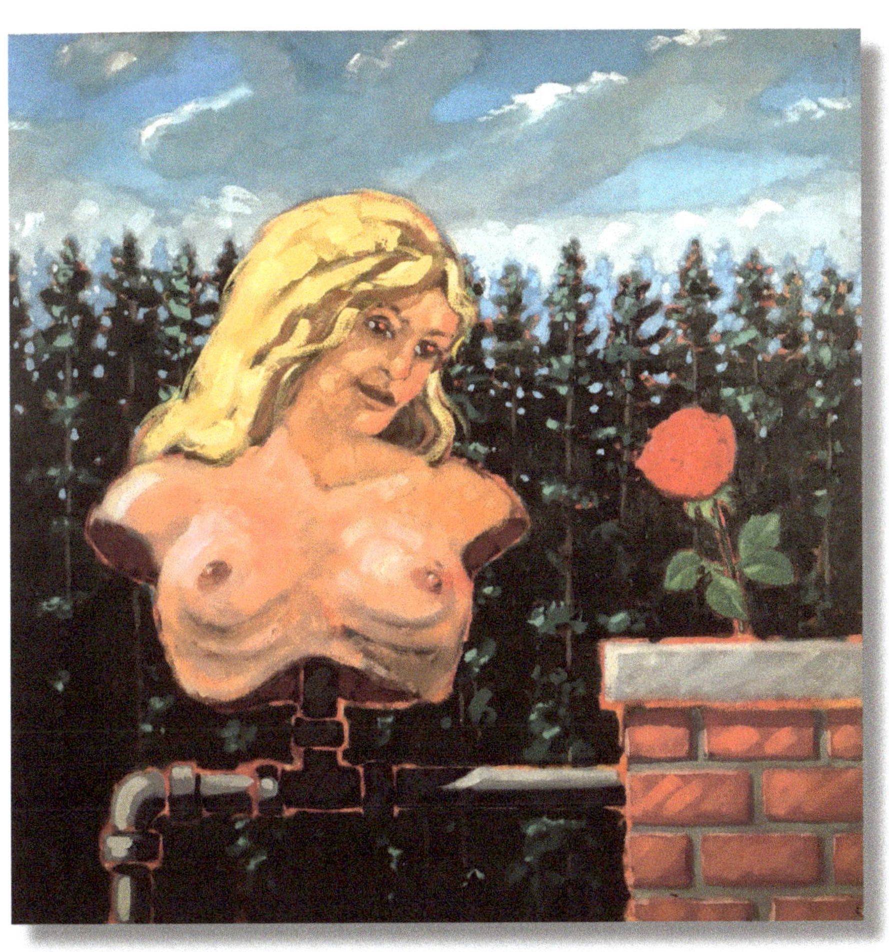

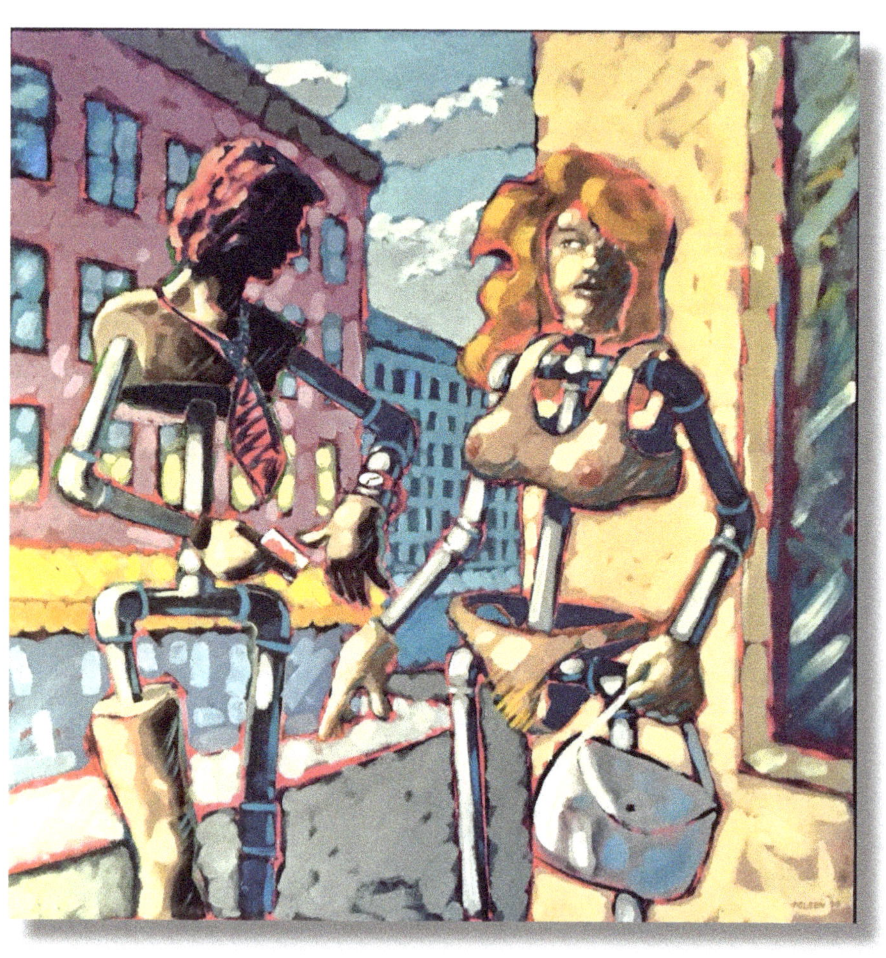

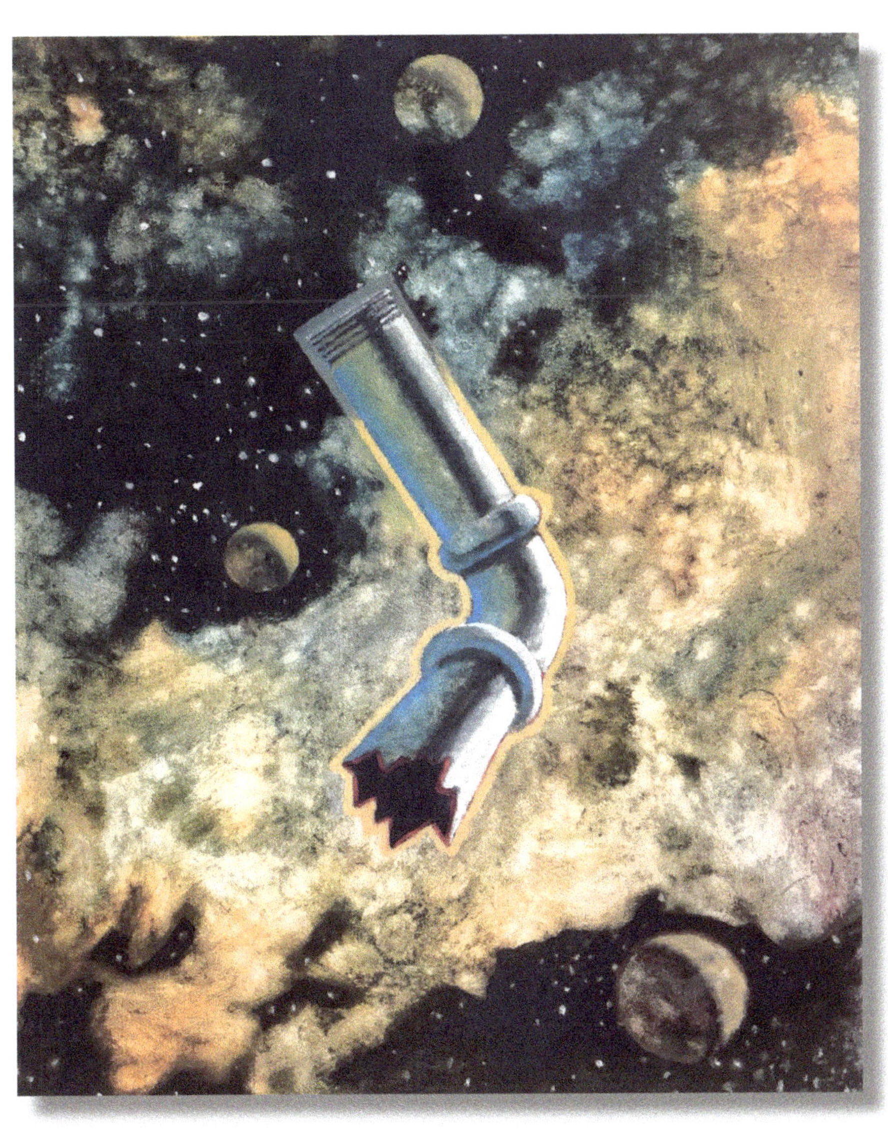

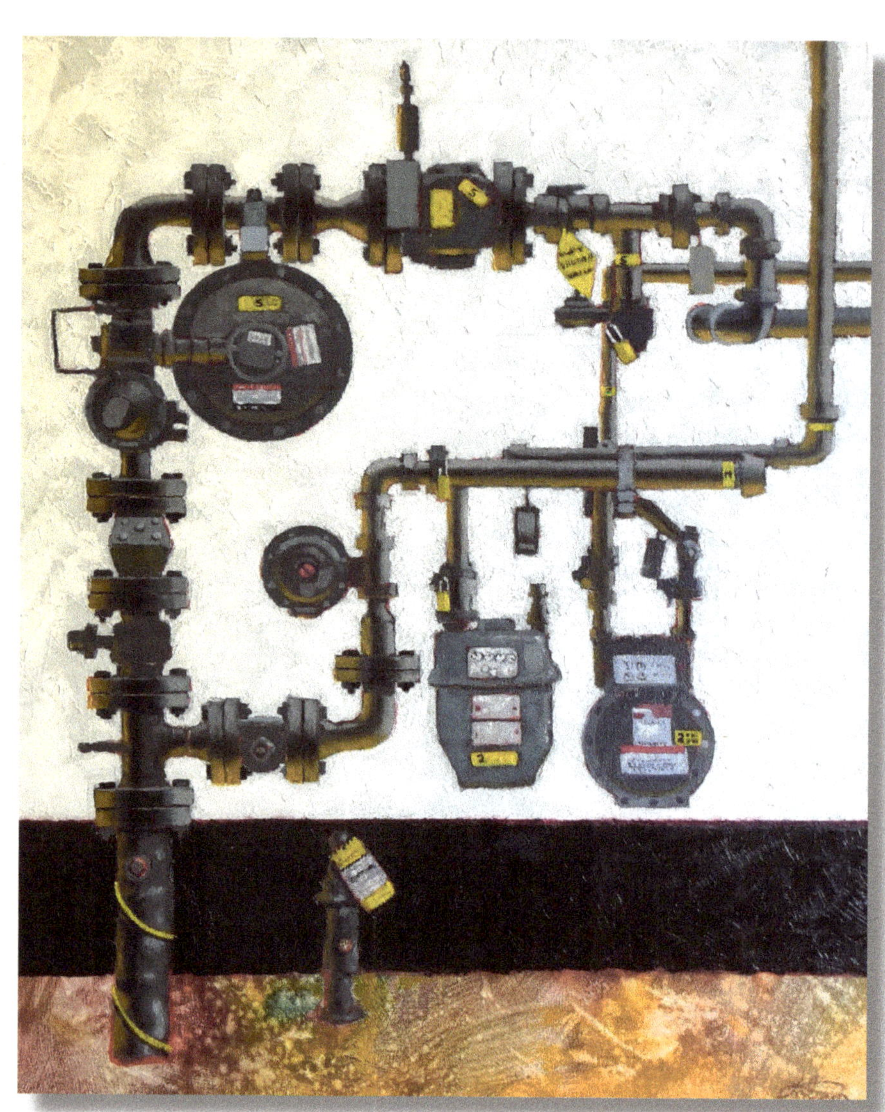

49

MAUK

After the CATS set, Big Air received more interest from clients curious about inflatables. Paul has many clients who proclaimed that he is the best inflatable fabricator they know. He received many "one of a kind" quality jobs from excellent clients. These included Cirque du Soleil, Radio City Music Hall, and Sony Interactive Entertainment. There is one specific designer in San Francisco who saw Paul as a person who could pull off the impossible. That is Mitchell Mauk from Mauk Design, Inc.

Paul is doing well enough financially that he bought his business property—four buildings on four acres. He remortgaged his house and paid off his shops in full.

Along with the occasional jobs, he continued his seasonal work for Becker, averaging 100 inflatable ornaments and toys a year for malls around the world.

Paul continued to fabricate floats for the Seattle and Portland MACY'S Parades. That included being in charge of finding the crews needed to pull this off; assembly, maintenance, and drivers. Big Air loaded trucks with the floats from their facility and delivered them to the Washington State Convention Center. The crew spent Thanksgiving week assembling the floats. They organized and drove them during the parade, then loaded them back in the trucks and delivered them to Paul's shops for storage.

* ✳ *

Paul first met Mitchell Mauk when he did a job for Sony Interactive Entertainment's PlayStation. He made an inflatable for each of the main characters of the video games, hitting the scene at the time. He made five characters, and Sony ordered two of each. They included Lara Croft, Spyro, and Crash Bandicoot.

It's a fun project, and they turned out great.

Over a year later, Paul received a call from Mitchell.

"I need your help," said Mitchell. "Can you make a sixty-foot-long Teflon molecule? It's due in two weeks."

"Do you have a photo?"

"Yes. I will send it to you now."

Seconds later, a digital photo is on my screen of a model of the molecule. It consists of spheres and tubes.

"I can make that. It's a pretty short lead time."

"I needed to figure something out," said Mitchell. "My design for a trade show in Las Vegas fell through. My client needs something."

"I'm pretty sure I can do that. Can you send me the model?"

"Yes, I can. What do you think it will cost?"

"$20,000."

"Okay. Go ahead and invoice me. I'll overnight the model."

When the model arrived overnight, Paul opened the box.

The model is made from Christmas ornaments. There are hundreds of tiny pieces in the box. The model had disintegrated.

Paul hopped in his truck and drove to Michael's arts and crafts store. Amazingly, he found wooden spheres and dowels that are in the exact proportion of the sample.

He drilled holes in the spheres to fit the dowels and recreated the model.

After painting it, he sent a photo to Mitchell.

"Looks great. Go for it."

This inflatable is an unusual job because he didn't use a fabric-based material; he used clear vinyl. The tubes are navy blue, and the spheres are light, transparent blue. The inflatable is coming together beautifully.

Paul contacted the installation company based in New York City. He sent them a technical drawing of how the molecule hangs. It'll be attached to a truss that is sixty feet long. Each sphere has a D-ring at the top, and the length of the support cable varies depending on the place it occupied in space.

The installation crew freaked out.

"We know this isn't going to work. If it doesn't, we're the ones who will look bad."

"It's going to work," Paul said.

They countered with, "You need to ship this to us so we can do a test inflation."

"Can do," Paul said. "I have two weeks to make this. It will arrive in Las Vegas just in time for the installation."

When Paul arrived at the convention center, the truss is in place with the cables hanging from their assigned spots. He spread the inflatable out to make sure it isn't twisted and attached all the cables.

The New York crew is standing around—arms folded—glaring at me. They thought he was going to embarrass them and ruin their reputation single-handedly.

Mitchell showed up, ready for the show.

"Okay," Paul said. "When I yell, go, raise the truss, and turn the three blowers on at the same time."

Paul gave the "go" sign, the truss began to rise, and the air blew into each tube, and then into each sphere. When it reached the designated height, the truss stopped, and there hung the most beautiful, awe-inspiring sight he had ever seen.

The jaws of everybody in the area dropped, followed by huge smiles. It is perfect. It looked better than Paul could have imagined.

The crew responded with handshakes and pats on the back. The most rewarding responses are the smiles—especially on Mitchell, who is running around taking photos.

After this show, the inflatable ships to the Jacob K. Javits Convention Center in New York City. The same crew is there when he arrived to install it—his newfound friends. Paul is treated with handshakes and smiles.

This exhibit received a national silver award from *Exhibitor Magazine* as the second-best exhibit in the nation that year.

Each job is an adventure. Paul is dealing with high-level clients and also dealing with the reality of being an employer.

Paul dove into the middle of its complexities even though he had never planned to be a businessman. When he first started making inflatable sculptures, he welcomed the challenges and viewed it as an adventure.

The good thing about his business is that clients called him. Paul didn't have to make sales calls. His clients were sold by the time they contacted Big Air because of his website and just plain old word of mouth.

Big Air employees are excited about having a job that is creative and fun. Seeing a project progress from a sketch to a finished product is rewarding, and everyone gathers together to see the first inflation of each project.

As time moves on, Paul began realizing the weakness in his business. His capacity to produce is not able to match the amount of business he is getting.

Paul needs employees who can take over certain aspects of fabrication, as well as people who can work with clients.

At the time, it all falls on Paul's shoulders.

Paul usually tries not to inundate himself with too much business. Jobs seem to space themselves out enough to make them manageable. But the more business he has, the harder it is to control the ensuing situations.

There is one job that is the epitome of what Paul is saying.

The producers of *Mystère*—a Cirque du Soleil production in Vegas—called Paul and asked if he could make a forty-foot snail to replace an old one they are using. The one they have is falling apart. The time and cost to maintain it made them realize that they might as well get a new one.

Paul sent them a formal proposal, followed by an invoice.

It is going on three weeks, and he still hasn't heard back from Cirque.

During those three weeks, Paul received a call for that year's Sony PlayStation exhibit. These are intense shows. This show will be his fourth year, and the exhibit is designed and coordinated by Pinnacle Exhibits.

Many businesses are involved. There's a company that handles the lighting, another company does the solid work, and Dillon fabricates the more specialty items. There are also shippers and installers. Pinnacle Exhibits designed the exhibit, and Mauk Design designed the project Big Air would be working on—a 1,500-pound afterburner.

Because of this, Paul has many conference calls with all of the vendors who are involved. They all have their priorities and are vying for importance. Everyone seems to feel that their role in the exhibit is the most important, and their concerns are to come first.

When the topic is on the giant inflatable afterburner, so many people make demands that Paul just sat back, feeling helpless.

He knew exactly how to fabricate this—what materials needed to use and how it would work.

The lighting people are the first to insist that their part in the project is the most important.

"We need to install the lighting before Big Air inflates the afterburner. It would take too much time to install it after inflation."

"How much weight are we talking about?" Paul asked.

"About 1,000 pounds."

"Can you make it lighter?'

"No. These are the lights we need to use."

Mitchell's input is, "We need to use a clear vinyl fabric for the base."

"That will be risky," Paul said. "If there is no fabric base, it will be too weak to support the inflatable."

"We need to do it anyway. We need to figure out a way."

"Okay, then. We need to lift the inflatable from the top. Attach it to a truss."

"No," responded the installers and the designers. "We don't want it to appear that it is hanging."

And so it went. There are a lot of assertions that weakened the chance of this working.

There are so many conference calls that nothing is finalized until three weeks before the due date.

Paul has already received the half down payment for the afterburner. The SONY job is underway.

Paul checked the mail a week after he began the SONY project and found a letter from Cirque du Soleil. Cirque sent a check as well.

The snail—named Alice—is the job Paul favors. Sony is an excellent account and offered future work possibilities. He has a history with them, but that meant he had to wrestle with their egos. They want to tell him how he should make an inflatable.

Cirque du Soleil, on the other hand, respected his experience and allowed Paul to take the bull by the horns and accomplish the mission.

Alice isn't due until two weeks after the Sony project, and Paul feels he is committed to both jobs. Paul is cornered. He had already received payment to start working on the afterburner, and Cirque du Soleil depended on him to remake Alice.

If Paul could design and pattern the afterburner in a timely fashion, he could put it in production and then do the clay sculpture for Alice.

Paul is on track to finish the afterburner when there is a prearranged visit from "The Team." There are two weeks to go until they install it in Los Angeles. The lighting people are not happy with the route Big Air had taken to present their lights, even though it had been preapproved. They changed their minds.

The Big Air crew spent the whole next week ripping out the old areas to accommodate the lights and remake them to the lighting company's satisfaction.

That left them one week to finish the inflatable.

After a week of working long hours—with overtime and no sleep—they rolled up and crated the afterburner as the truck waited at our door. There is no time left to do a test inflation.

Paul arrived in Los Angeles late in the afternoon. They had spread the inflatable afterburner on the floor. It actually looks beautiful.

The crews setting up the show are ready to leave. The company has a suite reserved at a Dodgers baseball game with vast quantities of food and drink.

Paul is exhausted from lack of sleep, which progressed to the point of him being wired and unable to sleep.

Chris from Pinnacle Exhibits asked if Paul is alright. He is also wondering how he thought the inflation would go.

All Paul can do is shrug his shoulders. He has no idea if it would work, but his gut instinct is that they pushed it too far.

The next morning, Paul began mounting blowers and attaching the inflatable to the broad stairway, the grand entrance to the exhibit.

About twenty lighting people are scurrying around.

"Wait, we need to install all the lighting before you inflate it."

They are all frantically assembling lights and wires.

"Relax!" Paul told them. "I need to make sure it works. If it does, I will drop it back down."

When the blowers are turned on, Paul's worst fears came true. As it started to rise, there is a loud pop, and it collapsed. The clear vinyl couldn't hold the weight—or the pressure.

Paul was distraught.

"Okay, plan B. What can we do?" asked Chris.

"Well, I can go home and work on another big job deadline before it's too late," Paul said.

Chris said that would be okay.

Paul did have a plan B: sew up the rip, sew support sleeves on top, and lift the inflatable in place using a truss. He could cut off the airflow to the base. By doing this, the air would seep into the base, and the pressure would be workable.

At the time, Paul didn't mention it. He's angry that he hadn't stood his ground when the other participants made their demands to construct the project. He let them talk him into doing things that Paul knew wouldn't work.

Paul is dead tired as he flew back to Seattle. The Cirque du Soleil job isn't due for two weeks. He would have stayed in LA if he had the time and wasn't so tired. Paul still regrets leaving it like that.

When Paul returned to Big Air, the crew is waiting and ready to proceed. They felt helpless without him.

Paul had them do some prep work while he was gone. When the afterburner was in production, he finished the clay for Alice. They were ready to pattern the shape and proceed.

Paul and his sewing machine operators flew to Las Vegas for a couple of days to go over details for the Cirque snail.

The project turns out beautiful. It is nice having control of the production.

50

PAINTING

efore Paul realized it, Big Air Productions, Inc. had been in existence for twenty years. Big jobs continued as he still worked on projects for Radio City Music Hall, Macy's parade floats, and Cirque du Soleil as well as rock tours and occasional trade shows and events.

In 2008, the economy went on the skids. It didn't affect Big Air at first, but in the next few years, the Becker Group's owner retired and sold his business to Global Experience Specialists (GES). They decided not to pursue the Christmas side of the company.

That's what Paul heard from GES anyway, but it turns out they began purchasing low-quality inflatable ornaments from Taiwan.

Macy's is having financial difficulties. They sent a person to Seattle to lay off the events people. To continue the parade, they had to keep Paul, but they cut and slashed Big Air's compensation for doing the work.

Paul gave Macy's notice that he is retiring, but will stay one more year to break in the Portland people. Big Air trained them to do the parade in Portland, so they understood how it all worked. They can run the Seattle parade.

The number of companies making inflatable shapes had grown rapidly since Paul began his venture in this field. By 2008, he had been in the business for thirty-six years (this included his San Diego experience). During that time, the designs had become computerized, along with much of the production. The final straw is when these companies sold inflatable shapes fabricated in Taiwan, China, and India. People didn't care about quality anymore. They wanted them quick, cheap, and dirty.

As Paul approaches retirement at sixty-five, he is tired of dealing with employees who at first respected his skill. As he became busier, Paul still made the clays and patterned the projects, but Big Air employees began complaining and thought they knew more than he did. Egos ran rampant. He found himself in the office, making bids, developing concept art, invoicing, and working with clients over the phone. Paul missed the hands-on aspect of creating an inflatable.

Paul also became tired of dealing with demanding clients and just didn't need it anymore. They expected shorter turn-around times and less expensive costs. He missed his old creative self. Paul wants to work alone and make quality art.

Paul began designing and building inflatable sculptures in 1982. He was a valuable asset for two companies who pioneered the industry and helped them grow into thriving companies before starting his own business in 1994. The work Paul does, and the high-end clients he has, went beyond what was expected.

In 2014, after many challenges and adventures, Paul retired and sold his shops, but not his business.

Finally, he can get back to his painting. Paul's barn made an excellent studio, and he began showing his work in galleries again. He is much happier but thankful for the unique experience of being on the ground floor of inflatable sculpture and having a significant role in creating it as an artist and businessman.

* ❊ *

Choosing art as Paul's life goal is only possible because of his determination and passion. He believes in himself.

Paul's artistic adventures have been grand adventures. Life is a roller-coaster full of ups and downs, full of thrills and remorse. That is what life is supposed to be. That is what shapes your spirit as you prepare to move on to whatever is next.

Having been born and raised in Wyoming and having chosen an art career is odd just by itself. This time travel through life started by growing up in a sparse and isolated landscape.

Paul experienced the magic and music of the sixties as a teenager. He was also at an age where he felt the effects and lessons of the Vietnam War, which created a generation surrounded by political turmoil and fear.

He experienced playing in rock bands to work his way through college and recorded two original CDs in Seattle from an original band formed by his son Kevin.

Through literature and traveling extensively through North America and Europe, Paul can comprehend the role art plays in many countries and societies. It is the act of creativity, perhaps a million years old.

Throughout the known history of the world, art has left traces of many ancient civilizations and places where humans did once exist. Art leaves valuable clues of how the people of these civilizations live. This force saturates every corner of the planet.

Most important to Paul is the work he does with the talents he is given. Paul did not waste these talents. Living and working in his studios were priceless experiences.

He had jumped out of the fishbowl called Wyoming and dove into the ocean. As a result, Paul not only learned a lot but he is also still learning. A whole new world is open to him.

Paul painted like a mad animal and shared it with the world through galleries and any establishment that is willing to show his work or give him a one-person show. People who know Paul only had to walk into his studio to see the passion he has.

So, here Paul is, retired and back to painting. His gift and work will evolve from the experiences he is honored to have—whether good or bad. They shape who he is today. Paul's paintings will reflect that history because he paints from his heart.

Galleries and museums have accepted Paul's work. His work—including small and large paintings and sketches—number in the thousands. The opportunities are there. He just needs to take advantage of them.

He jokingly said that his goal in life is to inundate his heirs with so many works of art that they won't know what to do with it all, especially if they are all quality pieces.

Paul's focus is on the experience and the process of making art. The end result is incidental.

Paul's art speaks for itself. He doesn't need to describe it. Even though his philosophy is to continue looking ahead, his past artwork is as much Paul's children as his son and three daughters are. His paintings and drawings have their own lives. These thousands of pieces can live many lifetimes beyond that of his descendants. Paul has no idea how many paintings he's sold or given away as gifts; there are many.

Once, while visiting a family in San Diego who he hadn't seen in years, he is drawn to the art on their walls. Paul walked up to a painting that caught his eye and said, "Wow, this is an interesting piece. Where did you get it?"

Paul looked at the signature. "Oh, yeah. I did that."

It's a strange thing to see a painting that he can't remember doing over thirty years ago.

The work Paul has done is acknowledged in different ways.

Four years in a row, he was asked to give lectures at the University of Washington on the use of algebra and geometry in inflatable sculpture fabrication. These included a separate panel discussion with other professionals comparing their direction and accomplishments.

The Northwest College of Art and Design invited Paul to speak on art and careers.

The Northwind Arts Center in Port Townsend asked him to give a three-hour lecture and demo of his painting process.

West Sound Academy gave him a one-person show that required giving the student body a lecture on the painting process and his life experiences as an artist.

Paul looks at other artists' work and feels unique in this crowd. He paints from his mind. The ability to do that is strengthened by his work with landscapes and the human figure. Too many artists paint from photographs. They are lovely paintings but show little of what is inside them.

Paul realized that painting is a form of meditation. What feels like a few minutes during the painting process turns out to be hours. When he finishes a work of art, he has more energy than when he started.

51

NAPLES

Paul missed being with Kevin while he grew up with his mother in Wyoming, but the first chance Kevin had, he came out to Seattle to be with his biological dad. He wanted to develop a relationship, and he did. During the twenty-six years that Paul has known him as an adult, Kevin grew into a man of courtesy, hard work, and love. Paul has always been able to communicate with him, and Kevin has always called him "Dad."

Kevin and his wife Annie, whom he met here in the Northwest, have four amazing sons. Kevin wants his sons to have a close relationship with their grandfather—a real grandfather and grandson relationship. Paul desires that too.

Kevin started work as a structural engineer in Seattle, and when his boys were old enough to be involved in outside activities, he took a job at Naval Submarine Base Bangor. The base is a short drive from his home, compared to his hour-and-a-half commute from his house in East Bremerton to Seattle. He wants to spend more time with his family.

After a couple of years, the Navy sent Kevin and his family to Naples, Italy. He will live there for five years. As a civilian contractor and a structural engineer, he traveled to jobs in Europe, North Africa, and the Middle East. Naples is his home base.

It isn't that easy for Paul to stay in contact with him and the family. Kevin and Annie did get on Facebook, and that closed the gap. They had an open invitation for Paul to visit them. As time flew by, Paul realized that Kevin's final year had almost ended. The time was quickly approaching for them to pack up and move back to the States.

Having retired from his business at the age of sixty-five, Paul had the time to take the trip to Italy.

The timing was perfect for Jessie as well. She has had a difficult time since dropping out of school, and she is still struggling to find her way.

Paul knew that this trip would be an experience she would never forget.

So, the trip to Europe came at a convenient time.

On this Europe trip, Paul planned to visit Venice, Italy. He repeatedly attempted to go there in 1988 when he traveled to Europe, but the railroad workers were on strike. He had also missed Naples and Western Italy.

Paul thinks Jessie will be delighted when she sees Paris and its fabulous museums, and he wants to revisit them as well.

So, Jessie and Paul decide that their first stop will be Paris, France.

The timing of their arrival was not the best. It's the same week as the terrorist attacks in Paris—Friday the thirteenth, November 2015.

However, the event didn't deter them from the trip.

They found a quaint little hotel room across the river from the Louvre and two blocks from the Musée d'Orsay. Jessie is impressed, and they both spent a lot of time viewing some of the best art on the continent.

Their favorite restaurant is a block from the hotel, and Jessie's favorite food is on the menu: clams and oysters. It also has Paul's favorites: escargot and French onion soup. The rest of the entrées and appetizers are delicious.

Jessie and Paul spent four nights in Paris and then caught the train to Rome early on their last morning.

The first leg of the journey took them to Milan. They had a two-hour layover and caught the next train to Rome after the sun had set. Jessie seemed to be disturbed and began crying. She seemed uncomfortable. It concerned Paul. She couldn't connect to Wi-Fi on the train, and another passenger helped her. That helped her mood. He thinks the trip is stressing her out.

When they arrived in Rome, both of them are exhausted. Initially, they had plans to spend a day or two to see the Colosseum and a few other significant sights.

They decided that Rome could wait. Paul found a hotel across the street from the station. After a refreshing night's sleep, they caught the train to Naples.

Actually, Naples isn't their destination; it's a small town on the outskirts of Naples called Castel Volturno. Kevin and Annie are waiting for them.

They couldn't ask for better tour guides.

Close to ending their five-year stint in Italy, Kevin and Annie had plenty of time to explore the local sights and visit many parts of Europe, including Venice.

The first order of business is to visit their favorite pizza restaurant. They described it as real Italian pizza, and it is incredible.

They decided not to go to the ancient city of Pompeii. It's enormous and tiring. Most of it had been dug up well before modern-day preservation techniques. Their tour guides (Annie and Kevin) took them to Herculaneum instead. Small portions of this city have been excavated, and the methods are more preservation-oriented. Paul can only imagine what life had been like during that time.

Annie is a great guide. She is a walking history book and describes the life and events of that time in detail.

Kevin took them on a day trip to the Amalfi Coast. That drive came highly recommended. He went there enough times to have a favorite restaurant with his favorite dish—pasta with clams.

The next must-see sight is the Naples National Archaeological Museum even though it is late evening, and they are pretty tired.

The museum is in the heart of Naples—a cramped madhouse full of people and bumper-to-bumper traffic.

The art and artifacts from Pompeii and Herculaneum soon overcame our tiredness. This museum has the best quality Greek and Roman sculptures Paul has ever seen.

Paul is so proud of Jessie. She made sure he wasn't left behind. Paul kept hovering around the remarkable sculptures as the rest of the group forged ahead. She continually came back, looking for him to make sure he is okay.

Other than these must-see sights in the Naples area, they relaxed and enjoyed the small town of Castel Volturno. Jessie and Paul strolled through the streets to their favorite coffee shop in the mornings and enjoyed the hospitality of the owner. One day, there is a street market with everything, from clothes to knick-knacks to seafood and vegetables.

Kevin and Annie's four boys also added to the atmosphere. They are well-behaved, animated, and provide light-hearted entertainment. Paul brought them all Seattle Seahawk jerseys as gifts from Seattle.

Then there is Thanksgiving. Kevin and Annie invited their friends to this yearly celebration. It is a wonderful day, and they met many friendly people. Annie also acted as their travel agent. Forget the train. They can take a short flight to Venice for forty-five dollars.

Paul gave her his credit card, and she booked a trip to Venice for Kevin, Jessie, and Paul.

Paul relished being with his son and daughter—in Venice no less. Kevin had been there a couple of times before, and he took over the tour. They ended up with an unbelievable room. It had a balcony hanging over a canal; the ceiling must have been fourteen feet high. A beautiful-colored glass chandelier hung from this ceiling.

They meandered around the narrow streets, ate in fabulous restaurants, and enjoyed the art.

Besides the ancient Italian art, Peggy Guggenheim has a beautiful museum of modern art in Venice. Paul heard it was once her residence.

One highlight is spending half a day in the Doge's Palace. It's an amazing history lesson, and Kevin insisted they take the tour.

Venice is everything Paul had expected and more.

Jessie and Paul parted with Kevin after three days in that beautiful city. Kevin accompanied them to the gate at the Venice airport. They needed to connect with their return flight to the States from Paris. Kevin flew back to Naples.

Paul and Jessie stayed in Paris for two more nights and chose the same hotel as before—with the Seine and the Louvre outside the window. They needed to relax before the long flight back to Seattle and spend more time revisiting the Musee d'Orsay and their favorite restaurant.

Jessie and Paul attempted to go to the top of the Eiffel Tower, but as they stood in line, Jessie felt sick. They caught a cab back to their familiar digs and packed for their flight the next morning.

52

RESTLESS

Paul had always thought he would retire in his dream house, the five and a half acres with an old farmhouse, a pond, and a stream that emptied into the Hood Canal. This property is amazing, with a full view of the Olympic Mountains and a forest teaming with wildlife.

He turned his small barn into the studio he always dreamt of.

After Paul's so-called retirement, he focused on his painting and became his old productive self. He is accepted into two galleries. One is the Roby King Gallery on Bainbridge Island and the other the Northwind Art Center in Port Townsend.

Paul also had the honor of exhibiting his work in two shows at the Bainbridge Island Museum of Art.

Showing at the museum was an opportunity Paul didn't see coming, and it happened from a fluke decision he made by entering a juried show in Kingston.

Kingston is a small town in Washington with a ferry that crosses the Puget Sound to another small town: Edmonds. Paul's daughters attended school in Kingston. The town has a summer festival that offers a local juried show for local artists.

At first, Paul thought it was an outdoor exhibit in the park where they showed crafts and a farmers' market. Paul shied away from this because he didn't like showing outdoors in a market setting; kind of snooty, he guessed, but he preferred galleries or indoor exhibits. As it turns out, the show is an indoor exhibit—not a gallery—they put up patricians to show the artwork. The show is in a community center whose walls already have knick-knacks decorating the interior.

A fellow artist, Shelly Wilkerson, is involved in coordinating the show. She has a gallery in Port Orchard and told Paul he should enter the show.

Shelly rescued a few paintings of his a while back that had been damaged by rats. The little rascals always seemed to find access to Paul's studio, the old barn on his property. Shelly restored a few damaged paintings and put them in her gallery.

So, Paul entered and received a second-place award at the Kingston festival. During the opening, Shelly told Paul that the juror wanted to meet him. This juror just so happened to be the curator of the Bainbridge Island Museum of Art, Greg Robinson.

A week after the exhibit, Greg called Paul, expressing interest in seeing more paintings.

Within a few days, Greg and the assistant curator visited Paul's studio and separated fifteen Northwest landscapes from the masses to be hung in the Bistro entrance of the museum. In the process, Greg kept eyeing the paintings from Paul's "Strata" series.

"You know, Paul; there is a space in another part of the museum where the 'Strata' paintings will fit perfectly." The space is a stairwell—not as bad as it sounds. It is large enough to present a perfect viewing area and allow an intimacy for the viewer that is better than the main galleries.

When the time comes to hang the show, a box back truck drove into Paul's driveway. Two women from the museum stepped out, put on white gloves, and safely packed each painting. The staff from the museum hung the shows.

The opening is spectacular.

Paul is asked to give a painting demo at the museum. He had done those before, and they worked out great. The demo at the museum didn't go as well as hoped. Paul blamed himself for not devising a plan. He just dove in swinging a brush.

He also gave a lecture on his work in the museum auditorium. That went very well. There is a reception afterward with friends, museum staff and members, and the general public.

Roby King Gallery took the opportunity to promote his work, and that resulted in several purchases. Cynthia Sears, the funder of the museum, bought two paintings, and a board member bought one. There were more sales through Roby King.

Yet something troubling is beginning to take shape.

An old wise man, or a sage, or maybe it was a guru, stated that once you have reached your goal, it is time to move on. If you persist in relishing that you reached your goal, you will become stagnant and unhappy.

It is then that Paul realized that the reason he enjoyed his life is not that he obtained his goal and is living happily ever after; it's because he realizes that it is the act of working toward a dream or goal that makes life so exciting.

It became too easy to wake up to a beautiful sunny morning in the Northwest and feel so good that he just had to open a bottle of red wine.

On other mornings, the rain sets a calm, contemplative atmosphere that is made even better by opening a bottle of wine or vodka.

Paul enjoyed a drink on occasion. He didn't like the feeling of getting too drunk or dealing with after effects. Usually, it is at a restaurant with a nice meal and a two-drink limit. He never drank while working, like when he had an inflatable job or worked in Galleries and picture framing. If he knew he would have responsibilities or a busy day ahead of him, he wouldn't drink the evening before.

Now that he is home painting all day, it became too easy to have a drink. Paul loves to prepare his meals—a lamb shoulder roast is his favorite with all the fixings—including a drink to sip on while he cooked.

There is a lot of work to do on the house and property. Blackberries bushes need to be kept at bay, and gutters need to be cleaned, to name a couple.

He loves going to art gallery openings that show his work. The conversations are enticing and challenging.

But still, something isn't quite right. Paul napped too much. His health and aging show signs of a body not meant to live forever. He is pushing seventy, and life became a bit harder with aches and pains nagging him. At night, Paul fell into bed exhausted by life. He would wake up two hours later, unable to sleep.

He finally developed an aversion to alcohol. It is easy to quit because it's making him sick.

— * ❋ * —

Paul knew what he had to do. He will die early if he continues on this path of reveling in his retirement. His life is not over, and there are still adventures to be had.

He needs to sell the house and move somewhere new and challenging. Paul requires interaction with life and artists. Maybe he could move back to Seattle and get a studio in the city, or he could move to Port Townsend, a beautiful small town teeming with artists with a gallery that represents him.

But Paul wants more of an adventure than that. Those options are too close to home. He wants to fling himself into the unknown where he didn't know anyone.

Paul's decision for his final adventure is Astoria, Oregon. He had visited this town on the Columbia River's mouth a couple of times, and he felt magic.

The mouth of the Columbia River is more than five miles wide in places. Most of the rivers, streams, snowmelt, and rain west of the Rocky Mountains surge down the Columbia and into the Pacific Ocean. The ocean has its own dynamics with its tides.

These forces meet each other, sometimes making the Columbia flow backward during high tide.

The Astoria-Megler Bridge, itself being four miles long and akin to a roller coaster ride, makes your stomach turn upside down.

Large tankers escorted by tugboats enter and depart the mouth of the Columbia. They are so close you can hit one with a rock. There are fishing boats, passenger ships, coastguard cutters, and sailboats.

This Northwest corner of the country has the oldest and most dynamic history west of the Rocky Mountains. The Pacific coastline is one of the most beautiful you will find.

Astoria is the endpoint of the Lewis and Clark expedition followed by three treks (one by boat around the tip of South America), all financed by John Jacob Astor.

The Chinook, Clatsop, and the Shoalwater Bay Indians inhabited the area at the time and still do, working to recover their traditions and languages.

I swear this place has ghosts, and a person can feel the energy, not only of the physical environment but also from the people who lived here.

So, Paul plopped himself down in Astoria. He realized it has a fantastic up-and-coming art community with original and dynamic artists, and he fit in like a piece of a jigsaw puzzle. The people of Astoria see him as unique. His painting style and philosophy are different than what they are used to, and Astorians like that.

Before leaving Poulsbo, Paul sold his house and paid off his debts. He also bought a 1500 Dodge Ram. He plans to continue driving to Port Townsend and Bainbridge to drop off and pick up paintings, and continue going to art walk openings.

Kukiko accompanied Paul when he drove down from Poulsbo to look for a studio.

They found one on the river that is better than he could have imagined. The space is more than a studio. It has a large gallery where he can display his work. He moved to Astoria with over a thousand pieces of art, including at least three hundred large paintings. The space has a fabulous view of the river and its continuous flow of traffic from five large windows.

After being in the inflatable business for more than three decades, Paul had more than thirty inflatable shapes. Many of these are smaller ornaments and toys, but some are large, like a forty-foot-long dinosaur and his twenty-five-foot-high bald-headed eagle.

A friend, Ray Hammer, a fantastic metal artist, helped him move the heaviest items to Astoria, including Paul's crosscut saw, his worktable, and sewing machine. The next couple of moves from Poulsbo are with a U-haul, filled mostly with paintings.

Paul's new studio is on Tenth Street and is particularly attractive because of a couple of galleries on the same block.

The McVarish Gallery is four doors down leased by Jill McVarish. Jill not only shows her paintings and other artists' works, but she also has her studio set up there. When you walk in, you will find her sitting at an easel, working on a painting. Her paintings are in oil and are large—some as big as five feet by six feet.

Jill's style has an antiqued look to it, painted in a dark renaissance style that pops with colorful figures, animals, and cartoon characters. She is in high demand and has a list of commissions that keep her busy—actually, more than busy.

As Paul organized his studio and painted the walls white, Jill would stop by at the end of the workday and invite him to meet her at WineKraft at Pier Eleven. WineKraft, owned by Rebecca Kraft, is two minutes away across the bridge from Paul's new studio.

The view will knock your socks off. This little trip with Jill happens almost every evening and includes a game of chess on occasion.

Paul falls into his usual routine of buying rolls of linen and wood to build stretcher bars. He is anxious to begin his first group of Astoria paintings.

When Paul first experienced Astoria, driving in from the north, four attractions immediately stand out. The first is the Astoria-Megler Bridge—a grand entrance. The town is built on hills looking over the Columbia with scattered colorful old-style houses. The river traffic is diverse, displaying enormous tankers and pilot boats escorting them through the treacherous mouth—and of course, there is the rest of the river traffic.

The skyline of the town, atop the highest hill, stands The Astoria Column, a tribute to the Lewis and Clark expedition. The most incredible 360-degree view in the area.

As a backdrop, Paul noticed Saddle Mountain.

Paul's first thought is to start painting these awe-inspiring sights, but he also realizes that most of the galleries in town have these same artist's images, and he doesn't want to paint what seems to be a common theme.

Rethinking this train of thought, Paul immediately began painting the tankers, tugs, the bridge, and Saddle Mountain. If he doesn't record these iconic images in his style, it will haunt him. He feels a need to record his version of Astoria visually. The Strata, Pipes, and surrealistic abstracts will follow.

53

ASTORIA

Every city or town that Paul resided in has an art walk, usually first Friday or the first Saturday of each month. Astoria's art walk is on the second Saturday.

Paul is a little late to get on the list for July, but he is told to open anyway, and word will get around. Jill brought balloons to put in front of his gallery and said she would steer the crowd in Paul's direction.

The Astoria Art Walks became the highlight of Paul's month. Seeing people flood in, or trickle in, invited fantastic conversations about his paintings, philosophy, and the world of art. He's meeting a lot of people in Astoria and also experiencing the beaches and inland areas. It's surprising how many people are from Portland.

Paul wants to maintain his relationship with the two galleries that represent him up north—Roby King on Bainbridge and The Northwind Art Center in Port Townsend. Every month, he drives to these galleries, drops off paintings, and attends the opening night events.

The shows are staggered, so it's first Friday at Roby King, first Saturday at Northwind, and second Saturday in Astoria.

His two shows at the Bainbridge Island Museum of Art ended their five-week stint in March. Because of the publicity from the museum and Roby King's promotion, including a one-person show in April, Paul sold five paintings at reasonable prices. The buyers included two purchases from Cynthia Sears (the museum's financer and the brainchild), a board member, and two sales from the normal population. Later on, the curator of the museum purchased two.

It's the end of November and getting chilly. Sea lions are making their usual ruckus: Jill and I are having a beer after work at WineKraft, enjoying the view and chatting.

"I'd like to do something with my inflatable ornaments and toys," Paul said as they discuss art, the world, or whatever. "Christmas is coming!"

These ornaments are leftovers from the inflatable decorations Big Air used to sell to malls around the world. They range from 6 feet to 15 feet high, about twenty-five of them.

"Hey, I know! You can exhibit them in The Secret Gallery. We don't have a show planned for December."

"Really, Jill? That would be perfect!"

The Secret Gallery is hidden behind Jill's gallery, and she just obtained the lease. This inflatable Christmas show will be the first show.

"Yeah, have at it."

"The room is in pretty bad shape, and I'll need to put a lot of eye bolts in the ceiling. I'll make sure they're safe."

The ceiling is about fourteen feet high with exposed slats and gaps, better described as large holes, in the ceiling. It's the same with the walls and floor. In fact, the walls look like they were raked over with a machine gun.

Both Paul and Jill like the rough condition of the room.

Paul spent the next week hanging the show. He couldn't get the quantity of work he wanted in the space because the ornaments are larger than he realized. There are twenty–five inflatable shapes Paul can choose from, and the room would only hold ten. The space between shapes is esthetically arranged for viewing; overfilling the room would not work.

The second Saturday Art Walk drew large crowds, and the Secret Gallery was the talk of the town. The show turned out to be a tremendous success. It was magical and new for Astoria.

Not only does Paul show his work in his studio but he also exhibits in several galleries and establishments in Astoria; at the moment anyway.

So Paul, for the time being, has found his home. He's not sure how long this will last since he is in his early seventies. His health is good for his age, but his muscles and joints ache. He experiences the loss of memory and makes a list every day of what he needs to do. It doesn't surprise Paul; It's been a bit worse in the past few years.

He's still painting the quality work he expects from himself, and when life gets rough, working on a painting seems to overshadow any adversity.

Paul found a figure drawing workshop and loves the practice and exercise of working from the model. It's at Clatsop College and has the magic other workshops have had for him. It's only two hours (instead of three) during the winter semesters.

As far as a homey sushi bar is concerned, he has yet to find that. Astoria has a couple but not ones with the vibes and magic he has experienced before; just as well, he's on a much tighter budget living on social security and whatever he can conjure up.

When his money began dwindling from his sold property up north, he began substitute teaching in Oregon schools. He has been called to teach at Astoria High School, Astoria Middle School, and the two elementary schools—Astor Elementary and Lewis and Clark.

Paul loves it. It gives him a much-needed social life with the students and the staff. As a substitute, there is no need for more adventure in his life. Every day is a challenge, and he returns to his studio exhausted but with a smile and good memories.

He's not teaching art, which he would prefer, but that would be easy for him, and there are only two art teachers in the Astoria school district. Subbing in Math classes, English literature, social studies, and even special education is like going back to school and learning all over again.

When Paul's lease is up, he is thinking of getting a camper for his pick-up and traveling the USA while painting his visual experiences. He needs to see how the next two years go.

Looking back on his life as an artist, he realizes that he has been faithful to his technique and philosophy since he arrived at his first studio in San Diego in 1973. At the time, he thought he was too scattered, going in too many directions at once.

Paul always started with his turpentine washes of splatters and textures. This technique is his Rorschach test to bring out images he sees in the mayhem—like seeing images in clouds. Paul then super-imposed his conscious intent over these unconscious images to have a two-way relationship, battling it out or compromising with each other. The energy flow is amazing. He is always excited to see how these images resolve themselves and how they will result in a finished piece of art. A form of existence that will survive for generations to come.

Each painting shows the highest quality Paul knows how to do so that the artwork will have the best chance of survival.

When Paul leaves this world, he will be leaving a psychological diary for the world to see—maybe someone can figure them out. He believes that, like a dream, when one looks back on it, it will all make sense, and to do that, he needs to be proficient in working from life, in the form of landscapes and figure drawing. It is only then that he is justified to do his surrealistic abstracts.

Most painters developed a style with a consistent technique; Paul combines his different effects and techniques to work with each other, like preparing a meal of meat and potatoes with a healthy salad and a rich dessert.

He combines washes with brush strokes and a palette knife thickness with glazes. Canvas textures sporadically play over the surface. All of this working with the dynamics of line, shape, and edges, and how negative space pops out to provide interest and dynamics—all combine in a unified order to produce a living piece of art.

These paintings are Paul's children, each with an individual life of its own.

www.ingramcontent.com/pod-product-compliance
Lightning Source LLC
Chambersburg PA
CBHW040728070726
47599CB00033B/1050